Flexible Citizenship

Flexible Citizenship

The Cultural Logics of Transnationality

AIHWA ONG

Duke University Press   *Durham & London*   1999

© 1999 Duke University Press

All rights reserved

Printed in the United States of America on acid-free paper ∞

Typeset in Minion and Quadraat by Keystone Typesetting, Inc.

Library of Congress Cataloging-in-Publication Data appear on the last printed page of this book.

The following chapters are reprints with minor revisions:

chapter 1 was originally published as "Anthropology, China, and Modernities: The Geopolitics of Cultural Knowledge," in *The Future of Anthropological Theory*, ed. Henrietta Moore (London: Routledge, 1995), 60–92; chapter 2 was originally published as " 'A Momentary Glow of Fraternity': Images of Nation and Capitalism in Asia," *Identities* 3, no. 3 (1997): 331–66; chapter 3 was originally published as "Limits to Cultural Accumulation: Chinese Capitalists on the American Pacific Rim," *Annals of the New York Academy of Sciences* 645 (1992): 125–45; chapter 4 was originally published as "On the Edge of Empires: Flexible Citizenship among Chinese in Diaspora," *positions* 1, no. 3 (winter 1993): 745–78; chapter 6 was originally published as " 'A Better Tomorrow'? The Struggle for Global Visibility," *Sojourn* 12, no. 2 (December 1997): 192–225.

Second printing, 2000

For Benjamin and Pamela

Contents

Acknowledgments

This book grew out of a paper I presented at the conference "After Oriental-ism," which was convened by Tani Barlow at the University of California, Berkeley, in May 1992. An early version of chapter 4 sparked ideas that I gradually took up in other chapters. The book was written in between raising two young children, teaching, advising graduates, and researching another project. I thank the Institute of International Studies, Berkeley, for paying for my China field trip in the fall of 1993. Ching Kwan Lee and Connie Clark provided useful contacts in Shenzhen. The University of California Pacific Rim Research Program subsidized a visit to Southeast Asia in the summer of 1997. I did not receive funds or time off for writing this work, but I have had a lot of critical encouragement.

I am grateful to Lisa Rofel for reading drafts of the manuscript and making valuable criticisms and suggestions. Donald M. Nonini, Brackette F. Williams, Ashraf Ghani, and Donald S. Moore also were generous in their detailed comments on parts of the manuscript. I also thank Jiemin Bao, Tani Barlow, Pheng Cheah, Akhil Gupta, Mary Hancock, Mark Leitchy, Lydia Liu, Vincent Rafael, Shih Shu-mei, Ken Wissoker, Diana Wong, and Mayfair Mei-hui Yang, who read different chapters and made helpful comments. The two final chap-ters were stimulated by conversations with Stephen J. Collier.

My children have grown a bit too fast in the interim, but they continue to be a source of comfort and wonderful diversions. Pamela, age six, has chan-neled some of her joyful exuberance into art and gymnastics. Benjamin, age ten, has shifted his interest from chess moves to the alignment of stars in the heavens. Their father, Robert R. Ng, sustains us all with music and humor.

Flexible Citizenship: The Cultural

Logics of Transnationality

On the eve of the return of Hong Kong from British to mainland-Chinese rule, the city was abuzz with passport stories. A favorite one concerned mainland official Lu Ping, who presided over the transition. At a talk to Hong Kong business leaders (*taipans*), he fished a number of passports from his pockets to indicate he was fully aware that the Hong Kong elite has a weakness for foreign passports.[1] Indeed, more than half the members of the transition preparatory committee carried foreign passports. These politicians were no different from six hundred thousand other Hong Kongers (about ten percent of the total population) who held foreign passports as insurance against mainland-Chinese rule. Taipans who had been busy doing business with Beijing openly accumulated foreign passports, claiming they were merely "a matter of convenience," but in a Freudian slip, one let on that multiple passports were also "a matter of confidence" in uncertain political times.[2] The multiple-passport holder seems to display an élan for thriving in conditions of political insecurity, as well as in the turbulence of global trade. He is willing and eager to work with the Chinese-communist state while conjuring up ways of escape from potential dangers to his investment and family.

Another example of the flexible subject is provided by Raymond Chin, one of the founders of the Better Hong Kong Foundation, a pro-China business group. I heard a radio interview in which he was asked about his investment in China and the future of Hong Kong under communist rule. Here, I paraphrase him: "Freedom is a great thing, but I think it should be given to people who have earned it. We should take the long view and see the long-term

1

returns on our investments in the mainland. Self-censorship and other kinds of responsible behavior may be necessary to get the kind of freedom we want."

This willingness to accommodate self-censorship reflects the displaced person's eagerness to hedge bets, even to the extent of risking property and life under different political conditions anywhere in the world. The Chinese in Hong Kong are of course a rather special kind of refugee, haunted by memento mori even when they seek global economic opportunities that include China. The novelist Paul Theroux notes that Hong Kong people are driven by the memory of previous Chinese disasters and shaped by their status as colonials without the normal colonial expectation of independence. They are people always in transit, who have become "world-class practitioners of self-sufficiency."[3] In this, they are not much different from overseas Chinese in Southeast Asia, who have largely flourished in postcolonial states and yet are considered politically alien, or alienable, when conditions take a turn for the worse. For over a century, overseas Chinese have been the forerunners of today's multiply displaced subjects, who are always on the move both mentally and physically.

The multiple-passport holder is an apt contemporary figure; he or she embodies the split between state-imposed identity and personal identity caused by political upheavals, migration, and changing global markets. In this world of high modernity, as one scholar notes, national and ethnic identities "become distinctly different entities, while at the same time, international frontiers become increasingly insignificant as such."[4] But are political borders becoming insignificant or is the state merely fashioning a new relationship to capital mobility and to manipulations by citizens and noncitizens alike?

Benedict Anderson suggests an answer when he argues that the goal of the classical nation-state project to align social habits, culture, attachment, and political participation is being unraveled by modern communications and nomadism. As a result, passports have become "less and less attestations of citizenship, let alone of loyalty to a protective nation-state, than of claims to participate in labor markets."[5] The truth claims of the state that are enshrined in the passport are gradually being replaced by its counterfeit use in response to the claims of global capitalism. Or is there another way of looking at the shifting relations between the nation-state and the global economy in late modernity, one that suggests more complex adjustments and accommodations? The realignment of political, ethnic, and personal identities is not necessarily a process of "win or lose," whereby political borders become "insignificant" and the nation-state "loses" to global trade in terms of its control over the affiliations and behavior of its subjects.[6]

If, as I intend to do, we pay attention instead to the *transnational practices and imaginings* of the nomadic subject and the social conditions that enable his flexibility, we obtain a different picture of how nation-states articulate with capitalism in late modernity. Indeed, our Hong Kong taipan is not simply a Chinese subject adroitly navigating the disjunctures between political landscapes and the shifting opportunities of global trade. His very flexibility in geographical and social positioning is itself an effect of novel articulations between the regimes of the family, the state, and capital, the kinds of practical-technical adjustments that have implications for our understanding of the late modern subject.

In this book, I intervene in the discussion of globalization, a subject heretofore dominated by the structuralist methods of sociologists and geographers. In *The Condition of Postmodernity*, David Harvey identifies flexibility as the modus operandi of late capitalism. He distinguishes contemporary systems of profit making, production, distribution, and consumption as a break from the earlier, Fordist model of centralized mass-assembly production in which the workers were also the mass consumers of their products. In the era of late capitalism, "the regime of flexible accumulation" reigns, whether in the realms of business philosophy and high finance or in production systems, labor markets, and consumption.[7] What is missing from Harvey's account is human agency and its production and negotiation of cultural meanings within the normative milieus of late capitalism. More recently, writers on "the information age" maintain that globalization—in which financial markets around the world are unified by information from the electronic-data stream—operates according to its own logic without a class of managers or capitalists in charge.[8]

These strategies—the decentralization of corporate activities across many sites, the location of "runaway" factories in global peripheries, and the reconfiguration of banking and investment relations—introduced new regimes in global production, finance, and marketing. These new modes of doing global business have been variously referred to as "globalization" by bankers and as "post-Fordism," "disorganized capitalism," and "flexible accumulation" by social theorists.[9] These terms are also significant in reflecting the new logic of capitalism whereby "nodes of capitalist development around the globe . . . [have] decentered capitalism . . . and abstracted capitalism for the first time from its Eurocentricism."[10]

Instead of embracing the totalizing view of globalization as economic rationality bereft of human agency, other social analysts have turned toward studying "the local." They are examining how particular articulations of the global and the local—often construed as the opposition between universalizing capitalist forces and local cultures—produce "multiple modernities" in different parts of the world.[11] Arjun Appadurai argues that such a "global production of locality" happens because transnational flows of people, goods, and knowledge become imaginative resources for creating communities and "virtual neighborhoods."[12] This view is informed by a top-down model whereby the global is macro–political economic and the local is situated, culturally creative, and resistant.[13]

But a model that analytically defines the global as political economic and the local as cultural does not quite capture the *horizontal* and *relational* nature of the contemporary economic, social, and cultural processes that stream across spaces. Nor does it express their *embeddedness* in differently configured regimes of power. For this reason, I prefer to use the term *transnationality*. *Trans* denotes both moving through space or across lines, as well as changing the nature of something. Besides suggesting new relations between nation-states and capital, transnationality also alludes to the *trans*versal, the *trans*actional, the *trans*lational, and the *trans*gressive aspects of contemporary behavior and imagination that are incited, enabled, and regulated by the changing logics of states and capitalism. In what follows, when I use the word *globalization,* I am referring to the narrow sense of new corporate strategies, but analytically, I am concerned with transnationality—or the condition of cultural interconnectedness and mobility across space—which has been intensified under late capitalism. I use *transnationalism* to refer to the cultural specificities of global processes, tracing the multiplicity of the uses and conceptions of "culture." The chapters that follow will discuss the transnationality induced by global capital circulating in the Asia Pacific region, the transnationalism associated with the practices and imagination of elite Chinese subjects, and the varied responses of Southeast Asian states to capital and mobility.[14]

This book places human practices and cultural logics at the center of discussions on globalization. Whereas globalization has been analyzed as consisting of flows of capital, information, and populations, my interest is in the cultural logics that inform and structure border crossings as well as state strategies. My goal is to tease out the rationalities (political, economic, cultural) that shape migration, relocation, business networks, state-capital relations, and all transnational processes that are apprehended through and directed by cultural meanings. In other words, I seek to bring into the same analytical framework the economic rationalities of globalization and the cultural dynamics that shape human and political responses. As a social scientist, I point to the economic rationality that encourages family emigration or the political rationality that invites foreign capital, but as an anthropologist, I am primarily concerned with the cultural logics that make these actions thinkable, practicable, and desirable, which are embedded in processes of capital accumulation.

First, the chapters that follow attempt an ethnography of transnational practices and linkages that seeks to embed the theory of practice within, not outside of or against, political-economic forces. For Sherry Ortner, "modern practice theory" is an approach that places human agency and everyday practices at the center of social analysis. Ortner notes that the little routines and scenarios of everyday life are embodiments and enactments of norms, values, and conceptual schemes about time, space, and the social order, so that everyday practices endorse and reproduce these norms. While she argues that social practice is shaped within relations of domination, *as well as* within relations of reciprocity and solidarity, Ortner does not provide an analytical linkage between the two. Indeed, her theory of practice, which is largely focused on the actors' intentions within the "system" of cultural meaning, is disembodied from the economic and political conditions of late capitalism. She seems to propose a view in which the anthropologist can determine the extent to which "Western capitalism," as an abstract system, does or does not affect the lives of "real people."[15] An approach that views political economy as separate from human agency cannot be corrected by a theory of practice that views political-economic forces as external to everyday meanings and action. Our challenge is to consider the reciprocal construction of practice, gender, ethnicity, race, class, and nation in processes of capital accumulation. I argue that an anthropology of the present should analyze people's everyday actions as a form of cultural politics embedded in specific power contexts. The *regulatory effects* of particular cultural institutions, projects, regimes, and markets that shape people's motivations, desires, and struggles and make them particular kinds of subjects in the world should be identified.

Second, I view transnationalism not in terms of unstructured flows but in terms of the tensions between movements and social orders. I relate transnational strategies to systems of governmentality—in the broad sense of techniques and codes for directing human behavior[16]—that condition and manage the movements of populations and capital. Michel Foucault's notion of governmentality maintains that regimes of truth and power produce disciplinary effects that condition our sense of self and our everyday practices.[17] In the following chapters, I trace the different regimes—state, family, economic enterprises—that shape and direct border crossings and transnational relations, at once conditioning their dynamism and scope but also giving structure to their patterning. These shifting patterns of travel, and realignments between state and capital, are invariably understood according to the logics of culture and regional hegemony. Given the history of diasporan trading groups such as the ethnic Chinese, who play a major role in many of the so-called Asian tiger economies, the Asia Pacific region is ideal for investigating these new modalities of translocal governmentality and the cultural logics of subject making.[18]

Third, I argue that in the era of globalization, individuals as well as governments develop a flexible notion of citizenship and sovereignty as strategies to accumulate capital and power. "Flexible citizenship" refers to the cultural logics of capitalist accumulation, travel, and displacement that induce subjects to respond fluidly and opportunistically to changing political-economic conditions.[19] In their quest to accumulate capital and social prestige in the global arena, subjects emphasize, and are regulated by, practices favoring flexibility, mobility, and repositioning in relation to markets, governments, and cultural regimes. These logics and practices are produced within particular structures of meaning about family, gender, nationality, class mobility, and social power.

Fourth, if mobile subjects plot and maneuver in relation to capital flows, governments also articulate with global capital and entities in complex ways. I want to problematize the popular view that globalization has weakened state power. While capital, population, and cultural flows have indeed made inroads into state sovereignty, the art of government has been highly responsive to the challenges of transnationality. I introduce the concept of graduated sovereignty to denote a series of zones that are subjected to different kinds of governmentality and that vary in terms of the mix of disciplinary and civilizing regimes. These zones, which do not necessarily follow political borders, often contain ethnically marked class groupings, which in practice are subjected to regimes of rights and obligations that are different from those in other zones. Because anthropologists pay attention to the various normalizing powers of the state and capital on subject populations, we can provide a different take on globalization—one that goes beyond universalizing spatial orders.

Fifth, besides looking at globalization, the point of this book is to reorient the study of Chinese subjects. Global capitalism in Asia is linked to new cultural representations of "Chineseness" (rather than "Japaneseness") in relation to transnational Asian capitalism. As overseas Chinese and mainland Chinese become linked in circuits of production, trade, and finance, narratives produce concepts such as "fraternal network capitalism" and "Greater China," a term that refers to the economically integrated zone comprising China, Taiwan, and Hong Kong, but sometimes including the ethnic Chinese communities in Southeast Asia. This triumphant "Chinese capitalism" has induced long-assimilated Thai and Indonesian subjects to reclaim their "ethnic-Chinese" status as they participate in regional business networks. The changing status of diasporan Chinese is historically intertwined with the operations and globalization of capital, and their cultural experiences are the ethnographic ground from which my points about transnationality are drawn.

Sixth, I challenge the view that the proliferation of unofficial narratives associated with triumphant Chinese capitalism reflect insurmountable cultural differences. I argue that on the contrary, discourses such as "Asian values," "the new Islam," "saying no to the West," and "the clash of civilizations" can occur in the context of fundamentally playing (and competing) by the rules of the neoliberal orthodoxy. Despite the claims of some American scholars and policy makers that the emergence of the Pacific Rim powers heralds an irreducible cultural division between East and West, these parallel narratives, I argue, disguise common civilizational references in a world where the market is absolutely transcendental.

Through an anthropology of emigrating families, transnational publics, state strategies, and panreligious nationalist discourses, the following chap-

ters will identify the cultural logics shaping individual, national, and regional relations of power and conflict. But before I turn to these themes, I will
briefly review how anthropology and cultural studies have approached the
topics that can be loosely gathered under the rubrics of "diaspora" and
"transnationalism."

Approaches to Transnational Flows and Diasporas

As the century draws to a close, there is a sense that the world we live in has
changed dramatically; it is as if the continental plates of social life are sliding
into new and unstable alignments. While sociologists and economists have
focused on globalization as changing corporate strategies, anthropologists
and cultural theorists are much more concerned about cultural shifts and
studies of migrations, diasporas, and other transnational flows. I identify
three main directions of inquiry.

U.S.-Centered Migration Studies

Largely an American project but increasingly one that is shared by Europeans, migration studies has recently shifted its focus from assimilation to
take into account the global context of border-crossing movements. Migration scholars view transnational processes associated with global conflicts and
the world economy as factors that affect the demographic and social composition of the nation-state. They pay attention to domestic attempts at managing
the influx of refugees, migrant workers, and foreign capital on the social and
political body of the nation. Such perspectives on transnational migrations to
the United States are framed in terms of either a world-system theory about
exploitative relations between "core" and "peripheral" countries or a neo-
classical economic theory of diverse labor supplies flowing toward an advanced capitalist formation.[20] Such studies view immigrants (of color) from
poor countries as victims of American corporate exploitation as well as racist
discrimination. They take the position that immigrant laborers, by making
important and diverse contributions to different aspects of American society,
deserve help in integrating into mainstream society. Their larger goal is to call
upon the state to provide different services to the newcomers and the majority
population to treat them with respect and acceptance as loyal Americans. The
studies also fend off or criticize American concerns about unchecked immi-

gration and rich countries' porous borders failing to keep out the world's poor. Claims about the weakness of the state in controlling immigration are counterbalanced by the charge that the state supports corporate interests that exploit the cheap labor of vulnerable immigrants.

New anthropological studies have intervened in the migration-studies framework; they focus on the links between transnational migration and political struggles. The authors of *Nations Unbound* make an ambitious connection between the postcolonial predicaments of poor countries, their export of labor to the metropolitan center, and the efforts of poor, exploited immigrants to support "nation-building" projects at home.[21] Although they are treated as racialized proletarian others in the United States, Haitians, Granadians, and Filipino immigrants are also active in sustaining households at home while engaging in political struggles against corrupt regimes. Poor immigrants are thus converted from being minorities to be assimilated into the host society into being some kind of universalized lower-class subjects who attain subaltern vindication both from struggling against racism in the United States and from transcending class and political barriers in their home countries. Also, in recent ethnographies of Mexican immigration, the focus is shifted from their role as farm laborers in the U.S. economy to their political consciousness of difference, not only from the American majority population but sometimes also from other Mexican collectivities. Michael Kearney explores the construction of a "transnational ethnicity" among Mexicans in California, while Roger Rouse traces the migration circuits and "bifocal" cultural consciousness of Mexican agricultural workers in the United States.[22]

However, these ethnographies of migration and identity making in America do not sufficiently deal with the ways in which the subjectivities of majority populations are also being reworked by neoliberalism in the United States. For instance, how are differentiated and competing notions of citizenship in the United States emerging within a dominant frame of American neoliberalism?[23] Whereas the movements of capital have stimulated immigrant strategies of mobility, many poor Americans are unable to respond in quite the same way and are instead "staying put" or "being stuck" in place, especially in rundown ethnic ghettoes.[24] What are the subjectivities associated with being stuck in particular U.S. contexts? Global capital and population flows have intensified the localization of resident minorities within the reconfigured political economy and have thus reinforced a citizenship patterning of whiteness and blackness in a more institutionalized sense than has been allowed for in studies of race.[25] Indeed, as some of the following chapters will show, the "out-of-placeness" represented by wealthy Asian immigrants in the American ethno-racial order induces a parallel sense of displacement among whites and blacks who have not benefited from globalization.

Cultural Globalization

But major anthropological accounts of transnationalism have been consumed less with migrants and their reception in host countries and more with issues of cultural flows and the social imaginary in a transnational world. For years now, anthropologists and others have argued that despite the widespread dissemination of the trappings of globalization—world markets, mass media, rapid travel, and modern communications—cultural forms have not become homogenized across the world.[26] The dispersal of Coke, McDonald's Restaurants, and American TV soap operas to villages in West Africa or to Cairo, Beijing, or Sydney is not bringing about a global cultural uniformity; rather, these products have had the effect of greatly increasing cultural diversity because of the ways in which they are interpreted and the way they acquire new meanings in local reception or because the proliferation of cultural difference is superbly consonant with marketing designs for profit making.[27] The rapid circulation of images, knowledges, and peoples has unraveled our more usual understanding of cultural production and reproduction within conventional political and cultural boundaries. In a world reconfigured by transnationality, how are anthropologists to handle the issues of instability, uncertainty, and flux in cultural reproduction and identity formation?

The most articulate proponent of what might be called "cultural globalization" is Arjun Appadurai, who states that his work deals with "a theory of rupture that takes media and migration as its two major and interconnected diacritics and explores their joint effect on the work of the imagination as a constitutive feature of modern subjectivity."[28] Appadurai borrows from Benedict Anderson's argument about the critical role of "print capitalism" in generating "imagined communities" of nationality in the modern era.[29] He theorizes the ways modern travel and electronic media mediate the production of cultural identity, locality, and the "virtual neighborhood" in a transnational era.[30] Coining terms such as "ethnoscapes," "ideoscapes," and "mediascapes," Appadurai highlights the tensions between the irregular and fluid shapes of population flows and communities of imagination that cut across conventional political and social boundaries.[31] By sketching in the deterritorialized conditions of imaginative resources and practice, Appadurai poses the problem of uncertainty in cultural reproduction outside the nation-state and stable cultural landscapes.

But the very suggestiveness of Appadurai's formulation begs the question of whether imagination as social practice can be so independent of national, transnational, and political-economic structures that enable, channel, and control the flows of people, things, and ideas. For instance, he ignores the fact that nations and states are still largely bound to each other, and he ignores the need to consider how the hyphen between the two has become reconfigured by capital mobility and migration. What are the structural tensions between a territorially based nation and a "deterritorialized" one? Furthermore, his accounts of cultural flows ignore class stratification linked to global systems of production. He makes no attempt to identify the processes that increasingly differentiate the power of mobile and nonmobile subjects. Indeed, he ignores the political economy of time-space compression and gives the misleading impression that everyone can take equal advantage of mobility and modern communications and that transnationality has been liberatory, in both a spatial and a political sense, for all peoples.[32] This assumption is belied by a recent United Nations human-development report that the gaps between the rich and the poor within and between countries are at an all-time high. An official remarks, "An emerging global elite, mostly urban-based and interconnected in a variety of ways, is amassing great wealth and power, while more than half of humanity is left out."[33] When an approach to cultural globalization seeks merely to sketch out universalizing trends rather than deal with actually existing structures of power and situated cultural processes, the analysis cries out for a sense of political economy and situated ethnography. What are the mechanisms of power that enable the mobility, as well as the localization and disciplining, of diverse populations within these transnationalized systems? How are cultural flows and human imagination conditioned and shaped within these new relations of global inequalities?

Besides the poor, women, who are half of humanity, are frequently absent in studies of transnationalism. Ethnographies on the feminization of labor regimes instituted by global capital were among the first to consider the reproduction of gendered inequalities across transnational space.[34] These works are seldom considered in masculinist studies of globalization, except to be mentioned in connection with the survival of third-world "patriarchy" in "small family firms" linked to flexible accumulation.[35] Again, the global-local dichotomy seems to suggest that third-world cultures merely accommodate global labor processes rather than participate actively in reciprocal production and reproduction of capital accumulation.

Feminist travel writing also underplays the intertwining of material and symbolic processes in translocal gender systems.[36] For instance, Inderpal Grewal traces the gendered construction of racial hierarchies in colonial India through the writings of British and Indian women traversing the British Empire.[37] For the contemporary period, Cynthia Enloe sketches in the broad outlines of transnational gender systems sustained by consumption and tourism, while Caren Kaplan has considered how the Western imaginaries of travel are highly gendered.[38] Such studies of imaginative gender geographies are innovative and are more important for claiming feminist global perspectives from the Western vantage point than for capturing the lived realities and localized subjectivities in those other places.

Diasporas and Cosmopolitanisms

Works best described as "diaspora studies" look at the subjective experiences of displacement, victimhood, cultural hybridity, and cultural struggles in the modern world. These works have been inspired by Paul Gilroy's new take on the African diaspora, as well as by the heterogeneous nature of black identity and cultures in different sites of dispersal and dissemination.[39] The writings of Gilroy, Stuart Hall, and others associated with British cultural studies are ultimately a historical reconstruction of the Atlantic as a zone of movement, connection, and complex structures of subordination wherein "a plurality of antagonisms and differences are distinctive features of black diasporan cultures."[40] This focus on the chronotope of movement and cultural contradictions within diasporan populations influenced the conceptualization of Ungrounded Empires, a volume on modern Chinese transnationalism that I edited with Donald Nonini.[41] But in contrast to the bipolar formulation of the black diaspora, we show that multiple geographies were and continue to be engaged by ethnic Chinese whose earlier diasporas are continually evolving into a network of family ties, kinship, commerce, sentiments, and values spread throughout regions of dispersal and settlement.

However, the influence on American cultural studies of the Center for Contemporary Cultural Studies in Birmingham, England, with which Hall and Gilroy are associated, has generally been limited. American studies of diasporan cultures have tended to uphold a more innocent concept of the essential diasporan subject, one that celebrates hybridity, "cultural" border crossing, and the production of difference. In the United States, the conjuncture of postcolonial theory and diaspora studies seems to produce a bifurcated model of diasporan cultures. Some scholars dwell on narratives of sacrifice, which are associated with enforced labor migrations, as well as on critiques of the immorality of development.[42] Others, who write about displacements in "borderland" areas, emphasize subjects who struggle against adversity and violation by affirming their cultural hybridity and shifting positions in society.[43] The unified moralism attached to subaltern subjects now also clings to diasporan ones, who are invariably assumed to be members of oppressed classes and therefore constitutionally opposed to capitalism and state power. Furthermore, because of the exclusive focus on texts, narratives, and subjectivities, we are often left wondering what are the particular local-global structural articulations that materially and symbolically shape these dynamics of victimhood and ferment.

Academic interest in how diasporas shape racialized, gendered, sexualized, and oppositional subjectivities is often tied to scholars' attempts to shape their own cosmopolitan intellectual commitment.[44] James Clifford is broadly concerned with the varied formation of cultural subjectivities in and through itineraries formed by the "detours and returns" that pass through intellectual salons and international hotels, as well as more humble ones formed by the "routes/roots of tribes, barrios, favellas, immigrant neighborhoods." His term "discrepant cosmopolitanisms" takes in all kinds of classed subjects whose specific histories and range of cultural practices evince "traveling-in-dwelling, dwelling-in-traveling," but Clifford is most interested in the multiply displaced writer meditating on political injustices encountered in travel.[45] Similarly, Bruce Robbins focuses on the cosmopolitan subjectivity of worldly, progressive intellectuals who are firmly anchored in their own societies but whose minds roam the world and whose political consciousness is shaped by the dialects of local interest and global vision.[46] Both Clifford and Robbins seek to link the study of cosmopolitanism with their belief in the cosmopolitan individual as a well-informed, politically progressive modern subject (whose precursors are two displaced Polish intellectuals, Joseph Conrad and Bronislaw Malinowski). This move reflects the desire to retrieve the intellectual's public role in the making of "internationalist political education" and thus of late modern cultures.[47] There is of course no necessary connection between the study of diasporan subjects and a cosmopolitan intellectual commitment, but cultural theorists appear to believe there is.[48]

Indeed, since the term cosmopolitanism has most recently been associated with those elite Western subjects who were the fullest expression of European bourgeois culture, capitalism, and colonial empires, we need to identify a kind of progressive cosmopolitan intellectual who, according to anthropologist Paul Rabinow, is "suspicious of sovereign powers, universal truths . . . moralisms high and low," as well as of his or her "own imperial tendencies."[49] As Rabinow notes, a "critical cosmopolitanism" combines "an ethos of macro-independencies with an acute consciousness . . . of the inescapabilities and particularities of places, characters, historical trajectories, and fate."[50] Such "inescapabilities and particularities" of displaced peoples are seldom captured in cultural-studies accounts, which seem primarily concerned with projecting the cosmopolitan intentions of the scholar.

The cultural-studies focus on diasporan cultures and subjectivities then seeks in the off-shore experiences of labor migrants, and in the worldly ruminations of intellectuals, the birth of progressive political subjects who will undermine or challenge oppressive nationalist ideologies (and global capitalism?). The new interest in diasporas and cosmopolitanism registers a special moment in interdisciplinary studies that seeks to invoke political significance in cultural phenomena that can be theorized as resisting the pillaging of global capitalism, as well as the provincialism of metropolitan centers. What is missing from these accounts are discussions of how the disciplining structures—of family, community, work, travel, and nation—condition, shape, divert, and transform such subjects and their practices and produce the moral-political dilemmas, so eloquently captured in these studies, whose resolutions cannot be so easily predetermined.

These three approaches—(trans)migration studies, globalization as cultural flows, and diaspora studies—have much to recommend them, especially for furnishing useful concepts and opening up a whole new critical area for anthropological research and theorizing. There are differences in their methods and frameworks, but there is also a surprising degree of agreement in their hopes and biases for the future. For instance, we see a break between those who use a political-economic framework to assess the impact of transmigration on host and home countries and the other two approaches that focus almost exclusively on the cultural, imaginative, and subjective aspects of modern travel and interconnections. The rift is wide enough for Marxist-oriented models to tend to map rather mechanistic relations of "the world system" onto their data on migration flows, while neglecting to convey the varied cultural expressions and handling of such relationships. In contrast, anthropologists who are solely concerned with cultural phenomena tend to brush aside political-economic systems and celebrate cultural difference, hybridity, and the social imaginary, which display "native" inventiveness, and sometimes resistances, to homogenizing trends. Seldom is there an attempt to analytically link actual institutions of state power, capitalism, and transnational networks to such forms of cultural reproduction, inventiveness, and possibilities.[51] This is a significant problem of method because it raises hopes that transnational mobility and its associated processes have great liberatory potential (perhaps replacing international class struggle in orthodox Marxist thinking) for undermining all kinds of oppressive structures in the world. In a sense, the diasporan subject is now vested with the agency formerly sought in the working class and more recently in the subaltern subject. Furthermore, there are frequent claims that diasporas and cosmopolitanisms are liberatory forces against oppressive nationalism, repressive state structures, and capitalism,[52] or that the unruliness of transnational capital will weaken the power of the nation-state.[53] Indeed, some claim that a "postnationalist order" is emerging "in which the nation-state is becoming obsolete and other formations for allegiance and identity have taken place."[54] In such formulations, freedom from spatial constraints (or "time-space compression," in David Harvey's term) becomes a form of deterritorialized resource that can be deployed against the territorially bounded nation-state.

But while such tensions and disjunctures are at work between oppressive structures and border-crossing flows, the nation-state—along with its juridical-legislative systems, bureaucratic apparatuses, economic entities, modes of governmentality, and war-making capacities—continues to define, discipline, control, and regulate all kinds of populations, whether in movement or in residence. There are diverse forms of interdependencies and entanglements between transnational phenomena and the nation-states—relations that link displaced persons with citizens, integrate the unstructured into the structured, and bring some kind of order to the disorderliness of transnationalism. In our desire to find definite breaks between the territorially bounded and the deterritorialized, the oppressive and the progressive, and the stable and the unstable, we sometimes overlook complicated accommodations, alliances, and creative tensions between the nation-state and mobile capital, between diaspora and nationalism, or between the influx of immigrants and the multicultural state. Attention to specific histories and geopolitical situations will reveal that such simple oppositions between transnational forces and the nation-state cannot be universally sustained.

Rethinking the Cultural Logics of Globalization

Only by weaving the analysis of cultural politics and political economy into a single framework can we hope to provide a nuanced delineation of the complex relations between transnational phenomena, national regimes, and cultural practices in late modernity. I go beyond the classical formulation of political economy as a domain of production and labor that is separate from society and culture—a mode of thought that has greatly influenced studies that attempt to assess the effects of capitalism on society. Because I view political economy as inseparable from a range of cultural processes, I share Arturo Escobar's critique of the Marxist code of signification, which constructs " 'economic' men and women [who] are positioned in civil societies in ways that are inevitably mediated, at the symbolic level, by the constructs of markets, production, and commodities. People and nature are separated into parts (individuals and resources), to be recombined into market commodities and objects of exchange and knowledge."[55] But we can reject this essentializing and homogenizing narrative about capitalist culture without throwing out an analysis of political economy.[56] An understanding of political economy remains central as capitalism—in the sense of production systems, capital accumulation, financial markets, the extraction of surplus value, and economic booms and crises—has become even more deeply embroiled in the ways different cultural logics give meanings to our dreams, actions, goals, and sense of how we are to conduct ourselves in the world.[57] Indeed, this book seeks to explore the multiple uses of the notion of "culture" in contexts of transnationality induced by the operations of global markets. The following chapters will discuss (1) the cultural logics of governmentality in the production of subjectivities, practices, and desires; (2) the cultural specificities of how capitalism operates among "Chinese" fraternal networks and publics across the Asia Pacific region; and (3) the deployment of "culture" or "civilization" by Asian governments and capitalists to implement new forms of governmentality and to resist American hegemony. But let me draw out these themes in relation to the ethnographic contexts of my investigation.

Transnational Processes Are Situated Cultural Practices

Transnational processes are situated cultural practices, so that the cultural logics of governmentality and state action in Asia Pacific countries are rather different from, say, those in a former world power such as England. Whereas in England, the effects of globalization may appear to threaten that country's economy and cultural identity, in Asia, transnational flows and networks have been the key dynamics in shaping cultural practices, the formation of identity, and shifts in state strategies.[58]

The case of the overseas Chinese is a particularly rich and complicated one for discussing transnationalism because not only have Chinese diasporas and their relationships with China and host countries historically been salient, but there is a huge body of scholarship concerning overseas Chinese, especially in Southeast Asia. Indeed, the transition to modernity in the Asia Pacific region was significantly marked by the ways in which the regional networks of diasporan-Chinese traders both transgressed the colonial administration of European "spheres of influence" and at the same time converged with colonial capitalist production and commercial systems.[59] Their family and trade enterprises both linked and transgressed the colonial prototypes of Southeast Asia nation-states, and they evolved over time with the transition from mercantilism to subcontracting to late capitalism. By the 1970s, diasporan Chinese "have come to play nodal and pivotal roles in the emergence of the new, flexible capitalism of the Asia Pacific region."[60] In a departure from the norm in post–World War II developmental states in, say, Latin America, Chinese economic and social networks introduced Southeast Asian subjects as key players in the Asia Pacific region and in the cultural work of producing alternative visions of Asian modernity.

New strategies of flexible accumulation have promoted a flexible attitude toward citizenship. For instance, Chinese entrepreneurs are not merely engaged in profit making; they are also acquiring a range of symbolic capitals that will facilitate their positioning, economic negotiation, and cultural acceptance in different geographical sites. I argue that in a transnational context, there must be social limits to the accumulation of cultural capital, so that ethnic Chinese who are practicing strategies of flexible citizenship find greater social acceptance in certain countries than in others.

While there are limits to their social mobility in the West, the growth of ethnic-Chinese networks and wealth in Asia has given rise to a narrative of Chinese triumphalism that celebrates a myth of fraternal solidarity across oceans.[61] But discourses about the neo-Confucianist basis of Asian capitalism have not gone unchallenged by Muslim leaders in Southeast Asia, who promote a counterdiscourse about a new Islam friendly to capitalism. At a broader regional level, East Asian and ASEAN countries often take a common moral stance—saying no to the West—to the epistemic violence wrought by neoliberal orthodoxy, but at the same time, they disguise their own investment in the rationalities of global capitalism.[62] Globalization in Asia, then, has induced both national and transnational forms of nationalism that not only reject Western hegemony but seek, in panreligious civilizational discourses, to promote the ascendancy of the East.

New Modes of Subjectification—Flexibility, Mobility, and Disciplines

Transnational mobility and maneuvers mean that there is a new mode of constructing identity, as well as new modes of subjectification that cut across political borders. Scholars look at the problematic nature of identity in late modernity largely in terms of mass consumer culture and the disorienting sense of displacement. Recent studies identify different modalities of flexibility associated with innovations in American culture and practice. For instance, scholars note that flexibility has become a household word that refers not only to the workaday world but also to the ways in which we consume commodities and organize our lives in late modernity. In his stunning thesis on contemporary culture, Fredric Jameson argues that relentless commoditization has led to the proliferation of cultural forms extolling fragmentation, (re)combinations, innovation, and flexibility in literature, art, architecture, and lifestyles—all variously expressing the "postmodern logic of late capitalism."[63] In the worlds of medicine and business, Emily Martin notes that "immune systems thinking," which idealizes flexibility, has pervaded the areas of body management, health, and corporate organization, thus shaping the ways in which Americans constitute their subjectivity.[64] In the heart of Silicon Valley, Judith Stacey observes that the upheavals wrought by the computer industry have induced the formation of flexible, "recombined" families.[65] While there appear to be different sources and domains for the rise of flexible concepts and practices in modernity, they all point directly and indirectly to the workings of global capitalism. But there has been little or no attempt to consider how different regimes of truth and power may set structural limits to such flexible productions and subjectivities.

My book will explore the flexible practices, strategies, and disciplines associated with transnational capitalism and will seek to identify both the new modes of subject making and the new kinds of valorized subjectivity. Among transnational Chinese subjects, those most able to benefit from their participation in global capitalism celebrate flexibility and mobility, which give rise to such figures as the multiple-passport holder; the multicultural manager with "flexible capital"; the "astronaut," shuttling across borders on business; "parachute kids," who can be dropped off in another country by parents on the trans-Pacific business commute; and so on. Thus, while mobility and flexibility have long been part of the repertoire of human behavior, under transnationality the new links between flexibility and the logics of displacement, on the one hand, and capital accumulation, on the other, have given new valence to such strategies of maneuvering and positioning. Flexibility, migration, and relocations, instead of being coerced or resisted, have become practices to strive for rather than stability.

Flexible citizenship is shaped within the mutually reinforcing dynamics of discipline and escape. While scholars of globalization have dealt with identity in terms of juridico-legal status, the disciplinary norms of capitalism and culture also constrain and shape strategies of flexible subject making. In other words, how can we combine the insights of Marx and Foucault in our understanding of subject formation? How are the strategies of capitalist exploitation and juridico-legal power (Marx) connected with the modes of governmentality associated with state power and with culture (Foucault)? Indeed, even under conditions of transnationality, political rationality and cultural mechanisms continue to deploy, discipline, regulate, or civilize subjects in place or on the move. Although increasingly able to escape localization by state authorities, traveling subjects are never free of regulations set by state power, market operations, and kinship norms. For instance, in different countries, schemes of ethnic and racial differentiation that define individuals as "Chinese," "Muslims," and so on both discipline and normalize their subjectivities as particular kinds of citizens, regardless of their mobility. The requirements of capital accumulation compel behavior and plans that privilege business-driven travel, family relocation, and the manipulation of state controls.

The identity of traveling Chinese subjects, however, does not merely reflect the imperatives of mobile capitalism or attempts to deflect state disciplining; it is also shaped by the powerful effects of a cultural regime that defines what it may mean to be Chinese in late modernity. Among overseas Chinese, cultural norms dictate the formation of translocal business networks, putting men in charge of mobility while women and children are the disciplinable subjects of familial regimes.[66] Over the past century, Chinese emigration to sites throughout the Asia Pacific region, including North America, has entailed localizing the women at home, where they care for their families, thus freeing the men to work abroad. While the sojourning men may themselves have been treated brutally in diaspora by the colonial powers, they also exerted patriarchal power over their wives in China. In many cases, the men had two (sometimes more) transnational families—one located in China, the other(s) in diaspora. The "China wife" and the "Singapore wife" represent the two female poles of an extended family strung across oceans—a situation that has endured through the eras of colonialism, revolution, cold war, and the New World (dis)Order.[67] Today, transnationalism has prompted a revival of the sojourning practice: Elite Hong Kong executives who jet all over the world sometimes transfer their families to "safe havens" in California, where the wives care for the families while earning residency rights. In some cases, the peripatetic father has set up another family "back home" in Hong Kong or China. The ungrounded personal identities of traveling men, and the new fixities of the Asian national elite emphasis on "Asian values," are the varied cultural logics produced by the encounter with globalizing trends and challenges.

Contrary to highly abstracted discussions of translocal gender systems, this work embeds the changing dynamics of gender relations in the imperatives of family, capitalism, and mobility. Family regimes that generally valorize mobile masculinity and localized femininity shape strategies of flexible citizenship, gender division of labor, and relocation in different sites. Transnational publics based on ethnicized mass media, networks of Asian professionals, and circuits of capital add a geometric dimension to Asian male mobility, power, and capital vis-à-vis women, not only in the domestic domain but also in transnational production, service, and consumer realms. New regimes of sexual exploitation—keeping mistresses, pornographic culture, prostitution—proliferate alongside translocal business networks. There are, however, ideological limits to masculinist representations of capital, not only from other emergent ethnic groups seeking alternative images of Asian entrepreneurialism but also from the American public, which is highly ambivalent about the influx of a new breed of affluent Asian immigrants. The Asian masculinist quest for global power and visibility clashes with the Western fear of being invaded—materially and symbolically—by Asian corporate power.

Postdevelopmental State Strategy: Zones of Graduated Sovereignty

Transnationality induced by accelerated flows of capital, people, cultures, and knowledge does not simply reduce state power, as many have claimed, but also stimulates a new, more flexible and complex relationship between capital and governments. The term *transnational* first became popular in the late 1970s largely because global companies began to rethink their strategies, shifting from the vertical-integration model of the "multinational" firm to the horizontal dispersal of the "transnational" corporation. Contrary to the popular view that sees the state in retreat everywhere before globalization, I consider state power as a positive generative force that has responded eagerly and even creatively to the challenges of global capital. Asian tiger states have evolved by aggressively seeking global capital while securing their own economic interests and the regulation of their populations.

There are grounds for identifying a postdevelopmental state strategy whereby governments cede more of the instrumentalities connected with development as a technical project to global enterprises but maintain strategic controls over resources, populations, and sovereignty. For instance, tiger economies such as South Korea and Malaysia have shifted from the state nurturing of domestic industries to a dependence on global capital and have thus become vulnerable to conditions shaped by financial markets. While Asian economic liberalism resists market dictatorship, Asian leaders negotiate different kinds of partnerships with global capital and, at the same time, let market rationality dictate their cultural regulation of society—especially of the middle classes, which are critical to development. Furthermore, countries such as Malaysia and Indonesia have responded to market demands and political resistances through a strategy of graduated sovereignty that subjects different segments of the population to different mixes of disciplinary, caring, and punitive technologies. Postdevelopmental strategies—whereby there is a decline in the state control over the technical project of development and an increase in the pastoral regulation of the population—are the pragmatic responses of developing economies to the challenges of globalization.

Zones of variegated sovereignty proliferate alongside moves toward greater regionalism as panreligious nationalisms seek to integrate nation-states in a loose web of cultural kinship and political culture. Ideological tensions between two major forms of governmentality are expressed in neo-Confucian discourses and claims about "the New Islam," narratives that are by and large shaped by nationalism driven by the imperatives of liberal economic competition. The phenomena associated with transnationality—mobile capital, business networks, migrations, media publics, zones of new sovereignty, and triumphant Asian discourses—all compel us to rethink the categories of the nation-state, culture, identity, and modernity in terms of their reciprocal production and reproduction in the new forces of global capitalism.

Anthropology has a special contribution to make to our understanding of transnationality, but perhaps we have been held back by the "macro" scope of the phenomenon and by a false sense of what constitutes the global and the local.[68] In this work, I try to show how our cultural insights and our attention to everyday practice and the relations of power can illuminate how the operations of globalization are translated into cultural logics that inform behavior, identities, and relationships. We have perhaps also been restrained by our tendency to self-critique and by the postcolonial critique that attributes all modes of domination to the West (colonialism, "the empire," Western capitalism, cultural imperialism) without paying close attention also to emergent forms of power and oppression that variously ally with *and* contest Western forces.[69] Anthropological knowledge is valuable precisely because it seeks to grasp the intertwined dynamics of cultural and material processes as they are played out in particular and geographic locations as part of global history. Because our focus is primarily on human agency and imagination, we pay ethnographic attention to how subjects, in given historical conditions, are shaped by structures of power—colonial rule, cultural authorities, market institutions, political agencies, translocal entities—and how they respond to these structures in culturally specific ways. Because we do not see culture as somehow separated from "rational" institutions such as the economy, the legal system, and the state, we are able to trace the cultural logics that inform different approaches—at the personal, community, national, and regional levels—to the processes of modernity and globalization. Anthropology, then, can provide a different, more ethnographically grounded and nuanced perspective to the universalism and homogeneity claimed by Western theory.

Thus, new narratives of Asian modernity, spun from the self-confidence of vibrant economies, cannot be reduced to a pale imitation of some Western standard (for instance, full-fledged democracy combined with modern capitalism). Ascendant regions of the world such as the Asia Pacific region are articulating their own modernities as distinctive formations. The historical facts of Western colonialism, ongoing geopolitical domination, and ideological and cultural influences are *never* discounted (only minimized) in these narratives, but they should nevertheless be considered alternative constructions of modernity in the sense of moral-political projects that seek to control their own present and future. Such self-theorization of contemporary non-Western nation-states, while always in dialogue and in tension with the West, are critical modes of ideological repositioning that have come about with shifting geostrategic alignments.

I have chosen to examine the everyday effects of transnationality in terms of the tensions between capital and state power because there is no other field of force for understanding the logics of cultural change. I focus on the agency of displaced subjects and attempts by the state to regulate their activities and identities as a way to explore the new cultural logics of transnationality. The pressures to cope with the contradictions between cultural homeland and host country, the governmentality of the state and the disciplining of labor markets, and the politics of imposed identity and the politics of self-positioning reflect the logics and ambivalence that flavor the cosmopolitan Chinese subjectivity. As a "Chinese" person whose primary frame of cultural identification is insular Southeast Asia, not China, I write as a diasporan subject moving in tangent to the claims of the home country, always poised to discern the governmentality of the state, culture, and capital and to struggle against submitting fully to any.

My larger goal is to redirect our study of Chinese subjects beyond an academic construction of Chineseness that is invariably or solely defined in relation to the motherland, China. Those of us outside China have been regarded as "a residual China" or as minorities in host countries, that is, as less culturally "authentic" Chinese.[70] Rather, I argue in this book, the contemporary practices and values of diasporan Chinese are characteristic of larger questions of displacement, travel, capital accumulation, and other transnational processes that affect large numbers of late-twentieth-century subjects (who are geographically "in place" and *dis*placed). Over the past few decades, the multiple and shifting status of "Chineseness" has been formed and embedded within the processes of global capitalism—production, trade, consumption, mobility, and dislocation/relocation—and subjected to various modes of governmentality that fix them in place or disperse them in space. According to Ien Ang, " 'Chineseness' has become an open signifier," acquiring meanings in dialectical relation to the practices, beliefs, and structures encountered in the spaces of flows across nations and markets.[71] There is an ever growing pluralization of Chinese identities, and people in mainland China, no less than diasporan subjects, are finding their division by gender, sexuality, class, culture, aesthetics, spatial and social location, politics, and nationality to be extremely meaningful.[72] By exploring experiences of some Chinese cosmopolitans, this book seeks as much to illuminate the practices of an elite transnationalism as to subvert the ethnic absolutism born of nationalism and the processes of cultural othering that have intensified with transnationality. My anthropology is thus situated obliquely to the hegemonic powers of Home and Exile. By oscillating between Western belonging and nonbelonging, and between the local and the global, anthropology as a mode of knowledge can provide a unique angle on new cultural realities in the world at large.

Part 1 begins with a criticism of the ways in which we construct knowledges about non-Western societies within unifying models of modernity and the postcolonial. New geopolitical configurations, I argue, require anthropologists and other scholars to shift from their vantage point of viewing the rest of the world as peripheries or sites for testing models crafted in the West. The rise of the Asia Pacific powers—China and the Southeast Asian tiger economies—are the ethnographic contexts for exploring alternative visions of modernity that both engage and challenge the West. Chapter 1 charts a post-Maoist modernity by analyzing changing modes of regulations and culturalist narratives. I argue that China's partial adoption of Southeast Asian models of development, together with its growing connections with overseas Chinese, has led to claims of a Chinese modernity that resolves the problem of de-racination. Chapter 2 takes a closer look at the tensions between the imagined community of the nation-state, which is territorially bounded, and that of the transnational community, which is open ended and therefore undermines the control of the state. Discourses about the moral economies of Asian countries both regulate citizens at home and construct a new hierarchy of relations between nation-states in the region.

In Part 2, I discuss how various regimes represented by the nation-state, the market, and the family provide the cultural logics that shape the migration strategies of Chinese elites bound for North America. Chapter 3 recasts Pierre Bourdieu's concept of different forms of capital within a transnational frame-work of cross-cultural travel and encounters. I maintain that in translocal strategies of accumulation, the migrant's ability to convert economic capital into social prestige is limited by the ethnoracial moral order of the host society. Chapter 4 discusses the governmentality of overseas-Chinese kinship and interpersonal relations (*guanxi*) as habitus that are instilled by regimes of accumulation, dispersal, and localization in the diaspora. A central practice in these regimes is the search for flexible citizenship whereby affluent migrants seek different locations for economic gain or political security and at the same time retain their flexibility to circumvent their disciplining.

Part 3 explores the new transnational publics created by intensified mobil-ity, the mass media, and capital flows. I view translocal ethnic-Chinese publics as fields of power relations "media-tized" by modern communications and travel. Chapter 5 draws on news reports, academic books, films, and eth-nographic research to trace the logic of family romances surrounding Chinese capitalism. By interweaving private sentiments and public politics, the ro-mance of traveling men reveals the political unconscious and regulatory forms of gender under late capitalism. In chapter 6, transnational publics—based on the mass media and professional and capital circuits—are viewed as norm-making systems that, through images and information, structure the cultural life of transnational Chinese in Asian and American contexts.

Part 4 outlines the post–cold war contours of cultural politics across the Asia Pacific region. American anxiety over an emergent Asia, represented by the Chinese economic giant, has made Samuel Huntington's "clash of civilizations" thesis influential in North American narratives about trade issues and human rights in Asian economies. Chapter 7 exposes Huntington's thesis as a postmodernist revival of American orientalism. I challenge his argument about unbridgeable civilizational differences by identifying a logic of post-Enlightenment economic rationality in the Asian tiger economies. Taking liberalism as a practical form of government rather than as a doctrine, I suggest that state regulation of the middle classes, translated into cultural terms, follows the rules of liberal economics. My final chapter deals with how the art of government, strained by the condition of transnationality, has to further stretch the bounds of political economy. Shifts in the relationship between governmentality and sovereignty have produced zones of differentiated sovereignty. Some of these zones are seedbeds for counterpublics that seek to articulate visions outside the structures of state and capital.

PART 1

Emerging Modernities

Anthropological Authority and the New World Disorder

When I was a child growing up in Malaysia, it seemed as though we were always trying to catch up with the West, which was represented first by Great Britain and later by the United States.[1] Although Malaya gained independence from the British in 1957 (and became Malaysia in 1962), British-type education and the mass media continued to construct our world as a failed replica of the modern West. This colonial effect of trying to learn from and imitate the global center has been a preoccupation of postcolonial elites seeking to articulate a destiny that is a mixed set of Western and Asian interests. Now a resident of the United States, my annual visits to Southeast Asia reveal that a different vision of the future is being articulated, an alternative definition of modernity that is morally and politically differentiated from that of the West.

The first half of this century saw the collapse of Western colonial empires; in the second half, we are witnessing the emergence of a multipolar world. What do these circumstances mean for anthropology as a Western theory of knowledge about culture? In *Culture and Imperialism*, Edward Said notes that a Western "structure of attitude and referencing" used the third world (cultures, places, peoples) as sources of materials to produce knowledge and as "cases" to explicate Western theory without recognizing non-Western actors as equal partners in cultural production.[2] In today's world, such a structure of attitude actually reflects a defensive Western cultural nationalism more than it reflects the supreme cultural confidence at the height of Western imperialism, the era dealt with by Said in his book. This chapter calls on anthropology to weave our empirical knowledge of the non-Western world into new geopolitical configurations. I argue that anthropologists and other scholars should shift from their vantage point of viewing the rest of the world as peripheries or sites for testing models crafted in the West. They can then make a unique contribution to an understanding of how the economic structures of development are integrated with the production of cultural identities.

The Moral Politics of Comparison

Anthropology as a discipline is mainly concerned with studying the non-West, especially the effects on it of colonialism, capitalism, and the cultural destruction visited by Euroamerican powers. Indeed, this rich and critical contribution to Western liberal tradition is a valuable corrective to ethnocentric assumptions that plague all disciplines, together with their representations of non-Western cultures and societies.

Our concerns about the effects of global structures of power and wealth have made us concentrate on the poor, the downtrodden, the marginalized, and the exploited in the third world.[3] This is a rich tradition that in many ways represents what is best and distinctive in American anthropology. Yet in a maturing field, we may want to broaden the scope of the anthropological understanding of power and deploy our disciplinary insights to investigate how the privileged half lives, exercises, and reproduces its domination—all increasingly on a transnational scale. Of course, Marxist anthropologists have always been concerned with the broad issues of political economy, but their focus has been on systems of trade, structures of production, and flows of commodities.[4] Rather less attention has been given to human agency and the cultural practices of the powerful, as well as how they have been shaped and given meaning by translocal relationships.[5] Nevertheless, the issue of human agency needs to be foregrounded much more in relation to different structures of global domination and hegemonies, looking not only at the powers of the weak but also of the strong.[6]

However, in a recent trend, the anthropology of modernity seems to be turning away from engaging with the changing global scene and seeking instead to focus on changes within the West, as if they can be understood independently of the West's entanglements and dialogue with the Rest. For instance, in response to the "crisis of representation," George Marcus and Michael Fischer call for "repatriating anthropology." In proposing this reorientation in anthropology, Marcus and Fischer convey the impression that the chief value of "cultural others" is in providing a foil to American modernity. The study of other cultures becomes "a strategy of defamiliarization" that anthropologists can use to engage in a cultural critique of their own Western society. Furthermore, if cultural others are to be used for this contrastive function, "they must be portrayed realistically, and in the round, sharing modern conditions that we experience also."[7] Here, Marcus and Fischer are cautioning against a largely obsolete tendency in anthropology to portray other cultures as existing in a noncoeval space with the West. But they also seem to assume that Western modernity is a universal formation and that the modernities of non-Western others can be understood only in relation to the idealized Western Model. Thus, although the comparative method is at the heart of anthropological knowledge, it has been a comparison that employs the West as the single measure of modernity against which other societies must be measured.

The moral politics of the entire field of discussion about modernity and transnationalism needs to be interrogated in a world where capitalism is no longer centered in the West but distributed across a number of global arenas. The hegemonic Euroamerican notion of modernity—as spelled out in modernization theory and theories of development[8]—locates the non-West at the far end of an escalator rising toward the West, which is at the pinnacle of modernity in terms of capitalist development, secularization of culture, and democratic state formation.[9] But even in the particular ways political-economic and cultural dimensions are combined, it is not possible to talk about a single modernity within the West. The contemporary impassioned conflicts and negotiations over immigrants, multiculturalism, women's rights, and the environmental effects of capitalism in the United States and in Europe speak to the composition and goals of development, culture, and the nation in different countries. In anthropology, we need to attend to how places in the non-West differently plan and envision the particular combinations of culture, capital, and the nation-state, rather than assume that they are immature versions of some master Western prototype.

Indeed, the crisis in American social sciences concerns how to represent (other) modernities when linear models of modernization, development, and the spread of democracy are no longer adequate to capture the range of political formations and self-positioning in different parts of the world.

For instance, both modernization theory, represented by William W. Rostow, and Marxist-influenced narratives of development, represented by Immanuel Wallerstein, ignore the ways in which Asian experiences cannot fit neatly into Western historicism (with its sequential history) and the core-periphery model.[10] Even when world-systems theorists talk about regional core-periphery formations, they fail to capture the complex interweaving relations of domination and subordination by transnational capital that blur the division between "core" and "peripheral" countries. Actual historical events, such as the collapse of communist systems, the revival of ethnic nationalisms, the relative decline of some Western powers, and the rise of Asian capitalism, have rearranged transnational relations of trade, development, and power. A recent op-ed piece in the *New York Times* criticizes the view that the United States is bound to lead the New World Order. Christopher Layne notes that "while Washington may believe its aspirations for world order reflect universal values, they reflect American preferences that may not comport with others' interests. . . . We [can't] indefinitely prevent new powers . . . from rising, or old ones . . . from staging comebacks."[11] In what ways can anthropology as a form of Western knowledge enact a decentering by attending to other narratives of modernity that are neither wholly derivative of the West nor based entirely on the interests of Western democracies?

Postcoloniality or Alternative Modernities?

In recent years, the study of postcoloniality has emerged as a new theory of relations between the West and the Rest. Emerging out of the writings of Indian "subaltern" theorists, postcolonial approaches have tended to use the particular experiences of colonialism in India as the model for understanding *contemporary* relations of domination, subjugation, and subjectivization. This metropolitan theory of third-world subalternity tends to collapse all non-Western countries (except Japan, of course) into the same model of analysis, in which primacy is given to racial, class, and national dominations stemming from the European colonial era.

In British cultural studies, "the postcolonial" refers specifically to nonwhite populations from former colonial territories that have relocated in the West; it recognizes that their historical experiences and contemporary productions are an irreducible and critical part of European modernity. Homi Bhabha identifies a "postcolonial contramodernity" in the works of black subjects in diaspora, and Paul Gilroy talks about the "double consciousness" of transatlantic black cultures as an irreducible part and critique of Western modernity.[12] For Stuart Hall, the postcolonial refers mainly to the effects of decolonization (through the influx of peoples from former colonies) on metropolitan countries such as England.[13] For these cultural theorists then, postcolonialism refers primarily to the ways colonialism has shaped contemporary minority-identity politics and the critique of Western societies.

More broadly, postcolonial theorists focus on recovering the voices of subjects silenced by patriarchy and colonial rule (*The Empire Writes Back* is the title of one popular collection);[14] they assume that all contemporary racial, ethnic, and cultural oppressions can all be attributed to Western colonialisms. American appropriations of postcolonial theory have created a unitary discourse of the postcolonial that refers to highly variable situations and conditions throughout the world; thus, Gayatri Spivak is able to talk about "the paradigmatic subaltern woman," as well as "New World Asians (the old migrants) and New Immigrant Asians (often 'model minorities') being disciplinarized together."[15] Other postcolonial feminists also have been eager to seek structural similarities, continuities, conjunctures, and alliances between the postcolonial oppressions experienced by peoples on the bases of race, ethnicity, and gender both in formerly colonized populations in the third world *and* among immigrant populations in the United States, Australia, and England.[16] Seldom is there any attempt to link these assertions of unitary postcolonial situations among diasporan subjects in the West to the historical structures of colonization, decolonization, and contemporary developments in particular non-Western countries. Indeed, the term postcolonial has been used to indiscriminately describe different regimes of economic, political, and cultural domination in the Americas, India, Africa, and other third-world countries where the actual historical experiences of colonialism have been very varied in terms of local culture, conquest, settlement, racial exploitation, administrative regime, political resistance, and articulation with global capitalism. In careless hands, postcolonial theory can represent a kind of theoretical imperialism whereby scholars based in the West, without seriously engaging the scholarship of faraway places, can project or "speak for" postcolonial situations elsewhere. Stuart Hall has warned against approaches that universalize racial, ethnic, and gender oppressions without locating the "actual integument of power . . . in concrete institutions."[17]

A more fruitful strand of postcolonial studies is represented by subaltern scholars such as Partha Chatterjee, who has criticized the Indian national projects, which are based on Western models of modernity and bypass "many possibilities of authentic, creative, and plural development of social identities," including the marginalized communities in Indian society.[18] He suggests that an alternative imagination that draws on "narratives of community" would be a formidable challenge to narratives of capital. This brilliant work, however, is based on the assumption that both modernity and capitalism are universal forms, against which non-Western societies such as India can only mobilize "pre-existing cultural solidarities such as locality, caste, tribe, religious community, or ethnic identity."[19] This analytical opposition between a universal modernity and non-Western culture is rather old-fashioned; it is as if Chatterjee believes the West is not present in Indian elites who champion narratives of the indigenous community. Furthermore, the concept of a universal modernity must be rethought when, as Arif Dirlik observes, "the narrative of capitalism is no longer the narrative of the history of Europe; non-European capitalist societies now make their own claims on the history of capitalism."[20]

The loose use of the term "the postcolonial," then, has had the bizarre effect of contributing to a Western tradition of othering the Rest; it suggests a postwar scheme whereby "the third world" was followed by "the developing countries," which are now being succeeded by "the postcolonial." This continuum seems to suggest that the further we move in time, the more beholden non-Western countries are to the forms and practices of their colonial past. By and large, anthropologists have been careful to discuss how formerly colonized societies have developed differently in relation to global economic and political dominations and have repositioned themselves differently vis-à-vis capitalism and late modernity. By specifying differences in history, politics, and culture, anthropologists are able to say how the postcolonial formation of Indonesia is quite different from that of India, Nicaragua, or Zaire. There are, of course, places for the use of the term postcolonial—for instance, in ethnographies about people who may see themselves as still haunted by the "ghosts" of colonialism or who live in agrarian situations where the forces of colonially instituted relations continue to play a significant role.[21] But in many areas of the world, we must move beyond an analysis based on colonial nostalgia or colonial legacies to appreciate how economic and ideological modes of domination have been transformed in excolonial countries, as well as how those countries' positioning in relation to the global political economy has also been transformed.

It appears that unitary models of the postcolonial and of modernity are ascendant at a time when many Asian countries are not interested in colonialism or in postcolonialism—having in their leaders' views successfully negotiated formal decolonization—and are in the process of constructing alternative modernities based on new relations with their populations, with capital, and with the West. In other words, the "alternative" in alternative modernities does not necessarily suggest a critique of, or opposition to, capital.[22] Rather, it suggests the kinds of modernity that are (1) constituted by different *sets of relations* between the developmental or postdevelopmental state, its population, and global capital; and (2) constructed by political and social elites who appropriate "Western" knowledges and *re-present* them as truth claims about their own countries. First, Asian tiger countries consider themselves as belonging to a *post* postcolonial era—one characterized by state developmental strategies, rising standards of living, and the regulation of populations in a post–cold war order of flexible capitalism. They would not consider their own current engagements with global capitalism or metropolitan powers as postcolonial but seek rather to emphasize and claim emergent power, equality, and mutual respect on the global stage. Many formerly colonized countries in Southeast Asia are themselves emergent capitalist powerhouses that are "colonizing" territories and peoples in their own backyards or further afield: Indonesia has invaded and colonized East Timor, while Malaysian, Singaporean, and Hong Kong entrepreneurs are factory managers in China, timber barons in New Guinea and Guyana, and hotel operators in England and the United States. These strategies of economic colonization by countries formerly colonized by the West represent new forms of engaging dissension at home and capital abroad—new arrangements that cannot be accommodated by a universalizing theory of the postcolonial.[23] More fruitful are attempts to understand new modes of biopolitical regimes that now discipline, regulate, and "civilize" peoples in varied contexts of the late twentieth century.

Second, elite discourses, by appropriating Western knowledges and terms—

for instance, race, science, technology, sexuality, democracy—recast and represent their nations as "modern" but "inside a local construction of 'east/west,' " according to Tani Barlow. She argues that through this suppression of the West, the localization of appropriated signs in Chinese contexts enables intellectuals to represent their nation as modern without being Western.[24] Through self-theorizing and truth claims, the elite views the nation not only as being in tension with Western hegemonies but as being an alternative modernity that is discursively represented in "locally hegemonic, historical projects."[25] The approach is therefore *not* a bipolar view of Western and non-Western modernities; rather, it is a method that considers how nation-states, in shaping their political economies and in discursively representing themselves as moral-political projects, while borrowing extensively from the West, also seek to deflect the West's multiple domination. We must go beyond treating "multiple modernities" as formations that are merely reactive to Western capitalism. Instead, we can examine the national and localization processes that actively negotiate new relations to capital and that make truth claims about distinctive modernities within local frameworks of the East-West divide.[26]

China in particular cannot fit into conventional notions about postcolonial societies because it was never fully colonized, nor as a major socialist state does it engage the global economy in quite the same way as smaller developing countries. In the "transition from socialism," post-1970s China, unlike the countries of Eastern Europe, has not suffered a dramatic weakening of the state in controlling either its population or the ideological orientation toward modernity.[27] In what follows, I will chart the rise of a post-Maoist modernity by discussing the changing state political-economic strategies and their interweaving with the elite's production and deployment of discourses about a distinctive Chinese modernity linked to overseas Chinese.

China's Embrace of the Authoritarian Asian Model

Since the turn of the century, Chinese intellectuals have played a major role as representers of the Chinese nation, both in the language of political economy and in the language of culture.[28] In different eras, their role as articulators of what is modern in China depended on strategies that used Western master narratives, that attacked China's past and customs, or that constructed "heroic polyglot subjects."[29] For much of the twentieth century, Chinese ideas about progress in the fields of development and political thought came from the West, by way of the former Soviet Union. During the Maoist era (1949–1976), the state was heavily influenced by the Soviet model of modernization, which sought political liberation from European domination through autonomous development that was delinked from the capitalist world economy.[30] On the one hand, establishment intellectuals stressed the development of science and technology to strengthen the Chinese socialist economy; on the other hand, they attacked what was constructed as Chinese tradition—feudalism and the customs of the past. These principles were encapsulated in the Four Modernizations (*sige xiandaihua*) policy, which targeted industry, agriculture, science and technology, and national defense for development but made no mention of democracy.[31] During the Great Proletarian Cultural Revolution of the 1960s, intellectuals attacked the Chinese past for containing "feudal" features. Campaigns to "do away with the 'four olds' and cultivate the 'four news' " (*po sijiu li sixin*) identified old ideas, old culture, old customs, and old habits that had to be replaced by socialist equivalents for China to attain its socialist modernity.[32] These narratives of a Chinese modernity shifted in the Dengist period (1976–1996), when elements that were formerly vilified became revered by elites bent on defining Chinese modernity in cultural, and not merely socialist, terms.

When Deng Xiaoping came to power, socialist nationalism was repositioned through a reengagement with global capitalism. Official discourses promoting the Four Modernizations began to valorize a traditional culture (*chuantong wenhua*) purged of its "feudal superstitions." A new phrase, "socialism with Chinese characteristics" (*you Zhongguo tese de shehuizhuyi*), signaled the sinicization of the modernization project and promoted national autonomy in rethinking development and controlling relations with the global economy. In his famous 1992 south China tour, Deng formally launched China's latest economic takeoff by calling for the construction of "a few Hong Kongs" as part of "one hundred years of market reforms and modernization."[33] Indeed, the resulting influx of capital from Hong Kong and from overseas Chinese was so great that a Hong Kong banker claimed that Hong Kong was "the prime driver of the greatest economic takeoff in world history."[34] Furthermore, undeterred by the 1989 crackdown at Tiananmen Square, Hong Kong investors led other Chinese capitalists from Taiwan, Singapore, Malaysia, Thailand, and elsewhere in pouring over U.S.$2 billion into Guangdong Province and in employing some three million mainland workers by 1991.[35] In Shenzhen, where the new vision was announced, there is a gigantic poster of Deng emerging like a Judeo-Christian god from sun-streaked clouds and raising his finger in seeming admonishment at the chaotic traffic in a major downtown intersection. The image symbolizes not the abandonment of state control but rather the release of market forces as a way to strengthen the state. In the socialist language, this is defined as developing "the productive forces," raising "the living standards of the people," and increasing "comprehensive national strength" so that China, following the model of Asian capitalism, will be a developed country by the early twenty-first century.

The Chinese state strategy of engaging global capitalism appears to be following the Asian developmental model whereby "strong state regimes [are] engaged in facilitating fast capitalist growth, some of it industrialization, in the era of the transnational corporation."[36] These "repressive-developmentalist states"—South Korean, Taiwan, Singapore, Indonesia—are characterized by their careful negotiation of relationships with foreign capital, their promotion of large professional middle classes, and their disciplining of their populations by varying degrees of political repression. Thus, the Chinese state strategy is mixed; it entails a particular combination of the developmentalist state, the disciplining of labor forces, the careful cultivation of transnational capital, the repression of human rights, and economic competition with the West.[37] In pursuing this strategy, China has participated extensively in the networks transnational capital has woven between East and Southeast Asian countries.

This authoritarian "Asian" model of development is based on an extensive disciplining of the population that goes beyond the socialist model of controlling birth, health, and labor mobility.[38] It requires a new regime of labor disciplining that is market driven rather than state driven. Whereas earlier socialist programs focused on mobilizing a largely undifferentiated population for massive state projects, current modernization programs display new forms of governmentality geared to the standards of the global labor market. They seek to improve and upgrade "the quality of the population"—focusing in particular on the 40 percent of the population who are 19 years old or younger.[39] Concerned that "the population is the source of China's backwardness," the state has launched campaigns to improve conditions in the fields of public health, education, family planning, law, and technology. The well-known one-child family policy, which formerly was aimed at reducing the birth rate, has become a tool to "prevent or reduce the number of births of the seriously sick or disabled children [in order to] improve the quality of the Chinese population." The ministry of public health defends this action as "totally different" from the Nazi eugenics policy.[40] Under the socialist system, workers were treated uniformly across industries, whereas the new market model seeks to correct and improve the quality of a segment of the vast labor force to make China competitive with other Asian labor regimes.[41]

In the countryside, the shift to market competition began with the household responsibility system. Households were urged to compete with each other rather than rely on diminishing social supports. Ann Anagnost reports that "the moral discourse on wealth" now honors the wealth-accumulating household.[42] Labels such as "ten-thousand-yuan household," "nouveau-riche household," and "civilized household" are the much resented indicators of a family's relative success or failure to meet the new Chinese living standards. In many cases, households have been able to improve their incomes because adolescent daughters or sons are working in factories and are thus contributing to China's competitiveness in the industrial sector.[43]

Furthermore, job security has been stripped from selected industries, plunging workers into labor markets now penetrated by global capital. In the Break the Three "Irons" Campaign, the state rescinded guaranteed employment (the iron bowl), guaranteed posts for managers (the iron chair), and guaranteed wages (the iron salary). Workers have complained about having to trade in an iron bowl for a porcelain one (elegant but fragile). By thus exposing workers to the uncertainties of the global market, the state puts its economy in direct competition with the flexible-market regimes operating in the wider Asia Pacific region. When Chinese newspapers now write about Chinese workers who are willing to work for less than U.S.\$80 a month, they are identifying thousands of young women who are flocking from all over China to the special economic zones along the coast. Increasingly, subcontracting firms consider Chinese women better workers than their counterparts in Southeast Asia, and more and more overseas-Chinese manufacturers are relocating their factories from Indonesia and the Philippines to south China.

Improving the quality of young workers by making them available for exploitation articulates with the imperatives of a new consumer culture. For instance, a visitor to Shenzhen's industrial zone observed in surprise, "A model woman worker dressed in gold and jade? Suddenly I understood. Model workers of the 1980s are good at creating wealth, and they also understand how to enjoy it. This is probably the charm of our times."[44] In the coastal cities that are now linked to Hong Kong and Taiwan by capital, trade, and the media, a thriving consumer culture has developed among young women. Whether employed in timber mills, electronics factories, or hotels, many rush to spend their earnings on consumer items such as beauty aids. In Guangzhou (Canton), there is "a virtual empire of Avon ladies" who serve a market of sixty million potential customers.[45] These sales representatives, who earn more than the majority of their customers, display Avon products on their faces and nails and promise that a "beautiful world" can be gained through working hard and making oneself over as a marketable product of Chinese capitalism. Here we see the delicate interweaving of female self-discipline, industrial regulation, and consumer manipulation that comes with global capitalism. Using ready-made images that target Asian consumers, corporations engender new needs and desires that socialize Chinese workers to the norms of mass consumption.

The increased integration of the Chinese economy with the rest of Asia (see chapter 2) produces an ideological need to differentiate China from capitalist Asia. In the post-Mao era, the role of rusticated intellectuals, restored academics, and social-science policy makers to speak for the Chinese people is expanding as attempts are made to distinguish the state and the nation; while reconstituted academic centers represent state policies, proletarianized intellectuals such as Wei Jingsheng speak for the people against the statist depredation.[46] As more and more Chinese reject the statist production of socialist truths and appropriate the newly valorized signs of sex, individualism, fashions, and pleasures that come with the consumer market, academic elites are reviving Confucianism (*rujia sixiang*) as a moral force "that can serve as a single source for building a new culture."[47] This revival and deployment of Confucianist discourse also renews the cultural and ethnic continuities between mainland and overseas Chinese, of whom the latter are viewed as the embodiments of a diffuse, enduring solidarity rooted in shared cultural traits. The business activities of overseas Chinese from Taiwan, Singapore, and other Pacific locations now link China to Pacific Rim modernity. As the boundaries between socialism and capitalism, and between China and overseas-Chinese communities, become blurred, Confucianism can be usefully invoked, with fruitful ambiguity, to simultaneously suggest the interbraiding of "Chinese" essence with the far-flung overseas-Chinese networks that accumulate capital throughout the region. Furthermore, Confucianism provides moral justification for the modes of gender domination associated with flexible labor systems and the consumer world of overseas-Chinese capitalism.

Plunging into the Ocean, Bridging Nations

Other elite discourses of Chinese modernity also are beginning to invoke the transnational lines of continuity in race/nation/culture between modern Chinese subjects and ethnic Chinese in Southeast Asia and beyond. In 1988, the popular Chinese television epic *He Shang* (River Elegy) seemed to echo sentiments yearning for a greater Chinese world of cultural progress. Written by media intellectuals rather than by state propagandists, the film reverses the conventional symbol of the Huanghe (Yellow River) as China's life force, history, and traditions. *He Shang* portrays the river as a symbol of China's tyrannical and stultifying agrarian civilization. Only when it enters the ocean does the Huanghe gain an openness and richness as it mingles with the waters of the Pacific. This film represents yet another wave of attacks on the reified Chinese past. As an intellectual "strategy of reversal" or a localized "Western" discourse attacking China's past,[48] the message is that China's modernity requires the nation to change its ancient course and merge into the "blue ocean culture" (*lanhai wenhua*). What exactly is meant by this blue ocean culture remains ambiguous. For many, it symbolizes the West—especially Western industrialization, science, and democracy—from which China must learn in order to be modern.[49] This is one discourse of modernity that seeks to push aside Chinese history and culture to embrace the West and to become like the West. However, I detect a more nuanced message: the blue oceanic societies that will guide China's modernity are the countries of the Asia Pacific region, which are widely viewed as having achieved Western material standards without losing their cultural heritage. The azure waters of the Pacific seem to invoke overseas-Chinese communities, in which Western elements are already localized and embedded. The conflicting reading of the film's message produced such a controversy that it was later banned and blamed for inciting prodemocracy movements in 1989.

The double message of *He Shang* is also reflected in the differing desires among members of China's vast society as to how to (re)envision China's future. The 1989 Tiananmen Incident, led by workers and students, seemed to point to the emergence of a new urban identity based on international symbols of democracy.[50] Perhaps. But there is a wide range of Chinese intellectuals who are engaged in the work of reenvisioning Chinese modernity, both against and for the state. This range includes repressed proletarianized intellectuals, independent novelists and writers, prodemocracy university students, and the growing state intelligentsia. Tani Barlow has argued persuasively that a college-educated bureaucratic elite has been using "the construction of Western social science discourse as the foundation of Truth" to guide social development and popular culture.[51]

This materialist realist view is echoed in the south, where a popular vision of Chinese modernity does not necessarily contain full-fledged democracy but rather talks about "the southern wind" of capitalism and consumerism blowing across China.[52] Historically, a Beijing-centered northern China has always been a symbol of the nation-state, whereas southern China, linked by diasporas to Southeast Asia (called *Nanyang,* or the Southern Ocean), has always explored its cultural margins and the future in relation to the Asia Pacific region.[53] This vision of a southern wind is inspired by the overseas Chinese, who, after centuries of being portrayed as traitors, are now considered the prodigal sons of China's modernity.[54]

A Huaqiao's First View of China

As a *huaqiao* (overseas Chinese), or a Straits Chinese born in Malaysia, my ideas about China were a mix of grim images of poverty and state oppression on the one hand, and a kinder, gentler Chinese people (than those in diaspora) on the other.[55] Over the years, academic study of China's modern history and society and Western media images of China had enriched this picture, but I remained convinced that visiting China for the first time would be a kind of spiritual homecoming. In 1993, armed with my American passport, I finally saw China. Not only did I not attain a spiritual connection with my parents' province, I felt a profound alienation. Of course, my mainland-Chinese friends and American academics said I visited "the wrong places"—the booming coastal cities of Guangzhou, Shenzhen, Shantou, and Xiamen rather than the "authentic" China of Beijing, Suzhou, or even Shanghai. This Beijingcentric bias is also promoted by Chinese studies, for which only the Mandarin-speaking region is the real China. But for me, south China is China, and it is real enough. Visiting the booming cities was like being caught up in the eye of the greatest typhoon in the history of capitalism. The people's headlong race to make money and trample on one another seemed to strip urban life of social grace. I have felt more at home in New York's urban jungle than in "my ancestral homeland." My sense of alienation was further enhanced by racial/cultural chauvinism and the pronounced importance of degrees of perceived Chineseness in shaping local views about wealth and modernity.

Overseas Chinese operate as an intermediary "contrast category" of Chinese modernity in a structural position between the mainland Chinese and the non-Chinese foreigners who embody Western modernity.[56] In all my encounters, the degree of my perceived racial and cultural Chineseness was used as a gauge of my wealth and prestige as a modern Chinese subject. Depending on how I dressed, I was taken for a Japanese or a Singaporean (rich) or a Malaysian Chinese (moderately wealthy) and would be treated with varying degrees of respect and charged accordingly for hotels, meals, and taxis. At one point, because I was dressed like a university student, the taxi driver was disdainful and could not believe I wanted to check into a famous hotel in Guangzhou. Overseas Chinese such as my sister, who always wore her designer suits and her fur coat (in the winter) on her visits to China, are identified as Chinese American (very, very rich). The gender discrimination is also particularly marked, and even on campuses, women clearly enjoy lower status than men. I was the exception: as a foreigner, I inspired interest because I could be a useful connection to an overseas university. Because they can better respond to such expectations of access to wealth or valuable overseas contacts, thousands of huaqiao entrepreneurs from Southeast Asia are much more enthusiastic about China than I was on my first visit.

Huaqiao as Bridge Builders

The opening of China to global trade is indelibly marked in the diacritics of returning diasporan Chinese. A new discourse, produced by the officially controlled media, has constructed a new term for these diasporan subjects—*haiwai huaren,* or "Chinese living overseas," an ambiguous label that removes the old stigma of huaqiao but retains the master symbol of irrefutable racial/cultural links to the motherland.[57] After being vilified by mainlanders, over-

seas Chinese are stereotyped as the embodiment of traditional Chinese familialism, business acumen, and talent for wealth making—the old Chinese folk
values that are now being officially valorized for building a bridge to China's
modern future.

An overview of mainland press clippings from the early 1990s discloses the
strategy of the media elite in producing truth claims about overseas Chinese as
a way to represent China's capitalist modernity. There are many stories of
returning huaqiao who help rebuild their ancestral hometowns and who
provide critical knowledges and contacts to resources in the outside world.
Overseas relatives, once they have revealed themselves, are reclaimed by mainlanders as people to whom one can rightly appeal for funds to pay for anything from rebuilding the local school to the funeral of a distant cousin whom
they have never seen. Through the invoking of kinship and hometown guanxi,
business arrangements become inseparable from and are euphemized as
moral relationships that facilitate the channeling of funds, favors, and people
across national borders.

A pretty typical banner headline proclaims "Let the Overseas Chinese Build
Bridges, Let Them Create Prosperity!" Something is lost in the translation,
but the pun on *qiao,* which refers both to overseas Chinese and to bridges,
merges diasporan subjects with a bridge to prosperity.[58] The article reports
that in Shanghai, almost half a million inhabitants have overseas connections
that form "a large invisible bridge" that is developing the city through Chinese capital from abroad. Other news reports refer to the huaqiao's capitalist
skills and flexibility, for example, "In the Overseas Chinese Hometown of
Quanzhou, the More Bridge Is Played, the More Flexible It Gets."[59] Here,
the Taiwanese investor's manipulation of capital is compared favorably to
bridge playing and the gains that are to be won by the hometown favored by
overseas-Chinese relatives. Other accounts construct overseas-Chinese investments in hometowns as acts of patriotism, inseparable from their reinvest-
ment in kinship and race/culture.[60] By investing in China, overseas Chinese
are "adding wings to the tiger," that is, to China as the new economic powerhouse in Asia.[61]

The discourse tying huaqiao capital to patriotism toward China often
waxes lyrical as traditions of loyalty among exiled subjects are invoked. One
news item opens with a poetic couplet:

> Time will not age the migrant's heart,
> High mountain passes cannot break the longing for home.[62]

Similar Confucianist sentiments are ritualistically invoked by the huaqiao themselves as they seek local acceptance and moral justifications for their economic ventures. At a reunion conference held in Fujian Province, a hua-qiao proclaimed: "We Fujian Chinese from Japan have for a long time raised the flag of love of motherland (*zuguo*), love of hometown (*qiaoxian*). . . . For the first generation of emigrants, [returning to China] is our dream come true. For the second, third, and even fourth generations, these ties can deepen their understanding of the hometown and the motherland."[63]

Cultural solidarity, filial piety, and everlasting loyalty to the motherland are key elements in the language of overseas capitalism, and traditional symbols are often displayed at investment-scouting meetings. After the above speech, the huaqiao from Japan planted pine trees in the city garden he and his compatriots rebuilt, which was aptly renamed "Love of Hometown Garden." The trees symbolize the claim and hope that the love of the hometown will be ever green and productive. The enduring symbols of Chinese roots stress the indestructible nature of ancestral home and kinship ties, thus casting the ultramodern flexible relations of capital accumulation in the timeless and unchanging representation of Chinese culture.

Besides the intermingling of the past and the present in discourses of huaqiao-mainland links, a parallel narrative elaborates guanxi as the touch-stone of Chinese cultural difference from Western modernity. Stories about returning huaqiao deal with their sojourns in the West, experiences that are often represented as resulting in a renewed ability to appreciate their Chinese-ness, which is expressed as an inescapable kinship and racial particularity. The following illustrates the theme that although Western scientific knowledge can be applied to help China develop, the huaqiao's retention of Chinese humanistic values is essential as a guide to China's future: Mrs. Yuan, who was trained as a linguist in the United States, returns to her father's Shanxi home-town, where she builds a new retirement home in his name. Having demon-strated that her filial piety has survived the diaspora, Mrs. Yuan notes that in the United States, the elderly live in beautiful environments but also in loneliness and neglect by their children. "Let us use the profound humanity of the Chinese people to attract elderly overseas Chinese people back to

China."[64] This tale sums up the message that the ideal modernity is one in which Chinese humanistic values triumph over modern science and Western callousness.

A similar view—one that brings race into the particular mix of science and culture that is desirable in Chinese modernity—is recounted in a newspaper article about Mrs. Li, who was trained as a scientist in America and returned to Hubei to set up a scholarship in her father's ancestral village. She had been "very moved at home by the government, which had led the people in constructing modern China." Besides giving lectures on advanced management techniques in China's major cities, Mrs. Li wanted to help young students "understand their motherland in relation to Western society." *March to Success,* a book based on her lectures, was selected as one of the ten most popular books in Beijing in 1988, according to the newspaper article. Li's message is that China is fundamentally different from the West. This difference is based on racial distinctiveness, a point she underlines by confiding that she sent her daughter to study in Beijing "to remind her that she is one of the Chinese people, with their black eyes (*hei yanjing*) and yellow skin (*huang pifu*)."[65]

The female protagonists in both stories embody Chinese humanism and the filial piety enshrined in the Confucian moral order. Their education by itself is not enough to cast them in the civilizing role of uplifting China's masses. In general, the news reports detail the signs of overseas-Chinese modernity—the scientific knowledge, the capitalist skills, the loyalty to the motherland, the Chinese humanism, the cultural and racial exceptionalism— that through their localization in the mainland context, link overseas Chinese to the mainlanders as modern Chinese subjects also constructing China's modernity.

But what is the perspective on overseas Chinese of ordinary people as they engage in actual networking to secure money, businesses, patrons, and trips overseas? In the cities where huaqiao congregate, the reactions to them are much more diverse than the elite views, veering between admiration and hostility; nevertheless, the refrain is that in order to modernize, China cannot do without their bridge-building capacities to leap from socialism to capitalist development. In the reinvigorated port city of Xiamen, across the Taiwan Strait, over the course of forty years of communist rule, locals have developed a view of Taiwanese people as smugglers and criminals preying on their coast. Now, the influx of Taiwanese money has transformed the city into a Little

Taipei, with skyscrapers, department stores, and karaoke bars. There is a pervasive sense of being colonized by these other Chinese. A customs official remarked that "they may be rich, but they aren't very polite. Lots of the Taiwanese who come over here are the dregs of society. They bring over the worst of the world, and when we see them smuggling or going out with hookers, naturally we are turned off."[66]

On a field trip to Xiamen in the fall of 1993, I was struck by how Taiwanese and Filipino Chinese businessmen appeared to be running the entire scene, from contributing to the reconstruction of the downtown and building housing estates to orchestrating the consumer culture around restaurants, shopping, and karaoke bars and calling the shots when it came to labor conditions in the new factories. I was told by local people that the Taiwanese Chinese had the local policemen in their pockets. They mentioned an incident in which a female worker who was protesting work conditions in a Taiwan-operated factory was beaten up by four supervisors. These men were taken into custody by the local police but were released after the intervention of the Taiwanese boss. No charges were pressed against them, and the worker lost her job without any form of compensation. A respected local scholar was prevented from checking conditions in Taiwan-operated factories because the authorities had been paid off to shield labor conditions from outside observers. Thus, although people welcome the Taiwanese investments and free-spending ways, they think that these huaqiao tend to exploit their women, create corruption, and intensify unequal relations in the province across lines of gender, class, and nationality.

A year previously, people up the coast in Quanzhou complained about the sale of dozens of failing state enterprises at rock bottom prices to a wealthy Indonesian Chinese. He was offered generous tax breaks to set up joint ventures with the city government. In protest, a worker made an anonymous call to the mayor's office, asking him, "Why don't you sell your wife too?"[67] This sense of capitalist rape creates a contradiction between the desire to woo foreign capital and local cultural values, thus subverting the earlier view that overseas Chinese are the embodiment of exclusively Confucian values that have perhaps been lost in China.[68]

When I asked local Xiamen informants whether the huaqiao's mistreatment of female workers could be traced to prerevolutionary practices, they insisted that Taiwanese managers had learned their management techniques and bad attitude toward women from the Japanese, who had colonized and modernized Taiwan in the early twentieth century. This interpretation is highly interesting because it linked Japanese colonialism with predatory capitalism and because it disavowed the possibility of any bad values associated with Chinese culture. Of course, when I asked Taiwanese managers (not involved in the incident) whether they were influenced by Japanese management policies in their factories, they scoffed at the idea, since in their view, only "Chinese" management would make sense to the people in China. Indeed, the Taiwanese, who share the same dialect with people in Fujian Province, consider their economic success in developing the area to be due in no small part to their understanding of local cultural traditions.

We see, then, at both the official and the informal level, a dual aspect to the euphemization of Chinese culture in relation to modernity. On the one hand, official discourses link China's economic takeoff to the Confucian values purportedly embodied by overseas Chinese, especially the humanistic guanxi networks that make them bring capital and other resources to jump-start China's development. On the other hand, at the informal, everyday level, Chinese culture is disassociated from the callous treatment local people, especially young women, who work for huaqiao capital and patrons; the bad aspects of huaqiao behavior must be attributed to colonialism and to some other, non-Chinese culture. This cultural defensiveness reflects the contradiction that while overseas Chinese are often sharp entrepreneurs who gamble with the fate of mainlanders, they are building the bridges necessary for the modernization of China. Warts and all, huaqiao symbolize both the window and the bridge to a distinctive kind of Asian affluence and modernity. In this vision of a continuum between mainland and Southeast Asian modernity, elite huaqiao women must express their loyalty to Confucian ideals while poor mainland women bear a kind of exploitation that is ideologically factored out of Chinese culture. This sanitized view of Chinese culture and its effects on the emerging modernity empowers the elites who stand to benefit from contacts with overseas Chinese.

"Leave the Country Fever"

The opening of China's borders, and the images of overseas-Chinese affluence, are a powerful magnet for mainlanders to "launch themselves into the ocean" (*xiahai*) of business and to cross the oceans themselves. The return of members from one diaspora has spawned new diasporas—of laborers, entre-preneurs, scholars, and families—from socialist China. A scholar in Fujian Province, which gained notoriety as the origin of the boat people who were recently smuggled to the West, told me that for ordinary Chinese, the country is viewed as a train on a fast track. It is leaving an agrarian society for a commercial and industrial one, which is represented by the blue ocean cul-ture. In Xiamen, Shenzhen, Shantou, and Guangzhou, I met young workers and students whose main goal was to plunge into the water, into the ocean itself, which can mean a number of things. For peasants and landlubbers, it connotes learning new skills, as well as the constant struggle to survive in the turbulent, often cruel conditions of social change. It is a place of suffering and risks, but it also promises great wealth, which is unobtainable in agriculture (or on the mainland, some seemed to imply). Jumping into the ocean can mean making the transition from farming, writing, or civil service to free enterprise, or it can mean actually leaving China to participate in the transna-tional world of global capitalism. For up-and-coming young Chinese, becom-ing an entrepreneur is synonymous with being modern and being caught up in "leave the country fever" (*chuguore*).

For those who do not find a bridge overseas in business, there are other ways of "leaving" China, for example, by participating in the "cultural mar-ket" (*wenhua shichang*) that has emerged in the coastal cities that are awash in overseas-Chinese capital and entrepreneurs. The explosion of desires associ-ated with becoming rich and leaving the country is garishly expressed in karaoke clubs that are icons of the imitative, mobile, and borderless form of Chinese modernity. In Shenzhen, which is considered the dreamland of China's future, karaoke bars are found on every city block and, sometimes, in every new building. It has become common for villages to have their own karaoke bars, which seem to have supplanted teahouses.

The karaoke bars and discos in China are not merely foreign forms of entertainment that the Chinese are mindlessly imitating.[69] Between mainland Chinese and the West are the overseas Chinese, who often mediate and trans-form Western cultural forms and express different, Asian modernity. That youth culture in Chinese cities is mediated by overseas-Chinese culture is evi-dent in the craze for KTVs (karaoke TV rooms for rent). Lip-synching along with a karaoke machine is an opportunity to participate vicariously in overseas-Chinese modernity since the video images and songs (mainly Cantonese pop songs called Cantopop) are produced in Hong Kong and Taiwan. Karaoke discos are usually attached to restaurants or private singing rooms. They have a dance floor where strobe lights and blaring disco music accompany gyrating dancers. These entertainment centers, along with their cultural content and practices, are slivers of Singapore, Hong Kong, and Taipei that have been transplanted to the mainland.

The karaoke bar is the first step into the glamorous overseas-Chinese world of wealth, modern sexuality, and sophisticated fashion. The entrance fees, which exceed a worker's monthly wage, are high, but the bars are very popular, especially with women eager to meet foreign men, preferably overseas Chinese. Young women who are students and office workers go to karaoke bars to learn about foreign culture, to meet boyfriends, and hopefully through marriage to "develop a bridge to leave China." While going to karaoke bars is very expensive, especially since one has to dress up in fancy clothes, it is viewed as an investment in a different future and an expression of many people's desire to leave socialist China and enter the world of overseas-Chinese modernity.

The karaoke craze has spread even to university campuses, where professors are provided with karaoke lounges. Imagine my surprise when on a major campus, after a daylong conference, young male and female scholars filed into a karaoke bar, urging me to join them. A professor picked up the microphone and sang to a videotaped film of Hong Kong on a huge screen where the camera panned slowly over the skyscrapers and beautiful harbor. He was soon joined by most people in the room, who sang in harmony and with feeling. They also lip-synched sentimental love songs without any trace of embarrassment, accompanied by videotapes of scantily dressed Hong Kong starlets posing in languid and inviting positions. When the video switched to a rousing song with feet-stomping, arm-waving, shirtless men roaring "We are Chinese people!" [*Women shi Zhongguoren!*], I felt it was time to leave. Though this was reminiscent of Red Guard performances, these young people singing and dreaming together appear to be pursuing individual dreams of success that are delinked from state planning. Karaoke seems to be the vehicle for the quintessential expression of a patriotism for a commodified Chinese culture associated with overseas affluence.

Karaoke equipment and entertainment are new ways to foster and cement guanxi, especially of the transnational kind. Luxury cars fitted with karaoke systems are an especially attractive gift from foreign managers to local officials. Karaoke bars are the places to bring acquaintances one wishes to cultivate. Thus, in addition to hosting the traditional round of banquets for potential partners, it has become de rigueur for overseas businessmen to take their guests to karaoke bars, where deals are finally signed.[70] Karaoke entertainment is a new way to "gain a lot of face."[71] Since much of guanxi depends on facial management and verbal agreements, happy karaoke images and sing-alongs are an ideal medium to establish good feelings of fellowship and solidarity.

As a window onto Chinese modernity and a medium for cementing transnational relationships (erotic and practical), karaoke uniquely expresses the combination of an individualist quest for wealth and success and the dependence of that quest on the cultivation of good guanxi across the water. Mayfair Yang notes the ambivalence toward guanxi on the mainland as being "born in conflict between a state-espoused 'public' collectivist ethnic and a 'private' ethics of personal relationships."[72] As a medium and practice of guanxi, karaoke expresses the privatized, personalistic ethics of Chinese subjects eager to participate in a modernity not bounded by the interests of the state but seeking to cross borders into overseas-Chinese modernity.

Modernity without Deracination

Opening the door to affluent overseas Chinese communities has prompted some chauvinist scholars to reconsider the sources of Asian modernity. Revisionist historians firmly reject the Weberian view that Confucianism and patrimonial bureaucracies obstructed the development of capitalism. Contrary to the popular view that Commodore Perry's visit was the catalyst for Japan's move toward industrialization, Japanese historians now trace the roots of East Asian modernity to the China-centered tributary and trade system that stemmed from inter-Asian voyages in the fifteenth century.[73] Europeans arriving in Southeast and East Asia were required to penetrate these tributary networks to participate in regional trade. These historians argue that intraregional competition between mainland-Chinese, overseas-Chinese, and Japanese merchant groups in the nineteenth century was the initial impetus for Japanese industrialization. This revisionist history is politically significant, for it reflects a new Asian confidence in seeking the roots of contemporary Asian modernity in regional economic and cultural exchanges while downplaying the importance of Western contributions.

Thus, the interweaving, cross-border narratives about Confucian culture and guanxi economism in Asia—whether in state pronouncements or in everyday practice—produce a vision of modernity without deracination in opposition to Western modernity. These narratives claim the utilitarian tools of Western economics and science but not cultural ideas and practices will be useful in shaping contemporary or future Chinese society. Rather, overseas-Chinese communities in Asia have become the pacesetters in articulating the larger contours of an organic unity of Chinese people scattered throughout the world. In elite discourses, overseas Chinese are viewed as possessing and deploying Western knowledge and skills without becoming inferior versions of Occidentals. Despite their cosmopolitanism and their sojourns in the West, these diasporan subjects have become clever at being capitalists, but they express their instrumental rationality in an inherently "Chinese" manner—a reverence for Confucian discipline and solidarity and the use of guanxi networks. Overseas Chinese are therefore considered the critical agents and cultural models who form a bridge to Chinese modernity. Huaqiao communities have provided the signs, forms, and practices of a distinctive modernity that learns from the West but transforms capitalism into a Chinese phenomenon. In this vision, the border-crossing joint ventures, trade networks, and consumer culture are all part of an ongoing reintegration of mainland- and offshore-Chinese populations and the development of a new regime of Chinese modernity that is based on the regional flows of Chinese cultural practices and network capitalism.

The theme of cultural genius and the making of a culturally exclusive capitalism raise fears among Westerners, who recognize that they are in a sense no longer calling the shots in Asia Pacific trade. A British economist notes that "the Chinese world may appear relatively westernized and modern to western eyes, but its inner spirit is quite different. The universalism and egalitarianism of the West is replaced by a sense of hierarchy and cultural affinity."[74] The emerging representations of Chinese modernity contradict postcolonial discourses that view third world nationalisms as prisoners to Western rationalist thought and the need to assimilate to the West in order to be modern. Chinese self-theorizing, which has evolved, rejects "the legitimacy of the marriage of (Western) Reason and capital" in defining what is modern.[75] Giving up Marxist theories of development, Chinese narratives identify Confucianism as the source of the moral authority, instrumental rationality, and network organization that is associated with powerful states and the dynamic, mobile capitalism that is reconfiguring the Asia Pacific region. By claiming a distinctive Confucian spirituality and instrumentality that is ultimately in dialogue with the West, such a normative *Asian* regime also acts as a check to Western claims of universality.

Conclusion

Tani Barlow is a China historian who challenges our propensity to view others through the prism of what we take to be our modernity. She observes that the "kinds of theories scholars deploy secure them in particular modernities."[76] In a world of emerging and receding global powers, alternate visions of modernity reflect the ways cultural visions of the present and the future are made in contexts of shifting geopolitical alignments. As anthropologists of the late twentieth century, we would not want to be secured in a singular modernity but would wish to explore the exchanges between different kinds of modernity. We need to move beyond conceptions of modernity that assume (1) that science and knowledge will disenchant the world and decenter culture from framing our understanding of it; (2) that the rest of the world will eventually be assimilated to an internationalized modernity originating in and determined by the West; and (3) that multiple modernities arise only through resistance to the West's universalizing trajectory. The varying perspectives on Chinese modernity—from the state, from the ordinary people, from overseas subjects—reveal that imaginaries and practices of modernity are developing in different sites, are in dialogue with one another, and, in an emerging region of the world, are challenging Western hegemony. There are, of course, other discourses and dissensions from lower classes, women's groups, and indigenous communities that contest the supremacist Chinese constructions,[77] but their dynamism only serves to confirm the ability of this particular Asian modernity to contain them, as well as to provide the concepts and to enunciate the modality that symbolically remaps their future.[78] The new narratives indicate more forcefully than ever that modernity is "a matter of signification," in which forms associated with Western modernization are renamed and reworked in local cultural contexts framed by an East-West opposition. At issue is who controls that which is signified as modern.[79]

Although focused on recent Chinese imaginings of modernity, this chapter has tried to suggest the historically specific cultural and regional framing of what being modern might mean to emergent powers. Some may misread this call for a mobile or nomadic anthropological thinking as falling back on cultural relativism and its implied stance of apolitical detachment.[80] But by standing outside a given modernity, anthropologists can critique not only the Western hegemonic knowledges that view the world as a foil or projection but also the kind of nativist ideologies of modernity that arise out of Asian capitalisms. Anthropology can play a critical role in building the intellectual tension between belonging and the detachment that comes from engaging with other kinds of constructed realities. The goal, which goes beyond de-familiarizing ourselves with our own society, is to explore our academic blind spots and our complacency, as well as to critically engage cultural chauvinisms elsewhere. While one can understand Asian resistances to Western domination, emergent Chinese modernity can enact a cultural hegemony that instills alarm and resistance elsewhere in the Asia Pacific region. A mobile anthropological sensibility retains radical skepticism toward unilinear history *and* toward the administrative forms of cultural authentication that have reacted against Western modernism. As a truly cross-cultural discipline, anthropology can explore the "weak" universals—especially the concept of minimal human rights[81]—as the grounds for an alternative sociality leading to a humane and just world.

Modern China is the product of the conjoining of modernist discourses originating in the West and native institutions . . . , historical social conditions . . . , and native reaction-formations. . . . Therefore, any diagnosis of power in contemporary China is a critique neither simply of the West nor of China's tradition, but of their offspring: China's modernity.

—Mayfair Yang, *Gifts, Favors, and Banquets*

The destiny of Singapore remains very much a rewriting and a re-imagining by each generation of what is possible. . . . How can it be otherwise for a nation that was born of imagination, erected on dreams and has created a network of internal, unseen information to reach beyond herself?

—Ban Kah Choon, "Narrating Imagination"

This chapter explores how, in contemporary Asia, Chinese culture and race have become critical raw materials in competing imaginaries of modernity. Social imaginaries have been called the "constructed landscapes of collective aspirations . . . now mediated through the complex prism of modern media."[1] I take modernity to be an evolving process of imagination and practice in particular historically situated formations that deploy preexisting ideological formations of culture and race. Whereas in the previous chapter I discussed cross-border cultural continuities in Chinese modernity, here I highlight the contradictions between two competing discursive systems that variously deploy Chineseness as a territorially bounded moral entity and as a deterritorialized moral economic force.² The first, a nationalist imaginary that emphasizes essentialism, territoriality, and the fixity of the modern state, is in tension with the second, a modernist imaginary of entrepreneurial capitalism that celebrates hybridity, deterritorialization, and the mobility of late capitalism.

For Benedict Anderson, the national community is not a given reality but has historically been imagined into being in the context of "print capitalism" and other forms of modern communications.³ But the kinds of national imaginaries Anderson is concerned with—in Indonesia and the Philippines—focus on the "good" civic nationalisms that emerged out of anti-imperialist struggles. He claims that "the dreams of racism actually have their origin in ideologies of *class,* rather than those of nation."⁴ But in an ancient civilization such as China, race consciousness has deep roots in historical struggles that established imperial borders against outsiders long before the emergence of modern society as configured by the convergence of capitalism and print technology.⁵ Indeed, Chinese antagonism toward "barbarians" and "foreign devils" has always been based on an ideological sense of the racial and cultural exclusivity of the *minzu* (race/nation) that cuts across class differences. This sense of imagined ethnic absolutism both predates and colors contemporary Chinese notions about the nation, whether in its territorial or civic variant. Furthermore, as Brackette Williams and others have argued, even Western European and American civic nationalisms depend on the invention of a unitary substance—the "blood" of kinship and race—to cement their links to a social and political unit and to an economic system.⁶ Most contemporary Asian nations exhibit an uneasy and unstable mix of civil nationalism emerging out of anticolonial struggles and the ethnic chauvinism of a dominant national group that reaches into the past, as among the Chinese or the Vietnamese, or that had to be invented under colonial rule, as in Malaysia.⁷

Furthermore, while Anderson uses the term "imagined community" for the imaginary work of a single, territorially bounded nation, I argue that national consciousness is also shaped by tensions with imagined transnational collectivities brought about by the reconfigurations of global capitalism. Indeed, his statement that "on the whole, racism and anti-Semitism manifest themselves, not across national borders, but within them" is contradicted by racial imaginaries that cut across state borders.⁸ Indeed, contemporary diasporan-Chinese chauvinism, while in tension with the claims of the Chinese nation-state, is also continuous with its racial consciousness. Racial discourses not only shape the internal divisions of imagined communities, as Anderson claims, but are also employed, for both oppressive and emancipatory purposes, in inscribing and managing social divisions in transnational space. In the Asia Pacific region today, two sets of narratives invoking Chineseness—as a territorial nation and as a transnational network—are in rivalry, but they are also in alliance, invoking stories about Chinese culture that shape regional consciousness about the ranking of races and nation-states. I will focus on the discourses of politicians, top executives, and scholars because they provide the ideological legitimacy for different imagined communities that are representative of broad patterns of alignment and cross alignments among nation-states and in relation to different capitalisms. I will explore how the conflation of Chinese race and culture—with their masculinist assumptions—is invoked in discourses defining (1) the modern biopolitical state in China and in Singapore, and (2) the transnational networks of flexible accumulation. I will end by suggesting that tensions between constructions of territorialized and fluid Chinese racial subjectivity are attempts to renegotiate relations between citizens and the nation-state, between state power and diaspora capitalism, and between a newly awakened Asian regionalism and Western powers in the Asia Pacific region.

The Reemergence of Race in the Chinese Nation

As China plunges into the global economy and becomes acutely aware of its relative backwardness, the early construction of the Chinese nation as a homogenized entity (of many "nations") is being replaced by popular representations of deeper differences between ethnic groups. For instance, the majority Han increasingly contrast themselves as modern/progressive subjects to the traditional/backward minorities such as the Miao, a process that Louisa Schein calls "internal orientalism."[9] At the same time, among the Han themselves, the freeing of social relations from pervasive state control has led to negotiations about Han consciousness that cut across China's national borders. There are also growing tensions between those who see in market reforms the route to China's future and members of the Communist Party who still adhere to a vision of a socialist future in which the state maintains central control over the economy and society.

Until the early 1980s, China's national identity was firmly determined by socialism and clearly defined by the territorial boundedness of "the mainland." It was disengaged from the global economy, where overseas Chinese were kept at a distance as China tried to establish relations with newly independent Southeast Asian countries.[10] China's isolation from the world's community allowed it to secure its identity in relation to its own population.[11] As a communist giant, it could also claim leadership of the struggling third world.[12]

This national identity, which was located in a particular territory (the mainland) and in a specific history (of the People's Republic), came under pressure with the establishment of Special Economic Zones (SEZS) near Hong-Kong. The integration of south China's coast with cities such as Tokyo, Singapore, Taipei, Bangkok, Kuala Lumpur, and Jakarta produced an influx of overseas-Chinese people and capital and Western investments, and uncontrollable flows of information and media images. Increased trade, communications, and traffic stimulated a rising demand for foreign goods, ideas, and cultures, as well as the desire to travel to other countries. As I argued in chapter 1, the presence and activities of overseas Chinese from mainly Southeast Asia have created all kinds of border-crossing networks that seem to subordinate political differences to trade interests. These ties between mainland and overseas Chinese, between mainlanders and foreign investors, and between Chinese socialism and foreign capitalism all helped to disrupt the political borders of the nation.

But from the very beginning, the Deng regime was careful to define Chinese modernity in a fixed territorial position vis-à-vis other nation-states in the world. Despite Deng's call for coastal cities to mimic Hong Kong, "socialism with Chinese characteristics" represents an attempt to domesticate freewheeling capitalism through state control, and to drive home the idea that capitalism is ultimately intended to increase the power of the Chinese nation-state. The goal is to significantly raise China's overall standard of living over the course of one hundred years so that the country can escape its developing status and thus strengthen its position with respect to other countries. This aim resonates with the ideological discourses of the ASEAN nations and Taiwan and echoes the earlier message of Meiji Japan, which is that the state must take control of capitalism to strengthen the nation.

China's new strategy of state strengthening by learning from other Asian countries also represents another reversal from the old Soviet model of modernization that privileged socialist egalitarianism over "bad" traditional culture. The setting aside of Marxist-Leninist language frees state discourses to valorize Chinese racial uniqueness and patriarchal cultural traditions as critical elements in modern nation building. In the early twentieth century, long-held ideas about the inseparable nature of the Han race, nation, and culture were reinforced in confrontations with foreign invaders, including European imperialists. Western theories of eugenics and social progress and Marxist models of historical materialism reinforced the conviction of many Chinese intellectuals that they were a biologically separate "yellow race/nation" that was failing in the competition with the "white race."[13] Attempts at modern reform posed a profound moral predicament for Chinese nationalists seeking to modernize without being westernized. In their new subject positions as appropriators of Truth (including Western scientific knowledges), Chinese intellectuals maintained a position of "Chinese learning for the fundamental principles, Western learning for practical applications" [*Zhongxue wei di, Xixue wei yong*].[14] This East-West framework allowed a vision of modernity that, according to Tani Barlow, was localized "within specific, autonomous, local political contexts." Thus, Barlow notes, the appropriation of Western racial thinking also resulted in the inscribing of the Chinese national racial essence into the new field of Chinese "culture" (*wenhua*).[15]

This race-based notion of an alternative modernity has been revived with the current rise of China in the global economy. Although objectively speaking, Asian authoritarian states are based on or borrow extensively from some Western state formations, by claiming to be "Asian," especially in their particular mix of rapid development and selective political repression, they break discursively with Western ideals of the modern and are thus able to claim a distinctive modernity rooted in the Asian race/nation/culture. In China, the embrace of the authoritarian Asian model of modernity, the crucial role of overseas Chinese in China's development, and the encounter with global capitalism have reinvigorated racial consciousness and its implications for the integrity of the national territory.

Thus, globalization, with its transnational flows and networks, engenders crises or renewal in national identities, either of which can revive racial consciousness. For instance, Stuart Hall notes that England, suffering from economic decline in the early 1980s, had regressed to a defensive and dangerous form of national identity that was driven in part by reliving the past through myth and in part by racism.[16] Paradoxically, China, which embarked upon a buoyant wave of global capitalism in the 1980s, is also experiencing a crisis of cultural identity—one brought about by the influx of foreign capital, overseas Chinese, and new commodities, images, and desires that bypass government rules. The growth of Chinese racial consciousness within China, and in a pan-Asian context, challenges the Chinese state to keep its political and territorial interests distinct from the promiscuous opportunism of overseas-Chinese capitalism. While China welcomes offshore-Chinese investments, mainland officials remain suspicious of overseas Chinese who appear to have little sentiment for the motherland.

Indeed, nationalist fears have been fueled by a vision of financial markets that challenge state control over what constitutes Chinese modernity. This is the trope of "Greater China" (*Da Zhonghua*) coined by Japanese economists to describe the increasing economic integration between China, Hong Kong, and Taiwan produced by globalization. The combined foreign-currency reserves of Taiwan, Hong Kong, and Singapore, together with those of China, it is claimed, would place the Chinese bloc far ahead of Japan as Asia's first-rank economic giant.[17] Some writers have gone so far as to claim that the overseas-Chinese community, not the nation-state, is "the mother of China's [economic] revolution."[18]

Chinese state interests, however, are vigorously expressed in public forums and in the press. Patriotic scholars are quick to reject Greater China as a bankers' fantasy, an illusion of outsiders greedy to cash in on China's booming economy. They fear that any ideological recognition of a wider "Chinese" capitalist zone will undermine China as a territorially based political entity. For instance, at a recent conference on the overseas-Chinese economy I attended at Shantou University, Guangdong Province, a local professor, Huang Kunzhang, asserted:

> From the national perspective, we reject the concept of Greater China. From the legal perspective, we cannot mix up different nationals [simply] because they have the same culture and language as we do. . . . [Similarly,] most Southeast Asian Chinese reject this concept. [But] Taiwan likes this view of Greater China. It is a business concept to capitalize on China's development. Western scholars see a stronger China and

project their own model of a larger China by exaggerating data on overseas-Chinese development. This problem must be seen at the level of government-to-government relations. We see things as a business matter. Overseas Chinese come not because they are patriotic but because of investment benefits. We need to clearly differentiate between different kinds of Chinese, between those who are nationals and those who are from overseas.[19]

Huang's contrast of "profits versus patriotism" has been picked up by other scholars who elaborate on the differences between Chinese from the mainland and Chinese from other countries. According to some, Chinese foreign nationals invest in China primarily for profits, not because they are loyal to the Chinese nation-state. They are opportunists and parvenus who are eager to enrich themselves while incidentally benefiting China. Others acknowledge that overseas Chinese have different degrees of attachment to the ancestral homeland; mainlanders cannot assume that all have China's real interests at heart. This view was reiterated for me in Quanzhou by the director of overseas Chinese affairs: "Overseas-Chinese emigrants must be distinguished by generations. The first generation has sentiment for China. The second generation, educated in the West, has not given up the concept of an ancestral home but its affection is not as deep. Only the parents have deep feelings; they want to make business and develop China quickly. We welcome them and their technical knowledge, that is, we welcome people with yellow skin (*you huang pifu de ren*)."[20]

Despite the tantalizing appeal of "our kind of people" and the racialist construct of overseas Chinese, the official view is that in practice, one cannot count on the loyalty of overseas Chinese, only on their desire to make a profit off China.[21] One participant, Chen Xiyu, of Xiamen University, later wrote that "constructing an economic zone based solely on race is theoretically weak and inconsistent with objective political and economic conditions." He insisted that despite the free flow of overseas-Chinese capital into China, the integrity of the nation-state must be defended.[22] Here, officials are careful to distinguish between citizens of China—those who were born in the country and are assumed to possess a patriotic interest in strengthening China—and those who count as Chinese because of their blood but whose loyalty to the Chinese nation cannot be presumed. Pro-official narratives thus put to rest

any supposition that the mainland concept of "socialism with Chinese characteristics" is necessarily an endorsement of the Greater China image of Chineseness with capitalist characteristics.

This fear of the erosion of the nation-state by mobile capitalism is shared by
the strong bureaucratic states of Southeast Asia. Again, there is the suspicion
that the difference between the concept of the nation as a kinship and blood
matrix and the concept of the nation as the country in which one is a citizen is
blurred for overseas Chinese. On the one hand, ASEAN countries worry that
capital flight to China will weaken their national economies, while on the
other hand, they are sending official delegations backed by huaqiao capital to
cash in on China's boom. The fear remains that an economically powerful
China will exert direct political domination over the region, thus weakening
the ASEAN countries' existence as independent nation-states. China's 1974
seizure of the Paracel Islands, and its more recent claim on the Spratly Islands,
has raised fears, as expressed by a Malaysian official, that China's resurgence
will "turn the South China Seas into a Chinese lake."[23] Singapore's prime
minister, in a rare expression of desire for America's presence in Southeast
Asia, notes that "when China becomes powerful in 20 or 30 years' time . . .
that's our worry; China may want to flex its muscles and then it will be a
troublesome world."[24] Thus Lee Kuan Yew, senior minister of Singapore, has
tempered his exultation over overseas-Chinese capitalism with a warning to
guard against "Chinese chauvinism": "We must be honest and recognize that
at the end of the day our fundamental loyalties are to our home country, not
to China."[25] While Southeast Asian nations are eager to cash in on China's
boom, they are also worried that the influx of overseas-Chinese investments
into China may lead to a reemergence of pre–World War II political support
for the mainland. The assumption of a continuity between the Chinese nation
and Chinese as a race continues to rankle both the mainland and Southeast
Asian states alike. China worries about being taken advantage of by overseas-
Chinese capitalists manipulating their racial advantage in China, while Southeast Asian nation-states resent overseas-Chinese racial loyalty to the growing
superpower in the region. Thus, Southeast Asian officials and scholars favor
using the term *ethnic* for their Chinese subjects; they reject the recently fashionable term *diasporan* as implying a disloyalty among ethnic Chinese, some
of whom may still be bound by sentiment to China. Huaqiao leaders make
statements to soothe fears of ethnic Chinese becoming political turncoats for

China: "They are doing it for profit. They aren't doing it for patriotic or sentimental reasons."[26] But overseas-Chinese capital investments in China have been protested in the Philippines and have featured prominently in the recent dramatic resurgence of anti-Chinese rioting in Indonesia. Chinese entrepreneurs pursuing flexible strategies of capital maximization have reinforced old suspicions about the loyalties of ethnic Chinese as citizens in their adopted countries.[27]

On the mainland, the state relies heavily on political campaigns and on its control of the news media to shape a sense of national community in a society opening to external influences. Since the 1980s, there has been a hiatus in official campaigns against "spiritual pollution" from the West. But whereas state regulation in the Maoist period focused on policing "bad" class subjects and "deviant" sexual subjects as a way to normalize national identity,[28] the state in the era of market reforms turns its attention to problematic economic and political behavior. This is not surprising, given the emergence of important new categories of people such as investors, professionals, sex workers, tourists, and urban consumers. Because they are located primarily in the coastal SEZs, they are seen to be particularly disruptive of a unified nation. However, these new subjects are critical to the booming Chinese economy both as producers and consumers, and the loosening sexual mores are considered part of a general liberation from the oppressive past and an aspect of the economic "opening" (*kaifang*). In Shenzhen, where overseas Chinese and newly rich peasants spend freely and carouse exuberantly amidst images of naked female torsos displayed in hotels, restaurants, and airports, the Quanzhou official I interviewed expressed the new state attitude toward the commodified "culture market" (*wenhua shichang*): "Let them [young people] have their desires! If they have money, they can do what they want. Just no more Tiananmens!" Policing not sexual freedom but political ideas and economic norms that might weaken the power of the nation is the focus of state concern as the new transnationalized spaces within the body politic destabilize a coherent national imaginary.

Official critique, then, is not of capitalism, which is viewed as necessary for strengthening the country, but of economic individualism and cultural excess. A recent "patriotic education" campaign resurrected Confucius as a guide to Chinese cultural identity in the era of flexible accumulation. As reported in the *People's Daily*, scholars in Beijing called for a "Confucian Renaissance" to combat the "money worship" associated with Western capitalism: "The Confucian school [*rujia xuepai*] does not oppose profiting through merchandise and money but advocates fairness in buying and selling, and neither is it opposed to making money and wealth but advocates that such practices be guided by morality." The official message is that there is a venerable Chinese way of making money that is specific to the historical and cultural boundedness of the nation: "The traditional culture of China's Confucian school has a two-thousand-year-old history, with a wealth of ancient books and records and an abundant system that can serve as a single source for building a new culture."[29] Such ideological work to narrowly define Chineseness as a singular racial-cultural formation that is deeply rooted in the heartland and history of the continent makes the state the ultimate authority and point of reference.

Like the state strategies of the ASEAN regimes, the Chinese state strategy rests on controlling the print and electronic media, which, if not carefully regulated, are powerful instruments for undermining the concept of the bounded and unified nation.[30] The current state campaign to promote "spiritual civilization" directs special criticism at artists, writers, and the news media for producing views about Chinese society and culture that are not state approved. At the same time, the state depends on the propagandizing efforts of print journalists, writers, and filmmakers to transmit the diversity of Chinese experiences into the imaging of the modern Chinese nation. For instance, a leading film producer recently completed a lavish movie on the Opium Wars, through which the British gained control of Hong Kong in the nineteenth century. Its opening was set to coincide with the end of British rule in Hong Kong, but even before it opened it had whipped up the mounting nationalist fervor over the return of Hong Kong to Chinese rule. Journalists, dubbed "engineers of the human soul," have also been recruited by the state-run Xinhua News Agency to promote patriotism, socialism, and loyalty to the Communist Party, rather than the sex, violence, and superstition of mass culture.[31] Thus, although capitalism increases state revenues, the state must rein in the print and electronic media, which corrode state authority, and seek to tame those overseas Chinese, and the mainlanders they influence, whose self-interested pursuits threaten the state's control of social and territorial integrity.

Such tensions between the state, on the one hand, and transnational capital and cultural forces, on the other, are deeply complicated by the paradoxical image of overseas Chinese. The latter are viewed as the racial embodiment of presocialist cultural traditions that are now critical to the strengthening of the Chinese nation, but also as amoral capitalist agents who can undermine China's territorial and state interests. Furthermore, the resurgence of Chinese racial consciousness overseas, stimulated by the reemergence of China on the world stage and by the economic activities of diasporan Chinese, cannot be disassociated from the racial pride that feeds China's imagined community.

"The Glow of Chinese Fraternity"

In diaspora, older racial images have also been dusted off to ornament contemporary forms of political economy in Southeast Asia. The key role of ethnic Chinese in flexible accumulation across the region and in China has stimulated new visions of a far-flung Chinese world. Lee Kuan Yew has anointed "the glow of Chinese fraternity."[32] This symbol of the new Chinese transnationalism retains a racial and masculinist bias and echoes images of "Chinese brothers" plying the oceans in earlier diasporas. These icons resonate nicely with the picture of Chinese executives convening in the skyscrapers of Taipei, Singapore, and Hong Kong. Their interlinked financial networks, called Greater China, describe a transnational space where capital and race are interbraided and brothers long scattered in diaspora are brought into association again. A summing-up at the Shantou University conference on the overseas Chinese economy asserted: "The big question is not Greater China but [the fact] that there are Chinese people inside and outside China [in Southeast Asia and elsewhere]. Overseas Chinese have the same language and same ancestral stock (*tongwen tongzhu*) as we do; they are like the married-out daughter (*jia chuqu de nüer*) who still has feelings (*ganjing*) for home. They are the same kind of people (*tongzhong*)."[33] While the diminutive feminine signifier is a mainland image of overseas Chinese, the focus is on the blood and sentimental ties that can develop even with "married-out-daughter" communities. Overseas Chinese are after all "the same kind of people" as mainlanders.

Although the tension remains between wishing to distinguish between the People's Republic of China and overseas Chinese, the historical linkages between south China and Hong Kong, Taiwan, and Southeast Asia have always lain at the bottom of overseas-Chinese consciousness. In the early days of the Chinese Republic, Sun Yat-sen called on overseas Chinese to support the republican struggle. Later appeals for help came when the mainland was invaded by the Japanese. Intellectuals, students, amahs, laborers, housewives, teachers, and businessmen contributed hard-earned dollars to "save the motherland." This prewar loyalty to the mainland is now again being tapped as Cantonese scholars urge that, with the help of overseas Chinese, "Guangzhou should be the cradle of China's new culture."[34] In this century, overseas-Chinese sentiments have been tapped and revived for purposes from saving the motherland to constructing a regional market economy linking Guangdong to Hong Kong, Taiwan, and Southeast Asia. In these proémigré discourses, racial origin, kinship bonds, historical solidarity, and economic relations have produced an undeniable transnational network that has burst beyond the bounds of the nation-state.

Implicit in these narratives invoking durable bonds between mainland- and emigrant-Chinese communities is the recognition of a new stage in East-West trade. For some mainland- and overseas-Chinese leaders, 6 June 1989 was memorable not so much for the Tiananmen crackdown as for marking the date when Japanese and American investors abandoned China. Overseas Chinese stepped up their investments in the mainland, helping to raise China's annual growth rates to double-digit figures. Lee Kuan Yew put it this way: "What ethnic Chinese from Hong Kong, Macau and Taiwan did was to demonstrate to a skeptical world that guanxi connections through the same language and culture can make up for a lack in the rule of law and transparency in rules and regulations." His statement also invoked the racial consciousness underlying transnational Chinese cooperation: "People feel a natural empathy with those who share their physical attributes. This sense of closeness is reinforced when they also share basic culture and language. It makes for easy rapport and the trust that is the foundation of all business relations."[35] Similar remarks about ethnic-Chinese businessmen belonging ultimately to one big family build an image of a transnational Chinese solidarity based on common racial origin, ethnic traditions, and alliances that penetrate bureaucratic rules and transcend ideological differences.

This capitalist-based imaginary is constructed out of words such as *guanxi, networks, neo-Confucianism, tribes, and multiculturalism*—academic terms that have been reissued by American business schools to describe the "East Asian miracle." American business academics such as John Kao and Joel

Kotkin mediate between the business-speak, or what Bruce Cummings calls "rimspeak,"[36] and the self-orientalizing discourses of ethnic-Chinese spokesmen in Southeast Asia. In the speech cited above, Lee Kuan Yew cites Kotkin's book *Tribes,* claiming that "networking between people of the same race has always existed."[37] He thus gains a scientific gloss from an essentialist construction of culture. Kotkin in turn cites Taipei attorney Paul Hsu, who "sees a new transnational 'Chinese-based economy' based on ties of common ethnic origin, language, and culture" that makes "the old government ideology of nation-states" outmoded.[38] In this corporate vision of Chinese transnationalism, highly mobile "races," not governments, will reconfigure relations between nation-states.

It is this continual invocation of Chinese cultural affinity and racial exclusivity that has disturbed some Western observers, who are struck by the increasing number of regional business meetings restricted to entrepreneurs of Chinese ancestry. Racial discourse often identifies the concept of a transnational race (a *greater* China) whose fraternal networks are the only means to penetrate China or Chinese-dominated economies. To reassure American entrepreneurs, Harvard business professor John Kao uses the term "open architecture" to suggest that there are openings for Westerners in Chinese networks.[39] Using this image, Hong Kong businessmen have invited Western firms to link up with guanxi networks so that non-Chinese can "both tap and create the opportunities" for access to resources and contacts in China.[40] Kao claims that the open architecture of networks has engendered a "symbiotic relationship" between U.S. and Chinese business partners. The latter are more culturally adroit than the Japanese in helping Westerners operate in the Asia Pacific markets, he says.[41] The Chinese transnational world is thus imagined through the regulation of racial and business-school languages.

Not surprisingly, triumphalist narratives about the successes of Chinese "network capitalism" become inseparable from claims about a reified kind of "Confucian" culture among overseas Chinese. Some Asian scholars, concerned about the backlash in Southeast Asia, emphasize the importance of "Western education" in overseas-Chinese capitalism. Wang Gungwu comments, rather equivocally, "I am not convinced that Confucianism itself contributed to entrepreneurship. . . . While Confucian values make us what we are, what makes a good entrepreneur depends on many factors which are not peculiar to Chinese entrepreneurs." Among these factors, Wang includes acquired skills in the English language and in Western business practices.[42] Wang's ambivalent remarks highlight the culturally hybrid makeup of overseas Chinese and yet promotes the kind of cultural essentialism—"Confucian values make us what we are"—it seeks to avoid. Similarly, multicultural experiences were also mentioned by Lee Kuan Yew, but in a way that seems to reify Chinese distinctiveness. Lee noted that overseas Chinese can teach the mainland "the economic value of multiculturalism, derived from coexisting with and absorbing the good points of other cultures."[43] The implication is that although ethnic Chinese have lived among other cultural groups, they have remained "Chinese" in a basic, unchanging way, since cross-cultural learning is only significant for Chinese economic advancement. In effect, cultural hybridity has been employed to highlight the economic peculiarity of the Chinese.

Such discourses, produced in a circuit that migrates from political centers to entrepreneurs' circles, constitute a regime of truth about a distinctive Chinese capitalism. Foucault has argued that apparently neutral discourses use rationalizations and categories (such as nature, race, culture, etc.) as truth claims that also operate as practices of regulation and control. In these transnational imaginaries, Chinese race, culture, and economic activities have become naturalized as inseparable or even the same phenomena, which are then deployed as "naturalizing powers"—regimes that appear "natural, inevitable, God-given"[44]—that shape the way people think about Chineseness, mobile capitalism, and their relationship to nations and to states. Next, I discuss how the truth claims of Chinese capitalism are brought into alignment with state interests to construct a kind of state-capital moral economy based on Confucian ideals. By contrasting such a Confucian state formation, the Singapore state also promotes a moral economic hierarchy among Southeast Asian countries.

Hierarchical Moral Economies: Hard versus Soft Societies

Besides discoursing on fraternal business networks, Lee Kuan Yew has also elaborated a thesis on how racial/cultural differences between societies are reflected in their capitalist performance. Lee has long formulated a theory of "hard" versus "soft" societies by reworking older colonialist themes that deployed terms such as *Asiatic, Oriental,* and *Mohammedan* as evaluative racial categories in relation to modern society. The British and other Europeans had defined Malays as "indolent" and "lazy" and contrasted the "softness" of their culture to the "industrious," "stubborn," and "callous" Chinese immigrants.[45] In the 1960s and 1970s, as prime minister, Lee began a campaign to build a "rugged society" in Chinese-dominated Singapore, both to forestall hostile forces in the surrounding Malay world and to inculcate behavior and norms that would make Singapore a modern capitalist society. This instance of what Don M. Nonini calls "reflex modernity,"[46] or the techniques whereby a postcolonial state reworks old colonialist themes to its own benefit, is also conspicuous for its gendered masculinist imagery of hard virility versus soft femininity. Lee's rugged-society model contrasted a disciplined, achievement-oriented work ethic among the Chinese to the "soft" society of the Malays. The colonial image of ethnic Chinese was recast into a positive image based on Confucian values of hard work and frugality that were on a par with the Western concepts of individual striving and meritocracy ("rugged individualism"). The colonial image of Malays was, however, retained. Such a (partial) postcolonial reconstruction arose in part from a subaltern opposition to colonial racism. By the 1970s, there was an element of righteous vindication when Lee visited Cambridge University, his alma mater, and chided the British for their decline in productivity and civility. Indeed, the Singapore vision of modernity soon dropped the Western value of individualism, and focused more explicitly on the assumed links between "Confucian" values and the rise of Asian industrialization.

Singapore's national identity since the 1980s has been geared toward promoting the development of a well-disciplined "Confucian" capitalist society. In an effort to create an authentic Chineseness among the culturally heterogeneous and westernized population, the state employed Harvard professor Tu Wei-ming to oversee programs sponsoring instruction and research in Confucian ethics and philosophies. The irony of a professor trained in the orientalist tradition of American East Asian Studies teaching Chinese subjects how to be Confucian seemed to escape notice as Singaporeans were persuaded that being Chinese was inseparable from being "Confucian." Such state-propagated ideas and narratives about Confucian culture are disciplinary schemes to shape and control a workforce geared to state-managed economic development and "state-fathering" of the social body.[47] State patriarchy is central to the form of state-sponsored export-oriented capitalism in Singapore.[48] The biopolitical force is most apparent in innumerable campaigns to improve the labor force—its language skills, its academic performance, its health practices, and its savings rate—and to ensure the "quality" of its repro-duction, as, for example, in the government drives to promote marriage and childbearing among female university graduates, who are mostly Chinese.[49] Such disciplinary schemes are represented within a moral economy of asym-metrical obligations between subjects and the state.

In his study of peasants in Southeast Asia, James C. Scott constructs a model of patron-client exchanges that is morally acceptable to villagers be-cause it is based on the assumption that their patron will guarantee their collective security in times of trouble. Scott claims that the agrarian moral order accepted social inequality because patrons provided crucial social and material guarantees to peasants in return for their labor, services, and loyalty. In a moral economy system, the subordinated groups perceive the unequal exchanges as collaborative and morally legitimate because they ensure se-curity for all.[50] Following Scott, one can say that there is also a *moral economy of the state,* in which a nationalist ideology embeds notions of state-citizen relations within a moral-economy ethos. I differ with Scott in that I believe that the dominant party, in this case the state, must continually produce the cultural values to engender and sustain adherence to a moral-economy ideol-ogy.[51] Moral codes do not merely emerge from preexisting cultural norms but must be invented and reinvented by the ruling elites, both in the ritual pro-nouncements about Asian cultural values and in policy mechanisms that reinforce the expected citizen compliance and worker productivity. In coun-tries such as Singapore, Malaysia, and China, citizens are persuaded that their governments will guarantee economic and social well-being in return for economic discipline and social conformity. Elite narratives construct a bal-ance between rights/freedoms and obligations/duties whereby the state en-sures the conditions for economic accumulation in return for tolerable con-straints and the selective repression of citizens' rights. The moral economy of the state at home is reinforced by the official evaluation of less morally justi-fiable regimes elsewhere in Asia.

In recent years, Lee Kuan Yew, now acting as an elder Asian statesman-at-large, has begun to pronounce on the relative economic performances of Southeast Asian countries. He assesses them not by comparing socialist with capitalist regimes, as was the case in the past, but by contrasting those possess-ing Confucian values with those that do not. Invited to Manila, Lee declared,

"Contrary to what American commentators say, I do not believe that democracy necessarily leads to development. I believe that what a country needs to develop is discipline more than democracy. The exuberance of democracy leads to undisciplined and disorderly conditions which are inimical to development." In Lee's view, the Philippines is handicapped both by its "American-style constitution," which undermines social discipline and stability, and by its "lack" of Confucian values; both factors account for the country being less successful than other developing Asian countries. "The ultimate test of the value of a political system is whether it helps that society to establish conditions which improve the standard of living for the majority of its people, plus enabling the maximum of personal freedoms compatible with the freedoms of others in society."[52] This manifesto of an Asian political system that balances collective (especially family) security against full-fledged individual rights was elaborated by another Singapore official. George Yeo, speaking to a European audience, also criticized Western-style democracy: "No democracy can function without strong moral underpinnings supported by the entire community. Democracies which see only rights without obligations eventually destroy themselves." Yeo offered Singapore as an experiment where both democracy and socialism "must become smaller. . . . In Singapore, we deliberately work our welfare policies through the family. The objective is to strengthen the family net, not weaken it."[53] An Asian form of democracy, then, is one with limits on both democracy and socialism, that is, limits on the expansion of individual rights and on claims on the state. The moral economy of the state is thus aligned with the moral economy of the family. Confucian moralism legitimatizes the state framing of its paternal order as a necessary response to the social changes—including objective realities such as the rising number of dysfunctional families—engendered by capitalism.

This invention and reinvention of official morality converge on the Asian family as the primary unit of regulation and as the vehicle of state power. It is the first of many levels of moral defense against individual interests. By attributing the economic success of Asian countries to smaller, more flexible, Asian forms of democracy, Singapore leaders reinforce their regime of truth, and they tap into the unconscious desires and nostalgia of the diasporan Chinese population. Such moral management is especially successful when comparisons are made between countries in terms of their assumed possession or nonpossession of Confucian culture. In Lee's view, the Philippines could soon be overtaken economically by a war-ravaged but "Confucian" country such as Vietnam.

Lee makes this point in an interview with the *Asian Wall Street Journal*: "[Vietnam] is a different society, differently geared [from the Philippines]. It is a high compression engine, not a low compression engine. It's hard-driving." He points to the Confucian "intangibles": "The coherence of a society, its commitment to common ideals, goals and values." Among these values is the belief in hard work, thrift, filial piety, and national pride as key factors in economic advancement. The interviewer then notes that "by implication, the Philippines is a *softer* place, not so *naturally* industrious and serious, with a doubtful ability to pull together in collective endeavor."[54] These remarks about differences in cultural values become essentialized as concrete, biopolitical differences as well. The interviewer then, posing the usual orientalizing questions, asks: "Why do Asians study harder? Why do they work harder? Why do they save more?" Except of course, the Philippines, which he calls the "celebrated failure." Such narratives on the moral economy underlying development or failure to develop do not mention how capitalism as an ideology of endless desires and as a system of exploitation, in combination with both biopolitical and oppressive state measures, may have played a role in the economic behavior of Asian subjects. Instead, by claiming the superiority of Confucian-based moral economies, these discourses define a hierarchy of moral and economic performances that coincide with racial difference in Southeast Asia.

The narratives tying Chinese cultural values to state stability and economic security are part of an ideological struggle to stitch together the inherently divergent tendencies of the state and market logics, as well as the tensions between an organic conservatism and individual desires.[55] As regimes of truth, narratives of moral economies express a "contradictory unity" whereby the state attempts to balance its political need for social control and stability against the dynamic and diasporic tendencies of capitalism. Observers have noted that the Singaporean state maintains power through orchestrating crises that become opportunities for the government to identify "threats" to state security, to marginalize potentially dissenting groups, and to instill self-surveillance in a population induced to feel continually under siege. Examples of these crises include the declining (Chinese) marriage and birth rates;[56] a "Marxist conspiracy" to subvert the state;[57] and the furor over "the Michael

Fay incident" (see below). The basic tension between the state desire for stability and the anarchic reign of the marketplace compels continual adjustment in relations between the nation and its subjects. What if, despite the orchestrated debates and educative processes, profits prevail over patriotism in the subjects' self-image?

This ranking of "Confucian" over "non-Confucian" countries installs a new status hierarchy in which the former are held up as models of Eastern capitalist modernity while those that follow American liberal democracy are at the bottom. This grid of cultural difference between countries also constructs the less successful, "soft" subjects—women, racial others—who exist within as well as outside of one's national borders. These subordinated subjects have to be civilized and regulated—by Confucian ethics and capitalist discipline—in patri-racial orders where the Confucianist merchant is the gendered, classed, and raced ideal.[58] While these nationalist narratives are directed at regulating populations within national borders, they are linked to similar discourses about Chinese networks and about Asian and Confucian values that, despite their different originating points, their discontinuities, and their tensions, are also renegotiating relations with the West.

Modernity and Orientalism: Spiritual Difference from the West

Although American interests continue to dominate the Asia Pacific region, recently, local leaders have proclaimed that the newly industrializing Asian countries are caught up in an "Asian renaissance." This cultural ferment means, in the words of an official, that "we're not saying that we're culturally superior. We're just saying we're not inferior."[59] As in earlier anticolonial movements, the current Asian cultural renaissance is based on nationalistic claims of an indigenous spiritual domain that is independent of Western domination.[60] Statements claiming Asian cultural difference from the West have been building for more than a decade, and they arise from different circumstances than those that gave birth to the Greater China imagery, but both sets of narratives are rooted in the shifting patterns of capitalist regimes in Asia.

The earliest seeds of an Asian postcolonial turning away from Western capitalist blueprints can be found in the launching of the Malaysian industrialization program. The prime minister proposed a Look East Policy, urging his subjects to emulate Japan—despite fresh memories of the Japanese wartime occupation of the country and much of Southeast Asia—as a model for economic development. The Japanese managerial philosophy, he noted, emphasized a strong work ethic and concern for the welfare of the workers—values that did not contravene the Islamic religion.[61] Japan soon became the major investor in Malaysia, Thailand, and Indonesia, helping to build the base of their industrial programs.[62] By the end of the decade, Japan's rising economic power and moral prestige in Southeast Asia had encouraged efforts to stand up to American domination, as, for example, in the publication of the book *The Japan That Can Say No*, a tract widely interpreted on the other side of the Pacific as "America bashing."[63]

With the economic emergence of China, however, most recent representations of Asian cultural difference are associated with China and the overseas Chinese, as well as a more broadly based notion of "Asian values." Narratives insisting on Asia's spiritual difference from the West often boil down to the reified Confucian values that are already popular with the business leaders and the media in Singapore and Malaysia. As often enunciated by Malaysian and Singaporean leaders, these values consist of "the family, education, high savings, hard work, home ownership, and clean living."[64] Western scholars would associate this list of attributes with Thatcherite and Reaganite formulations for dealing with excessive economic individualism and the insecurities generated by globalization.[65] Indeed, throughout much of this century, Western scholars have identified these features among the universalistic norms of modernity. Now appropriated and dressed up in timeless orientalist guise by Southeast Asian regimes, they operate as normalizing truth claims to regulate the newly affluent populations. Furthermore, the rise of the entrepreneurial state associated with peripheral Fordism in Asia has created its own ideological doctrine of "the Asian Way," defined as "an intricate ideology . . . to justify why it is no longer possible to compete with Asians under the old rules."[66] This new interest in collectively defending Asian free trade is also reflected in the redefinition of "East Asia." The term has been expanded beyond its cold war boundaries to include China, Japan, Korea, Taiwan, Hong Kong, as well as Southeast Asian nation-states—a region whose combined gross domestic product is expected to be 33 percent of the world economy by the year 2010.[67] That the concept of Asian values is deeply invested in market competition was dramatically highlighted by East and Southeast Asian reactions to the American threat to withdraw Most Favored Nation (MFN) status from China in retaliation for alleged human rights violations.

Human rights have become the core issue in articulations of Asian cultural difference from the West. Global debates about human rights in Asia allow local leaders to publicly resolve the contradictions between the community and the state, between spiritual and material interests, and between the unfettered individualism associated with the West and the self-censuring political culture in Asia. A year after the World Conference on Human Rights in 1993, the Chinese premier Li Peng instructed the visiting Australian foreign minister: "There is not just one model of human rights. The Vienna statement includes the basic views and demands of many developing countries on the issue of human rights. It expressly points out that 'the right of developing countries to develop (*fazhan quan*) is part of and inseparable from human rights.' While emphasizing general human rights, we cannot neglect the characteristics of the country and region and the importance of historical, cultural, and religious backgrounds. We cannot neglect each country's conditions and cannot demand a singular model of human rights."[68]

This view that economic development—nay, capitalism—is a fundamental human right is echoed by Southeast Asian governments, who claim that economic development is "the only force that can liberate the Third World."[69] In a novel reworking of older anti-imperialist rhetoric, postcolonial leaders see themselves as continuing to resist Western domination through capitalist development. Furthermore, their rejection of the Western human-rights campaign as a trade weapon also implicitly criticizes the new Western evil other, that is, the privileged and lazy working classes who are demanding all kinds of protectionism at the expense of Asian development.[70]

Thus, from Beijing to Singapore, a chorus of voices is asserting that capitalism is a human right, while the U.S. human-rights campaign is denounced as "an instrument to perform power politics" and force less powerful countries to accept an imposed Western standard.[71] For the first time, a group of East and Southeast Asian leaders is speaking out collectively against American "arrogance": the Malaysian finance minister called efforts to link changes in human-rights or labor policies to U.S. market access as "condescending and even arrogant," while others claimed in international forums that Asian economic ascendancy owes little to the "arrogant West." Even among the normally tactful Japanese, resigning Japanese prime minister Hosokawa gave a parting shot: "It is not proper to force Western- or European-type democracy onto others."[72] These voices raised in righteous anger not only are contesting Western notions about human rights and democracy, they also express fears that the West's continuing domination will derail Asian capitalism, which has become, in their narration, synonymous with Asian modernity.

Furthermore, to prevent the West from capturing the moral high ground, Asian scholars claim that indigenous humanistic traditions actually inform Asian capitalism. In an article in *Beijing Review*, an official government publication, Dong Yunhu defines an alternative notion of human rights that is rooted in Asian civilization: "Although the human rights concept centering on individuals originated in the West, the humanitarian spirit, such as the value of human dignity in India, and Confucian humanism in China, has long been a part of Asia's cultural tradition. In these humanitarian traditions, humanism and kindheartedness were regarded as the natural features of man. The idea that 'the aged should be well supported, children should be brought up, the able-bodied should be given an opportunity to bring his ability into full play, and the disabled should be helped,' also encouraged people to be concerned about society and others before themselves." Dong goes on to link these spiritual traditions to the rights of the modern nation-state: "The cultural tradition of respect for individual rights while *guaranteeing* the state, social, family, and other collective rights has played an important role in promoting economic and social progress in the region and will continue to promote its further revitalization." He is confident that Southeast Asian leaders would agree with him that a balance between individual rights and socioeconomic rights is the Asian model of development. "This collective humanitarian tradition is helpful for Asia and has promoted a high economic growth rate and the improvement of living standards."[73]

There is thus a move beyond the simple reiterating of Chinese/Confucian values toward the articulation of a pan-Asian "humanitarian model" that is based on ahistorical and homogenizing descriptions of Asian cultures to legitimize overall state policies of capital accumulation, labor, and social control. The invocation of Asian values often becomes a carte blanche to legitimatize any action of a ruling regime. Some discourses come close to orientalizing Asian traditions as timeless and irrefutably embodied in all Asians. The incantations regarding strong families, loyalty to elders, discipline, frugality, the work ethic, and so on are also pointed critiques of the West.

The most articulate voice in such cultural criticisms belongs to Kishore Mahbubani, a Harvard-educated official in the Singaporean Ministry of Foreign Affairs. He has published articles in America titled "The Dangers of Decadence: What the Rest Can Teach the West" and "The United States: 'Go East, Young Man.'"[74] Mahbubani insists that an America suffering from "unfettered individual freedom" and its resulting "massive social decay" ought to learn about social values from its Asian neighbors. Mahbubani makes valuable observations about American society from an Asian perspective. Nevertheless, although he talks about the recent historical upheavals that have compelled Asian societies to break with past "mental ossification," he also invokes a sixth-century Confucian vision of a well-ordered, unabashedly patriarchal society as a guide to contemporary Asian societies and even to the United States.[75] Here, we are reminded again of the biopolitical concerns of state-sponsored capitalism that underlie the rhetoric of the Asian-values discourses—now generalized to be synonymous with major Asian spiritual traditions. By raiding the rich storehouse of Asian myths and religions, these discourses can find legitimization for state strategies aimed at strengthening controls at home and at stiffening bargaining postures in the global economy.

Stitching Together Disjunctures at Home

These imageries—of the nation-state, of Greater China, and of Asian values— which are produced from different sites, are in varying degrees of tension with each other and ultimately have points of application "at home." How do claims of the Asian way and a moral unity against the West engage the interests of subordinate groups in their own countries? In what ways do they set the terms of thinking and talking about Asian capitalism and cultural difference? How do regimes of truth "stitch together" the contradictory disjunctures between market logics, individual interests, and the biopolitical needs of the state?[76] One way triumphalist narratives of nation and capitalism deal with contradictory forces is to remain silent about realities such as the social upheavals; the historical and ongoing exploitation of Asian labor, women, and children; the rampant consumerism; the public incivility; the cut-throat individualist competition; the rising divorce rates; and the cultural hollowness that flourish in south China and the Asian tigers as they do in other places undergoing rapid capitalist development. One may well ask how "Confucian" are the everyday practices of the majority of overseas Chinese if we go beyond the narrow definitions of discipline and diligence and remember that Confucianism also means a turning away from materialism and a narrow concern with the family. The majority in Southeast Asian Chinese communities have never read Confucius; their beliefs and practices are a heterogeneous mix of interacting Chinese elements, elements from other cultures, and state definitions of "national" culture.[77] Furthermore, the purported "welfare-oriented" model of Asian business entails not only paternalism but also the exploitation of indebted workers in a multiplicity of family businesses.[78] In both state-sponsored capitalist ventures and family-firm operations, the exploitation of young female workers and children is pervasive and in some cases, has been intensified by flexible strategies of capital accumulation based on informal networks and subcontracted production processes.[79] These subaltern groups, who bear the main burden of Asian capitalist success, are almost never mentioned in dominant discourses of the Asian way. Though indispensable to capitalist success in the region, they are rendered invisible and speechless—an effect of the "symbolic violence" of triumphalist Chinese modernity.[80]

Another way hegemonic discourses weave around problematic areas is to secure their regimes of truth to certain political positions, which shows the overwhelming importance of national stakes. For instance, in late 1993, there was a major fire in a Shenzhen factory owned by a Hong Kong subcontractor. The fire killed over eighty female workers who were trapped by barred windows and sealed doors. Human-rights groups contend that 90 percent of foreign joint ventures in China flout safety rules with the help of corrupt local officials. Their victims are usually young female workers who have migrated from poor inland provinces. Because most have no residence permits, their illegal status is used by employers to discipline them by threats of exposure and expulsion.[81] When I was in Guangzhou a couple of months after the Shenzhen fire, TV talk shows and the media appeared to be mainly concerned with defending the state and foreign investors. Journalists and officials noted that there were adequate laws protecting workers' safety, and failure to implement the rules caused the tragedy. Others shielded foreign companies from blame, noting that doors and gates were welded shut to prevent workers from stealing products. There was hardly any mention of the youth and gender of the workers, who were referred to as "migrants," a stigmatizing term in coastal China. Many of the fire victims could not be identified because their names were not on record. There were no demands by local women's groups to defend their interests. Although young women are the paradigmatic workers of China's industrial boom, they are rendered faceless even when sacrificed to the greed of officials and investors. Elite pronouncements are often taken as disinterested statements that protect Asian cultures when in fact, their effects have been to reinforce state power in legitimizing official policies and suppressing dissent.

Singapore has emerged as the chief English-language articulator of a Chinese modernity. The international coverage of the caning of Michael Fay for vandalism has made tiny Singapore the representative of what the West thinks Confucian discipline and efficient capitalism are all about. In Singapore, the Fay case was skillfully handled by political leaders and writers as an educative process highlighting the difference between the soft, decadent West and the strong East. The standoff with the United States over an appropriate means of punishment for vandalism was cast as a David-and-Goliath contest: "A small state stood up to the bullying of a super-power whose media was largely blinded by an avowal of individualism."[82] Although a 1986 study showed that just over one-quarter of those surveyed supported caning as an appropriate punishment for vandalism, this figure rose to 79 percent in a recent poll, "probably because Singaporeans felt affronted by the bully-boy tactics adopted by the U.S. media over the caning of Fay."[83] Differences over crime and punishment were orchestrated into a lesson on deep cultural differences toward individualism, social order, and the symbolic domination of the West. The government handling of the incident "focused minds on the issue of law and order" and convinced the majority of Singaporeans that their interests lay with those of the ruling party. The government-controlled press allowed one timid dissenting voice to slip in: "We say . . . 'ya, ya, he deserves it . . .' but deep inside wonder about the direction of punishment-versus-crime here."[84] A list of differences between Singaporean and American cultures was printed in the papers: Singaporeans are more "compassionate," lack "cynicism towards authority," and need to maintain the "moral authority of the Government."

Moreover, in Singapore, "families of criminals are more likely to feel they have been shamed before society, rather than blame it."[85] As in China, the state uses the print media to reinforce the cultural rightness of its policy.

The Shenzhen fire in China and the Michael Fay incident in Singapore are local occasions that allow national disciplinary hegemonies to conjoin discursively coincidental interests between subordinate groups and the nation-state. In both cases, national discourses about the differences in Asian capitalism have mobilized wide public support. They have also increased the public's demand for parity and respect from the Americans in a way that was never attempted in postwar Japan. This shifting, multinational cultural representation of the emerging Asian way has caused the news magazine *Asiaweek* to define the emerging transpacific economic formation as "Asiamerica! The Next Century's Super-culture."[86]

Conclusion: A Momentary Glow?

The many modernist visions—of the Chinese nation, of transnational Chinese capitalism, of Asian spiritual difference—emanate from sites of unequal power in the Asia Pacific region. Separately and collectively, these circuits of symbolic power are claiming the region, which is no longer an unchallenged domain of American capitalism but the eastern frontier of Asian expansion. The varied ideological work of imagining heterogeneous and complex Asian experiences into a stable and coherent set of collective values and goals is defining an alternative modernity to that of the West.

I do not use the term *alternative modernities* to suggest that these ideological positions represent an absolute moral or epistemological difference from those in the West.[87] Asian modernist imaginations, which insist upon their cultural/spiritual distinctiveness, are contradictory self-orientalizing moves. A common ethnographic assumption holds that speaking subjects are unproblematic representers of their own culture, whereas I argue that their truth claims, like those of ethnographers, are articulated in webs of power. Indeed, answering the question, Who owns culture? (and articulating its particular truths) is an open-ended, contestory process. Perhaps because of Western orientalist assumptions about the enduring nature of Asian cultures, Asian leaders who deploy cultural and racial discourses to regulate home societies and to project their national power are treated with less skepticism than if such strategies were used by Western states. Alternative, then, is used here to refer to an oppositional dynamic to existing hegemonies within the field of geopolitical forces; it is a counterforce arising from sites that are not without their own particular mix of expansive and repressive technologies.

Indeed, in a world of Western hegemony, Asian voices are unavoidably inflected by orientalist essentialisms that infiltrate all kinds of public exchanges about culture. I use the term *self-orientalization* in recognition of such predicaments, but also in recognition of the agency to maneuver and manipulate meanings within different power domains. Statements about Chinese modernity are an amalgam of indigenous ideas, Western concepts, and self-orientalizing representations by Asian leaders. Such formulations of modernity should not come as a surprise since the Asia Pacific region as a geopolitical entity was constructed by Euroamerican imperialism and capitalism.[88]

Early in the twentieth century, Enlightenment concepts of liberty and progress, as well as social-Darwinist views of inequality among nations, informed the thinking of many intellectuals in China and Southeast Asia. Currently, what are claimed to be Chinese/Asian values, or the "Asian form of democracy," are derived from Western notions of progress. The standard postwar tract on modernization—in the sense of belief in progressive evolutionary development, rationality, property ownership, family stability, and social order—owes much to an American reformulation of Western bourgeois thought. Many ideas, such as the imperative of economic development, the need for scientific and technological progress, and the progress toward rational management of society, can be found in books such as Rostow's *Stages of Economic Growth: A Non-Communist Manifesto* or repackaged in Margaret Thatcher's and Ronald Reagan's speeches. Furthermore, claims that Chinese/ Asian modernity is based on cultural difference disguise the fact that although indigenous societies have their own essentializing notions about culture, many of the remarks are self-orientalizing in that they reify Western concepts of Chinese guanxi networks, neo-Confucianism, and the like. Thus, narratives of Asian modernity contain many of the elements in Western discourses because they are informed by and are continually produced by negotiating against Western domination in the world.[89]

I therefore use the term *alternative modernities* to denote not so much the difference in content between Asian and Western modernities but the new self-confident political reenvisioning of Asian futures that challenges the basic assumption of inevitable Western domination. Modernity is a polysemic term in Asia, as elsewhere, and I have merely touched on a small set of imagined modernities linked to a range of Chinese societies and their increasing interactions. In Asia, state narratives insist that Asian modernity is an alternative to the West because in their view, capitalism is a system that should strengthen state control, not undermine it. Thus, the major difference between Asian modernities and those in the West lies in the way Asian state biopolitics and economic competition are routinely recast as timeless cultural practices and values, and events generated by the breaking down of national borders are managed through institutionalizing Confucian moral economies, which are set off against Western liberal democracies. These hegemonic moves seek to instill cultural solidarity and control in diverse populations while deflecting Western domination in the economic and political realms. Symptomatic of the effects of such triumphalist cultural discourses are statements such as one by a Hong Kong writer who asserts that despite national borders, the system of trade interests that allows profits and trust to grow between countries within Greater's China's "community of Chinese" (*Zhongguoren gongtong di*) is "a system that would restore something like the offering of imperial tribute, so that China maintains the regional order of the Asia-Pacific area."[90]

These discursive practices of state and capital converge in pronouncing that the cultural logic of Asian capitalism is collectivism and stability (as opposed to fragmentation and flux in the West).[91] This hegemonic moment is attained when leaders of different countries find in the master Chinese symbols "points of articulation" between various locales in Asia.[92] As the ever astute Lee Kuan Yew notes, this "*momentary* glow of fraternity" may not outlast China's emergence as a superpower.[93] Nevertheless, such a hegemonic moment describes an alternative map of symbolic power, inscribing the "hard" surfaces of triumphalist Chinese capitalism and cultural chauvinism across the Asia Pacific region. What we have then is a paradigm change in capitalism as the West knows it. Heretofore, the world-systems model has posited the West (and Japan) as the center and the non-West as the periphery. More recently, the Western capitalist concept of globalization denotes a world dominated by transnational capitalist operations, regardless of geopolitical differences. It is a historical irony that at the point when a new Asian hegemony is emerging out of the particular imbrications of state and capital in the Asia Pacific region, so much Western academic attention remains riveted on the

West itself or mesmerized by the West's colonial past and present in "the peripheries." Chinese modernities are new racial imaginaries and regimes of domination that decenter Western hegemony in the global arena. A synergy of political, economic, and ideological processes is producing a geopolitical center in East Asia. Will the momentary glow of fraternity forged in alternative Chinese modernities and in renegotiating American global domination become the Asia Pacific hegemony of the new century?

PART 2

Regimes and Strategies

Fengshui and the Limits to Cultural Accumulation ☰ 3

In northern California, the so-called Hong Kong money elite resides in an exclusive community on the flank of the San Francisco Peninsula mountain range. All the homes in Peninsula Peak cost over a million dollars; some, much more.[1] The choicest houses are set into the sides of the hills, with the mountains as a backdrop and a view of the bay. The *fengshui* (propitious placement determined by geomancy) is excellent. In southern Chinese folklore, mountain ranges are inhabited by dragons—mythical creatures highly valued for their power, as well as for their association with royalty and ancestors. Hong Kong itself is considered blessed by nine dragons who inhabit the hills facing the deep harbor.[2] Seeking to tap similar veins of riches overseas and facing impending rule by mainland China, Chinese from Hong Kong have crossed the Pacific to make this former white enclave their new home.

Initially led by real-estate agents, and later by word of mouth, the influx of wealthy Chinese from Hong Kong, Taiwan, and Southeast Asia has spread to cities and upscale communities all over the state. They account for 15 percent of Peninsula Peak's population, which is around ten thousand.[3] Mansions in an Asian/Mediterranean style stand amidst clearings where few trees remain unfelled. This was a sore point with locals, as was the fact that many of the houses were paid for in cash, sometimes before the arrival of the new occupants. In March 1990, one such home was the site of a fund-raiser for a prominent Chinese American Democratic incumbent in the state government. The cars parked on the winding road included ten Mercedes-Benzes, a couple of Rolls Royces, several BMWs, and one Jaguar. There were also a Volvo and two Japanese cars, one of them mine. Though everyone there was fluent in English, practically all spoke Cantonese, and we could have been at an exclusive gathering in Hong Kong.

I spoke to one of the younger people at the party. Like many teenage émi-grés, she was actively taking lessons—piano, tennis, singing, and dancing—to be able to participate in the social activities of upper-class life. But she surprised me by confessing that she and her Chinese American classmates in another affluent suburb had also signed up for modeling classes. They were not really interested in becoming models, for that would lower their social value, but they were intent on learning how to dress, walk, and generally comport themselves in ways that would make them "more acceptable to the Americans." Chinese parents frequently encourage their children to display social poise and public confidence by urging them to perform before guests after dinner. Indeed, the young woman I spoke with was very well groomed and was determinedly presenting herself to each guest, as if to practice her lessons in social mixing among this cosmopolitan crowd. Propitious location, the trappings of wealth, and appropriate body language are the cultural forms immigrants must gain mastery over if they are to convert mere economic power into social prestige, as determined by the host society.

Different Forms of Capital

This chapter looks at Hong Kong emigrants in terms of their flexible strategies of accumulation in both economic and cultural senses. Chinese traders in transnational settings have been viewed mainly as skillful "handlers of money,"[4] but rarely have they been seen as agents actively shaping their self-identity in a cross-cultural context. In fact, sinologists tend to conflate overseas-Chinese practices with an essentialized notion of Chinese emigrant culture as one characterized by "the versatility and entrepreneurial qualities of their family firms" but otherwise culturally conservative even in highly dynamic transnational environments.[5] What is often missing in accounts of diasporan experiences is a focus on Chinese diasporan subjects as active manipulators of cultural symbols. I argue that an important feature associated with the flexibility of Hong Kong emigrants' strategies is their acquisition and deployment of what Pierre Bourdieu calls "symbolic capital." In *Distinctions: The Social Judgment of Taste,* Bourdieu maintains that in modern France, upper-class dispositions and habits (habitus), together with the acquisition and display of certain credentials, luxury goods and social trappings, are practices that attest to the social distinction of subjects.[6] Symbolic capital thus invites honor while disguising its links with the kinds of accumulation we often associate with crass money dealing. As an ideological system of taste and prestige, symbolic capital reproduces the established social order and conceals relations of domination. Elsewhere, he also notes the "interconvertibility" of such symbolic capital with economic capital in the narrow sense, even though the former "gives every appearance of disinterestedness by departing from the logic of interested calculation (in the narrow sense) and playing for stakes that are non-material and not easily quantified."[7] Nevertheless, symbolic capital operates according to market logic, something Bourdieu underlines by using terms such as "capital," "acquisition," "credit," "profits," and "balance sheet" to describe the activities surrounding symbolic values that generate high social returns.[8]

Bourdieu's insights into symbolic capital are addressed to the practice of capital accumulation in a social system that was conceived in a relatively homogenous and static fashion. He is primarily concerned with how the criteria of what constitutes good taste and breeding may shift while the pathways laid down for attaining high status remain structurally the same. What are the effects of cultural accumulation in a cross-cultural, transnational arena where there is not one but many sets of competing cultural criteria that determine high symbolic value in multiple class- and race-stratified settings? For Chinese emigrants operating in Western metropolitan circles, symbolic values are set not only by Paris but also by London, Berlin, New York, and Los Angeles. Asian arrivistes find themselves seeking the kinds of cultural capital that are determined across the oceans in order to be sufficiently adept in socially navigating the norms of these foreign societies. In other words, when the world is the arena of strategies of accumulation, subjects coming from less privileged sites must be flexible in terms of the cultural symbols they wish to acquire. To put it another way, Euroamerican cultural hegemony determines and judges the signs and forms of metropolitan status and glamour. Hong Kong emigrants seek the kinds of symbolic capital that have international recognition and value, not only in the country of origin but also in the country of destination and especially in the transnational spaces where the itineraries of traveling businessmen and professionals intersect with those of local residents. These transnational arenas are not only business environments but settings where competing hierarchies of cultural distinction assess the symbolic status of locals and, more critically, that of newcomers, no matter how cosmopolitan they are in practice. In upper-class social settings— whether in Singapore, Hong Kong, or Bangkok—guests are frequently decked out in the latest fashions of Giorgio Armani, Yohji Yamamoto, and DKNY, not in local imitations, as was the case in the less-affluent past. Thus, while the "global cultural economy" of people, products, and ideas may be character-ized by disjunctures,[9] regimes of consumption and credentialization are defi-nitely hierarchized, with Europe and America setting the standards of interna-tional middle-class style. Indeed, it is the cultural structuring of distinction and taste in the metropolitan countries and their global hegemonies that makes the snob value of a Harvard MBA, a Mercedes-Benz, or a Rolex watch effective in Beijing, Bahrain, Boston, or Buenos Aires. Of course, there are local configurations, so among some aristocratic European circles, flaunting one's American business degree may be considered petit bourgeois rather than haute culture, and the tides of fashion may quickly make certain brand names or styles outmoded, to be replaced by other trends. Nevertheless, these shifts and rhythms in international middle-class circles are dictated by fashion designers, marketing practices, and news media based in Western metro-politan centers. Hong Kong professionals, called "yompies" (young outwardly mobile professionals), are armed with Luis Vuitton luggage and shod in Gucci shoes and more often than not brandish a cell phone, whether bound for downtown or across the Pacific. Indeed, for many middle-class Chinese in Malaysia, Singapore, Hong Kong, and the Philippines, the ultimate symbolic capital necessary for global mobility is an American college degree, which guarantees that the holder has acquired the cultural knowledge, skills, and credentials that enable the transposition of social status from one country to another.

Second, I modify Bourdieu's concept of symbolic capital around the ques-tion of convertibility. He observes that the various "capitals"—economic, cultural, symbolic, and social—are different kinds of resources that are mutu-ally convertible and that they can also be converted into personal power and can thereby define one's life chances or social trajectory.[10] For example, under specific conditions, the cultural capital of a foreign university degree can be converted into both economic capital (wealth) and social capital (prestige and eligibility for legal citizenship). However, I would like to argue that under the current conditions of "time-space compression" associated with flexible accumulation, it is primarily economic capital that is being converted into all other forms of capital, not the other way around.[11] Hong Kong emigrants in pursuit of economic capital hope also to acquire the symbolic forms that will enable their flexible positioning vis-à-vis different sites, markets, and cultures.

Bourdieu is primarily interested in cultural capital in the embodied state, that is, in the form that is called cultivation, which depends on hereditary transmission (although it can also be acquired "in the absence of any deliberate inculcation").[12] However, when accumulation strategies are the means for propelling one across cultural and geopolitical spaces, the deliberate acquisition of cultural capital is very common indeed. It starts with parents sending their children to the "right" school (British missionary) and inculcating in them the "correct" foreign language, academic interests, and social behavior. The would-be immigrant often acquires an intensified sense of him- or herself as body capital that can be constantly improved to meet new and shifting criteria of symbolic power.

Third, Bourdieu has never suggested that there are any structural limits to the accumulation of cultural capital other than the shifting criteria of what constitutes cultural capital in time and place. His notion of symbolic capital is wedded to the idea of what he calls the archaic, or "good-faith," economy and static reproduction.[13] But where there is accumulation and credit, there must be loss and debit. Indeed, the reproduction of social power, especially for the newcomer deploying start-up symbolic capital, is never guaranteed or certain, especially when he or she embodies other signs—for example, skin color, foreign accent, and cultural taste—that may count as symbolic deficits in the host society. Thus, in transnational movements, newcomers may have acquired cultural capital that they have difficulty converting into social capital because there is a perceived mismatch between the distinction of their symbolic capital and their racial identity, which may be associated with low social value in the host group. Because there is dissonance between their personal features and their possession of cultural capital—for example, an apparently Asian subject who speaks fluent Dutch—such individuals may even be judged culturally incompetent. This glaring inconsistency destroys the misrecognition that cultural capital is legitimate competence based on the biological singularity of the possessor and "the prestige of innate property."[14] Limits to cultural accumulation, then, are especially apparent to immigrants when there is a mismatch, from the hegemonic standpoint, between the symbolic capital and its embodiment. Nonwhite residents and immigrants in the West are accustomed to being asked, Where are you from? or on extreme occasions being told "to go home" because they do not match the ideal image of, for instance, an American citizen. The point is not that money cannot buy everything, but that accumulation of symbolic capital can only go so far in converting prestige and honor into social capital that will increase access to institutionalized relationships of mutual acquaintance and recognition in particular cultural economies. Furthermore, a reverse kind of discrimination occurs when someone such as Dutch Indonesian intellectual Ien Ang goes to Singapore and has to defend herself for her inability to speak Chinese.[15] Thus, the blending of a racialized person with a certain set of symbolic capital must be read as acceptable by the receiving society before any social prestige can accrue to such an embodiment of "correct" taste and accomplishment.

Fourth, I would like to propose two additional kinds of cultural capital that Bourdieu has not yet mentioned: location and philanthropy. As mentioned above, fengshui is extremely popular among Hong Kong people, who, as refugees living on some of the most expensive real estate in the world, are exquisitely concerned with the importance of location. The revealed value of a choice location is as real estate; its hidden value is as a confluence of good fortune and social power. Location, then, is a form of intertwined economic/cultural capital, and for Hong Kong emigrants, choosing the destination, the community one settles in, and the house itself are careful calculations that can never be reduced simply to economic considerations. Since placement is a form of spatial power, choosing a location is part of the strategy for cultural accumulation whereby the subject tries to influence the social milieu in which he or she embeds him- or herself.

Like potlatch, philanthropy is a practice of cultural accumulation that depends on giving away (thus dissipating) one's economic resources. As a gesture of public selflessness, philanthropy is a dramatic form of cultural accumulation that can be a strategy of last resort after other forms of capital (educational, symbolic, etc.) fail to improve an individual's social status. As with the selection of location, philanthropy depends on a discerning choice, and the selection of particular charities on which to shower one's favor is a gesture of symbolic affiliation that may reinforce or cut across social divisions. Giving to charity, then, is a mode of cultural accumulation that can be pretty effective in breaking down barriers to acceptance after newcomers with start-up symbolic capital realize the limits to converting cultural capital into social distinction.

Finally, Bourdieu's concept of habitus and capital acquisition seems to work seamlessly when applied to French society, which he analyzed as a fairly stable social-class system where everyone knows his or her place even if the cultural codes of distinction may shift from time to time.[16] But what happens when strategies of cultural accumulation run up against regimes of racial difference and hierarchy, so that the possession of cultural capital is rendered somewhat ineffectual for being embodied in racially inferior agents? The experiences of Hong Kong migrants, probably among the most acquisitive consumers anywhere, help to complicate the picture regarding the effectiveness of accumulation strategies in transnational arenas.

Strategies of Accumulation and Mobility

While anthropologists have talked about the imaginaries and cultural landscapes emerging out of transnational "flows," less attention has been paid to the agents who are part of these movements and who must manage the cross-currents of cultural winds at home, in transit, and upon arrival in what may be only a temporary place of residence. In postcolonial Southeast Asia, most people who have made it into the middle class are Western educated and thus prepared for studies abroad in Australia, Great Britain, and North America. Especially since the late 1960s, when the turmoil of the Great Proletarian Cultural Revolution spilled over into Hong Kong, middle- and upper-middle-class families began sending their children for education abroad. This "soaking in salt water," or immersion in overseas experience, has become a rite of passage for the young from well-to-do families, a kind of sojourning abroad that is paralleled and sustained by itineraries of international business.[17] Families participate in decade-long itineraries shaped by a mix of strategies that stagger the departures of children, expand entrepreneurial activities overseas, and relocate members and homes in choice locations abroad. It is a cultural logic of many ethnic Chinese in Southeast Asia to organize their families according to strategies of time and space so that over time, the family is distributed over a longer distance or wider expanse of space. These strategies of accumulation, dispersal, and relocation, which are stimulated by the dual impulses of escaping political instability and pursuing livelihoods, are most recently and dramatically displayed by emigrants from Hong Kong.

Under British rule (1842–1997), Hong Kong was itself a destination of refugees from China. From its takeover by the British in 1842, Hong Kong has been a transit point for refugees and commercial flows. It is today a great metropolis, the hub of transnational corporations in Asia, and the third largest financial center in the world (after New York and London). Given its particular mix of refugees, manufacturing, and financial markets, Hong Kong nurtures subjects who are obsessively engaged in accumulating capital and real estate as ways of making a living and building a nest egg against unexpected contingencies. The travel writer Paul Theroux argues that given their memories of previous disasters on the mainland, Hong Kong refugees are not typical refugees. Hong Kong "has really been another way out of China—and especially a vantage point for these people in transit to find another place to live."[18] But we must qualify the popular view that the outflow of people from Hong Kong (almost as many return) is caused solely by the communist takeover of Hong Kong. Through generations of escaping Chinese upheavals, Hong Kong people, like overseas Chinese in Southeast Asia, have developed an art of improvisation, flexibility, and mobility that is inseparable from the commercial world that evolved under European rule and flourished under postcolonial circumstances in Southeast Asia.[19]

Indeed, the south China diaspora dating from the last century must be the historical context to view this latest wave of out-migration.[20] More specifically, the contemporary reemigration of Hong Kongers to the West is a process whereby Chinese transnational strategies have become integrated with the "flexible accumulation" systems of late capitalism. David Harvey argues that since the 1970s, capitalism has become globalized through innovative financial and organizational practices. Securities are now traded twenty-four hours a day, and "flexible responses in labor markets, labor processes, and consumer markets" have greatly increased.[21] These conditions favor geographical dispersal, small-scale production, and the pursuit of special markets in a highly uncertain competitive environment—all qualities already possessed by the hundreds of thousands of Hong Kong Chinese family firms. Indeed, Hong Kong since the 1960s has been the wildest realization of freewheeling capitalism anywhere in the world and was (until the transfer of most production units to the Chinese mainland) the global capital of the subcontracting system of production. In the 1980s, satellite communications have allowed relatively small family enterprises to participate in a truly global arena, which was once the preserve of multinational corporations.

While Hong Kong is the biggest investor in mainland China (of which it is now part), many business families are turning increasingly to Australian, American, and European markets, which are viewed as sites of long-range investment and family plans. Thus, strategies of Chinese emigration are driven by a mix of economic and political reasons that express not merely entrepreneurial savvy but also the professional and cultural competence to maneuver in global settings. Although emigrant families rely on economic capital for conversion into cultural capital, their ability to acquire new symbols of power often outstrips their ability to decode and manipulate cross-cultural meanings in foreign locations. This jeopardizes the social reproduction of their power abroad.

For many ethnic Chinese in Hong Kong and Southeast Asia, both the well-off and the not-so-rich, strategies of accumulation begin with the acquisition of a Western education, usually in a missionary school, that will launch a youngster into a boarding school or college in the metropolitan West.[22] The most successful Hong Kong emigrants had their education in British prep schools, where they acquired the correct cultural capital that would facilitate educational and occupational success abroad. The Diocesan Boys' School, the Diocesan Girls' School, and St. Paul's (coeducational) were the top institutions where prominent families sent their children. There, they acquired the trappings of British public schools, as displayed in British-accented speech, a smart turnout, and a muted arrogance that primed them for dealing with Western elites in a way that traditional Chinese businessmen found hard to muster. Since the early 1960s, schoolchildren have been passing around well-thumbed copies of *Lovejoy's Guide to U.S. Colleges* to pick out the colleges they would attend. The strategy to acquire an American degree is often inseparable from choosing a particular location in which to attend school. Most children and their parents favor the big cities, where there are large Asian communities, or the sunny states that share similar weather conditions with home. The prestige of the intended university—say, Yale—is balanced by the features of the location: Is it close to relatives? Good real estate? Chinese shops and restaurants? Once one is admitted somewhere (the quality of the college is often secondary to the attraction of the location), he or she recruits siblings and friends to the same college or nearby institutions. California is the most popular destination because of its huge Asian population, good real estate, and sunny weather.

Since 1990, in anticipation of the return of Hong Kong to China rule, over one thousand emigrants a week have left Hong Kong—an outflow that is referred to as "the China tide," washing up on the shores of Australia, Canada, and the United States. Many take advantage of the Family Reunification Act to enter American cities, and ten thousand permanent visas a year are granted to Hong Kong immigrants, many of whom head for the San Francisco Bay area, which is home to about a quarter of the nation's Asians.[23] While children head off to high schools and colleges, their parents focus on buying real estate. For Hong Kong investors, buying commercial and residential property is a means to diversify their portfolios, as well as a kind of "health insurance" for capital and family. Besides commercial property, immigrants also acquire family homes so that residency can eventually lead to the possession of green cards. Education, degrees, property, and green cards, more than wealth itself, are the cultural capital sought as steps toward being accepted by the host society.

However, Chinese students and professionals entering the United States lack the appropriate racial and cultural origins that are the stereotypical markers of racial prestige in Western democracies, and the effectiveness of their accumulation strategies is conditioned and limited by their racial and social origin. The dissonance between these racialized immigrants and the cultural skills they wish to acquire produces structural limits to the conversion of economic wealth into social prestige. Let us first look at how the politics of location reduces the immigrants' ability to convert economic capital into cultural capital.

The Politics of Location: Restructuring the Ethnic Landscape

In recent years, property values in Hong Kong and Singapore have soared so high that American properties are considered bargains. While wealthy investors spend tens of millions of dollars on commercial property, middle-class investors come to California to seek stable investments and to find political refuge and good schools for their children. American locations are thus viewed as blessed in two senses: as the sites of relatively inexpensive property and as the sites of moral/political security for immigrant families. The

fengshui practices of Hong Kong immigrants reveal a deep concern for securing not only their own economic fortune but also the fortune of the family. In
Peninsula Peak, I visited a large ranch house bought by a Hong Kong socialite,
which was ideally set into a hillside facing the bay. She pointed out, however,
that the house design could cause the good fortune of the place to dissipate
and thus weaken the boundaries of security produced by the fengshui of the
site. A huge staircase ended too close to the front door, allowing energy and
good fortune to flow away from the home. She counteracted such bad forces
by placing a chandelier and a large mirror in the hallway. In the home of
another Hong Kong immigrant, the staircase, which was similarly positioned,
was covered with a wall of mirrors to deflect forces that could weaken the
fengshui of the site. Such cultural logic, and practices to transform the design
of American homes, indicate that for these immigrants, choosing an American location is inseparable from securing the safety and well-being of their
families. In Peninsula Peak, this concern was reflected in the struggles of
Chinese parents with local school boards, which are monopolized by white
parents, and in the attempt to set up Chinese language lessons and sports
gatherings that cater to immigrant children. The politics of location—to escape political uncertainties in Asia, to obtain a green card, to educate children
in good schools, and to live in safe homes—thus influence the immigrants'
strategies of accumulating American property. However, this quest for economic and cultural capital in the American landscape destabilizes the sense of
political security for American residents.

By the 1980s, the influx of Asian capital and professionals into California
had brought about an ethnic restructuring of many downtown and suburban
landscapes. While many poor Asian immigrants still head for Chinatown,
significant numbers of overseas Chinese arrive as representatives of a different
structure of immigration that is tied to the economic boom in Asia.[24] According to a recent survey, approximately four hundred thousand ethnic Chinese
live in southern California, of whom 87 percent are foreign born, hailing from
Hong Kong, China, Taiwan, and Southeast Asia.[25] Many are well-educated
professionals who live in upscale neighborhoods, attend American universities, work in high-tech companies, buy up expensive real estate, and eat in
sophisticated Chinese restaurants. They have established entirely Asian communities in formerly white suburbs. Monterey Park and the San Gabriel
Valley, which are the sites of huge investments from overseas Chinese, have

been described as "an extension of Asia."[26] The infusion of Pacific Rim capital, then, produces the concrete forms of an ethnic social life. These include daily rituals such as using stores and services where the Chinese language is spoken, sending kids to Chinese language schools, and arranging family gatherings in Chinese restaurants. All the while, one is linked by news and electronic media to the wider Chinese diasporan world. The structure of feeling and the cultural sensibility are those of transplanted communities of migratory Chinese elites from different Asia Pacific sites, rather than of communities that grew out of the American political economy or body politic.

The Asian character of these new immigrants offends, at an almost unconscious level, a deep sense of what the American nation—in terms of race and territory—is all about. In *City of Quartz*, Mike Davis betrays his sense of political unease in his description of "the Japanese colonization of Downtown": "'Offshore' capital, not just the Japanese but the Chinese, Koreans, Canadians and Manhattanites as well, now have the capacity, in the context of Los Angeles's wide-open economy, to suddenly transform any scenario by huge buy-outs or injections of new investments (witness Shuwa's billion-dollar landing in Downtown in 1976 or Trump's sudden arrival in 1990)."[27] Another writer bemoans the transformation of Los Angeles into "the capital of the Third World," made up of constituent parts of "Confucianism's fabled indifference to everyone outside a given family group, Latin American political intolerance, and Western European nihilism."[28] Such anti-immigrant musings also characterize the reception of well-off immigrants in northern California. Trepidation has been expressed about "bright young investors" from wealthy Hong Kong families controlling about ten percent of downtown San Francisco, primarily hotels and commercial buildings, which gives rise to a phenomenon that newspaper columnist Herb Caen calls the "Hongkongization of San Francisco."[29] Asian immigrants have also acquired smaller properties in rundown neighborhoods such as the Tenderloin, hoping to cash in on the expected gentrification in years to come. Complaints about escalating real estate prices, absentee landlordism, and Asians as interlopers with "deep pockets" have made these investors tight lipped about their purchases.[30]

Resentment against the changing ethnic control of downtown property is also expressed against immigrant families who build multiunit residential homes in the city. For years, neighborhood representatives in San Francisco have worked to impose a Residential Control Amendment (RCA) to the city's already strict zoning codes. Most of those opposed to these moves are Chinese Americans and immigrants who consider the amendment an attempt to halt the ethnic reshuffling of urban neighborhoods: "We look at the RCA as a selective process of discriminating against ethnic Chinese and Hispanics, who tend to have extended families living together. They talk about preserving the neighborhood character. Well, whose characters are they talking about?"[31]

Such homegrown NIMBY (not in my backyard) resistance is especially strong against affluent Chinese immigrants from Hong Kong and Taiwan who settle in formerly white suburban centers throughout the state. Malls with names such as Pacific Renaissance or Pacific Rim are filled with mainly Asian-operated stores, supermarkets, beauty salons, service agencies, movie houses, and restaurants that are clearly modeled on elite commercial enterprises in Hong Kong, Taiwan, and Japan. Most of the commodities, as well as the decor and self-presentation of these businesses, are imported directly from Asia, and their customers hail from overseas-Chinese communities all over the region. In contrast, the chauffeurs, back-room workers, and busboys are Latinos, drawn from another community of immigrants to serve the needs of a mainly Pacific Rim clientele. NIMBY protests against such urban developments use a range of tactics, including zoning codes to slow growth and English-only movements to keep cities such as Monterey Park from becoming the "Chinese Beverly Hills."[32]

But the politics of location have developed beyond the nativist backlash against the urban transformations wrought by Pacific Rim capital and communities. The "Asian connection" between Pacific Rim corporate interests and American city bosses was forged in the 1980s. The newcomers have found that when it comes to investments, flexible coalitions with local players are essential and that in an era of multiculturalism, even racially motivated attacks can be turned to their advantage. The arrival of affluent Chinese immigrants in the 1980s coincided with attempts by the mayors of cities such as Los Angeles, San Francisco, and San Jose to court "Pacific Rim capital" and seek contributions from the new Asian immigrants. Hong Kong investors, who are mostly sympathetic to Republican values, nevertheless will contribute handsomely to politicians of either party who have a liberal stand toward "Asian Americans."[33] In San Francisco, such contributions have won Chinese immigrants seats on city commissions, where they represent the interests of the wider Asian American public. But Chinatown activists charge that the Hong

Kong entrepreneurs are merely "making political alliances to enhance business opportunities" rather than representing the interests of small groceries, restaurants, and gift shops.[34] Nevertheless, the affluent new immigrants justify "money politics" maneuvers on the grounds that there has not been enough Asian American representation in city institutions: "I don't know if there is a real vision or some grand strategy [among the Hong Kong newcomers]. . . . What is happening though is a large group of Chinese feel that we have got to be a little more visible and play a larger role in local politics. We just want to be members of the local community. I don't think we will ever be the major players. We may be one of several major players."[35] Down south, in Monterey Park, Timothy Fong found that coalitions between American city bosses, big developers, and Asian investors wielded racism as a weapon to push through progrowth policies.[36]

Nevertheless, partnerships with city bosses in their accumulation strategies have not shielded the immigrants from being perceived as culturally, linguistically, and racially Asian and therefore "out of place" in the American ethno-racial hierarchy, a scheme that locates Asian subjects as a "good," but subordinated, minority. In the commonsensical view of ethnic succession, recent arrivals from non-Western countries are expected to enter at the bottom of the socioeconomic ladder and wait their proper turn to reach middle-class status.[37] Affluent Asian immigrants who arrive in the country already possessing the economic and social attributes associated with Americans occupying the top ranks of society thus confound the expectation of an orderly ethnic succession; they also call into question the proper location of minorities in the ethno-racial hierarchy. By locating themselves in white suburbs rather than in Chinatown, and by making a living not as restaurant workers but as Pacific Rim executives, well-to-do Asian newcomers breach the spatial and symbolic borders that have disciplined Asian Americans and kept them on the margins of the American nation. This "out-of-placeness" of new Asian immigrants reinforces the public anxiety over the so-called thirdworldization of the American city, a term that suggests both economic and ethno-racial heterogeneity, over which white Americans are losing control.[38] Accustomed as they are to being economically and socially superior to Asian immigrants, middle-class whites seek in the English-only and antidevelopment campaigns to express anxiety over their own displacement in geographical and economic terms. Globalization has greatly blurred the distinction between Americans and foreign-born immigrants or newcomers who invest, work, and live in this country.[39] The key issue, perhaps, is not language or real estate; rather, it is how the arrival of affluent immigrants challenges white Americans' understanding of themselves as privileged American natives who should take no back seat to foreigners, especially Asians. But will the accumulation of cultural, and not just economic, capital by these well-heeled immigrants change such nativist perceptions?

Cultural Competence in the Polyethnic City

> When was the last time . . . fabulously rich people, talented, with their families, were looking to live and work in your city?—Hong Kong–born banker

In their everyday lives, affluent Asian newcomers find themselves viewed as members of a minority ethnic group, rather than as cosmopolitan people from Asian tiger countries. As extremely class-conscious subjects, they are offended by the popular American image of the Chinese as railroad and laundry workers.[40] Despite their high social and economic profile in Hong Kong, these newcomers find that their welcome by the local Anglo upper class has been cool. Long viewed as coolies, houseboys, and garment workers, but now upgraded to members of a law-abiding and productive model minority, each new wave of Asian immigrants has to contend with the historical construction of Asian others as politically and culturally subordinate subjects. Arriving with their family fortunes, American degrees, and can-do business attitudes, Hong Kong investors still cannot erase the coolie stigma that clings to the image of Asians in America. How do these Asian immigrants deal with the limited effect their cultural accumulation has on opening doors to elite circles in the host country?

Bad Taste or the Homeless in an Affluent Neighborhood?

As home buyers and property developers, Chinese immigrants have encountered regulation by civic groups upset at the ways their cities are being changed by transnational capital and taste. In wealthier San Franciscan neighborhoods, residents pride themselves on their conservation consciousness, and they jealously guard the hybrid European ambiance and character of particular neighborhoods. In their role as custodians of appropriate cultural

taste, which includes governing buildings, architecture, parks, and other public spaces, citizen groups routinely badger City Hall, scrutinize urban zoning
laws, and patrol the boundaries between what is aesthetically permissible and
intolerable in their districts. By linking race with habitus, taste, and cultural
capital, such civic groups set limits to the whitening of Asians, who, meta-
phorically speaking, still give off the whiff of sweat despite arriving with start-
up symbolic capital.

Public battles over race/taste have revolved around the transformation of
middle-class neighborhoods by rich Asian newcomers. At issue are boxy
houses with bland facades erected by Asian buyers to accommodate extended
families in low-density, single-family residential districts known for their
Victorian or Mediterranean charm. Protests have often taken on a racialist
tone, both registering dismay at the changing cultural landscape and making
efforts to educate the new arrivals to white upper-class urban norms. While
the activists focus on the cultural elements—aesthetic norms, the democratic
process, civic duty—that underpin the urban imagined community, they encode the strong class resentment against large-scale Asian investment in residential and commercial properties throughout the city.[41] A conflict over one
of these monster houses illustrates the ways in which the state is caught
between soothing indignant urbanites seeking to impose their notion of cultural citizenship on Asian nouveax riches and attempting to keep the door
open for Pacific Rim capital.

In 1989, a Hong Kong multimillionaire, Mrs. Chan, bought a house in the
upscale Marina District. Chan lived in Hong Kong and rented out her Marina
property. A few years later, she obtained the approval of the city to add a third
story to her house, but she failed to notify her neighbors. When they learned
of her plans, they complained that the third story would block views of the
Palace of Fine Arts and cut off sunlight in an adjoining garden. The neighbors
linked up with a citywide group to pressure City Hall. The mayor stepped in
and called for a city zoning study, thus delaying the proposed renovation. At a
neighborhood meeting, someone declared, "We don't want to see a second
Chinatown here." Indeed, there is already a new "Chinatown" outside the old
Chinatown, in the middle-class Richmond District. This charge thus raised
the specter of a spreading Chinese urbanscape encroaching on the heterogeneous European flavor of the city. The remark, and its implied racism,

compelled the mayor to apologize to Chan, and the planning commission subsequently approved a smaller addition to her house.[42]

However, stung by the racism and the loss on her investment, and bewildered because the neighbors could infringe on her property rights, Chan, a transnational developer, used her wealth to mock the city's self-image as a bastion of liberalism. She pulled all of her investments out of the United States and decided to donate her million-dollar house to the homeless. To add insult to injury, she stipulated that her house was not to be used by any homeless of Chinese descent. Her architect, an American Chinese, told the press, "You can hardly find a homeless Chinese anyway."[43] Secure in her overseas location, Chan fought the Chinese stereotype by stereotyping American homeless people as non-Chinese and challenging her civic-minded neighbors to demonstrate the moral liberalism they professed. Mutual class and racial discriminations thus broke through the surface of what initially appeared to be a negotiation over normative cultural taste in the urban milieu. A representative of the mayor's office, appropriately contrite, remarked that Chan could still do whatever she wanted with her property, adding, "We just would like for her not to be so angry."[44] The need to keep overseas investments flowing into the city had to be balanced against the neighborhood groups' demands for cultural standards. The power of the international real-estate market, as represented by Chan, thus disciplined both City Hall and the Marina neighbors, who may have had to rethink local notions of what being enlightened urbanites may entail in the era of Pacific Rim capital.

Philanthropy for Scaling the Cultural Heights

Other Chinese investor-immigrants, unlike Chan, try to negotiate the tensions between local and global forces and to adopt the cultural trappings of the white upper class so as to cushion long-term residents' shock at the status change of the racial other, who up until recently was represented by images of the laundry man and the garment worker. Chinese developers who live in San Francisco are trying harder to erase the image of themselves as "economic animals" who build monster houses, as well as the perception that they lack a sense of civic duty and responsibility. They try to maintain their Victorian homes and upscale English gardens, collect Stradivarius violins and attend city operas, play tennis in formerly white clubs, and dress up by dressing down their nouveaux-riches appearance. Nevertheless, they use the term "glass ceiling," which is often used by women and minorities whose rise in corporations is obstructed by an invisible barrier of discrimination, to describe the social barriers to their acceptance by top-drawer society. One investor notes, "We have the qualifications to compete. But it'll take a few more generations to crack the old boys' network. Meanwhile, we are creating our own networks."[45] Others talk about "hitting a wall," for the perceived barriers to their social mobility are both vertical and lateral. They feel excluded from business contacts and exclusive neighborhoods but also from the major cultural events that are linked with the city's white upper crust. A British representative of Hong Kong remarked to me that when businessmen complain about the glass ceiling, "that is their way of saying, 'I am culturally inadequate' in the United States." His disdain reflects the effects of British neocolonial policies that had also excluded Chinese, no matter how prominent they were, from the British clubs in Hong Kong. Here, we see the merging of transnational racial schemes in which the British and Californian upper class view Asians, no matter how rich or educated, as second-class world citizens.

This global racial ranking has reinforced the isolation of the affluent newcomers in the United States. A Hong Kong businessman protests, "If the established San Francisco power doesn't invite us to their [opera] balls, we have our own balls. If they don't want to do business with us, we do business among ourselves. If they don't let us into Pacific Heights, we create our own Chinatown."[46] Some have indeed retreated into their own networks and clubs, where they have attempted to re-create the elite circles of their homeland. Their Hong Kong alma maters provide the basis for many of these business and social networks, tennis and other sports groups, and mahjongg and other social clubs.

In my interviews with this so-called Asian-money elite, a key message was that if the locals find them objectionable on racial or cultural grounds, they find their Pacific Rim money less objectionable. One of the people I interviewed was Ian Mak, the manager of a leading Asian bank that is seeking to sink deeper roots into the Asian community in North America by providing better rates for loans and services. Gazing at the sweeping cityscape from his wraparound window, Mak saw money politics as a way to make Asian wealth accessible to a northern Californian society that is still unaware of the depth of its future dependency on Asian economies. After his appointment, with two other Hong Kong Chinese, to the city Chamber of Commerce, Mak said, "A vibrant city like Manhattan, Los Angeles, when they are booming like crazy, they need the kind of diversity and new money coming in. . . . [It's a matter of] whether [northern Californians] realize what they have to change in order to become international. . . . [If they] realize they are losing a lot of market shares to Los Angeles and they want to do something bigger . . . [they will] have to be far more international. . . . It is not a question of whether they want to accept or resist Asians, it is [a question of] if one decides to change, then the economic success of the Asian countries provides the most ready answer."[47] Another Hong Kong–born Chinese, a favorite of the mayor, also complained about the insularity of San Francisco compared to, say, Vancouver, Canada, which has become more firmly integrated with the Pacific Rim economies: "The Bay Area can compete, as it is a location of choice. But San Francisco is not that international. We have a 'continental mentality.' . . . We need to think globally, starting with education. . . . Our kids should study geography, a second language. They should study abroad. When I was in school in Hong Kong, we studied trade winds, the movement of the seas—the world."[48] But the concept of the United States as basically a nation of European settlers and the racial distrust of Asians limit the welcome of Asians as important figures in the American economy. Mak told me that while the local elite may desire European investment, the reality is that Japanese and Chinese are the major players in California. The state's future is linked more closely to the Pacific Rim countries than to Europe.

Other immigrant investors point to the effect that their infusion of money has had on rundown parts of the city, where it has led to urban renewal and created jobs where none existed before. They see themselves as increasingly indispensable as leaders, especially to the diverse Asian populations in California. A major hotelier, Kenny Bao, whom I interviewed cited his support for Cambodians and Vietnamese refugees living in the poor neighborhood near his hotel. (He did not mention his protracted battle against the formation of a union by his hotel staff, a quarter of whom are Asian.) Sitting in his plush office, surrounded by Chinese paintings and objets d'art that symbolize wealth and luck, he conducted our conversation while gazing at figures for the Hong Kong and New York stock markets scrolling across two huge TV screens. As I balanced a cup of English tea on my knee, he expressed a view of the Chinese entrepreneur as a patriarch of less-fortunate people: "If you believe in me you can believe in the next twenty or thirty years. As a foundation, [workers] don't have to worry about job security . . . jumping ship to another company to get promotion, because if we keep the right guidelines for the company to grow, then they don't have to worry about so much politics and bureaucracy within the organization." He went on to say that Asians "are all the same" in terms of having cultural values like diligence, frugality, and strong family values.[49] This picture of a pan-Asian, homogenized population in California seems to reinforce the image of overseas Chinese as the arbitrators and controllers of capital and labor across the Pacific. Recognized throughout the city by his gold Mercedes-Benz, Bao and his family have invested heavily in the United States on the certainty that Anglo and African American leaders "recognize they will have to rely on Asians to give momentum to California in the next decade or two."

While these immigrant tycoons stress their economic importance to local society, others find it important to engage in the practice of cultural citizenship, that is, in ways of belonging according to the dominant cultural criteria. The Asian move into philanthropy outside Chinatown was spearheaded by Hong Kong immigrants in a city where almost 30 percent of the inhabitants are Asian. As the traditional sources of support from elite white families have shrunk, city institutions such as the San Francisco Opera and the ballet company have begun fund-raising efforts among Asian Americans. A few affluent Hong Kong immigrants have boldly entered old white-money domains through participation on boards or organizations. Many of these investors have been trained in Hong Kong and in the United States to be technically competent in the business world but not in the humanities or arts. Their tastes run along the lines of "The Blue Danube" and Hong Kong movies and soap operas. However, through showy contributions to a few strategic cultural institutions, these newcomers can demonstrate a cultural competence they may or may not actually possess. I interviewed a surgeon who, with Kenny Bao, was one of the first two Chinese Americans to sit on the board of the city symphony. When he complained about the lack of Chinese contributions to the symphony, I had to remind him that there were hardly music lessons in Chinatown or other poor urban schools. But he defended his position by saying that rich Hong Kongers can "give back to society" some of the benefits they have enjoyed in the United States. Bao and Leslie Tang-Schilling, the daughter of a Hong Kong industrialist, who is married into a prominent San

Franciscan family, have both expressed a conviction that their patronage of the arts will promote more "Asian art" in the city cultural programs. Such acts of cultural investment are aimed at winning the social approval of the city's white leaders rather than demonstrating cultural competence or building prestige through supporting ethnic-based organizations.[50] Thus, by converting economic capital into high cultural capital, the new immigrants hope not only for social acceptance but also for the reproduction of precariously positioned social prestige.

Other Pacific Rim money is funneled toward major educational institutions. Tang-Schilling, a developer in her own right, leads the move to soften the hard-edged image of Chinese investor-immigrants by focusing on children and students. She is the organizer of a Christmas gift-giving campaign for poor children in the Tenderloin. Her family has contributed a few million dollars for an imposing new health center on the Berkeley campus of the University of California. Other overseas-Asian families have donated large sums (from half a million to a few million dollars) to the construction of facilities devoted to chemistry, the life sciences, computer science, and engineering at Berkeley and at Stanford University. On the Berkeley campus, there are buildings called the Tang Health Center; the Chan Auditorium, and the Tan Chemistry Building. On the East Coast, a gift of $20 million was made to Princeton University by Gordon Wu, a Hong Kong tycoon whose money could perhaps have better benefited long-neglected universities on the Chinese mainland.

Whereas an earlier generation of overseas-Chinese tycoons went home to build academic centers in China,[51] today's Asian investors wish to buy symbolic capital in Western democracies as a way to facilitate racial and cultural acceptance across the globe. Like earlier European immigrant elites, who also looked for symbolic real estate, overseas-Chinese donors show a preference for "hardware" (impressive buildings bearing their names) over "software" (scholarships and programs that are less visible to the public eye).[52] The difference is that subjects associated with third-world inferiority have scaled the bastion of white power. Such showcase pieces have upgraded Asian masculinity, layered over the hardscrabble roots of the Asian *homo economicus,* and proclaimed the Asians' arrival on the international scene. Nevertheless, there are limits to such strategies of symbolic accumulation, and a white backlash has been expressed in a rise in random attacks on Asians. By leaving an

Asian imprimatur on prestigious "white" public space, the new immigrants register what has for over a century—one thinks of the plantation workers and railroad men, the maids and garment workers, the gardeners and cooks, the shopkeepers and nurses, and the undocumented workers laboring in indentured servitude, whether in the colonies or in cities such as New York and Los Angeles—been a space of Asia Pacific cultural production within the West.[53]

Conclusion

The westward migration of Pacific Rim capital and professionals also entails the fabricating of cultural personae who can operate effectively in transnational fields and whose strategies of cultural accumulation seek to reproduce in overseas sites their high status at home. In California, Chinese investor-immigrants use wealth, political alliances, and the patronage of high culture to deflect some of the persistent racial bias against them as Pacific Rim interlopers. They soon discover that just as there are limits to flexible accumulation in business, so are there limits to cultural accumulation for gaining prestige in the polyethnic American city. Chinese immigrants deploying cultural forms that are not considered as "belonging" to their ethnic group cannot easily convert such symbolic capital into high social standing in Anglo circles. Their cultural performance as a new faction of the Californian elite is discredited by a perceived difference in their "money politics" and their "cronyism," as well as in their accent and the color of their skin. A Hong Kong manager told me, "They want your Pacific Rim money, but they don't want you." Can the Pacific Rim money, not just its objective value, be detached from the body of the ambivalently received Asian immigrant?

In the 1980s, much of the Japanese corporate investment in California represented a form of disembodied Pacific Rim symbolic value because in the large majority of cases this investment was not accompanied by the actual relocation of Japanese subjects. The "China wave," on the other hand, brings both alien capital and alien bodies; thus, Chinese investors have encountered social barriers to cultural accumulation as a strategy of flexible positioning. Hong Kong émigrés discover that their wealth cannot easily be converted into cultural capital, just as their fengshui-aligned locations cannot make up for their being "out of place," spatially and symbolically, in the American ethno-racial scheme. For many middle-class Americans, unease over being displaced in their neighborhoods and in their native social order, and anxiety over the American city as being "too open" to foreign capital and influence, are linked to a wider undercurrent of panic over "losing out"—in jobs, wages, home ownership, and wealth—to the economic dynamism of the Asia Pacific countries, as embodied in the Asian newcomers. The presence of Pacific Rim investors, perhaps more than any other wealthy immigrant group, makes ordinary Americans question their assumption of an insular North America that is exempt from the disruptions of globalization that are happening "elsewhere." The immigrants' strategies of accumulation and relocation imply alternative notions of citizenship within the dominant frame of "American" neoliberalism and suggest that citizenship benefits, even for the entrenched white middle class, have become more precarious in a world of circulating multinational subjects. Ultimately, the new Asian rich make whiteness a more problematic concept in the era of globalization.

4 The Pacific Shuttle: Family Citizenship, and Capital Circuits

Destabilizing Chineseness

During a recent late summer in the Ukraine, an angry mob dragging down a statue of Lenin reenacted the political collapse of the Soviet Union, while vendors selling Bolshevik trinkets reinvented the economy. David Chang, representing the Asia Bank in New York, was in town to snap up apartment houses and real estate before the dust settled. "Governments come and go," he said, "but business stays."[1]

In California, "the Silicon Valley way of divorce" among new Chinese immigrants has led to one failed marriage out of five. One "typical" Chinese couple—he is an engineer; she, an accountant—used to live in a half-million-dollar house with two well-schooled children. They invested in a second home and vacationed in Lake Tahoe. When the wife asked for a divorce, it was not because her husband had an affair, or at least not with another woman. "My husband works on his computer in the office during the day, comes home at 8 P.M., and continues to sit in front of his computer after dinner. . . . I am a 'computer widow' who is never asked how she is doing, nor what has happened to the family lately."[2]

In both stories, postmodern elements jostle for attention. These elements include *displacement* (Asians in Western worlds), *fragmentation* (families broken up by emigration and divorce), *difference* (male and female subjectivities), and *impermanence* (in everyday arrangements). Were these reports about people other than Chinese, they would attract no more than a passing glance. But to me, such postmodern snapshots are a jarring reproach to academic descriptions of Chinese identity, family, and cultural practices.

Much scholarship on Chinese subjects has been shaped by the orientalist concern with presenting the other as a timeless, unchanging culture. Recent attempts to revise the static image of Chineseness nevertheless still confine the analysis of ways of "being Chinese" within the clearly defined Chinese contexts of the nation-state and culture.[3] An essentializing notion of Chineseness continues to dog the scholarship because the Chinese past, nation, singular history, or some "cultural core" is taken to be the main and unchanging determinant of Chinese identity. Sometimes we forget that we are talking about one-quarter of the world's population. What is conveyed is the sense that people identifiable as "Chinese" exist in their own world, and even when they participate in global processes, they continue to remain culturally distinct. I suspect that the grand orientalist legacy continues to lurk in a field, dominated by historians, that is convinced of the singularity of this great inscrutable other. Younger scholars and feminists who seek to provide more complex, historically and geopolitically contingent accounts of Chinese cultural practices are often merely tolerated, if they are not marginalized for threatening to disrupt the stable tropes of high sinology. Perhaps not so ironically, as I have mentioned above, ambitious Asian politicians have made much political capital by borrowing academic representations of Chineseness for their own self-orientalizing projects (see chapter 2). Grand orientalist statements are dialectically linked to the petty orientalisms generated by transnational corporate and advertising media, which make pronouncements about Oriental labor, skills, values, families, and mystery. The slogan for Singapore Airlines is "Singapore Girl, what a great way to fly."

But stories about capital, displacements, and hybridity explode the reigning notions about being Chinese. How do discrepant images reflect the changing social, economic, and political relations in which Chinese subjects are important participants? Today, overseas Chinese are key players in the booming economies of the Asia Pacific region. In what ways have their border-crossing activities and mobility within the circuits of global capitalism altered their cultural values and class strategies? This chapter explores how the flexible positioning of diasporan-Chinese subjects on the edge of political and capitalist empires affects their family relations, their self-representation, and the ways in which they negotiate the political and cultural rules of different countries on their itineraries. In contrast to Edward Said's depiction of the objects of orientalism as silent participants in Western hegemonic projects,[4] I trace the agency of Asian subjects as they selectively engage orientalist discourses encountered on travels through the shifting cultural terrains of the global economy. Yet their countercultural production should not be interpreted as a simple reproduction of "the ways we are situated by the West" but as complex maneuvers that subvert reigning notions of the national self and the other in transnational arenas.

Perhaps more than other travelers and migrants, international managers and professionals have the material and symbolic resources to manipulate global schemes of cultural difference, racial hierarchy, and citizenship to their own advantage. Today, flexibility reigns in business, industry, labor, and the financial markets; all incorporate technologically enhanced innovations that affect the way people are differently imagined and regulated and the way they represent and conduct themselves transnationally.[5] But whereas international managers and professionals may be adept at strategies of economic accumulation and maneuvering, they do not operate in free-flowing circumstances but in environments that are controlled and shaped by nation-states and capital markets.

For instance, the form and meaning of citizenship have been transformed by global markets and floods of skilled and unskilled workers crossing borders. Although citizenship is conventionally thought of as based on political rights and participation within a sovereign state, globalization has made economic calculation a major element in diasporan subjects' choice of citizenship, as well as in the ways nation-states redefine immigration laws. I use the term *flexible citizenship* to refer especially to the strategies and effects of mobile managers, technocrats, and professionals seeking to both circumvent *and* benefit from different nation-state regimes by selecting different sites for investments, work, and family relocation. Such repositioning in relation to global markets, however, should not lead one to assume that the nation-state is losing control of its borders.[6] State regimes are constantly adjusting to the influx of different kinds of immigrants and to ways of engaging global capitalism that will benefit the country while minimizing the costs. For instance, nation-states constantly refine immigration laws to attract capital-bearing subjects while limiting the entry of unskilled laborers. From the perspective of immigrants such as well-heeled Hong Kongers, however, citizenship becomes an issue of handling the diverse rules, or "governmentality," of host societies where they may be economically correct in terms of human capital, but culturally incorrect in terms of ethnicity.[7]

To understand the tactical practices of this diasporan managerial class, we must locate them within and one step ahead of the various regimes of truth and power to which they, as traveling persons, are subject. Michel Foucault uses *regime* to refer to power/knowledge schemes that seek to normalize power relations.[8] By appealing to particular "truths" that have been developed about science, culture, and social life, these systems of power/knowledge define and regulate subjects and normalize their attitudes and behavior. The regimes that will be considered here are the regime of Chinese kinship and family, the regime of the nation-state, and the regime of the marketplace—all of which provide the institutional contexts and the webs of power within which Chinese subjects (re)locate and (re)align themselves as they traverse global space.

As Donald M. Nonini has argued, each kind of regime requires "the localization of disciplinary subjects," that is, it requires that persons be locatable and confinable to specific spaces and relations defined by the various regimes: the kinship network, the "nation," the marketplace.[9] In this sense, "flexible citizenship" also denotes the localizing strategies of subjects who, through a variety of familial and economic practices, seek to evade, deflect, and take advantage of political and economic conditions in different parts of the world. Thus, we cannot analytically delink the operations of family regimes from the regulations of the state and of capital. One can say, for example, that Chinese family discipline is in part shaped by the regulation of the state and by the rules of the global marketplace, but the convergence of Chinese family forms with flexible strategies of capital accumulation enables them to bypass or exploit citizenship rules—whatever the case may be—as they relocate capital and/or family members overseas. So while I talk about flexible citizenship, I am also talking about the different modalities of governmentality—as practiced by the nation-state, by the family, by capital—that intersect and have effects on each other, variously encoding and constraining flexibility in global (re)positioning. By analyzing different modalities of flexibility *and* governmentality under conditions of globalization, I identify contemporary forms that shape culture making and its products. First, how does the regime of diasporan Chinese kinship structure, deploy, and limit flexible practices?

Middling Modernity: Guanxi and Family Regimes in Diaspora

One form of elite-Chinese sensibility developed in the context of the late nineteenth century, when interregional commerce flourished under European colonialism in East and Southeast Asia. The entry of Chinese into mercantile capitalism ruptured the traditional links of filiation among Chinese subjects, Chinese families, and the Chinese social order. In nineteenth-century China, the Confucian concept of filial piety (*xiao*) governed the relations of superior and subordinate (father/son, husband/wife, older/younger brothers). Because the family was considered a microcosm of the moral order, filial piety also figured in the relations of citizens to rulers.[10] But in nationalist discourse, elites striving to imagine a modern Chinese nation found that patriotism had little appeal in a climate of "semicolonialism," Japanese invasion, general lawlessness, and economic and social upheaval.[11] Republican China's founder, Sun Yat-sen, bemoaned the difficulty of extending loyalty to family into a loyalty to the new nation; he sadly compared the Chinese people to "a sheet of loose sand." European imperial domination and political humiliation did incite early modern anti-imperialist, antipatriarchal movements, especially among university students in Beijing. But among the commercial classes in the treaty ports, filial piety in the Confucian sense was narrowly focused on familial well-being and family interests, as well as on family firms outside China. Filial piety thereby became the substance for shaping other ways of being Chinese in the world.

A diasporan-Chinese modernity—in the "middling" sense of pragmatic everyday practices[12]—developed among emigrant Chinese in the colonial worlds of East and Southeast Asia. In city ports and colonial enclaves, Chinese subjects facing political mistreatment and intense competition for survival evolved an instrumentality in norms concerning labor organization, family practice, links between family and the wider economy, and dealings with political authorities.[13] London-trained anthropologist Fei Hsiao-tung was highly critical of the loss of Confucian ethics among this merchant class:

> To such ports a special type of Chinese was attracted. They are known as
> compradors. . . . They are half-cast in culture, bilingual in speech, morally unstable. . . . Treat ports . . . are a land where the acquisition of wealth
> is the sole motive, devoid of tradition and culture.
>
> [Nevertheless] they occupy a strategic position in China's transi-

tion. . . . As their children grow up, they give them modern education and send them abroad to attend Western universities. From this group a new class is formed. . . . But being reared in a cosmopolitan community, they are fundamentally hybrids. In them are manifest the comprador characteristic of social irresponsibility.[14]

The Chinese comprador class became notorious for the systematic ways its members amassed personal power and wealth at the expense of the new republic. By forming profitable links overseas, merchant and industrial families repositioned themselves as subjects of global trade rather than as loyal subjects of the Chinese motherland. Political and economic instabilities, and a weakly developed patriotism, encouraged merchant families to develop links to overseas colonial empires. This turning away from Confucian social ethics toward a family-centered notion of Confucianism found its greatest expression among overseas-Chinese communities that developed under Western capitalism in Southeast Asia.

Modern Chinese transnationalism thus has roots in these historical circumstances of diaspora and European colonial capitalism; in the postcolonial era, Chinese family enterprises became fully integrated with the larger global economy. Chinese traders recruited labor gangs, organized construction and mining crews, built merchant houses, and also ran brothels, gambling houses, and opium dens—all activities that transgressed the localizing regimes of colonial powers—while at the same time, they became more firmly integrated within the colonial economies.[15] Their regional networks for labor and capital accumulation enabled Chinese traders to be the "wild men" who continually challenged political regimes and eluded their regulation.[16] As nationalism in China became channeled into party politics, many Chinese sojourners did express their patriotism by contributing funds to the leaders of the struggling republic. But in the colonies, paternal bonds and interpersonal relations structured networks for interregional trade and provided the institutional basis for a sense of a larger, diffused, "imagined" community of huaqiao.[17]

In the postcolonial era, most Southeast Asian states have remained suspicious of the political loyalty of their Chinese citizens, partly because of those citizens' economic domination and extensive overseas connections. Only Singapore and Taiwan, both of which possess a Chinese majority, have used Confucian education to inculcate state loyalty, which they maintain is analogous to filial piety. But in most countries, especially in Islam-dominated Malaysia and Indonesia, the discourse of nationalism draws on colonial models of race-based and multiethnic nationhood.[18] Thus, the cultural politics of being Chinese varies in different countries, but for many overseas Chinese, there is no obvious continuity between family interests and political loyalty (especially since most overseas Chinese have experienced anti-Chinese discrimination in their host countries). Outside of Taiwan and Singapore, there is a disengagement between Chinese cultural interests and national belonging in host countries identified with dominant ethnicities such as Vietnamese or Malay. For instance, in Malaysia, lower-class Chinese subjects often seek to evade the localizing mechanisms of the state that stigmatize them as "more Chinese" (i.e., less assimilated than upper-class Chinese) and hence subject to regulation as second-class citizens. This diffused sense of being diasporan Chinese has also been shaped by their flexible, mobile relations across political borders and by the kinship regime of truth and control.

Launching family businesses on the edge of empires, Chinese subjects depend on a careful cultivation of guanxi and instrumentalist family practices. These habits, attitudes, and norms are not a simple continuation or legacy of some essentialized bundle of "traditional" Chinese traits. Guanxi networks in Southeast Asia are historically contingent; they are a kind of (post)colonial habitus, that is, they are the dispositions and practices that emphasize pragmatism, interpersonal dependence, bodily discipline, gender and age hierarchies, and other ethnic-specific modes of social production and reproduction in diaspora and under foreign rule.[19] Such overseas-Chinese habitus have ensured that the emigrant family has survived for generations while evading the discipline of the colonial (and later, the postcolonial) states, with their special regimes of othering Chineseness.

Produced and shaped under such conditions, the familial regimes of diasporan Chinese based on guanxi are not without their own violence and exploitation of workers, family members, kinsmen, and so on. In the early days of colonial capitalism, guanxi networks deployed Chinese emigrants in the "pig trade" (supplying coolies to labor camps throughout Asia), thus subjecting many to brutal control, lifelong indebtedness, poverty, and crime while enriching their patrons.[20] Guanxi, as a historically evolved regime of kinship and ethnic power, controls and often traps women and the poor while benefiting fraternal business associations and facilitating the accumulation of wealth for Chinese families in diaspora.

In everyday life, however, there is widespread misrecognition of guanxi's violence, while its humanism is widely extolled by ordinary folk, businessmen, and cultural chauvinists alike. Such symbolic violence[21]—the erasure of collective complicity over relations of domination and exploitation—is also present in academic writings that unduly celebrate guanxi as the basis of the recent affluence of overseas Chinese.[22] Misrecognition of business guanxi as basically a structure of limits and inequality for the many and of flexibility and mobility for the few is part of the ritual euphemization of "Chinese values," especially among transnational Chinese and their spokesmen (see chapter 2).[23]

Indeed, guanxi regimes and networks have proliferated within the institution of the subcontracting industry, the paradigmatic form of flexible industrialization throughout the Asia Pacific region. Many Chinese firms enter light manufacturing by subcontracting for global companies, producing consumer items such as jewelry, garments, and toys in "living-room factories."[24] In recent years, guanxi networks have been the channel for subcontracting arrangements between overseas-Chinese capital and enterprises in mainland China. A Sino-Thai tycoon, who is the largest investor in China, invokes guanxi to explain the growth of his conglomerate on the mainland. He compares his own business style to what he sees as the inflexibility of Western firms: "American and European companies have adapted themselves to a very sophisticated legal-based society. . . . In China there is no law. There is no system. It is a government by individuals, by people."[25] Thus, the guanxi institution, as invoked and practiced, is a mix of instrumentalism (fostering flexibility and the mobility of capital and personnel across political borders) and humanism ("helping out" relatives and hometown folk on the mainland). Although guanxi connections may be mixed with patriotic sentiment, overseas-Chinese investors are also moved by opportunities for mobilizing cheap labor in China's vast capitalist frontier (see chapter 1). It is probably not possible to disentangle nostalgic sentiment toward the homeland from the irresistible pull of flexible accumulation, but the logic of guanxi points to sending capital to China while shipping the family overseas.

It may sound contradictory, but flexible citizenship is a result of familial strategies of regulation. Michel Foucault suggests that we think of modern power, in its "government" of population and the welfare of that population (biopolitics), as productive of relations, rituals, and truths.[26] I consider the rational, normative practices that regulate healthy, productive, and successful bodies within the family and their deployment in economic activities for economic well-being as family governmentality. The biopolitics of families, however, are always conditioned by wider political-economic circumstances.

The rise of Hong Kong as a global manufacturing center was secured after British colonial rule put down and domesticated trade unions and student activists during the 1960s, a state strategy that was common throughout Asia.[27] In subsequent decades, refugee families from all classes adapted through hard work, fierce competitiveness, and tight control over the family to improve overall family livelihood and wealth. Hong Kong social scientists use the term "utilitarian familialism" to describe the everyday norms and practices whereby Hong Kong families place family interests above all other individual and social concerns. One scholar observes that economic interdependency is the basic structuring principle—expressed as "all in the family"—a principle that mobilizes the immediate family and relatives in common interests.[28] An individual's sense of moral worth is based on endurance and diligence in income-making activities, compliance with parental wishes, and the making of sacrifices and the deferral of gratification, especially on the part of women and children. In her study of factory women, Janet Salaff found that daughters are instilled with a sense of debt to their parents, which they "repay" by shortening their schooling and earning wages that often go toward their brothers' higher education.[29] These writers seem to identify these family practices as something inherent in "Chinese culture"; they ignore the effects of state discipline and a highly competitive marketplace on refugee families. Such family regimes among the working classes have been responsible for the phenomenal growth of Hong Kong into a manufacturing giant. Among the upwardly mobile, biopolitical considerations inform family discipline in production and consumption. Besides acquiring the habitus of continual striving, children, especially sons, are expected to collect symbolic capital in the form of educational certificates and well-paying jobs that help raise the family class position and prestige. In imperial and republican China, the accumulation of degrees was an established way to rise from peasant to mandarin status or a way for merchants to rise socially in the eyes of officials.[30] In

Hong Kong, the entrepreneur's rise to the highest status is determined solely by his wealth, regardless of how it has been accumulated, although he too may take on the trappings of mandarin learning.[31]

Familial regimes that regulate the roles of sons and daughters for the family well-being can also become discontinuous with or subvert the biopolitical agenda of the state. The British government's laissez-faire policy encouraged the population to pursue wealth with "flexibility and vigor" and, until the eve of the return of Hong Kong to Chinese rule, to express political freedom as a market phenomenon. This market-driven sense of citizenship was until recently viewed not as the right to demand full democratic representation but as the right to promote familial interests apart from the well-being of society.[32] Middling modernity thus places a premium on material goods and on an instrumental approach to social life, as indexed by the ownership of Mercedes-Benzes and market shares. There is a joke that professors spend more time playing the stock market than teaching. Risk taking and flexibility in the entrepreneurial sense induce an attenuated sense of citizenship. A young, single civil servant posted to San Francisco confided to me, "I don't think I need to associate myself with a particular country. I would rather not confine myself to a nationality defined by China or by the U.K. I am a Hong Kong person. I grew up there, my family and friends are there, it's where I belong. . . . [But] I lack a sense of political belonging due to the British colonial system. But we have thrived on the system—in terms of the quality of life . . . roughly fair competition . . . in terms of moving up through the educational system . . . even though Hong Kong is not a democracy."[33] This person planned to get a British passport and try his luck wherever he could practice his talents. Like many savvy Hong Kongers, he was outwardly mobile, aligned more toward world market conditions than toward the moral meaning of citizenship in a particular nation. Such middling, disaffected modernism has been shaped within the politics of colonialism and the nation-states over a refugee and diasporan population, and yet these strategies are adept at subverting the political regimes of localization and control.

English Weather: National Character and Biopolitics

Since the 1960s, ethnic Chinese from Hong Kong and Southeast Asia have sought residential rights in Western countries to escape political discrimination and anticipated upheavals that could disrupt businesses and threaten family security. But with the rising affluence of Asian countries and the relative decline of Western economies, they may find that economic opportunities and political refuge are not both available in the same place—or even in the same region of the world. With the return of Hong Kong to mainland-Chinese rule, many Chinese professionals would like to continue working in Hong Kong and China but have parked their families in safe havens in Australia, Canada, the United States, and Great Britain. Many, however, found that their search for overseas citizenship is constrained by the immigration policies of Western countries that are equivocating over capital and ethnicity.

The contours of citizenship are represented by the passport—the regulatory instrument of residence, travel, and belonging. Citizenship requirements are the consequence of Foucauldian "biopolitics," in which the state regulates the conduct of subjects as a population (by age, ethnicity, occupation, and so on) and as individuals (sexual and reproductive behavior) so as to ensure security and prosperity for the nation as a whole. Under liberal democracy, biopolitical regulation (governmentality) helps construct and ensure the needs of the marketplace through a policy of acting and not acting on society.[34] For instance, in Hong Kong, the British liberal government has always alternated between government action and necessary inaction in the commercial realm to maintain the wide-open capitalist economy. The question of Hong Kong Chinese emigration to Great Britain, then, must be considered within the dialectics between liberal governmentality and transnational capitalism.

As the residents of a remnant of the British Empire, Hong Kongers were designated British Dependent Territory Citizens (BDTC), with limitless rights of travel but no right to reside in Great Britain. After the reimposition of mainland-Chinese rule, these same residents came to be called British Nationals (Overseas) (BNO), with their conditions of domicile and travel unchanged. Hong Kong Chinese are thus normalized as an overseas population that is in, but not of, the empire; their partial citizenship rests on differences of territoriality, coloniality, and (unmentioned) British origins.

British immigration policy is on the threshold of structurally determining the relationship between class and race so that phenotypical variations in skin color can be transformed into social stratifications based on the assumed capital and labor potential of different groups of immigrants. Postwar immigration laws institutionalized racial difference through the progressive exclusion of "colored" immigrants from the Commonwealth.[35] In the early 1960s, under public pressure to restrict colored immigrants (who were said to overwhelm housing and state benefits), the Conservative government withdrew the right of colored U.K. passport holders to enter Britain. A few years later, the same government granted the right of entry and settlement to several million "white" people from South Africa. This action was defended by a government white paper that maintained that expanded Commonwealth immigration creates social tensions; the immigrant presence had to be resolved if "the evil of racial strife" was to be avoided.[36] Although the language of immigration law was not explicitly racist, the distinction between whites and coloreds from the Commonwealth and their assumed differential contribution to racial tension (*race* was frequently used to refer only to coloreds, not to whites) clearly reproduced a class hierarchy whereby race was given concrete institutional expression.

In this transnational discursive formation of race, Chinese from Hong Kong were coloreds, yet they were clearly differentiated from Afro-Caribbean immigrants because of their significant role in overseas capitalism and their perceived docility under British rule in Hong Kong. In the 1960s, the restriction on immigration from the Commonwealth countries limited Hong Kong arrivals mainly to restaurant operators and employees.[37] In addition, thousands of students were sent by their parents for higher education in Britain. By the 1980s, fear of Hong Kong's imminent reversion to Chinese rule and the potential threat to the Hong Kong economy generated steady emigration, mainly to Western countries. Soon the monthly outflow of Hong Kongers reached one thousand; this jeopardized confidence in the Hong Kong financial market, which British interests were heavily invested in. The colonial government saw the problem as one of "brain drain" and fought to stem the outflow by appealing to orientalist reason. An official commented that "the [Chinese] have an overwhelming pragmatic concern for family and personal development—the same pragmatic self-interest that has made the Hong Kong economy so successful."[38]

In England, immigration policy was modified in 1990 to grant British citizenship to some Hong Kong subjects, mainly as a gesture to stem the outflow from Hong Kong and stabilize faith in the Hong Kong economy. Again, biopolitical criteria that served market interests determined who was awarded citizenship. A nationality bill granted full citizenship or "the right of abode" to only fifty thousand elite Hong Kongers and their families (about a quarter-million out of a total Hong Kong population of almost six million). The members of this special subcategory of Chinese were carefully chosen from among householders (presumably predominantly male) who had connections in British government, business, or some other organization. A point system for different occupations, such as accountancy and law, discriminated among the applicants, who had to have a high educational standing and had presumably to speak fluent English. They were mainly in the age bracket of thirty to forty. Thus, these individuals were selected for their capacity to be normalized as British citizens and their ability to participate in the generation of transnational capital.

British immigration law thus produced a new discourse on overseas Chinese, who were eligible for citizenship only as *homo economicus.* Although the British Labour Party criticized the bill's "elitist" emphasis on the immigrants' educational and professional backgrounds, it did not address the larger subject of how interest in transnational capital colors the perception of race. Although still not fully implemented, the new nationality law constructs a different legal subjectivity of citizenship—as less than *homo economicus*—for Chinese already in the country.

Homi Bhabha has noted that English weather invokes the "most changeable and immanent signs of national character" and is implicitly contrasted to its "daemonic double": the hot, tropical landscapes of the former colonies. English weather represents an imagined national community under threat of "the return of the diasporic, the postcolonial."[39] Prime Minister Margaret Thatcher, anxious to quiet a restive public over the admission of more coloreds into the "bless'd isle," defended her bill in Parliament by wondering why the Chinese would trade sunny Hong Kong for Great Britain, "a cold and cloudy island." She reminded the British that the nationality bill was intended as an "insurance policy" to keep would-be Chinese citizens in Hong Kong up to and beyond 1997.[40] In other words, full British citizenship for even those Chinese meeting the biopolitical criteria was citizenship indefinitely deferred; the nationality law operated as insurance against their ever becoming full British citizens. It was clear that a cold welcome awaited them.

China Recalls Prodigal Sons

Even before the "tidal wave" of emigration following the Tiananmen crack-down in 1989, China tried to stem the exodus of capital and professionals from Hong Kong. Through its mouthpiece, the Xinhua News Agency, the People's Republic repeatedly appealed to all Hong Kongers who had gone abroad to reconsider their decision, to "come back, to work for the prosperity of the land of [their] birth."[41] An official blamed the flight of Hong Kong Chinese on the instrumental ethos bred under Western influence. He charged that Chinese residents had been led astray by capitalist countries offering investment opportunities to attract Hong Kong skilled labor and capital.[42] China viewed the British nationality law as a insult to Chinese sovereignty and a shameless attempt by Britain to cream off Hong Kong's talent. It threatened expulsion of those who possessed British citizenship after 1997.[43]

Generally, China took a paternalistic tone with errant Chinese capitalists, who it promised would be "forgiven" for seeking foreign citizenship; "prodigal sons" who returned were favorably contrasted with the "traitors" who had abandoned capitalism in China altogether. While China appealed to filial piety and held out promises of capitalist opportunities, thereby hoping to retain Hong Kong subjects, Britain held out promises of citizenship and democratic rights, thereby hoping to ensure a place for British interests in the Pacific Rim economies.

Many Hong Kongers opted to work in China while seeking citizenship elsewhere. Caught between British disciplinary racism and China's opportunistic claims of racial loyalty, between declining economic power in Britain and surging capitalism in Asia, they sought a flexible position among the myriad possibilities (and problems) found in the global economy. Flexible capital accumulation is dialectically linked to the search for flexible citizenship as a way to escape the regime of state control, either over capital or over citizens. In Hong Kong, a small industry arose to disseminate information about the legal requirements and economic incentives for acquiring citizenship abroad. Just as Hong Kong–registered companies sought tax havens in places such as Bermuda, well-off families accumulated passports not only from Canada, Australia, Singapore, and the United States but also from revenue-poor Fiji, the Philippines, Panama, and Tonga (which required in return for a passport a down payment of U.S.$200,000 and an equal amount in installments).[44] The Hong Kong authorities uncovered a business scam that offered, for a sum of U.S.$5,000, citizenship in a fictitious Pacific island country called Corterra. Wealthier travelers sought out actual remote islands, safe havens that issued passports with little commitment in return. Kenny Bao of the hotel family chain confided in me that his brother was a friend of the king of Tonga, who gave him citizenship in return for a major investment. A political refuge secured, his brother continued to operate the family's multinational hotel business out of their Hong Kong headquarters, managing properties in Britain and China but having citizenship in neither. Thus, Hong Kong Chinese, for whom the meanings of motherland, country, and family had long been discontinuous and even contradictory, sought legal citizenship not necessarily in the sites where they conducted their business but in places where their families could pursue their dreams. Among the elite and the not-so-elite, this meant a politically stable and secure environment where a world-class education could be found for the children and real estate was available for homesick housewives to speculate in.

Plotting Family Itineraries

Big-business families provide the clearest examples of a careful blending of discipline in familial practice and flexibility in business and citizenship. Li Ka-shing and the late Sir Y. K. Pao, both of whom rose from refugee poverty to immense wealth, are considered perhaps the most brilliant examples of entrepreneurial border running in the Chinese diaspora. Many tycoon families emerged in the 1960s, when businessmen amassed fortunes in real estate just as Hong Kong's manufacturing industries helped make the colony a household word for inexpensive consumer products.[45] In interviews with the sons of some of these wealthy families, I found the familial regime of control to be very firm, even as the family businesses were taking off overseas. Fame and business-power relations are inseparable, and the company founding father is a patriarch who regulates the activities of sons who must be trained and groomed to eventually take over the family business. Filial piety is instilled through the force of family wealth. From the top floor of his San Francisco high-rise, Alex Leong, a mild-mannered middle-aged investor, told me, "I remember, even when I was in junior high [in Hong Kong], my objective was to follow my father's footsteps and be in business . . . to take over the family business rather than to try to work for someone else or to do my own thing. Because I think it is very important for sons to carry on the family business, something that has been built up by your father. To me, that's the number one obligation. . . . If your family has a business, why would you go work for somebody else and leave a hired man to look after your family business? To me, that doesn't make any sense."[46]

Alex comes from a prominent family that traces its lineage back to a grand-uncle who was once the governor of Guangdong Province. Alex's father went to school in Germany, but after the communist victory in 1949, he took his family to Australia. His father then explored business opportunities in Brazil, where the family lived for a few years. They finally returned to Hong Kong, where his father went into the real estate business and set up a firm called Universal Enterprises. Filial piety dictated that Alex and his brothers take on the roles mapped out by their father. Alex explained that it is a common practice for big-business families to distribute their sons across different geographic sites: "The fathers make a very clear subdivision whereby one brother doesn't infringe on the others, fearing that there would be too much fighting among them. For instance, my oldest brother works in Hong Kong. I take care of everything in North America. We always talk, but we know whose responsibility it is here and over there."[47]

In Kenny Bao's family—the one in which the eldest son obtained a Tongan passport and remains in Hong Kong to run the family hotel chain in the Pacific region—Kenny, based in San Francisco, takes care of the North American and European hotels and the youngest brother, who came on board later, is managing the family business in southern California. Daughters, no matter how qualified, are never put into management positions in the family business, which is considered their brothers' patrimony.[48] Three Hong Kong–born women are running investment businesses in the San Francisco Bay area, but they have established their own firms using seed money from their fathers. Their businesses are not part of the family enterprises founded by their fathers. Leong refers to one of these women as "one of the men" because she has been highly successful in what is still considered a male vocation.

Although Leong cannot imagine doing anything else, he confesses that he sometimes feels "stifled" by the fact that the reins of control are in his father's hands: "When you have a father as a boss, to me that's a double boss, right? You can't just say, 'I don't agree, I quit,' and resign. . . . You can't just walk away from your father. And then a father who has been in business for so long, he'll never recognize you as an equal, so you are always in a subordinate position." The familial regime is so powerful that even sons who try to slip its net are sometimes pulled right back into conformity. Leong's youngest brother graduated from college a few years ago, but having observed his older brothers' predicament, he has resisted working in the family business. The young man expressed his rebellion by working in a bank, but under the paternalistic eye of one of his father's wealthy friends. Leong expects that "eventually, when my youngest brother joins in, it is our objective to continue to expand here in the U.S. and to wind down in Hong Kong."[49] Scholars of rural China maintain that a man who has inherited family property rather than acquired his own fortune enjoys more power over his sons,[50] but here in the tumult of the global economy, it is the self-made tycoon who appears to exert strong control over his family throughout his lifetime. He directs and regulates the behavior of his sons, who are sent out across the world to carve out new niches for the family business empire. Leong's father has been retired for some years now, but the sons continued to consult him on major selling and buying decisions. A political analogue to this system of boss rule is the continuing power of the former prime minister of Singapore, Lee Kuan Yew, who still appears to exert tremendous *towkay* (boss) power over his state enterprise.[51]

Thus, the masculine subjectivity of this elite diasporan community is defined primarily in terms of the individual's role as a father or a son, that is, his role in maintaining the paternal/filial structure that both nurtures and expands family wealth. Unlike daughters, who inherit a small share of the family fortune (about a third of the sons' inheritance in Leong's family) and then have nothing to do with the male estates, sons must remain active, integral parts of the family business throughout their lives. To be passive—for example, to draw an income without being involved in the daily operation of the business—is to play a feminine role, like sisters (who marry out) or wives (who may manage the finances but rarely take on management roles). However, as uncertainties increase in Hong Kong and more sons break away and emigrate on their own, a few young women have taken over running their family businesses.[52] But the familial system has traditionally relied on men, and in families without sons, even "foreign devil" sons-in-law who have proved their loyalty to the family business can take the place of sons. For instance, the business empire of Sir Y. K. Pao, the late shipping and hotel magnate, is now run by his two Caucasian sons-in-law. One can say that filial piety has been bent and channeled to serve the governmentality not only of the family but of global capitalism as well.

Families in America, Fathers in Midair

The modernist norms and practices of diasporan Chinese anticipate their relocation, along with capital infusions, into the Western Hemisphere. Earlier Chinese immigrants to the United States were largely laborers, with a sprinkling of merchants. Today, Chinese investors and professionals arrive as cosmopolitans already wise in the ways of Western business and economic liberalism.[53] With new modes of travel and communication, familial regimes have become more flexible in both dispersing and localizing members in different parts of the world. Hong Kong papers talk about the business traveler as an "astronaut" who is continually in the air while his wife and children are located in Australia, Canada, or the United States, earning rights of residence.

The turn toward the United States began in the 1960s, when teenagers from middle- and upper-middle-class families applied to American schools and colleges. Alex Leong's father often told him, "Your future is really going to be outside Hong Kong. So you should be educated outside, as long as you maintain some Chinese customs and speak Chinese."[54] The well-off used their children's overseas education as an entrée into a Western democracy, buying homes for the children and setting up bank accounts and exploring local real estate. Upon graduation, sons were expected to help expand the family business in their country of residence. After graduating from the University of California, Berkeley, and the University of Wisconsin business school, Leong set up a local branch of his father's company in San Francisco. Because he is not yet a citizen, his parents plan to retire in Vancouver, Canada, where residential rights can be had for an investment of Can$300,000. They expect to join him eventually in the Bay Area, while the sons take greater control over running the family empire. This mix of family and business strategies allows them to weave in and out of political borders as they accumulate wealth and security.

Many entrepreneurs, however, continue to shuttle between both coasts of the Pacific (because it is still more profitable to do business in Hong Kong) while their wives and children are localized in North America. The astronaut as a trope of Chinese postmodern displacement also expresses the costs of the flexible accumulation logic and the toil it takes on an overly flexible family system. The astronaut wife in the United States is euphemistically referred to as "inner beauty" (*neizaimei*), a term that suggests two other phrases: "inner person," that is, wife (*neiren*) and "my wife in the Beautiful Country (America)" (*neiren zai Meiguo*). Wives thus localized to manage suburban homes and take care of the children—arranging lessons in ballet, classical music, Chinese language—sarcastically refer to themselves as "widows" (and computer widows), which expresses their feeling that family life is now thoroughly mediated and fragmented by the technology of travel and business.

In a Canadian suburb, some widows have formed a group called Ten Brothers to share domestic problems and chores in the absence of their husbands. "We have to start doing men's work like cutting grass in the summer and shoveling snow in the winter. So we call ourselves 'brothers' instead of sisters."[55] This sense of role reversal induced by flexible citizenship has also upset other prior arrangements. In the Bay Area, wives bored by being "imprisoned" in America parlay their well-honed sense of real estate into a business sideline. Down the peninsula, the majority of real-estate agents are immigrant Chinese women selling expensive homes to other newly arrived widows. Here, too, flexibility reigns as wives keep trading up their own homes in the hot residential real estate market. A Hong Kong industrialist told me that he has moved five times over the past sixteen years as a result.

In some cases, the flexible logic deprives children of both parents. These are teenagers who are dropped off in southern Californian suburbs by their Hong Kong and Taiwan parents and who are referred to as "parachute kids." One such child who was left to fend for herself and her brother refers to her father as "the ATM machine" because he issues money but little else. Familial regimes of dispersal and localization, then, discipline family members to make do with very little emotional support; disrupted parental responsibility, strained marital relations, and abandoned children are such common circumstances that they have special terms. When the flexible imperative in family life and citizenship requires a form of isolation and disciplining of women and children that is both critiqued and resisted, claims that the "Confucian affective model" is at the heart of Chinese economic success are challenged.[56] The logic of flexibility expresses the governmentality of transnational capitalism within which many elite families are caught up, and their complex maneuvers around state regulations reveal the limits and pathos of such strategies.

American Liberalism and Pacific Rim Capital

I have argued elsewhere that in the United States, neoliberalism plays a role in shaping our notion of the deserving citizen. The history of racial conflict also tends to produce a perception that different kinds of ethnic and racial groups embody different forms of economic and political risks.[57] Following Foucault, I consider liberalism to be not merely an ethos but a regime of normalizing whereby *homo economicus* is the standard against which all other citizens are measured and ranked.

At the beginning of the twentieth century, the Chinese had the dubious distinction of being the first "racial" group to be excluded as undesirable and unsuitable immigrants to the United States. Earlier, Chinese immigrants had been welcomed by capitalists and missionaries as cheap, diligent, and docile laborers, but they were eventually attacked as unfair competitors by white workers in the railroad and mining industries. During the cold war, the public image of Chinese oscillated between that of the good Chinese, who were represented by America's Guomindang allies, and that of the bad Chinese, who were associated with "Red China."[58] In the 1960s, the emergence of a middle-class Chinese population provided contrast with the growth of a nonwhite "underclass," a term used mainly for inner-city blacks.[59] The media popularized the term *model minority* to refer to Asian Americans, who were perceived as having raised themselves up by their bootstraps, thus fitting the criteria for good, or at least deserving, citizens.[60] Images of Oriental docility, diligence, self-sufficiency, and productivity underpin contemporary notions that the Asian minority embodies the human capital that makes good citizens, in contrast to those who make claims on the welfare program.[61]

Through the next decade, the influx of immigrants from Hong Kong and Taiwan, many of them students bound for college, swelled the ranks of middle-class Asian Americans.[62] The rise of a Chinese-immigrant elite—many of them suburban professionals—coincided with the restructuring of the American economy and its increasing reliance on skilled immigrant labor and overseas capital. In the public mind, the Asian newcomers seemed to embody the desired disciplinary traits of an increasingly passé model of American character. For instance, in the aftermath of the Tiananmen crackdown, a letter to the *San Francisco Chronicle* defended the admission of Chinese (student) refugees: "The opportunity to welcome the best and the brightest of China and Hong Kong into our area is fantastic. These are motivated, energetic, courageous people, with strong cultural traditions of taking care of their families, working hard, and succeeding in business. We need more of these values in our midst, not less."[63] It appears to me that "traditional" American values are to be found in these newcomers, who are coming with different kinds of capital but perhaps not so strong "cultural traditions." Earlier images of the Chinese railroad worker, laundryman, houseboy, and garment worker have been replaced by the masculine executive, a *homo economicus* model inspired in part by the so-called neo-Confucian challenge from across the Pacific.[64]

Increasingly, the reception of skilled and capital-bearing Chinese newcomers represents the triumph of corporate discourses and practices that invoke the Pacific Rim and its Oriental productivity and new wealth. For instance, under pressure from corporate and Asian lobbies, U.S. immigration laws were modified in 1990 to attract some of the Pacific Rim capital that was flowing toward Australia and Canada, where the laws are less stringent. A new "investor category" allows would-be immigrants to obtain a green card in return for a million-dollar investment that results in the creation of at least ten jobs. On Wall Street, seminars directed at Asian Americans offer suggestions on how to "get U.S. citizenship through real estate investment and acquisition." A consultant urges, "Think of your relatives in Asia. If they invest in you, they get a green card and you get a new business."[65] As in other Western countries with finance-based immigration, citizenship has become an instrument of flexible accumulation for the nation-state; it is a way for the nation-state to subvert its own regulatory mechanisms in order to compete more effectively in the global economy.

Narrating Cosmopolitan Citizenship

In what ways has the arrival of the diasporan Chinese reworked the cultural meaning of "Asian American" and produced a new discourse of Pacific Rim romanticism and even symbolic violence? Whereas Said has described orientalism as a one-sided and self-reifying process, I have tried throughout this chapter to represent the discursive objects themselves as cocreators in orientalism. This has been, after all, part of their flexibility in negotiating the multicultural worlds of European imperialism. For centuries, Asians and other peoples have been shaped by a perception and an experience of themselves as the other of the Western world.[66] The new prominence of Asians in world markets has enabled Chinese subjects to play a bigger role in identifying what counts as "Chinese" in the West.[67] Diasporan-Chinese academics now use orientalist codes to (re)frame overseas Chinese as enlightened cosmopolitans who possess both economic capital and humanistic values. Wang Gungwu, the former chancellor of Hong Kong University, describes overseas Chinese living "among non-Chinese" as "a modern kind of cosmopolitan literati" who have embraced the Enlightenment ideals of rationality, individual freedom, and democracy.[68] Perhaps. Scholars based in the United States claim that "Confucian humanism" will create "an Oriental alternative" to the destructive instrumental rationality and individualism of the West[69]—in other words, a kinder and gentler capitalism for the twenty-first century. One wonders whether these scholars have bothered to visit factories run by Chinese entrepreneurs and observed whether their practices are really that "humanistic" and uninformed by the logic of capital accumulation.

These grand claims circle around and occlude the complex, wide-ranging realities of East Asian capitalism—or at least its Chinese variant. For instance, Hong Kongers hail from a colonial territory where there has been little nurturing of Confucian humanism and democratic values. Until Tiananmen, many had developed a radically apolitical stance toward the state. Just as Hong Kong is viewed as a place to maximize wealth, so the Western democracies to which many Hong Kongers are bound are considered "gold mountains" of opportunity. The subcontracting system of production used in Hong Kong and Taiwan and now in China is among the most exploitative of women and children in the world.[70] In Hong Kong, "democracy," for many entrepreneurs, often means freedom from political constraints on making money; the state and wider society are of concern only when they can be made relevant to family interests.[71] In the view of the business elite, the modern social order is built upon the domination of those who possess intellectual and economic power, and wealthy people are models for envy and emulation rather than enemies of the poor.[72] Like investors all over the world, Chinese businessmen who engage in philanthropy are seeking to escape property taxes and to gain social status as prominent members of society; it is a stretch to construct these acts as acts of Confucian benevolence. As billionaire Li Kashing says, "There is no other criterion of excellence [except money]."[73] But such prideful discourses on diasporan-Chinese elites as humanistic citizens persist, and they are intervening in narratives about the role of Asian Americans in the United States.

From across the Pacific, corporate America answers the call to reconsider Chinese immigrants as exceptional citizens of the New World Order imaginary. Of course, the reception is not unambivalent, for global trade is viewed as war.[74] This contradictory attitude was expressed by David Murdock, chairman and CEO of Dole Foods, at a conference on Asian Americans in Los Angeles. Murdock personifies corporate America: his company has operations in more than fifty countries and employs thousands of employees in the Asia Pacific region. He warned that in a world of many big economic powers, the technological edge has shifted to the East. There are, however, more than seven million Asian Americans. He continued: "We need to be more competitive. We need people who understand the languages, cultures, the markets, the politics of this spectacular region. Many Asian Americans have language ability, cultural understanding, direct family ties, and knowledge of economic conditions and government practices throughout Asia. This knowledge and ability can help Americans achieve political and business success in the region. . . . Their insight and ability can [help] in opening doors for the U.S. [and in] building a new structure for peace in the Pacific."[75] By defining a role for Asian Americans as good citizens and trade ambassadors, Murdock's speech situates them in the wider narrative of the Oriental as trade enemy.

At the same conference, Los Angeles City Councilman Michael Woo, who was then seeking to be the first Asian mayor of Los Angeles, picked up the narrative by reframing the question: "What then is this new person, this Asian American, in the new era of the Pacific?" The question, which is reminiscent of European queries about Anglos earlier in the century, subverts the view that whites are the undisputed key players on the West Coast. Woo, whose family has close ties with Asian capital, went on to propose "a new hybrid role" whereby new Asian immigrants (rather than long-resident Asian Americans, he seemed to suggest) can act as "translators, go-betweens [between] one culture and another, using skills that have brought us to such prominence and success in the business world and in the professions and entering into the public arena" to become mediators in community relations.[76]

Asians are "bridge builders," Woo claimed.[77] In his view, the Asian American "middleman minority" is not the besieged ethnic group of academic theorizing.[78] Woo was using the term in the larger global sense, coming dangerously close to the meaning that evokes compradors, those members of the Chinese elite who acted as middlemen between colonial governments and the masses in Asia. Calling colonial go-betweens *muchachos*, Fred Chiu notes their role as "the ideal-typical mediating and (inter)mediating category/force in the reproduction of a world of—out-going as well as in-coming—nationalism and colonialism."[79] And of course the term "bridge" has gained new resonance for overseas Chinese in their new prominence as transnational capitalists. As I mentioned in chapter 1, in Chinese, the word for bridge puns with the word for overseas Chinese, and diasporan Chinese have been quick to play on the metaphor of bridging political boundaries in their role as agents of flexible accumulation and flexible citizenship. The bridge-building metaphor appeals to the members of an Asian elite who set great store in being engineers, doctors, managers, and bankers and who see themselves as self-made men who are now building the infrastructures of modern affluence on both sides of the Pacific. Woo saw a continuity between Asian economic and cultural middleman roles. He noted that trading skills developed in the diaspora "in the midst of cultures very different from their own" included not just those of use in "the handling of money, but also skills in sizing up people, negotiating a deal, and long-term planning." He suggested that these "survival skills" could be "transferred" to non-Asians.[80] Woo thus echoed the *homo economicus* construction of Chinese immigrants and elevated their role in the American social order.

Such narrativization is never simply complicit with hegemonic constructions but seeks to reposition Asian immigrants and Asian Americans as new authority figures while suggesting declining human capital and leadership qualities among Anglos. By calling Asian Americans the new Westerners, Woo implies that the Anglos have been surpassed in diligence, discipline, moral capital, and even knowledge of the changing multicultural world that is critical to America's success. His narrative carves out a space of Asian Americans as mediators in American race and class relations. The bridge-building citizen evokes the tradition of American communities and the ideal of a civil society in which neighbors look out for each other.[81] Asian American leaders, Woo seemed to suggest, could build bridges between racial minorities and the government. By identifying Pacific Rim bodies with Pacific Rim capital, the concept of bridge builders gentrifies Asian American identity in both its local and its global aspects—in moral contrast to less-privileged minorities, with their dependence on the welfare state.[82] When Woo's talk ended, the largely Asian audience rose up and clapped enthusiastically; they voted to replace the model-minority label with the label bridge-building minority, a term that apparently enables Asian Americans to share the transnational role of diasporan Chinese in building the Pacific Century.[83]

Conclusion

The emigration of Chinese corporate elites out of Asia has entailed the cultural work of image management as they seek wider acceptance in Western democracies and in different zones of late capitalism. By revising the academic images of overseas Chinese as money handlers, trading minorities, and middlemen, corporate spokesmen paint a picture that mixes humanistic values with ultrarationalism and portrays the ideal *homo economicus* of the next century.[84] Such self-representations are not so much devised to collaborate in the biopolitical agenda of any nation-state as to convert political constraints in one field into economic opportunities in another, to turn displacement into advantageous placement in different sites, and to elude state disciplining in order to reproduce the family in tandem with the propulsion of capitalism.

Of course, whereas for bankers, boundaries are always flexible, for migrant workers, boat people, persecuted intellectuals, artists, and other kinds of less well heeled refugees, this apparent mix of humanistic concerns and capitalist rationality is a harder act to follow. For instance, Don Nonini has identified the tensions and pathos experienced by middle-class Malaysian Chinese whose familial strategies of emigration are intended to help them escape second-class citizenship as much as to accumulate wealth overseas.[85] Although Chinese small-business owners consider themselves locals in their Malaysian hometowns (e.g., as "natives of Bukit Mertajam"), many are vulnerable to anti-Chinese policies and feel that they have no choice but to send their children overseas, where they may feel less discrimination. These businessmen postpone joining their children in places such as New Zealand that do not feel like "home." Their loyalty to home places in Malaysia is ironically disregarded by state policies that discriminate against them as lower-class ethnics in a way that does not affect wealthy Chinese, who are viewed as more "cosmopolitan" and open-minded about Malay rule. As Jim Clifford has reminded us, there are "discrepant cosmopolitanisms,"[86] and the cosmopolitanism of lower-class Chinese from Malaysia is fraught with tensions between sentiments of home and pressures to emigrate. This is not to say that members of the Hong Kong Chinese elite do not have patriotic feelings for the Chinese motherland but rather that the investor emigrants are well positioned to engage in a self-interested search for citizenship and profits abroad—a strategy that will enhance their economic mobility and yet sidestep the disciplining of particular nation-states.[87]

Among this elite group (though not limited to them), such a mix of ultra-instrumentalism and familial moralism reveals a postnationalist ethos. They readily submit to the governmentality of capital, plotting all the while to escape state discipline. In the most extreme expressions, their loyalty appears to be limited to loyalty toward the family business; it does not extend to any particular country. Kenny Bao, the hotelier in San Francisco, explains that he can live in Asia, Canada, or Europe: "I can live anywhere in the world, but it must be near an airport." Such bravado constructs the bearable lightness of being that capital buoyancy can bring. Yet the politics of imagining a transnational identity that is dependent on global market mobility should not disabuse us of the fact that there are structural limits, and personal costs, to such flexible citizenship.

This essay should not be interpreted as an argument for a simple opposition between cosmopolitanism and patriotism (taken to an extreme, either is an undesirable or dangerous phenomenon). I have argued that a Confucian cultural triumphalism has arisen alongside modern Chinese transnationalism in Southeast Asia. Some scholars have been tempted to compare the role of the modern Chinese economic elite to that of medieval Jewish bankers, whose activities protected free trade, along with liberalism and other Enlightenment values, in the Dark Ages. We should resist such a comparison. Although contemporary Chinese merchants, bankers, and managers have burst through closed borders and freed up spaces for economic activities, they have also revived premodern forms of child, gender, and class oppression, as well as strengthened authoritarian regimes in Asia.[88] A different kind of cosmopolitical right is at play. The point is not that all Chinese are painted by the same broad brush of elite narratives but that the image of the border-running

Chinese executive with no state loyalty has become an important figure in the era of Pacific Rim capital. What is it about flexible accumulation—the endless capacity to dodge state regulations, spin human relations across space, and find ever new niches to exploit—that allows a mix of humanistic relations and ultrainstrumentality to flourish? Indeed, there may not be anything uniquely "Chinese" about flexible personal discipline, disposition, and orientation; rather, they are the expressions of a habitus that is finely tuned to the turbulence of late capitalism.[89]

PART 3

Translocal Publics

The Family Romance of Mandarin Capital ≡ 5

Cosmopolitics and the Subaltern Unconscious

In *Anthropology and Politics,* Joan Vincent identifies the 1980s as the era of
"cosmopolitics."[1] She sees the cosmopolitical turn as most promising for
ethnographic research on the political economies of third-world countries.
Vincent's remarkable contribution to anthropology has been grounded in
intensive fieldwork in Zanzibar, Uganda, and Ulster and archival research on
Ireland and the Philippines. Clearly, anthropology is the discipline to track
down, delineate, and expose the complex politics of colonial imperialism and
capitalism inside and outside the European homeland. Less well known, perhaps, is Vincent's extensive influence among students (graduates of Barnard
College, Columbia University, and other institutions), who have been inspired, encouraged, and guided to study the cosmopolitics of subaltern classes,
peasantries, and women "confronting global capital" in communities around
the world.[2] I was one of those privileged students, and my work has always
shown the traces, I hope, of Vincent's political sensibility. In this chapter, I
want to recast some of Vincent's ideas about the strategic importance of "men
in motion," in the "moving frontier" of colonial capitalism, as well as the
question of class consciousness in late-twentieth-century capitalisms.[3]

    In her study of British rule in colonial Uganda, Vincent wondered what
factors in colonial capitalism accounted for the lack of class consciousness
among subaltern groups.[4] Influenced, perhaps, by Marx's comparison of
French peasants to "a sack of potatoes"—"they cannot represent themselves,
they must be represented"[5]—Vincent suggested that the mobility of capitalist

agents disguised the class character of imperial capital, leaving local groups unconnected to each other even as they were objectively exploited by the same system. By arguing that the mobility of capital and its agents was dialectically linked to the fixity of subaltern groups, in both geographical *and* ideological senses, Vincent identified the critical process whereby transnational capital reinforces the mobility of some at the expense of many, a power mechanism that is especially significant in the era of late capitalism.[6]

The ideological murkiness of traveling agents of capitalism, and the "class unawareness" of subaltern groups, are complex ethnographic questions that challenge us to move beyond a class-centered analysis. While other scholars of colonial and postcolonial societies have dealt with issues of class consciousness in relatively stable situations of class exploitation,[7] Vincent's focus on the moving frontiers of capitalism vividly problematizes analytical linkages between capitalist mobility and the political (un)conscious of subaltern groups. Indirectly, her work on Teso poses the question, How does one account for political consciousness when the material links to capital are so attenuated as to seem invisible to the dominated?[8] This question suggests the obverse, that is, What happens when the material relations of exploitation are keenly felt and yet are not symbolically linked to a politics of class identity? This is an especially important theme in the contemporary world, where so much of what we take to be reality is complexly mediated by the dynamic flows of images that make all systems of referents highly fragmented, destabilized, and not directly connected to the structure of production.[9] While it is fashionable among orthodox Marxists to reject such observations as "postmodernist," I maintain that the days are over for calmly plotting a structural relationship between the "objective" and the "subjective" aspects of (class) consciousness. Capital remains fundamental to our understanding of contemporary social life, and it is sensible to think of capital as highly sped-up, constantly mutating sets of material, technological, and discursive relations, of production *and* consumption, in which everything is reduced to an exchange value. Donald Lowe refers to this phenomenon in the United States, where accelerated production/consumption has annihilated use values, as "the hegemony of exchangist practices."[10] Even when we move away from the centers of global capitalism, subaltern groups in the new transnational publics shaped by capital, travel, and mass media cannot develop political consciousness in a way that escapes the mediations of ethnic identifications, mass culture, and national ideologies. Indeed, transnational capitalism in Asia has been linked not so much to the rise of class hostility but to other forms of cultural struggle that privilege gender, family, ethnicity, and nationality.[11]

The problem of subaltern consciousness, then, is not merely one of the "invisibility" of dominant relations to subalterns or the impossibility of the "authentic" representation of subalterns by nonsubalterns;[12] rather, it is also one of linking "subaltern" imagination not to the structure of production but to what Foucault calls "knowledge power." In the contemporary world, where so much of everyday consciousness is mediated by "print (and electronic) capitalism," discursive knowledges constitute a field of power that defines entities such as the family, gender, ethnicity, race, and nationality and thus constitutes the political consciousness of class-differentiated subjects.[13] How are social identities rooted in objective class differences shaped not by an ideology of class exploitation but by the corporatist hegemony of exchangist values? I find Fredric Jameson's notion of "the political unconscious" especially useful for unmasking ideological messages embedded in cultural narratives about the traveling subject of contemporary Asian capitalism.[14] Although Jameson is interested in uncovering the political unconscious—a structure of psyche that is historical—in literary works, I wish here to uncover the political unconscious in commercialized cultural and political forms linked to mobile Chinese families that have recently dominated public cultures in Southeast Asia. What are the ideological messages in the figuration of traveling masculine subjects and entrepreneurial families? What do they tell us about the popular imagination of power, authority, and desires in the brave new Asian world of authoritarian states and free-flowing capitalism?

The Governmentality of Family Romances

This rise of Chinese corporate forms in the Southeast Asian public landscape has been sudden and quite startling. I remember visiting Malaysia in 1992 on Chinese New Year and being amazed by the huge commercial displays of Chinese words, figures, and banners on major hotels and stores. Despite Malaysia's large Chinese minority, the public display of Chinese symbols had been muted throughout the 1970s and 1980s, when Malaysianization policies established Malay language, personalities, and cultural icons as the appropriate vehicles for public prestige and pageantry. The new prominence of Chinese iconography outside "Chinatown," I was told, was a sign of welcome for Taiwanese businessmen, who have become the main investors in Malaysia, overtaking the Japanese. Ironically, while blatant displays of Chinese artifacts in public culture have been suppressed for fear of inciting local ethnic-Chinese chauvinism, commercial images of Chineseness as symbols are permitted and even encouraged for their links to transnational capital and entrepreneurs, in effect casting them as " 'thoroughly modern' Asians."[15]

This flamboyant display of Chinese corporatism indexes a new accommodation between translocal capital and the developmental state, an alliance that enables cosmopolitan Chinese iconography to dominate public culture. These, however, are not apolitical images of culture and consumption but are imbued with messages about the stereotypical "Asian" family order, gender hierarchy, and subscription to a particular state vision of communitarian capitalism. Indeed, just as the world of Walt Disney disseminates capitalist ideology,[16] the new Asian public culture creates a realm where cosmopolitan images promote a kind of ideological conformity that is especially powerful because it is cast in the language of family romance and modern adventure.[17]

Embedded in these public cultural forms are political messages about power, masculinity, and a mobile economic liberalism. As Foucault has reminded us, economic liberalism is not simply a theory of political and economic behavior but "a style of thinking quintessentially concerned with the art of governing."[18] The objective of political economy resituates "governmental reason within a newly complicated, open and unstable politico-epistemic configuration."[19] One can say that a kind of laissez-faire governmentality infuses the market behavior of overseas Chinese, among whom a premium is placed on norms that allow the free play of market forces, flexible activities, and the self-discipline of the profit maximizer. In Adam Smithian thinking, the state is ideally a solicitous institution that makes corrective adjustments to open channels to free trade, but its interventions should be limited so as not to hamper the workings of market rationality. Indeed, while nation-states such as Singapore, Malaysia, and Indonesia may be politically repressive now and again, the state ensures the freedom of economic activities across the region. Prime Minister Mahathir Mohamad of Malaysia calls such a combination of "not-so-liberal democracy" and government intervention into the economy "communitarian capitalism."[20] These ideas about the inseparable links between economic liberalism and authoritarian rule are disseminated through public cultures that recast capitalist strategies and state control as family romances.

The new Asian publics are increasingly contexts through which, in Lynn Hunt's words, "private sentiments and public politics" are interwoven and struggled over by different class, ethnic, and nationality groups.[21] Following Hunt, I use the construct of family romance(s) to mean the collective and unconscious images of family order that underlie public politics.[22] Narratives of affluent Chinese families provide a kind of structure to political imaginaries, which (like nationalism) can crosscut and neutralize the interpellations of class, gender, and ethnicity.[23] Family romances do not operate in an apolitical manner but inform the way people imagine the operations of power between individuals and the state, between different ethnic groups, and of course between men and women. Below, I suggest that family romances—as articulated in public displays, images, and narratives—are vehicles that variously encode political messages about (1) a fraternal tribal capitalism; (2) Chinese-native elite alliances; (3) the moral economy of the state; and (4) working-class women's dreams. These are different facets of "the family model of politics,"[24] and they speak to the differing notions of authority and legitimacy among transnational capitalists, their bureaucratic partners, and the new middle classes; they also shape the notions of authority and legitimacy of subaltern subjects in Asian modernity.

The Romance of Family Empires

Over the past two decades, Southeast Asia has seen the emergence of about a dozen major Chinese business families whose multinational holdings place them among the world's richest people. Chinese-owned companies that enjoy the patronage of politicians have become "larger than all but the biggest local branches of the global MNCs [multinational corporations] which proliferated throughout the region" in the 1980s.[25] Their owners include Robert Kuok and the Kwek brothers of Malaysia and Hong Kong, Liem Sioe Liong and William Soeryadjaya of Indonesia, and the late Chin Sophronphanich and the Lamsam family of Thailand.[26] Taken together, overseas-Chinese corporate families and professionals are the new economic elite in Asia (outside Japan); their activities, mobility, and stories are the stuff of a regional thinking about "communitarian capitalism."

The symbolic qualities of Chinese corporate families—interpersonal relations based on fraternity and mandarin ideals—are key elements in a political imaginary of regional development and interethnic dependence between rulers and capitalists. This Chinese capitalist triumphalism arose in the context of a sustained economic boom that began in the 1970s, when Singapore and Hong Kong joined South Korea as the new "dragons" in Asia. In the next decade, as Malaysia, Thailand, and Indonesia won the label "minidragons," ethnic-Chinese business groups began to exercise their critical role in forming economic linkages that supplemented and went beyond the strategies of the developmental states. In 1991, the Singapore Chinese Chamber of Commerce held the first global meeting of Chinese chambers of commerce from all over the world, inviting participants from seventy-five countries. This meeting of business interests was represented as a model of postcolonial fraternal bonds that overcame regional and political differences. A leader of the Singapore Chamber of Commerce told me that there was no language barrier at the gathering because the Chinese entrepreneurs were all bound by kinship, in the double sense of having both blood and fictive fraternal bonds.[27] As I mentioned in chapter 2, this rediscovered brotherhood in the context of transnational capitalism has been dubbed a "momentary glow of fraternity"; it asserts a transnational autonomy vis-à-vis the less-flexible patriarchal authority of the state.[28]

Emboldened by their successes in forming transnational networks, overseas entrepreneurs boast of using fraternal links to bypass or do without political and legal regulations. In an interview, a member of the Singapore Chamber of Commerce recalled for me: "Overseas Chinese grew more confident and more concerned about their identity. Globalization requires going beyond just national identity in enlarging our scope and permutations of what we're trying to do. Although investments are directed by our government regionalization policy, most important linkages are made through company levels, and again at the local level through human relations."[29]

Ethnic-Chinese solidarity based on male bonding and networks has created what Joel Kotkin calls "the most economically important of the Asian global tribes" and has made the "old government ideology of nation-states . . . outmoded."[30] This use of the term *tribe* to refer to traveling ethnic businessmen constructs an essentialist concept of cultural difference and brings to mind the band of brothers who ritually sacrificed the original father figure in

Freud's *Totem and Taboo*.[31] Fraternal networks are represented as the modern Asian way of doing business man to man, usurping the paternalistic role of the government in economic activities. The familial morality of Chinese capitalism, then, is not that of the autocratic father but rather the fraternal flexibility that forms alliances across ideological, political, and ethnic borders.

The oxymoron *Confucian merchant* is a sign of the extravagance of Chinese capitalism.[32] That Confucian philosophy puts traders at the bottom of the occupational hierarchy and regards their singular pursuit of wealth as the very antithesis of Confucian values has not been an obstacle to business-news images of capitalists as reborn Confucians. In narratives of East Asian triumphalism, Chinese merchants are likened to mandarins whose high status stems not only from their fortunes but also from their representation of a reworked Confucianism of the "all-men-are-brothers" sort.

The merchant mandarin par excellence is Robert Kuok, a Malaysian-born tycoon who has been called "the embodiment of a Confucian gentleman" in the region's authoritative business magazine, the *Far Eastern Economic Review*.[33] The cover of the issue in which this assessment appears displays Kuok dressed in an emperor's yellow dragon robes in the regal pose of an ancestor figure. His spectacular economic success has been attributed not only to his masterful cultivation of relationships with capitalists and politicians but also to his loyalty to business subordinates and to his sense of business discretion. The family romance behind this merchant prince celebrates the values of discipline, pragmatism, and economic success; it opposes political idealism and the impractical goals of the anticolonial revolutionary. The trader and the revolutionary are key figures in overseas-Chinese history.[34] The story of Robert Kuok and his younger brother Willie is presented as a morality tale of overseas Chinese who are torn between a foolish anti-imperialist struggle (Willie) and practical adjustments to imperial rule and global capitalism (Robert). The sensible influence is represented by Kuok's mother, a "very austere, very religious" and "old-fashioned" woman, that is, an authentic Chinese parental figure of piety and moral uprightness.[35] It is instructive that maternal, rather than paternal, influence is constructed as the key influence on sons in this diasporan-Chinese family. Emigration from China breaks with the traditional patriarchal power associated with the lineages and the ancestral temples of the home culture.

The Kuok brothers were educated in elite colonial British schools (where

Robert's classmates included future politicians such as Lee Kuan Yew). The Second World War, which precipitated the process of decolonization, set the brothers off on radically different paths. While Robert worked with the occupying Japanese forces and learned from their rice trade, his younger brother, Willie, entered the jungle to join the anti-imperialist Communist Party of Malaysia as a propagandist. By the end of the war, both brothers had gained fame. Willie's death at the hands of British troops was announced in the British House of Commons. A few years later, Robert Kuok established a major sugar mill and, through rapid expansion, soon became the "sugar king" of Southeast Asia. Expanding his strategic ties to overseas-Chinese traders and indigenous politicians, Robert Kuok has built an empire based on commodities, shipping, banking, and property development, with offices in Hong Kong, Beijing, Paris, and Santiago.

This story, which has been reported in the international press and circulates among overseas Chinese, contrasts "good" and "bad" overseas-Chinese male subjects. Robert Kuok is the reassuring image of a new diasporan masculine ideal—open to all kinds of advantageous alliances, tempered by an astute judgment of human relations, and always nurturing social relations with associates. This mandarin image was further promoted by *Forbes*, the world's leading business magazine: "Nearly all the first-generation tycoons, such as Indonesia's Liem [Sioe Liong], Malaysia's Kuok, and Hong Kong's Li Ka-shing, have the same image: trustworthy, loyal, humble, gentlemanly, skilled at networking and willing to leave something on the table for partners."[36]

In his study of the intertwining of nationalism and sexuality in Nazi Germany and Great Britain, George Mosse notes that bourgeois manhood was often represented by values of restraint and self-control. "Manliness was not just a matter of courage, it was a pattern of manners and morals" that appealed to the middle classes as virtue and respectability, or the control of passion.[37] In Chinese dynastic romances, the manly virtues of the new bourgeoisie are a mix of restrained flamboyance and benevolence toward those who are less well endowed. This vision of a gentrified tycoon culture—a world away from the hubbub of Chinese commercial streets—appeals to the new middle classes, who have been keeping up with global "middling" norms of the good life.[38]

Such images of family morality—restraint, fraternity, princeliness—both represent and resonate with the fantasies of Chinese families, with their nostalgia for a remembered glorious culture, and with the ways they understand economic and political experiences. There is growing evidence that the middle classes in Southeast Asia now look to (Chinese) business families rather than to the families of sultans or kings as models for appropriate modern Asian masculine conduct, practices, and values. Chinese communities in Malaysia take great pride in the Kuoks, who are viewed as homegrown sons who have become global empire builders. They closely follow the business decisions and property acquisitions of the Kuoks (that is, of Robert, the surviving brother, and both brothers' children), seeking clues as to how to conduct themselves and attain economic success. Furthermore, the media prominence of the Kuoks, together with that of the Lis of Hong Kong, the Liems of Indonesia, and so on, has given ethnic-Chinese minorities in Southeast Asia a new respectability; spurred by the new political tolerance toward Chinese business, even the assimilated are "coming out of the closet" as "Chinese." For instance, with the end of military rule, more and more Sino-Thais are asserting their Chinese origins, and culture in Bangkok has become "more openly Chinese."[39] In visits to Singapore or Hong Kong, ethnic Chinese from ASEAN countries can discard their batik or Thai-silk shirts, drop their indigenous names, and speak Chinese dialects and perform kinship rituals, especially around business banquets. More and more, in cities such as Kuala Lumpur and Bangkok, and in trips back to the mainland, corporate power is stamped with Chinese business practices and rituals.[40]

Even indigenous ASEAN leaders, long suspicious of ethnic-Chinese business, now strategically position themselves as closer to Chinese corporate practices. Malaysian and Singaporean leaders use the category "East Asian" to refer to their own countries, seeking to link their "minidragon" status to the economic boom in China. Malay businessmen are taking up Mandarin to do business and learn from ethnic-Chinese entrepreneurs. Recently, the Malaysian deputy prime minister invoked the Chinese sage Lao Tse to urge "the youth of East Asia" to combine spiritual with material success. He said that they should struggle for both free trade (against Western protectionist policies) and ethical values (against the complacency that comes with affluence).[41] This yoking of free trade with reified Chinese values is one example of attempts by Malaysian leaders to proclaim that theirs is "a noncapitalist market economy" that is founded on the communitarian but flexible relations of the "bamboo network."

Cross-Ethnic and Cross-National Fraternities

What do these images of fraternal capitalism and economic dynasties tell us about the ways elite power sharing is imagined? In postcolonial Southeast Asian nation-states, whether monarchist or republican, discussion of dynastic rule is often tightly controlled, if not banned outright. In Thailand, subjects are forbidden to discuss the power and authority of the monarchy, while in Indonesia and Singapore, the state does not tolerate any commentary about the political and economic privileges of ruling families. In recent years, Lee Kuan Yew has sued foreign scholars and newspapers for writing about alleged nepotism in Singapore's political system.[42] While any discussion of patriarchal political rule is suppressed, there has been an explosion of stories about business dynasties.

Economic dynasties and alliances, not dynastic politics, are the narratives of elite power. Even as stories celebrate the restraint of the merchant princes, they also valorize the extravagance of their corporate networks. As is clear from the above, this fascination with Asian business empires is often fed by Western publications such as the *Far Eastern Economic Review,* which is owned by Dow Jones and Company, the Wall Street firm. In many ways, the family model of Asian capitalism is also a creation of Western media barons and reflects a mix of orientalist fantasy, business instrumentalism, and an American spin on economic opportunities and contacts in Asia. The *Review* has a new series called "Family Ties," devoted to "Asia's family-held business groups." One such story, about a Hong Kong beverage entrepreneur, is subtitled "Grandson of Indentured Servant in Malaysia Epitomizes the Overseas Chinese Success Story."[43] This rags-to-riches story is repeated many times because "probably at no point in history have so many families accumulated so much wealth in a single generation."[44] These stories are an endorsement and a celebration of the transnational expansion of business families beyond their host countries and beyond even the region. More fundamentally, they constitute a regime of truth about the ascent of a new kind of transnational fraternal alliance in the new Southeast Asia. They also note the role of strategic links to officials and the importance of cross-ethnic relations—business partnerships, marriages, kinship relations—in the rise of the new Asian tycoons.

The image of merchant princes has helped legitimize the new moral order of capitalist-state alliances. Although Islamic leaders in Indonesia have for years criticized the links between Chinese bosses (*cukong*) and the Soeharto family, the fortunes of the Indonesian ruling class are intertwined with and dependent on their contacts with Chinese businessmen.[45] Under the cukong system, Chinese bosses bankroll and otherwise support Indonesian politicians in exchange for patronage and protection from excessive attacks on the Chinese. The biggest cukong is Liem Sioe Liong, whose great fortune has been tied to that of President Soeharto's family. Their partnership began during the Second World War, when Soeharto was an army man in the provinces and Liem was a commodities trader and suspected gunrunner.[46] The rise of Soeharto as president and the growth of Liem's Salim Group of companies are intertwined events that have led to many suspicions among the indigenous (*pribumi*) business community. The economic fortunes of the Soeharto family have also expanded as a result of the cukong connection that won the late Madam Hartinah Tien Soeharto the nickname "Mrs. Ten Percent" in reference to commissions she gathered through wielding nepotistic influence. The Soeharto children are partners in many of the Salim Group ventures. While the Soeharto government has suppressed Western press reports about Soeharto family business interests, such cukong arrangements have aided in the rise of many Chinese firms, which, with their ability to attract foreign investments, have led Indonesia's economic resurgence.[47]

Across the water, Malay-Chinese business alliances, called Ali-Baba partnerships,[48] have also been a key to the rise of powerful companies. For instance, one top Malay stockbroker not only has his de rigueur Chinese business partner but also a Chinese wife (Robert Kuok's daughter); in addition, he has access to top Malay government officials.[49] Someone else who participates in an Ali-Baba partnership is Francis Yeoh. Despite being an ethnic-Chinese Christian in a predominantly Muslim, Malay-chauvinist state, he has been called "the master builder of Malaysia [who] thrives with a little help from his friends."[50] Indeed, like virtually every successful corporate heavyweight here, he is a familiar presence in the halls of political power and is an intimate of Prime Minister Mahathir. That symbiosis of political power and entrepreneurial energy is a phenomenon that has spread throughout much of Southeast Asia and helps explain the region's economic dynamism. These stories suggest that fraternal alliances between (Chinese) businessmen and (indigenous) bureaucrats are partnerships that thrive because fraternal business links are meshed with authoritarian political structures.

But in a globalized economy, such business-government fraternizing is not limited to Southeast Asian countries. The overseas-Chinese corporate practice of providing credit and payoffs in exchange for political favors and protection has spread to the United States. Liem's banking partner, Mocthar Riady, was caught up in a recent uproar over giving "soft money" to the Democratic Party (see chapter 6). But precisely because the alliances between Chinese financiers and politicians in Southeast Asia have their limits in attracting capital from overseas, and because Chinese firms have become modern transnational corporations, they are moving beyond their own governments to seek relations with politicians in a number of countries. In transnational business fraternities, governments are resources that can be made to share power through capitalism.

Although indigenous communities in Southeast Asia continue to be suspicious of Chinese traders, their gentrification as merchant princes casts a glow of respectability and modernity onto generals and politicians often suspected of economic incompetence and corruption. The wider acceptance of Chinese business by political elites is reflected in the number of Beijing-bound trade delegations from ASEAN countries that are composed of ethnic-Chinese businessmen. Government-business partnerships are touted in the Malaysian press as the new vehicles for strengthening the national economy through the expansion of transnational contacts that build on Chinese networks. Ethnic Chinese in partnership with state enterprises are viewed as less disloyal, especially if, like Liem, they are careful to invest in their home country while exploring other opportunities abroad.

Another feather in the cap of the Chinese tycoon is his new image as a multicultural leader who is an effective mediator for governments, and not only between, say, Kuala Lumpur or Jakarta and Beijing. As their operations expand overseas, the press celebrates their ideologically indiscriminate flexibility in doing business: "Robert Kuok appears to blend just as easily with Cuban leader Fidel Castro and Chinese Premier Li Peng as he does with Malaysian Prime Minister Datuk Seri Mahathir Mohamad and Indonesian President Soeharto. . . . 'Robert Kuok has funded the entire world,' a Malaysian broker points out. 'He is everyone's friend.' "[51] Overseas-Chinese entrepreneurs are the new heroes, glad-handing world leaders while spreading fraternal friendship and business to any spots that remain resistant to global capitalism.

The Family Romance of the State

The romance of Chinese families is also deployed by academics and government officials to organize popular understanding of political morality. Since the 1980s, states such as Taiwan and Singapore have undertaken Confucianizing campaigns as a way to shape the cultural imagination of citizenship. These discourses allow the state to produce disciplinary knowledges and ideologically align family and state interests along a single moral continuum. In Singapore, an educational campaign was launched to promote religious knowledge and moral education through the systematic introduction of Confucian studies into the school curriculum. This strategy reached beyond the school gates through the promotion of research to support these Confucianizing claims.

In Singapore in 1994, a book on Chinese pioneers in capitalism was published to great fanfare—"They are selling like hotcakes," a scholar told me. Drawing on the life stories of forty-seven Chinese businessmen, *Stepping Out: The Making of Chinese Entrepreneurs* was presented as a collective morality tale of Singapore's success. The authors claimed that these businessmen's Confucian morality had been essential to their capitalist success, which in turn, had contributed to national strength. These rags-to-riches Singaporeans were constructed as paragons of Confucian virtue—self-sacrificing, honest, trustworthy, respectful—who were impelled by a moral ethos of "doing life . . . with others, for others, because of others." These capitalist pioneers were defined as examples of a Singapore Everyman, benevolent patriarchs who treated their business partners and workers "like brothers." The authors claimed that the "Confucian merchant" of contemporary Singapore was formed in a moral order that emphasized trust, confidentiality, and the social control of subordinates.[52] This relentlessly male vision of society—one that traces family genealogies from fathers to sons, who are construed as male-to-male partners—excludes women from the public sphere; women are constructed, almost by omission, as exclusively creatures of the private sphere, who never step out. Sociologist Claire Chiang, one of the authors of *Stepping Out*, seems quite content with this romantic picture she has helped produce. In an interview, she confided that in the course of her research among the business families, "there is no mention of the daughters holding the [reins]. But daughters are often on the cashier's side, holding the purse."[53] This rigid public/private division along gender lines, with female power being relegated to the realm of the domestic budget, conjures up a fantasy about "traditional" Chinese gender roles, in which women remain fixed within the household. The book received the imprimatur of Goh Keng Swee, the architect of Singapore's modern economy, who maintained in a foreword that Singapore's economic affluence is proof that the moral basis of entrepreneurial success in Singapore was "founded on the Confucian ethic" of these male pioneers.[54]

Such a scenario makes public masculinity and private femininity the foundation of state. Indeed, there is a clear attempt to coordinate what I have called "the moral economy of the family" with the moral economy of the state (see chapter 2). For besides constructing the Confucianized family as the backbone of economic development, the state reiterates its policies of strengthening the family by providing guarantees of social security and order.[55] A Singapore official describes Singapore as a capitalist society built upon "socialist" families: "For many East Asian societies, it is not only the family that is socialist, it is the extended family and sometimes the extended clan."[56] The fact that women are an important part of the workforce, that divorce rates are rising, and that government campaigns promoting marriage among the professional elite fail to make a big dent in the number of unmarried women does not deter such profamily claims. On the contrary, it is the very anxiety engendered by such trends that accounts for the twinned ideologies of feminine domesticity and masculine public life.

The romance of the invented Confucian family is an ideological expression of the state's promotion of extended family formation through its housing, educational, and savings schemes.[57] These themes, which integrate the family romance with state policy, are further developed in profamily campaigns that encourage marriage and reproduction among professional women; these women are urged to return home, almost as a patriotic duty, to make babies who are deemed to be of a higher "quality" than those of lower-class women. By providing ideological and institutional supports to families threatened with individualism and fragmentation, the state restores faith that the moral power of Confucian ideology can forge a successful alliance with capitalism so that fraternal power can flourish in the public sphere without the threat of bad mothers undoing gender difference and hierarchy in the home. Geraldine Heng and Janadas Devan have coined the term "state fatherhood" to describe the state engineering of racial demographics, family, gender, and class relations in Singapore.[58]

Working Women's Dreams of Traveling Romance

Thus far, I have discussed how different romances of the Chinese family express messages about fraternal power, interethnic alliances, and the gendered public-private division that betray unifying themes of an emerging political imagination in Southeast Asia, which is grappling with the forces of late capitalism. In what ways do these masculinist imaginaries resonate with the consciousness of working-class women, who, after all, form the bulk of the labor force in Asia? In his study of petit bourgeois and working-class Malaysian Chinese, Don Nonini identifies a dialectic of mobility and location that is highly gendered. He observes that their familial strategies send men overseas for education and work, while women are required to stay at home and care for the remaining family members.[59] How, one may ask, does the family romance resonate with working-class women who also migrate but whose experiences are different from those of traveling men? Do men in charge of mobility represent a kind of symbolic capital working women may identify with? I turn to the experiences of working-class women in south China, a region undergoing major transformations as a result of economic activities by ethnic Chinese from Southeast Asia.

In the fall of 1993, I visited China's most successful special economic zones, which are based in coastal cities such as Shenzhen, Xiamen, Guangzhou (Canton), and Shantou, where tens of thousands of young women from the inland provinces have descended to work in factories that are mainly financed and operated by overseas-Chinese capital. For instance, in Shenzhen, the roaring metropolis of China's future, right across the water from Hong Kong, 80 percent of the investors are Chinese from Hong Kong and the Asia Pacific region. These "Chinese from overseas," who are so vaunted in the mass media, are viewed in an intensely ambivalent way by local women (see chapter 1). In their workaday world, female workers in Shenzhen want to maintain distance from Hong Kong and overseas-Chinese managers, visitors, and businessmen. According to Ching Kwan Lee, young migrant women from the impoverished interior consider overseas Chinese to be outsiders who do not share their culture or appreciate their own very different backgrounds.[60] Furthermore, as Lee's research has shown, overseas managers enjoy enormous discretionary power over the treatment of workers on the shop floor, as well as over their chances of remaining in the cities. Many female workers prefer to be supervised by their own kinsmen or townsfolk who work in the same factory. Indeed, regimes of control based on kinship and localistic ties are pervasive throughout the manufacturing industry, for personalistic relations increase workers' compliance and also lift the burden of direct confrontation from overseas-Chinese bosses. The cultural divide is deepened because female workers feel that their foreign bosses are unable to empathize with their problems and their very limited options in the labor force. There is also the image of overseas-Chinese men as uncontrollable agents of sexual exploitation, now made more flexible and invasive by the flows of capital.

In the Women's Federation (*Funü Lianhehui*) office of Shenzhen, the director told me that Hong Kong and overseas-Chinese men were perceived as good catches by local women, although "their cultural standards are not so high." This was her way of saying that for young women, these men are chiefly attractive because of their money and mobility. "Hong Kong visitors are bad for public morality. There are about ten thousand truck drivers coming into Shenzhen each day, and they contribute to prostitution."[61] The booming mistress trade is sparked by the Hong Kong men's "railroad policy" of keeping a mistress at each stop on their circuit, and there is a "concubine village" near a container-truck border crossing where many Hong Kong men have set up a home away from home, sometimes with children.[62] Some of these women may take second jobs as agents for their patrons' businesses in China. Such practices recall the early days of Chinese sojourning in Southeast Asia, when families were left in different sites in the diaspora. It is one of the many ironies of late capitalism that premodern family forms and female exploitation, which the communist state had largely erased in the cities, are being resurrected.

In the Deng era, the mass-entertainment industry has redefined the passive and self-sacrificing young woman, an icon of the precommunist era, as a cultural ideal. After having viewed *Yearnings,* a phenomenally popular TV series about family upheavals in post-Tiananmen China, Lisa Rofel notes that the family and female self-sacrifice have become new symbols of national unity. She argues that an underlying theme in the melodrama is the emergence of a strong and controlled masculinity that may lead the battered nation into the future.[63] We must note, however, that the urban population in coastal China seems to favor foreign programs beamed from the Star TV satellite network, which has created a whole new trans-Asian public through its bewildering variety of Asian and Western offerings, including MTV, talk shows, movies, and so forth. In Shenzhen, working women watch Hong Kong soap operas for cultural scripts on how to be independent modern women. I visited a beauty parlor set up by three enterprising female migrants in one of the hastily built workers' apartment complexes to serve the increasing demand for personal grooming. While attending to the customers, the hairdressers watched Hong Kong soaps on television and made a running commentary on what they imagined to be women's greater choices and strategies in overseas-Chinese communities. For these young women, who had left their rural villages for the bright city lights and begun the difficult climb toward middle-class status, the lure of capitalism lay in the possibility for self-reliance, not self-sacrifice. They were preoccupied with figuring out strategies and networks for crossing into this brave new world. While young women routinely rely on family, neighbors, and friends to leave their villages and survive in the industrial cities, many are now seeking new relations that are not based on already constituted kinship or social bonds. Among Shenzhen's female working class, most kinship and hometown networks lead straight back to the village; at best, they prove to be only a weak source of coercion and support in the workplace.[64] Women who desire wealth and travel to rich places outside China answer to a different family romance.

For these women, overseas-Chinese men represent a vision of capitalist autonomy and a source of new "network capital."[65] In an interesting reformulation of Pierre Bourdieu's concept of symbolic capital,[66] Siu-lun Wong and Janet Salaff use network capital to mean acquired personal networks based on friendship, school ties, and professional contacts (rather than networks formed from links based on family, family name, and hometown).[67] They argue that the accumulation of network capital has been a critical practice of well-to-do Hong Kongers in their emigration strategies. Working-class women in coastal China are less well positioned to build on professional contacts, but many depend on personal charms to create new personal connections. So even a road-trip Romeo from Hong Kong can be an irresistible catch because he literally and figuratively embodies the guanxi (ideally through marriage) that will lead to the dazzling world of overseas-Chinese capitalism.

Marriage to a traveling man enables one to expand one's accumulation of network capital and can also benefit the members of one's family, who eventually may also emigrate to the capitalist world, where their desires for wealth and personal freedom can be met.

So mobility, wealth, and an imagined metropolitan future, rather than love or class solidarity, account for the lure of family romances. Feelings of regional, cultural, and class differences from overseas-Chinese men may remain, but not sufficiently to deter working women from marrying them to "develop a bridge to leave China," a common expression used by the women I met. One of the three hairdressers I visited was corresponding with a Chinese Canadian and a white American she met in a bar. I later learned that she had begun a courtship with a male cousin who had emigrated to California, and she eventually flew to San Francisco to marry him.[68] Hers was a particularly creative weaving of acquired and created networks in a successful emigration strategy. Another young woman I met, who is considered a classic north China beauty, has a faithful, perfectly respectable Chinese boyfriend who works in the government. This beauty, however, frequents bars; she hopes to meet an overseas-Chinese man who can help her leave China.

That karaoke bars are the sites of mobility and new wealth is apparent from their video equipment and their clientele of foreign businessmen, hustlers, and upwardly mobile women. Indeed, the bar has taken over from the workplace, where worker politics have become too contaminated by Communist Party and capitalist interests to protect the collective interests of workers. Instead, many working women prefer the "state-free" arena of bars and discos to work out individual strategies of eluding economic exploitation, at least of the factory kind. The romance of mobile capitalism, then, conjures up a felicitous brew of imagined personal freedom and wealth, a heady mix that young women imagine traveling men can provide the passports to. This particular conjunction of working women's middle-class dreams and mobile men has reinforced conditions ripe for the masculinist thrust and scope of sexual and class exploitation throughout Asia.

Conclusion

I have traced the different family romances between corporate brothers, state and capital, and men and women that have proliferated in the public cultures of the new Asia. These unifying themes indicate that the family imaginary both expresses and normalizes the tensions between fluidity and rigidity, the public and the private, economic power and political power, exploitation and romance, and domination and subordination. David Harvey notes that the flexible operation of late capitalism is exceptionally creative in its destruction of rigidities. But he has not considered how cultural messages that romanticize mobile capital can also reinforce, ramify, and reinstall various relations of inequality and thus promote a new kind of conformity to flexible accumulation and state authority. Cultural forms labeled Chinese or Confucian in modern state regimes, corporate networks, and individual practices express and shape a political unconscious that construes male corporate power as benevolent, enlightened, and progressive for individuals and for the state. While capitalism has increased female employment at most levels of the labor market, its institutions and family metaphors have also made more mobile, more extensive, and more complex the sexual and class exploitation of women and the working population. The romance of merchant mandarins and the Confucian family defines men to be in charge of both wealth and mobility, while women are localized in domestic situations or workplaces commanded by men. These visions of social and family order resonate with aspirations of different classes and underlie the sense of a distinctive transnational Asian publicness that obscures the divisions of class and gender. Such family romances reinforce the dark secrets of family, nation-state, and global capitalism that promise wealth, security, and escape but deliver exploitation, despair, and entrapment. By stripping off the veil of romance, we reveal that the mobile forces of capitalism, as Joan Vincent has documented and theorized in her life's work, are alternately destructive and creative of the class, ethnic, and gender relations that constitute the very transnational networks that have developed within and alongside global capitalism.

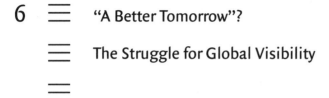

6   "A Better Tomorrow"?

The Struggle for Global Visibility

Anthropologists have used terms such as "mediascapes," diasporas, and "borderzones" to explore cultural forms that spill across the borders of community and country.[1] Here, I wish to discuss the production of transnational spaces that are not so much defined by flows as by the emerging regimes of normativity that engage the state in a variety of ways. In the "informational age"—a world increasingly organized by print, film, and media technology[2]—new fields of power shape social norms by means of circulating images, narratives, and information. Just as capitalist processes structure our political economic orders, representations—in mass media, technical knowledge, and corporate culture—are social facts that play a role in forming our cultural subjectivity.[3] Material and symbolic forms associated with globally emergent groups constitute ethnicized translocal publics that, by restructuring ethnicity across space, have an unsettling effect on political schemes of ethnic difference.

Roland Robertson has argued that for over a century, globalization, in the sense of the structural making of the world as a whole, has been dominated by Euroamerican powers through the spread of capitalism, Western imperialism, and the development of a global media system.[4] The world was viewed in terms of the West vis-à-vis less developed parts of the world, a relationship commonly referred to as the geographical, racial, and conceptual opposition of North and South. With the emergence of the Asia Pacific economic powers, the East-West axis has become salient, but it is still within a Western global image tied to a static notion of white supremacy. The integration of Asian countries into the flow and exchange of information, capital, and cultural communication has engendered ethnicized publics that play a role not only in shaping cultural norms across translocal fields of power but also in negotiating cultural normativities on the global stage, so that "Asian" cultural and economic forms now intrude into "Western" spaces.

The concept of the public has for a long time been thought of as an arena of discourses and exchanges outside state control but bounded by the borders of the nation. I identify three important features of transnational publicness in the informational age.

Publics and Normativities

The informational age explodes Habermas's normative requirements of the public sphere as an arena within which "rational critical discourse" by citizens (sharing capacities for consent and speech) can be conducted to influence state policies and programs.[5] This is an ideal-type situation that has never existed anywhere in practice, even in the Western democracies.[6] In the Asia Pacific region, the increasing dependence of state power on transnational capital and modern media has opened up new spaces for expressing a range of cultural and market interests that often influence state action.[7] By not limiting public-sphere activities to "rational" critiques of the state or those critiques that are "free" of the state's penetrations, my concept of publicness allows us to consider the various regimes of cultural normativity that have different relations to state power.

Publics are nonstate fields of power in which images, information, and practices—now highly mediated by print, electronic, and film media—participate in the production of cultural norms that affect the way we view things and act in our everyday life. By normativity, I mean the structuring of norm making through the circulation of images and discourses about objects, features, and goals associated with particular categories of things and people. For instance, Manuel Castells identifies a managerial public formed in the stratospheric space of global elite networks, where "cultural codes are embedded in the social structure in such a way that the possession of these codes opens the access to the power structure."[8] The attitudes, images, and behavior generated in such a corporate public constitute a particular regime of global normativity that competes with other kinds of translocal publics, as well as with national cultural orders.

Transnational Struggles for Visibility

The public sphere as "a field of discursive connections," in Craig Calhoun's words, is carried by informational technology that provides access to global visibility.[9] John B. Thompson identifies "the space of the visible" as a "non-localized, non-dialogic, open-ended space . . . in which mediated symbolic forms can be expressed and received by a plurality of non-present others."[10] In the informational age, getting strategic information to the global media—TV, film, newsprint, website—is controlled less by politicians than by media and corporate elites who regulate, for instance, the diversity and type of cultural images in "a new galaxy of communication."[11] Media barons and tycoons are the technical agents who are "in charge of" time-space compressions.[12] They are also in charge of "struggles for visibility" to produce alternative images, ideas, and practices associated with transnational culture.[13] In short, emergent publics are not merely an effect of mass media flows but rather translocal fields in which media and corporate networks compete (with each other and with state power) in the production, distribution, and regulation of particular kinds of images, norms, and knowledges across political spaces.

The Systems World and the Lifeworld Conjoined

In his formulation of modern society, Habermas separates the market and material functions from the "lifeworld" of moral and cultural making.[14] Contrary to this picture of highly segregated orders, I consider translocal publics to be communicative networks that vitally reintegrate the systems world and the lifeworld *across* political boundaries. They are arenas where the reorganization of capital, technology, and cities ("postmodernity") and the extreme commodification of culture ("postmodernism")[15] converge, since the technologies of subject making are dependent on the material processes of capitalism. At the same time, if globalization precipitates crises in subjectivity—"all that is solid melts into air"—translocal publics now mediate cultural disorders through the production of normative orders that are often associated with particular categories of people. In the new Asia Pacific, emerging cultural forms both challenge and engage state power and in the process also rework the cultural tensions between "the East and the West."

Obviously, there are a variety of emergent Asian publics, but my focus will be on the new *Chinese* publics popularizing ethnic themes—expressing ambivalence over capitalism, the embodiment of new capitalist power, and the global reach of Asian capital—that are received by diverse audiences. My study of translocal regimes shaping social consciousness is necessarily partial,[16] and in this chapter I will focus more on the production and dissemination of cultural attitudes and norms about "Chineseness" than on the interactive dimensions or the reception of normative messages. Such publics represent a new cultural phenomenon, freed of local moorings, that articulates and problematizes ethnic consciousness in the world at large. I first consider a translocal public based on an overseas-Chinese mass media that plays on the tensions between ethnic-Chinese morality and an Americanized capitalist modernity. This theme of Americanization reemerges in the circulation of ethnic-Chinese professionals and investors as global players within the Asia Pacific region. A third public is formed by the linkages between Asian capital and American political interests. All three types of publicness build on informational technologies that challenge existing borders between corporate and state power, on the one hand, and between Asian and Western cultural differences on the other. The new ethnic norms—media images, corporate figures, and political practices—disrupt and reconfigure as well Western codes of cultural difference.

"Soap Operas without Borders"

The rise of middle-class consumers throughout Asia has greatly expanded the Chinese mass-media world. The economic power of overseas Chinese, as regional capitalists, has migrated into the realm of popular culture. The media public attuned to Chinese-language news and entertainment is vast and growing rapidly on the Internet as well. Craig Calhoun, among others, notes that the international audience of overseas Chinese was "mobilized significantly by the media" to support student protesters in the Tiananmen crisis of 1989.[17] It would be a mistake, however, to limit consideration of public cultures to overtly political documentaries, debates, and events and to ignore noncritical discourses that link the lifeworld and the systems world. The films produced by Shaw Brothers and Golden Harvest and the Hong Kong and Taipei TV programs that are beamed by satellite all over the Asia Pacific region rely mainly on entertainment, not political news, to explore different dimensions of cultural identity. This sense of a broad cultural public that is dependent on TV, films, magazines, and videotapes also attracts diasporan-Chinese communities in the United States.[18] In recent decades, this media-based public has engendered a new collective sense of Chineseness among diverse ethnic Chinese in south China, Hong Kong, Taiwan, Malaysia, Singapore, and elsewhere in Southeast Asia.[19] Ethnic Chinese, like other people, are inhabitants of a diversity of communities and are defined by a plurality of discourses that situate them in different subject positions. The new media visibility of Chinese entrepreneurs, professionals, and entertainers has added another sense of Chinese community that is not place-bound but that in fact disembeds the process of identity making from the local matrix of social relationships. The growth of Chinese media—in Mandarin, Cantonese, and English—reveals that a new translocal identity is defined not so much by language or national origin (one or two Chinas; ethnic Chinese or nationals of China) as by kinship rituals and cultural values that are variously represented in mass media markets.[20] There are the hugely popular kung fu and gangster movies from Hong Kong that are watched by millions of Asians, an audience so vast that Hong Kong kung fu star Jackie Chan is the most popular actor in the world. As Chinese cultural identity becomes destabilized, fragmented, and blurred outside of nationalist definitions, the mass media has become an extremely important realm for reworking subjectivity. I argue that the great appeal of these movies for diasporan-Chinese communities lies not only in their action genre; they are also popular because they are a medium for exploring reified Chinese values (cast through the lens of Hollywood) in conditions of displacement and upheaval under capitalism.

As a genre, kung fu and gangster movies are all about brotherhoods, hierarchized allegiances, and kinship loyalty, which are frequently ways of defending against the authority of the state and uncertainties in society at large.[21] These relations among fictive gang brothers are continually challenged not only by the claims of their families but by their corrupt, greedy, and cruel bosses, whose only loyalty is to capital accumulation. Most of the movies explore the criminal link between Chinese big business and gangsters, but a careful distinction is made between the profit-driven motives of the boss and the moral principles that constrain the behavior of the brothers. In John Woo's movies, for example, the businessman or criminal boss is interested in profits and cutting into somebody else's markets, while the gangsters in his employ ultimately answer to the higher principle of fraternal loyalty. In the hugely popular film trilogy *A Better Tomorrow,* the hero, played by Chow Yun Fat, is a man who holds on to his principles while struggling to survive in a brutal world of gun smugglers, mobsters, and heartless tycoons. Chow has played thieves, gangsters, and outlaw cops in different movies, but these are only ways of surviving in the capitalist world; his integrity as a Chinese man who is profoundly loyal to his brothers is never sacrificed. In *Hard Boiled* (1994), for instance, Chow as Tequila is a diehard cop who will stop at nothing to see justice done in avenging the murder of his partner. The stories usually end with Chow going down in a blaze of gunfire while defending or avenging his younger brother in crime.

Gangs are not "just like families";[22] they are often celebrated as exceeding in loyalty and importance of actual parent-child or conjugal relationships. Gangsters are recruited through an apprentice system in which an older member ("big brother") trains and protects a newcomer ("younger brother") in the arts of fighting, survival, and most important, brotherly love and sacrifice. In the first *A Better Tomorrow* (1986), the Chow protagonist, Mark, tells Ho, his younger partner, that "being a big brother is not something you can learn from a book" but is something that can be learned only from bitter experiences in "our world." The moral of the story, which is woven in and out of a series of violent gun incidents, is Mark's unrelenting sacrifice on behalf of Ho. When Ho is hauled off to jail, Mark takes revenge on their turncoat compatriots and has his legs shot out from under him. In their emotional reunion, Ho says, "Even if I break my legs, I can never repay you." The two men resume their warm friendship, eking out a marginal living rather than returning to criminal activity.

The past, however, has come between Ho and his younger brother Kit, a cop who is still bitterly suspicious of him. Mark and Ho resist attempts to force them back into gang activity because Mark wants Ho to reconcile with Kit. He urges him, "Don't mind me. Pay attention to your brother. You *are* brothers." But gangster brothers prove more loyal than blood brothers. Kit continues to distrust Ho, noting, "I am the cop; he's the thief. We walk on two different paths." To effect a reconciliation between the brothers, Mark tries to help Kit bring in the real criminals. In a fierce shoot-out, Ho and Mark rescue Kit from the mobsters. As Mark lectures Kit on his brother's loyalty to him, he is shot through the head. In a final act of brotherly love, Ho kills the syndicate boss—revenging Mark—*and* turns himself in to the police, thus sacrificing himself so that no suspicion will fall on Kit.

In *A Better Tomorrow III* (1988), the theme of brotherly love is again explored, this time between Mark and his cousin Mun, who are both in love with a female mob leader, Kitty, in wartime Saigon. Kitty is a successful gold smuggler and, like the heroes, a sharpshooter who kills dozens of men without a twinge of regret. She is depicted as a hardheaded survivor in diaspora, unable to love because of the pain of loss. At one point, Kitty and Mark discuss the plight of overseas Chinese, who are forced to "play the game" of making money by crooked means with "rules they do not control." They are subject to attacks and bribes by government agents and are forced to buy their way out of most situations. "Overseas Chinese struggle all their lives to get ahead. . . . If this was our country, we wouldn't have to leave." Kitty shows that she has a heart of gold after all and provides the funds that allow the men's uncle to leave South Vietnam. In Hong Kong the uncle watches on TV the communists, who appeared to be winning the war in Vietnam, and complains, "Why return to Hong Kong when it too will revert to communist rule in twenty-five years?"[23] He does not feel that he has "come home" because his drugstore is still in Saigon. Soon after, the uncle is killed by mobsters who had followed him from Vietnam, and Mark vows to take revenge: "Blood debt must be paid by blood."

This script is meant for overseas-Chinese audiences who resonate to the themes of holding on to family values of unswerving loyalty and revenge despite the upheavals and uncertainties of life in the diaspora. In Chinese gangster movies, the hero is lucky if he survives at all in the course of defending fraternal justice, but he almost never gets the woman. For instance, in *A Better Tomorrow III,* Mark and Mun return to South Vietnam to avenge the death of their uncle, but Kitty is killed in a shoot-out with mobsters. In the final scene, both men escape in the last helicopter out of Saigon, mourning over Kitty; their brotherly bond has been strengthened by their having loved and lost the same woman.

The overall message of the kung fu and gangster movies is that the Chinese values of fraternal solidarity and justice are both vulnerable and vital in the chaotic world of Asian capitalism. By holding on to these values, Chinese culture is all that provides a moral counterweight to the heartlessness of capitalism and the upheavals of diaspora. There is an implicit criticism of capitalism for shredding lives in its relentless pursuit of profits. In contrast, the criminal activities of the heroes are presented as necessary for survival in a difficult world, but they never corrode the sense of brotherly solidarity and fair play. This theme of ambivalence about Asian modernity underlines the need for Chinese men to support each other in a violent world that is parallel to but distinct from that of actual families of women and children.

The diasporan-Chinese subject is a man who is first and foremost a brother to other displaced men, not a citizen of a nation-state, nor even a husband to a wife. Wives and girlfriends stay at home minding their children—and sometimes aged in-laws—while men form relations of intense loyalty with their brothers in the world outside. The rationale of these stories is that social bonds based on kinship must be nurtured outside, and often against, the everyday demands of the family and the legal requirements of the state. The fraternal links and solidarity forged in battles against criminals, authorities, and the world at large build a rational system that is an alternative to the state structure. A political subtext of the Hong Kong gangster film is the way Chinese gangsters and syndicates manage to run circles around British imperialists and their stooges, thus subverting the white man's rule and his economic might. This theme of Chinese prowess in kung fu is also a major reason for the wild popularity of kung fu books by Louis Cha, whose novels have sold almost a hundred million copies in Asia. The plots of his fifteen novels "always involve so-called Barbarians trying to invade the Han lands. They're about how the Han Chinese try to fight back."[24] Similarly, the inescapable message of kung fu movies is that through a mix of native canniness, suffering, and fraternal loyalty, the Chinese will yet turn the tide against imperial domination; this is a theme that resonated especially strongly with Hong Kongers, despite their trepidation over their impending reversion to mainland rule. Fraternal capitalism, and its basic values of trust and justice, form a kind of ethnic moral economy that competes with Western domination.

But are the normalizing messages of these movies purely about Chinese values or are they rather seen through the lens of American Westerns and do they thus echo American frontier themes? It is no secret that John Woo, like film directors the world over, honed his skills by studying American movies and in the process picked up techniques as well as modernist themes. If we do an intertextual analysis of the naming of the protagonists mentioned above, we see stock characters with Western names: Mark, Kit, Kitty, and Tequila.[25]

Western themes include the importance of male bonding for surviving in a lawless world, men fighting for a space in which domesticity is safe, and making a last stand against outsiders and the authorities.[26] These good, old-fashioned American frontier values are transposed or rather merged with representations of ethnic-Chinese fraternal culture, which is seeking to survive but is also willing to sacrifice for a better future for the family. The normalized male subjectivity presented in these movies is one in which the vitality of the Chinese/American survivalist enables a rootless population to fight off wild men, outmaneuver the state, and ride the upheavals of a world without frontiers.

Whereas the American theme is submerged in kung fu movies, the rapid invasion of predominantly American satellite-TV programming has foregrounded cultural hybridity and racial mixing in Asian mass-media culture. By the early 1990s, satellite broadcasting systems had made programs from anywhere in the world available to the entire Asia Pacific region. Hong Kong became the major site for transmitting an English-dominated TV culture that appeals to younger audiences, often encoding and embodying Asian modernity and capitalism in cultural hybridity. Today, MTV Asia—distributed through five separate channels—claims about fifty million viewing households in Asia.[27] The music videos broadcast are mainly mainstream Western pop but contain a rich vein of Mandarin and Cantonese ballads, Hindi movie music, and pop songs from Southeast Asia. When I visited China's coastal cities in the fall of 1993, the names Star TV, MTV, and KTV (karaoke TV) were on the lips of young workers, Chinese yuppies, and even older people. It was a shock for me, an overseas Chinese (with preconceptions about prudish and humorless Chinese TV programs), to view MTV Asia from my hotel room. It was hosted by young, fast-talking, Eurasian disc jockeys who easily slipped in and out of English, Cantonese, and Mandarin.

Broadcasting from Hong Kong, satellite television has created a segmented and diverse audience that has fallen under the oligopolistic control of media moguls. However, as Castells points out, "Each culture and social group has a specific relationship to the media system" and "the widespread practice of 'surfing' . . . introduces the creation by the audience of their own visual mosaics."[28] However, the variety of audience reactions that arise from particularized interactions between media messages and cultural codes from outside the media circuit does not prevent media moguls from trying to shape audience identity to bring it in line with the exigencies of unbridled consumption and state interests.[29] In the age of globalization, media images and messages are customized to fit the sensitivities of affluent postcolonial audiences who are wary of messages suggesting white supremacy.

Star TV, Asia's first satellite television service, beams programs to thirty-eight countries. Audiences from Bahrain to Burma to Beijing all tune into Star TV to watch CNN and *The Bold and the Beautiful*. China recorded an audience for *Falcon Crest* of 450 million.[30] Nevertheless, racially and culturally hybrid figures—Michael Jackson, Whitney Houston, Connie Chung—are the stars of these media systems. In a 1993 interview with *Hemisphere,* the in-flight magazine of United Airlines, former Star TV CEO Richard Li, scion of the Li Ka-shing family of Hong Kong and Vancouver, observes, perhaps tongue in cheek, that Asians have a lot more in common than they have differences. He states that his goal is to decrease cultural misunderstanding among the 2.8 billion people reached by his satellite-TV system. Clearly, he sees his company's role as one of resynthesizing cultural identities and recasting them as something new—a modern "pan-Asian" subject at home anywhere in the continent. By playing Asian pop songs and showcasing multiracial, multilingual TV anchors, Star TV reaches highly diverse cultural and political audiences that range from hill tribes in Nepal to middle-class families in Bangkok to leaders in Beijing. Li asks, "Are we promoting indigenous music? Well, provided it can be pan-Asian, we are. Take a singer like Cristina. She's Thai. But then she's hot. She's also part Chinese and French, and her music is international even though the language is Thai. Again take Cui Jian in China. The language is Mandarin but the music is also very accessible."[31] Audience accessibility is essential to media consumption, but of course it doesn't guarantee acceptance of the message. However, regardless of audience reception, both MTV Asia and Star TV seem to promote images of culturally hybrid Eurasian subjects through their programs.[32]

It was conflict over the local control of cultural messages that caused the rift between MTV Asia (owned by MTV News of Viacom Inc.) and Star TV (acquired by Rupert Murdoch from the Li family in 1994).[33] To compete with MTV Asia, Murdoch introduced Channel 5 with two new signals, one in Mandarin, the other in Hindi; both used videos by top Western performers but were increasingly Asian in content. Together with Star TV's English-language channel, these two new signals were expected to provide twenty-four-hour video service to an estimated 42 million households across Asia and the Middle East.[34] A Star TV executive noted, "When will [MTV Asia] realize that you can't run programming for Asia, or other regions for that matter, out of an office in Manhattan?"[35] Local distribution has given Murdoch and his Hong Kong media moguls a major role in the casting—through Star TV, its MTV programs, and karaoke lip-synching performances—of mixed-race subjects, who come to represent a kind of transnational Asian modernity. Furthermore, Murdoch has been so ferocious in gaining control of the vast Asian markets that he has even adjusted his TV content to accord with the wishes of local governments. He agreed for Star TV to drop its BBC news segment after Chinese officials objected to its "biased" reports. The images distributed by Star TV, while culturally diverse and hybridized, seem to configure a de-politicized consumerist modernity that treats Asia as a rijsttafel of cultures, languages, and ethnicities and avoids issues of political difference.

The entertaining excursions through Asian modernity are highly gendered—in the production of desirable objects and in attracting a pan-Asian male gaze. Who better to represent modern Asian multiculturalism than Eurasian females, those doubly liminal figures in the Asia Pacific region who are at once stigmatized for their racial ambiguity (exoticism) and are yet valorized as Westernized subjects (in build, looks, and cultural practice)? Certainly they are viewed as more accessible to Asians than white women, for whom their images operate as a stand-in.[36] On MTV and Star TV advertisements, the Eurasian woman is a figure of desire for the transnational Chinese male subject, whose travels and new affluence have stirred hopes for cross-racial encounters. The conjurers of such mobile masculine fantasies are Chinese venture capitalists such as Richard Li, who, as noted above, was interviewed in 1993 by the in-flight magazine of United Airlines, which was seeking more routes to Asia. Li, then only twenty-three, represents the new cosmopolitan Asian: "I've lived exactly 50 percent of my time here [in Hong Kong], and 50 percent in North America. . . . Do I feel Westernized? Well, Hong Kong has always been a very international city. I mean, I would feel as comfortable living in Shanghai, Los Angeles, London, or Zurich. . . ."[37] Familiarity with global financial centers requires a culturally flexible corporate subject. More cross-culturally nimble than the Japanese, who also control an extensive media empire that is studded with Eurasian subjects (who are seen as both ideal and comic figures by the domestic audience), ethnic-Chinese media barons have reached a vaster, more diverse Asian audience through a galaxy of satellites.[38]

The Chinese audiences of MTV Asia and Star TV are merely the most visible of translocal spheres presided over by other ethnicized elites in Asia. The Indian cinema (emanating from "Bollywood," in Bombay, and from alternative filmmakers) deploys iconic images associated with the moral dilemmas of upwardly mobile families, the rural and urban poor, and ethnic conflicts.[39] The lively Malay film and TV industries normalize images of modern subjectivities associated with a moderate Islam that can coexist with globalization.[40] By raiding Asia's rich and diverse cultural treasures, the media public emanating from Singapore seems to lay claim to a neo-Confucian "sinic" modernity that is sometimes a "(self-) parodic incorporation of the 'authentic.' "[41] The Hong Kong–centered media public discussed above appears less ironic in its production of cultural codes and more frantically multicultural in its normalizing images and messages. Despite the imagery of cultural hybridity and racial mixing, the overall framing of messages suggests that the identity at stake is that of an Americanized Asian subject who is under twenty-five, watches MTV, wears jeans, owns a car, wields a wireless phone, and haunts shopping malls. An American economist calls these new consumers "a global MTV generation. They prefer Coke to tea, Nikes to sandals, Chicken McNuggets to rice, credit cards to cash."[42] Fusing Oriental mystique and Western style, the mass-media public then recasts modern Chineseness as a cultural half-breed—the Asian postmodern subject who will bring home the trophy. These normalized images suggest the ethnic power of an ascendant capitalist group in negotiating and bridging the political, cultural, and economic ruptures of Asian modernity.

The Global Arrival of Asian Professionals

The struggle of elite Chinese subjects for global visibility can also be traced on two other fronts: their emergence as a new class of professionals in transnational corporations and their new prestige as world-class corporate movers and shakers. In these economic spheres, normativity is not merely generated through the profusion of certain images but also depends on the "realizing" of certain rules that target, shape, or regulate conduct in practice.[43] Such practical normativities in corporate behavior are the effects of the globalization of the service and capital markets. Thus, a new category of Western-educated ethnic-Chinese professional has emerged in the service of American, European, and Japanese corporations operating within the Asia Pacific region. The *Wall Street Journal* notes that "for the multinationals, the ethnic Chinese are invaluable as intermediaries who can guide them through Asia's sometimes treacherous business landscape and help build bridges to new markets—especially mainland China."[44] These corporate professionals embody the normative ideals of flexibility in an informational age—in the sense of being both *technically* adaptable to a variety of forms, functions, skills, and situations and *culturally* adaptable to a variety of countries in Asia and in the West.[45] American companies in Asia consider ethnic-Chinese employees as "the kind of smart, flexible work force extolled by [former] U.S. Labor Secretary Robert Reich."[46] An American executive based in Penang, Malaysia, a major site of electronic manufacturing in Asia, says this about ethnic Chinese: "In some ways, they're more like Americans in that they live to work."[47] A local manager of Motorola claims that with ethnic-Chinese employees, "we are perfectly positioned to penetrate low-wage areas elsewhere in Asia, and especially China."[48] He is, of course, not just talking about their technical skills but referring to their multicultural knowledges that make them so "American" to Western companies and yet culturally attuned to practices in different Asian countries.

Penang is the world's largest producer of disk drives for companies such as Hewlett-Packard, Seagate Technology, Quantum Corp., and Kamag USA. It is also a center for training Asian white-collar workers for Western companies operating in the region. As high-tech firms replace Western professionals with local ones, ethnic Chinese occupy all managing-director positions not taken by the dwindling expatriate staff, and they also fill many other top positions. Besides representing a savings cost for American companies, these professionals can be easily routed to any site in the Asia Pacific region and still operate at a level required by their American companies. While training is not limited to ethnic-Chinese professionals, the latter have come to represent the regional class that embodies the professional practices and standards required by Western companies operating in the Asia Pacific region.

A Chinese employee of the Hewlett-Packard subsidiary in Penang was recently featured in the *Wall Street Journal* for inventing an electronic device that won him companywide fame: "Thirtysomething and single, he lives a life similar to those of many American professionals: He works long hours, dresses casually, and relaxes by jogging and scuba diving."[49] At the same time, these Asian professionals are cultural intermediaries between Western managers and the vast cheap labor markets these managers are seeking in more and more Asian countries. The world's largest supplier of brand-name apparel, Levi Strauss & Co., depends on Asian professionals to oversee its roughly seven hundred contract factories in south and Southeast Asia.[50] Many of the factory operators are ethnic Chinese or Koreans, and Levi Strauss deploys Singaporean and Malaysian Chinese, who tend to be multilingual and familiar with regional customs, to be health and labor inspectors.[51] In short, these professionals represent the Asian version of the globe-trotting American executive class, only they are much cheaper and probably more effective in Asian markets.

Groomed as symbols of the new Asian professionalism, ethnic-Chinese personnel thus chafe at company practices that define their expertise as American-like but still position them "downstream" from Western corporate standards. Some have won accolades for designing more efficient electronics products, and they have been made heads of international divisions, with authority over Asian and American workers. Such recognition for a few has not, however, been enough to mitigate a sense of ethnic and racial discrimination by Western employers. Hewlett-Packard engineers told me that tensions have arisen because Chinese employees in the Malaysian plant feel that they understand the products they manufacture and the Asian markets much better than Americans at company headquarters in Boise, Idaho. Charging their American bosses with having an unwarranted sense of cultural superiority, they constantly negotiate to have more of the designing work and pilot lines shifted to the Malaysian site.

Whereas American firms have standardized the performances of their Asian employees, this standardization cannot easily be translated into the kind of corporate recognition and prestige enjoyed by "real" American employees. Thus, mounting ethnic pride minimizes the workers' identification with American capital and stresses instead their embodiment of globally competitive standards. These Asian professionals see themselves as a highly mobile professional class that hops from job to job and company to company globally and bargains for the salaries, training, and other perks formerly associated with Western expatriate workers. Thousands of Chinese from Hong Kong, Taiwan, Singapore, and Malaysia form an expatriate professional class who are training mainland Chinese in all kinds of industries ranging from hotel management to running the stock market in Shanghai. They are introducing a kind of corporate normativity to Chinese capitalism that mixes the professional flexibility favored by Western companies with the Chinese emphasis on networking and guanxi. The proliferation of such corporate norms among mainland-Chinese professionals has made them into competitors with overseas Chinese working for foreign firms in China. Although new kinds of Asian professionalism are also developing in South Korea and India (not to mention the *salaryman* culture in Japan),[52] ethnic-Chinese professional and managerial classes now represent corporate governmentality (techniques and procedures for governing conduct) in many parts of Southeast and East Asia.

On a more elevated level, the rise of Asian industrial moguls—some of whom are now ranked among the world's top ten billionaires[53]—has resulted in attempts to develop their images as savvy global managers and cultural connoisseurs. For example, the imprint of Hong Kong developer Li Kashing can be seen outside Hong Kong—in the renovated Vancouver downtown, in a huge mall in Beijing, and in redevelopment plans for a San Francisco island. On a bigger scale, Thai Chinese businessman Sumet Jiaravanon, the head of a vast empire, the C.P. Group, is the largest foreign investor in China. C.P. Group industries—chicken feed, motorcycles, petroleum, and telecommunications—can be found from Harbin to Hong Kong, from Indonesia to Turkey.[54] No longer content to be regarded as faceless, colorless global players, Asian tycoons demand to be treated as equals by Western companies. Malaysian developer Francis Yeoh became famous in the corporate world for two acts that took place when he sought help for building two huge power plants in Malaysia. First, after having been snubbed by the director of the U.S. company General Electric, he awarded a multimillion-dollar contract to Siemens A.G. of Germany.[55] Second, by refusing to give in to discriminatory terms set by Western investment banks, he raised one billion dollars for Malaysian institutions.[56]

Francis Yeoh has claimed global media attention in other ways. In 1994, he celebrated the opening of a Pangkor Island resort by throwing a world-class party. Malay sultans, ministers from Asian countries, and Asian multimillionaires and socialites, as well as the former lord mayor of London, were among his guests. For the evening entertainment, a stage was specially constructed over tennis courts. When the curtain parted, Luciano Pavarotti strode on stage clutching his signature handkerchief. As the guests roared their welcome, Yeoh was reported to have said, "This for me is a dream: to have Pavarotti here, in Malaysia." Yeoh's dream probably had little to do with the tenor's accessibility to the Malaysian public and everything to do with the visibility of overseas Chinese who are able to command world-class performances. He refused to divulge what it had cost him: "I cannot reduce this event to monetary terms. It's priceless."[57]

The cultural capital was incalculable because among transnational publics, visibility is everything, and it can now be shaped by Asian elites. The pinched face of Chinese capitalism exploded with the lightbulbs of celebrity, and when it recomposed itself, it had gained the high gloss of the international jet set, while Malay sultans and British aristocrats were momentarily bathed in the glow cast by Chinese corporate power.[58] This is an instance of what Stuart Hall calls, in a quite different context, the process of "imaginary political re-identification, reterritorialization, and re-identification" with state power,[59] since the staging of the metropolitan ambitions of Chinese capital is also a way for reconnecting with political elites from different places.

The Asian Face of Globalization

The influx of Pacific Rim capital to the West, which reverses the flow of U.S.-generated capital to the Asia Pacific region, has, however, induced anxiety and ambivalence in the social imaginaries of the Euroamerican world. The arrival of the Asian new rich radically challenges the depoliticized view of globalization as the McDonaldization of the world. Accustomed as we are to the domination of American corporate interests in the world at large, the Asian investments in Western cities have shaken up Western assumptions about the link between race and capitalism, as well as notions about white global supremacy. For instance, alongside Arab acquisition of leading department stores, Asian capital has bought up British institutions such as the Churchill and Gloucester Hotel, and it has funded Asian art wings at the Victoria and Albert Museum and the British Museum. Britain has long been accustomed to rich folk from Hong Kong and India, and it has adjusted to the reality of Asian capital infusions more easily than other European countries, which already fear a ceding of parts of their sovereignty to the European Union. Recently, public anger was expressed in France at the proposed sale of the state-owned

Thomson Multimedia consumer electronics company to Daewoo of South Korea. Nationalist leaders such as Jean-Marie Le Pen ascribed this transnational buyout to ruthless "Korean" methods.[60]

Similarly, while the United States prides itself on being more predisposed to global markets, accepting calmly the acquisition of the phone company MCI by British Telecom, the arrival of Asian capital has induced anxiety about the random effects of globalization. In the 1980s, when Japanese corporate interests installed themselves in the Rockefeller Center, in downtown Los Angeles, in Hollywood, in the Seattle Mariners, and in automobile plants in the south, a huge outcry went up over the Asian "takeover" not only of American real estate but also of Western icons. When Japanese executives bought Van Gogh's *Sunflowers* it was the last straw, and there were dark warnings about the United States becoming a "techno-colony" of Tokyo.[61] But by and large, Japanese investments and influence buying in Washington, D.C., were not accompanied by Japanese bodies. The current influx of the Asian rich along with their capital has created an ambivalence among longtime residents. A recent poll reveals that more than 80 percent of the Americans surveyed admired Asian Americans for "placing a high value on intellectual and professional achievement" and for having "strong family ties." But the model-minority image is becoming cloudy because almost half of the Hispanics and African Americans polled considered Asian Americans "unscrupulous, crafty, and devious in business."[62] Recent media stories about East Asian immigration highlight the violence, the illegality, and the exploitativeness of Asian businessmen as represented by Chinese labor smugglers. Reporting about Korean vigilantes in the Los Angeles uprising further compounds the negative image.[63] The ambivalent political-moral image of Asian Americans is now being further confused by rich Asian newcomers whose insertion into American society has not followed the orderly ethnic succession beloved of the American national ideology. Instead of coming in at the social basement level and working their way up through the second generation, affluent Asian immigrants plug directly into the upper reaches of American society and thus have an unsettling effect on middle-class whites as well.

Asian American leaders attempt to fend off negative cultural perceptions by recasting professional newcomers from Taiwan and Hong Kong as people skilled in networking, in making flexible accommodations, and in bridge building across cultural divides and national borders. They also seek to upgrade the profile of Asian Americans in general by influencing politicians. Working behind the scenes to influence public perceptions of the new Asian immigrants are lobbying groups such as the Asian Pacific Leadership Council (APLC). Formed in Los Angeles by immigrant Chinese investors, business owners, lawyers, and other professionals, the APLC seeks to flex the political muscle of the Asian American community by linking it to Pacific Rim capital. These newcomer professionals are mainly in their thirties and forties, are Western educated, and are "big money hitters," with personal ties to Hong Kong, Taiwan, and Indonesia. They represent themselves as enlightened corporate strategists who are redefining the multicultural economy and future of California. Through the late 1980s and early 1990s, they contributed generously to politicians running for office and to members of Congress. I interviewed one of the leaders, an attorney, who said, "We Asian immigrants want more political access, using money to make a voice for ourselves as a group."[64] The APLC is regularly consulted by the California state government about Pacific Rim capital and immigration issues, and it has helped educate state officials about international trade by bringing them to Asia.

A political goal of these transnational yuppies is to provide money to increase the overall representation of Asian American interests. The attorney I interviewed claims that before the APLC was formed, Asian Americans never had the money to contribute to political campaigns in all fifty states. Now, APLC members have met with national leaders such as Senators Edward Kennedy and Alan Simpson and have hosted gatherings where U.S. congressmen (described by the attorney as "dripping saliva") meet big Asian players.[65] The APLC's strategy is not to align itself with either the Democrats or the Republicans: "We don't sink or swim with a single party." Rather, they swim with whoever gets to them first in terms of seeking campaign contributions: "We're new, we want to have friends and impact."[66] Modeling itself on Jewish American interest groups that are both respected and feared for their massive contributions, the APLC hopes to raise the kinds of funds from businesses that will impress politicians. Indeed, by the early 1990s, Asian American contributions to political campaigns were second only to Jewish American contributions.

But the APLC takes care not to fall into the "fat-cat model" of favoring issues that affect only the rich. Connections are maintained with other Asian American groups to raise the overall political effectiveness of the minority community. However, it is clear that the Asian immigrant entrepreneurs see themselves as playing a high-stakes role in hobnobbing with corporate and political leaders and influencing policies; they leave grassroots work to the older Asian American groups. APLC leaders see themselves as a younger, richer, and more experienced group that is a big brother to homegrown Asian American groups. "Foreign-born Chinese are more assertive and have more confidence than Asian Americans," says the attorney I interviewed. He boasts, "What works is who you have contacts with and the message 'Okay, I'm really trying to be American now.' "[67] Being "American now" means playing the "diversity" card. "With American politicians, we always say we're Asian [rather than Chinese]," says the attorney. He says he tells people that as a group, Asians will "enrich the state [of California] as a whole."[68]

Here, the new Asian immigrant, following the Jewish American model of accession to great economic and social heights, stumbles because he does not know the lessons longtime Asian Americans have learned so well. Whereas Jewish Americans have, by the late twentieth century, blended into the white ethno-racial American landscape,[69] it remains unclear whether Asian Americans can become similarly "whitened," since Asians are not generally viewed as possessing the "race privilege" that can convert economic capital into greater cultural legitimacy.[70] In the American race-based tradition, the processes whereby immigrant groups can, over time, convert economic resources into cultural prestige are determined by their possession of the "vital" attributes of whiteness and European origin associated with mainstream cultural normativity.[71] As Brackette Williams has argued, nonwhite populations may accede to positions of greater socioeconomic success but not necessarily greater social legitimacy.[72] Furthermore, the quest for acceptance by groups ethnicized as Asian Americans is handicapped by the public's failure to distinguish between American Asians and foreign Asians. It is also clear that with the continuous influx of Asian immigrants, and with ongoing transpacific ties, Asian Americans themselves seldom make that distinction. Certainly, the fact that most of the APLC's members are simply residents and not citizens does not prevent them from seeking to influence politicians. The recent uproar over illegal Asian contributions to the Democratic National Committee reflects America's deep ambivalence about whether Asians or Asian Americans can ever be morally distinguished or ever become "legitimate" Americans.

Many of the charges as to whether "the Asian connection" (a rather far-flung net that links subjects from Indonesia to Taiwan to Hong Kong to

Thailand to China) sought to influence American foreign policy suggest a fear that transnational Asian networks threaten the American moral order. This threat is expressed as a moral threat because the operations of flexible accumulation are said to be irreducibly Asian in nature and to have nothing in common with Western practices. Thus when *New York Times* columnist William Safire talks about Asian "tin pot dictators" and "Asian cronyism,"[73] he wishes to make essential certain corporate practices as having inherently Asian qualities; this kindles American anxieties about Asians introducing their corrupt practices into the democratic heartland. Obviously an informed newsman, Safire fails to make the link between the "Asian connection" in American political life and what may be called the American "tradition" of intervening in the politics of many nation-states. Months after the furor over Asian influence buying first broke out, the *New York Times* got around to mentioning that the American government itself has bought influence in over one hundred countries since the Second World War.[74]

Indeed, when, in 1997, fingers were pointed at illegal campaign contributions by Indonesian Lippo Group executive James T. Riady and his former employee John Huang, Indonesians must have been amazed at the double standard of American political morality. An anthropologist just back from Jogjakarta, Robin Madrid, reported that college students there could not believe the self-righteous tone of the American uproar, considering the decades of American intervention into their country's affairs.[75] After all, under President Eisenhower, the United States, guided by the CIA's flawed intelligence, intervened in the Indonesian civil war—with the unintended result of strengthening Indonesia's army and its presidency while destroying parliamentary democracy. There is also strong evidence that the United States shipped arms to Muslim youth groups who took part in the massacre of communist suspects after the abortive Untung "coup" of 1965.[76] Currently, President Soeharto's repressive New Order in Indonesia receives strong support from the American government and has benefited from a huge influx of American investments.[77]

Under Soeharto's patronage, ethnic Chinese such as Liem Sioe Liong and Mocthar Riady have amassed huge business conglomerates. As a hated minority who are said to monopolize business, ethnic Chinese find that they cannot do business without the political patronage and protection of government officials. Liem and his Salim Group have bankrolled Soeharto and his family for years. Other powerful conglomerates include Mocthar Riady's Lippo Group; Riady is Liem's banking partner. Many Americans first heard of the Lippo Group when it was learned that Mocthar's son James had contributed half a million dollars to the 1996 Democratic presidential campaign, the first in the chain of revelations about illegal campaign contributions by overseas Chinese. For ethnic-Chinese capitalists such as Riady, and for his counterparts in Southeast Asia such as Thailand's Dhanin Chearvanont of the C.P. Group, seeking an invitation to the White House is merely an extension of their practice of seeking politicians' help to safeguard conditions for doing business in Asian capitals.

But Southeast Asians cannot claim a monopoly on such bureaucratic-corporate cronyism since for decades, American corporations have been buying "face-time" and influence on Capitol Hill and in capitals around the world.[78] Contrary to media representations of corporate-official alliances as exclusively Asian arrangements, these alliances have become normalized practices in the era of globalization, when flexible economic accumulation is coupled with the flexible accumulation of political favors in the world's capitals, especially Washington, D.C. Yet Americans assume that the United States can intervene massively in the politics of another country (Indonesia is no banana republic, but the fourth largest country in the world) and still express moral outrage over the suspected influence of Asian money on their own government. It appears that the essentialization of transnational corporate influence buying as an *Asian* practice allows American commentators to differentiate between American political or military interventions abroad and what they consider a moral-political invasion of the United States by crafty Asians. While the Asian campaign-contribution controversy poses the larger question of "where does their (Asian) capital end and our (American) political interests begin" in a globalized world,[79] self-righteous Americans appear to be worried about a moral contamination by Asians of the heart of American political culture.

The Orient, long regarded as exotic and backward, has again suddenly become a menacing presence in our midst.[80] The anti-Asian mood generated by the campaign scandal is a symptom of a larger refusal to accept the conditions produced by globalization, specifically, the shifting ethnic coordinates of global power, as well as the complex ways that capital, bodies, and cultures now penetrate the other's space. Globalization upsets the global moral hierarchy associated with the West civilizing the other. For much of the past century, American military campaigns and adventures in the Asia Pacific region have been portrayed as civilizational missions to uplift the natives (the Philippines), to beat back fascism (Japan), and to struggle against amoral communists (Korea, Vietnam, and China); all were said to have occurred in the name of spreading enlightenment and democracy. Whereas European corporate elites have long sought to buy power in Washington, D.C., Asian individuals such as John Huang and James Riady embody an unwelcome Asian moral contamination of our Western space of civilization.

No longer confined to the borderzones of managed cultural encounters, powerful Asian subjects now circulate in the stratosphere of Western society. Asian subjects appear to have escaped their localization in the American moral order, thus breaching the spatial and symbolic borders that confine them as a model minority. By moving "out of place," affluent Asian newcomers upset the ethno-racial hierarchy that has disciplined Asian Americans as a docile minority. The flexible capitalist operations embodied by Asian investors challenge the stability of the American ethno-racial hierarchy; the replacement of Chinese laundry and garment workers by Pacific Rim executives in cities such as Monterey Park has been startling to American whites. The public uproar over the Asian role in campaign funding registers not merely outrage at illegal contributions but also anxiety about the American city as a space that is overexposed to Asian capital and influence. Instead of being confined to Chinatowns, Asian American capital and cultural norms have reconfigured American cityscapes to such a degree that native whites feel displaced from their symbolic and material domination of public life.[81] The anti-Asian backlash is swept up in a wider panicked state around the economic and cultural implications of globalization, which foreshadow the decline of white supremacy in the Asia Pacific region.

Thus, the ineffable sense of cultural exclusion that haunts Asian Americans is always reinforced whenever the American public feels morally invaded by foreign Asians. Fearing, in Wang Ling-chi's words, "the restoration of Asian Americans as foreigners,"[82] Asian Americans seek to distance themselves from influence-buying foreign Asians. Their leaders protest that they are good citizens, insisting that "our concerns about health, education, immigration, voting and housing" are distinct from the influence buying of globe-trotting Asian yuppies.[83] But by taking a defensive posture in being "real" Americans, they unwittingly reinforce the public perception of Asian Americans as "foreigners within." By insisting that Asian Americans are "good natives" in contrast to "corrupt" foreign Asians, this strategy fails to save Asian Americans from taking the heat for the campaign contribution controversy. It reinforces the ever present disciplinary mechanism that regulates Asian American political subjectivity as one that is always precariously balanced on the thin line between patriotism and betrayal. As the World War II incarceration of Japanese Americans clearly demonstrated, American political culture in times of crisis views Asian Americans as identical to Asians. Asian American identity is always vulnerable to accusations by white supremacist groups such as the militia movement, who complain of the "anti-American" activity of the federal government in robbing them of their land with the help of "foreign capital."[84] The vital rationalities of nation and race in America are such that whiteness controls the terms of governmentality and the disciplining of ethnically marked subjects, regardless of their citizenship status. They continue an old tradition that has construed Asians variously as "foreign labor," "foreign enemies," and now "foreign capital."

The strategy of Asian Americans to distance themselves from the new Asian transnational publics, although logical within American racial politics, nevertheless discloses an ongoing political vulnerability that merely reifies the ethno-racial divide between Asian Americans and white Americans while studiously ignoring the objective reality that a majority of Asian Americans are now linked to transnational family networks.[85] By defending themselves as *Asian* Americans, an ethno-racial category, rather than as American citizens with universal political claims as members of the nation, Asian Americans continue to be trapped by an American ideology that limits the moral claims to social legitimacy of nonwhites. Indeed, even as the crosscurrents of global capital and migration blur the economic and social boundaries between Asia and North America, white anxiety seeks to reinscribe an East-West normativity and to reinstate the moral division between Asian and white American citizens. Ethnicized translocal publics—based on Chinese capitalist transnationalism in the Asia Pacific region—have unexpectedly engendered in mainstream American society not more ease with an upscale multiculturalism but rather a newly ethnicized sense of whiteness under siege in the world at large.

Conclusion

The information age has facilitated the rise of translocal publics from non-Western sites of power; cultural normativities associated with ways of being transnational Chinese vie for a new visibility on the global stage. The three publics discussed above are produced and sustained by ethnic-Chinese technical and corporate agents all promoting regimes of Americanoid images, attitudes, and practices in consumption, business, and transnationality that intrude into spaces of Western cultural normativities based on white supremacy. The visibility of Asians as global movers and shakers, however, becomes a specter that triggers a crisis in American public consciousness and challenges the hegemonic link between whiteness and global capitalism. Streaming into the United States, transnational Asian publics have had, ironically, the effect of reinstituting an East-West divide.

But the growth of the transnational public sphere does not always incite an adversarial response from the body politic. These zones of new normativities do not *necessarily* or *directly* offset state power, whether Asian authoritarianism or Western democracy. These publics beyond the state build on the logics of globalization and the information technologies and thus have a more complex relationship to state regimes than those confined within political borders. The circulating images, information, and capital, which alternatively express the mass consumption, ambivalence, and global reach of Chinese subjects, constitute a challenge to national ethno-racial orders, but they can also work very well with state authorities in Asia. Transnational ethnic publics increasingly invoke cross-cultural skills, wealth, and access to state power as ways to engage—in geostrategic fashion—the states that count. Never in simple antagonistic relation to state interests, the publics discussed above operate parallel to state structures, producing translocal cultural forms that crosscut, negotiate, and/or destabilize the moral orders of nations. They thus undermine an older global consciousness about East-West divisions and the inevitability of white supremacy.

PART 4

Global Futures

China as Evil Empire

In Giacomo Puccini's opera *Turandot*, the beautiful but cruel Chinese princess has her unsuccessful suitors beheaded and their gruesome momentos displayed around "Peking." Much blood flows as suitor after suitor fails to solve the three riddles that are the keys to her heart. Coming from the West, the Prince of Persia, Calaf, answers the three questions and wins not only the princess's hand but her love as well. To Calaf's cries of "You are mine! Mine!" the icy Turandot breaks down:

> In your eyes shone
> the light of heroes.
> In your eyes I saw
> the proud certainty of victory . . .
> and I hated you for it . . .
> and for it I loved you,
> torn and divided
> between two equal fears:
> to conquer you or be myself conquered . . .
> and I am conquered . . . Ah![1]

China is an evil empire to be conquered by the transformative moral power of the West.[2] When I was a student in New York, I was intrigued by the popularity of two operas with Asian themes, *Turandot* and *Madam Butterfly*.[3] A true opera lover does not, of course, take the story lines literally; these are, after all, vehicles for expressing universal themes of love, tragedy, and transcendence.[4] As icons of Western civilization, they are loved by the Lincoln Plaza crowd and beamed on TV to highbrow audiences throughout the country. But the themes bothered me, a student from Asia, for all kinds of obvious reasons. I felt that on some subliminal level these operas must inform or resonate with worldly New Yorkers' attitudes toward "the Orient." The world has changed, Pacific Rim countries are rising, but the great popularity of both operas seems to resonate with a persistent view about one civilization asserting its power over another. One can hardly fail to notice the hierarchical and gendered relationship between the West and the two Asian countries depicted in these operas. Though conquered by love of the West, Turandot is more powerful than Butterfly; a princess and her kingdom are not as easily subjugated as a geisha isolated in her home. Turandot is cruel and complex, whereas Butterfly is sweet and innocent.[5] Ancient China was powerful; early modern Japan, weak vis-à-vis the West. Sooner or later, Asian women get invited by American dates, despite their Vietnam-era angst, to see these operas (or, God forbid, *The Mikado*) as harmless fantasies about the East.[6] But the clashing cymbals/symbols of cross-cultural encounters prevent me from enjoying the operas as just sublime music. There is such a thing as post-Puccini blues.

It is an irony that in an era of globalization, we are once again revisiting Oriental and Occidental societies as rival cultural regimes. Samuel Huntington's "clash-of-civilizations" thesis declares that the dominant form of post–cold war tension will be neither ideological nor economic but cultural, as emergent non-Western powers "join the West as movers and shapers of history."[7] Huntington's scenario has cast a spell in Washington, where China is perceived as the biggest "rival civilization."[8] An unlikely coalition has formed between Republican conservatives fearful of China's military threats to Hong Kong and Taiwan and human-rights activists concerned about the Chinese treatment of dissidents at home and in Tibet. They are joined by another group that is worried about China, as the new Asian powerhouse, replaying the Japanese threat of the 1980s through buying economic and political influence.[9] The campaign against China as an evil empire has stirred up foreign-relations experts, journalists, and lobbyists to such a degree that the result may be actual conflict, rather than the kind of global coexistence that Huntington ultimately calls for.[10] Such are the uncertain powers of academics to shape an understanding of the world.[11]

In Asia, Huntington's thesis has stimulated responses from members of the political elite who are both influenced and frustrated by the West's attempts to understand emergent Asia Pacific nations. It is reported to be popular among the leaders of the People's Liberation Army, whose paranoid antagonism toward the West may very well have been stoked. The responses from Southeast Asian leaders, however, have been more sophisticated. While they reject the view that a collision between East and West is inevitable, they use the occasion to critique the West, and they deploy the orientalist assumptions in Huntington's model to their own advantage—both in administering their subjects and in forming multilateral alliances.

In this chapter, I will first expose the orientalist binary thinking in Huntington's global sociology. The next section challenges Huntington's claims that Western values are absent in Asia, where societies are fundamentally shaped by "indigenous values." I argue that liberalism—a key legacy of post-Enlightenment thought—is a pervasive influence in the government of some Asian democracies. Taking liberalism as a practical rationality (rather than as a political philosophy), I will identify regulatory strategies that treat society as an object of government, so that state-designed cultural forms shape attitudes and behavior that is adjusted to liberal economic competition. My goal is to show that while both Huntington and certain Asian leaders give voice to this discourse of civilizational differences, a logic of economic liberalism underlies both. In the process, I merely suggest but do not engage in a historical interpretation of how the supersession of one form of liberalism by another, in each setting, has taken place.

Huntington's Taxonomy: Revisiting Orientalism

The clash of civilizations is a post-modernization theory that sees not a convergence of countries in the process of modernization but rather divergences caused by profound cultural differences. During the cold war, U.S. foreign policies were informed by a teleological scheme that envisioned only two paths of development, which culminated either in communism or Western capitalist modernization. William W. Rostow's *Stages of Economic Growth: A Non-Communist Manifesto* placed faith in the global spread of capitalism as the engine that would diffuse Western values of rationality, progress, and liberty.[12] But in the aftermath of the fall of communism in Eastern Europe and Russia, and the apparent global triumph of American-style capitalism, Huntington's thesis insists that there has been a failure of westernization.[13] Although the "free market" is a Western legacy, Huntington does not see its widespread adoption as an index of the successful dissemination of Western values. He focuses on the Enlightenment ideals of liberty, equality, reason, progress, and human rights, which the non-West has not embraced along with capitalism. In a world no longer effectively regulated by Western cultural hegemony, he identifies the new risks represented by rising non-Western powers that the West must learn to "accommodate" for the sake of geopolitical coexistence.[14]

As a discourse of knowledge/power, the clash-of-civilizations model returns to the nineteenth-century legacy of grand orientalist themes that stress difference and separation and create objects—"civilizations"—of knowledge and control.[15] For Huntington, civilization is "the broadest level of cultural identity people have" that is defined both by common objective elements, such as language, history, religion, customs, and institutions, and by the subjective self-identification of people.[16] A civilization may consist of several nation-states (for example, Western, Latin American, Arabic, Islamic, and Confucian civilizations) or only one (Japan). "Torn civilizations" are a blend of different cultural and religious traditions, for example, the "Eurasian" countries of Turkey and Russia, with their mix of Western, Orthodox, and Islamic traditions.[17]

Even when one reserves one's skepticism about whether any civilization can be anything but a blend of different ethnicities, cultures, and traditions, there remains a major problem with the way Huntington has cut up the world. Sinic civilization seems to have spread like a heavy smog through East Asia, but Japan, a country much influenced by Chinese Confucianism and culture, is a separate civilization. There is no mention in Huntington of the Southeast Asian civilizational complex that is a melange of Hindu, Buddhist, Islamic, and Christian religions intermixed with animistic traditions. Instead, Indonesia, which is only nominally Muslim, is considered by Huntington to be a subdivision of Islamic civilization. And, except for North Africa, which is encompassed by the Islamic crescent, much of the continent falls outside of anything that can be called civilization. Western civilization, according to Huntington, is made up of the European and North American segments. One can hear the howls of protest, especially from the European entities lumped under Anglo-American hegemony. Latin America is considered an adjunct to Western civilization.

Despite his list of different civilizations, Huntington's taxonomy is ultimately based on the old "West-versus-Rest" model, which depends on an assumption of the lack of historical dynamism in regions (such as "the Orient") that are defined by the center as peripheral.[18] Whereas Europeans underwent revolutions and came up with Enlightenment ideas and standards, non-Western civilizations, after a hiatus of imperialism and colonialism, are reverting to a precontact "civilizational consciousness." This is because, following these civilizations' political independence from the Western powers, a "second-generation indigenization phenomenon" is rejecting the values, institutions, and practices that came with European imperialism and colonialism.[19] In a rather cut-and-dried scenario, Huntington presents two paths to moral development: in the West, a unilinear progress leads to irreversible moral standards, whereas a cyclical dynamic determines the development of non-Western civilizations. Instead of incorporating the Enlightenment values that are disseminated by the West, contemporary Asian societies are reverting to old values, which appear not to have been modified or changed by historical encounters with the West. Indeed, Huntington claims that contact with the West has intensified civilizational consciousness in religion. The globalization of capitalism has increased the animosity between peoples, and by uprooting people from local identities, it has engendered the "roots phenomenon," especially among the postcolonial elites. Religious nationalism and economic regionalism reinforce common culture among subjects. While the non-West has evolved economically by adopting European institutions and capitalism, the result in the cultural realm has been the revival and consolidation of religious—that is, nonmodern—values.

Furthermore, the uniqueness of the West is set off against a series of deficiencies in the Orient. In *The Sociology of Religion*, Max Weber blames the lack of antimagical rationality in "Oriental religions" for the failure of Asian societies to develop capitalism.[20] But whereas Weber blames Islam and Confucianism for stifling the growth of capitalism, Huntington blames the same religions for failing to evolve modern political rationality in a now exuberantly capitalist Asia. Huntington notes that the emerging Asian powers have developed chiefly by the acquisition of "the wealth, technology, skills, machines and weapons that are part of being modern."[21] This development is not westernization because it is marked by the alleged absences of the Enlightenment values of liberalism, egalitarianism, liberty, and human rights.

While Huntington is ostensibly seeking to "provincialize Europe," his condemnation of the historical backwardness of the Orient resurrects the model whereby, in Talal Asad's words, the West as "a singular collective identity defines itself in terms of a unique historicity."[22] Asad has criticized Western theory for naturalizing Enlightenment residues and assuming their universal applicability by inscribing binary oppositions that deny historical dynamism to non-Western peoples.[23] He reminds us of Marx's comment that "men make their own history but not under conditions of their own choosing,"[24] but this does not mean that subjugated peoples do not live and struggle within their own cultural traditions and effect social change. In this sense, Huntington's model is a step back from modernization theory, which at least assumes that the non-West can be "civilized" by the West and acknowledges the dynamic articulation of cultures. By casting Asian societies as resistant to political learning, Huntington dramatizes their cultural threat, which the West, especially the United States, must test its mettle against.

Huntington's theory is heir to Western discourses that both infantilize and feminize a subjugated Orient—Turandot brought to her knees. Over the past century, America's repeated encounters with Asia have been viewed as a series of maturing tests for the nation and its masculinity. Ron Takaki argues that by the end of the nineteenth century, fears about a flagging combative spirit under corporate capitalism fed "the masculinist thrust toward Asia," as Americans sought moral and economic conquest in the Philippines and in China.[25] The Japanese bombing of Pearl Harbor further reinforced the view of the moral depravity of Asian Pacific cultures. In *Sentimental Imperialists,* James Thomson, Peter Stanley, and John Perry maintain that the American nationalist ideology views its postwar encounters in Asia as youthful adventures, that initially brought a loss of hope, then maturity and national unification (represented in part by the absorption of Asian refugees and immigrants), for the new superpower.[26] Henry Kissinger characterized the war in Indochina as "testing our manhood in Asia," while President Johnson was reported to have likened the bombing of Vietnam to "screwing a whore." The symbolic and materialist linkages of such themes are particularly dangerous and disturbing, and their sexualized imagery manifests itself in a bravado of violence against particular kinds of bodies that are marked as radically different and located outside the West.[27]

But Huntington cautions that the rules of the game have now changed with the emergence of the newly militarized, and thus masculinized, non-Western powers. He warns not only of the so-called challenger civilizations of Islam and Confucianism but also of their potential allies. Less powerful "swing civilizations" include Russia, India, and Japan, which will line up behind one or the other of the top civilizations, depending on the geopolitical advantages of the alignment.[28] Huntington warns of the threat of alliances that exclude the West, thereby replacing the old Soviet Union–China communist partnership: "The most prominent form of this cooperation is the Confucian-Islamic connection that has emerged to challenge Western interests, values, and power."[29] Since we can no longer presume to culturally convert the East, Huntington urges the United States as a global power to accept Islamic and Asian civilizations even as they are seeking the universal dissemination of their values.[30] In short, the post–cold war world confronts global risks beyond environmental degradation or the arms race; a civilizational risk of a deeper, masculinist kind increases uncertainty and anxiety over the survival of Western civilization itself.

Huntington is writing in a period when the West is haunted by what has been called "reflexive modernity," in which criticisms of modernity proliferate at institutional and personal levels and detraditionalized Western societies are engaged in self-evaluation—as demonstrated by the rise of the women's, the multicultural, and the environmental movements.[31] In "The West: Unique, Not Universal," Huntington argues for a self-strengthening and a preservation of post-Enlightenment traditions and values in the global context of an ascendant Asia where the expansive power enabled by capitalist growth is not held in check by Western humanist values.[32] Having drawn the fault lines of civilization, Huntington recommends not conflict but accommodation and coexistence with the militarily powerful "non-Western modern civilizations . . . whose values and interests differ significantly from those of the West."[33] The irony is that the reception of Huntington's model routinely overlooks his call for accommodation and coexistence and focuses instead on the threat of global conflict suggested by his neat compartmentalization of "civilizations"

Table 1   Huntington's Typology of Civilizations

West	Non-West (Islamic-Confucian)
Cumulative cultural change	Cultural persistence
Western values:	*Their negation/absences:*
liberalism	illiberalism
rationality	irrationality
social equality	social inequality
individual rights	collective rights

according to deep differences in political philosophy and opposing sets of moral-political values (see table 1).

Despite his earlier writings on economic development in the non-West, Huntington underplays the profound importance of European and American imperialism in shaping global differences as well as commonalities across societies and cultures. By dismissing the cultural legacies of European imperialism and the uneven adoption of Western traditions by colonized countries, Huntington's thesis is a totalizing theory of the Orient that is more nationalistic than useful in understanding the diversity and complexity of modernities in the non-West. He argues that "modernization and economic development neither require nor produce cultural westernization. To the contrary, they promote a resurgence of, and renewed commitment to, indigenous cultures."[34] Such an analytical division occludes the fact that cultural ideas, attitudes, and practices have been in circulation, primarily through trade and conquest under European imperialism and colonialism, for centuries. One may ask whether societies or institutions can modernize—by operating liberal economies, for instance—without in some way adopting post-Enlightenment attitudes and values.

When Huntington talks about tensions between civilizations, he is actually talking about the actions and policies of non-Western governments, politicians, and cultural elites who are rising up in a "cultural backlash" against Western cultural imperialism.[35] By equating civilization with the truth claims of ruling elites, Huntington unproblematically assumes that elites are the "authentic" owners and re-presenters of "indigenous cultures." But can we talk about "indigenous cultures" in a generic way when such forms of labeling are themselves acts of power, whether at the national or global levels? For a political scientist, Huntington is not sufficiently attentive to the webs of power whereby truth claims are made in the interests of certain classes, ethnicities, and regimes, whether in the West or in the East. Often, he is satisfied with using elite definitions of culture, rather than examining how cultural rhetoric and ethical-political considerations are part of the social regulation of society. His notion of culture as an independent variable is contradicted by the ways in which culture is routinely deployed as a resource by political elites and by market forces in domestic, regional, and global arenas.

Liberalisms: Individual Liberty or Governmentality?

To challenge Huntington's assertions about the absence of Western political values in the East, I will focus on Asian countries that do not profess commitment to the doctrine of liberalism but whose technologies of government—in rendering autonomy as "the objective for a variety of governmental projects"[36]—reflect their commitment to a liberal market rationality derived from the West. But first, what does Huntington mean by liberalism, which he says is missing in Asian societies? On a visit to Southeast Asia, Huntington called Asian democracies such as Singapore, Malaysia, and so on "illiberal systems," and he contrasted them to American democracy, which he described as having "free, fair, and competitive elections [that] are only possible if there is some measure of freedom of speech, assembly and press, and if opposition candidates and parties are able to criticize incumbents without fear of retaliation. Democracy is thus not only a means of constituting authority, it is also a means of limiting authority."[37]

Liberalism for Huntington, and for many social scientists, refers to a sphere of individual liberty and limited government. For theorists such as John Rawls, this doctrine of liberal individualism means that individuals, as free and equal citizens, must share basic rights, liberties, and opportunities.[38] In contrast to this concept of citizenship based on the "unencumbered self," communitarian critics, drawing on the civic-republican theory of politics, propose "a notion of the citizen as one for whom it is natural to join with others to pursue common action in view of the common good."[39] This debate, which opposes Western liberal individualism to communitarianism, frames most discussions about differences between political cultures in the West and in Asia, and Huntington's clash-of-civilizations model is one variant of this view. But, as Barry Hindess has argued, there is an ambiguity in the doctrine of liberalism that poses both a political community of naturally autonomous subjects and a political community that promotes rationality, self-control, and responsibility.[40] By ignoring the regulative aspects of liberalism, both Huntington and Asian communitarian theorists can rhetorically dismiss the role of liberal rationality in regulating subjects in Asian societies, pointing instead to the exclusive role of Asian values in shaping a collectivist ethos.

Second, by making an analytical opposition between the market economy and cultural values, and between liberalism and social inequality, policy experts such as Huntington can not only claim the absence of liberalism in Asia, they can blame the social inequalities generated by capitalism entirely on reified Asian ("non-Western") cultural values. By identifying liberalism as being concerned only with protecting civil rights, Huntington argues that there is a fundamental political difference between the West and the Rest, where cultural values are seen as privileging the collective.[41] But this strict demarcation of Western individualism and Asian collectivism skirts the fact that capitalism itself is wedded to liberalism and that capitalism, as a dialectical process of endless production and destruction, is itself a source of profound social inequality that produces differential access to the means of material and symbolic production.[42] Indeed, liberal market rationality, which is a product of the post-Enlightenment period, is now hegemonic in the world and has engendered unequal values not only in the non-West but also in the West. While Huntington is right in arguing that Asian states did not entirely adopt the Enlightenment ideal of the legal autonomy of subjects, he underplays the states' critical role as midwife to capitalism and the centrality of market rationality in the making and regulation of their societies. Huntington's assertion that Asian forms of government are entirely the legacy of Asian civilizations and are not *also* the legacy of European rule disregards the liberalism that addresses itself to the problems of governing the economy as a quasi-natural entity (the "hidden hand" of Adam Smithian economics). It is in this sense that the Asian cases are liberal and thus share a common logic of economic and political rationalities with the West. What Huntington and others point to as the "natural" result of persistent Asian values I consider is the practical accomplishment of liberal governance in postcolonial and postsocialist Asia. To thus frame the debate, we need to think about (economic) liberalism as a problem of "too much" government.

If, following Michel Foucault, one considers liberalism not as a political philosophy but as an art of government, then liberalism is not something that can be reduced to a perfect realization of a doctrine called liberalism; rather, it includes the array of rationalities whereby a liberal government attempts to resolve problems of how to govern society as a whole.[43] A useful definition of a liberal government is given by Graham Burchell: "Liberal government is pre-eminently economic government in the dual sense of cheap government and government geared to securing the conditions for optimum economic performance. There is a sense in which the liberal rationality of government is necessarily pegged to the optimum performance of the economy at minimum economic *and socio-political* cost."[44] Thus, if some Asian countries operate according to the principles of economic liberalism, the sociopolitical conditions must also be produced by the working out of liberal rationalities. I therefore argue that the so-called nonliberal features of Asian democracies—such as the limited individual rights that have been dubbed "Asian values"—should be considered the sociopolitical effects of an array of strategies, programs, and techniques that regulate society in a way that reflects the liberal logic of economic competitiveness. But the task is to explain why liberal economies should coexist with a form of state regulation that makes Asian democracies appear "illiberal" when compared to Western neoliberal democracies (see below).[45]

If we recognize Asian tiger economies as liberal formations dedicated to the most efficient ways of achieving maximal economic performance, then what are the modes of social regulation that ensure that such growth will be attained at minimum economic and sociopolitical cost? Nicholas Rose and others maintain that as "a rationality of rule," liberalism is fundamentally concerned about "a series of problems about the governmentality of individuals, families, markets, and populations."[46] In Western liberal democracies, social regulation is largely attained, at a distance, through the authority of expertise in an array of strategies, programs, and techniques that shape economic, familial, and social arrangements.[47] In Asian liberal economies, I argue, social regulation is not so much dispersed in a multiplicity of agencies but rather gathered into the state apparatus, and problems of governmentality are presented as problems of religion and cultural difference from the West.

Table 2 contrasts features of social regulation in advanced Western neo-liberal societies and in Asian liberal societies. Analytically speaking, we are

Table 2   Key Contrasting Features of Social Regulation

Liberal Southeast Asia	The Neoliberal West
Expanding middle classes	Middle classes in crisis
a) Dependent Subjects:	*a) Self-Fulfilling Subjects:*
ethics of self-reliance	ethics of personhood
authority of experts	expert of the self
subject of a given culture/nation	agent in his/her own government
b) "The Caring Society":	*b) The Post–Social Welfare Society:*
bureaucratic benevolence	privatized management of risks
government accountability	self accountability

comparing early industrializing neoliberal democracies, where the welfare state has sought to even out the inequalities produced by capitalism and the middle classes are now in crisis, with late-developing authoritarian regimes in Asia, where the expansion of the middle classes is part of the state project of development. In contrast to the rational, calculating subject of the neoliberal West, who pursues a highly precarious individualism in which the individual is an expert of the self,[48] Asian tiger economies promote a rational subject who is shaped by the authority of the state as cultural regulator. Whereas in Western neoliberalism, privatized risk management has become a much more important technology of (self-) regulation, thus encouraging subjects to be in charge of their own lives, in Southeast Asian democracies, technologies of security promote subjects who, while self-reliant, are dependent on the culturally sanctioned collectivity represented by the state. Furthermore, whereas in the West, the welfare state is in retreat and individuals are increasingly left to fend for themselves in the era of globalization (see below), in Asian liberal systems the "caring-society" model of social regulation allows the state to take account of the skills, consumer power, and interests of the middle classes as a way to attract faster development.

Nay-Saying and Postdevelopmental Strategy

The public repudiation of Western rationality and culture has become something of a trend in Asian elite circles. In 1996, a Chinese best-seller titled *China*

Can Say No expressed a high level of Han chauvinism in criticizing American trade policies.[49] Referring to China's scientific and cultural glories of the past, the book claimed that "in the next century . . . Chinese thought and Chinese entrepreneurial abilities will deeply influence the world, becoming the sole force leading human thought." Furthermore, in a direct challenge to American economic power, the authors asserted, "We don't want MFN, and in the future we won't offer it to you either."[50] The intertwining of cultural chauvinist discourses and trade conflicts reflects a fundamental clash of economies that are represented and experienced in cultural (and even racial) terms. The authors of *China Can Say No* were inspired by the book *The Voice of Asia*, which was published a year earlier by Prime Minister Mahathir Mohamad of Malaysia and politician Shintaro Ishihara of Japan.[51] Ishihara, of course, is the author of *The Japan That Can Say No*, the first Asian book to publicly reject American-imposed trade policies.[52] Mahathir and Ishihara vigorously reject Western "liberal" values (in the narrow sense of political freedom), insisting that Asian cultural values underlie an Asian model of capitalism; they maintain that an Asian renaissance is challenging Western domination of the region. This criticism by a crescendo of nay-saying Asians reflects the common stance taken by the Asian economies toward the Group of Seven (the Western industrialized powers and Japan) and the trade barriers represented by NAFTA (the North American Free Trade Association) and the European Union. Led by Mahathir, the Southeast Asian countries formed their own caucus within the Asian Pacific Economic Cooperation (APEC) group of economies, hoping to secure better trade conditions with the Western powers. More recently, the authors of *China Can Say No* have published another book, titled *China Can Still Say No*, this time attacking *Japan* for its trade practices.[53] As the rhetoric of cultural difference becomes inseparable from trade wars, the fundamental issue is not irreducible civilizational divisions but rather how the state, seeking optimal growth, uses cultural "expertise to translate society into an object of government."[54]

The liberal rationalities of many postcolonial Asian states have evolved in conjunction with Western ones since the Second World War. They reveal the imprint of the political modernity that came with Western colonialism and the adoption of socialism. Capitalist development and the rise of the middle classes in Asia have, however, followed a different trajectory from that experienced by Western countries. Whereas in Europe, capitalism emerged from independent urban merchant and trade guilds and from struggles over the centuries for bourgeois democracy, in the late-developing nations of Asia, the state has played a major role in transforming premodern agrarian societies, colonial bureaucracies, and, lately, party rule into capitalist formations—all within a few generations.[55] In what Barrington Moore has called a "revolution from above,"[56] state-driven transitions to socialist or capitalist development in Asia have also included the formation of middle classes, whose structural position and loyalty are much more firmly tied to state projects than were the structural position and loyalty of the early bourgeoisie in the West.

In the Asian liberal economies, then, the state's nurturing and its regulation of the middle classes are essential to economic competitiveness. One should view with skepticism fears for the future of Hong Kong, now returned to Chinese rule as a "special administrative region" (sar). In a letter to the *New York Times* a reader notes: "Hard though it may be for some to swallow, British blood, toil, and tears seeded Bombay, Bermuda, Malaysia, New Zealand, Singapore, Sydney, and of course, Hong Kong. Seven of today's 10 most competitive economies derive their origins from the legal structure, trading, and ideas of the British Empire."[57] This self-serving and unbalanced view of the civilizing mission does not, however, refute the reminder that Western liberalism—the mode of government that promotes economic growth—has taken root in Asia and that it plays a major role in shaping realities there today. Singapore has been ranked as one of the most competitive economies in the world, and Hong Kong, whose sar status is relatively autonomous of Beijing, continues to be one of the most liberal economies. My goal is not to dismiss the political problems in Asian democracies but rather to point to their institutional roots in economic liberalism and the increasing need to regulate the demands of the expanding middle classes.

The earlier picture of postcolonial Asian countries—South Korea, Taiwan, Singapore—was one of strong developmentalist states. Following the Latin American prototype, Herbert Feith argues that the "repressive-developmentalist state" arose in conjunction with state-driven, export-oriented industrialization, which involved the disciplining of new workers and the maintenance of new technical, professional, and bureaucratic elites to manage state apparatuses and interface with transnational corporations.[58] Asian tiger states such as South Korea and Taiwan have become "strong" by creating cohesive political alliances with corporate capital; this has played a role in the formation of a bourgeoisie. Indonesia, Singapore, Malaysia, and Thailand represented varying degrees of the strong centralized state that has engineered the rise of middle classes, formed strategic alliances with capital (both domestic and foreign), and thus facilitated conditions for profit maximization. I will not discuss the varied arrangements and relative successes of such industrialization programs in different economies;[59] the point is that by taking draconian measures against labor to serve the interests of transnational corporations, these nation-states have become "strong" in both the political ("authoritarian") and the economic ("industrializing") senses. In a carrot-and-stick approach, strict laws against labor and political activism have been balanced against overall increases in the standard of living. Scholars of Southeast Asia have occupied themselves with determining the balance between development and repression in each nation-state: Malaysia, for instance, has been described as being ruled by a "repressive-responsive regime," meaning that authoritarian rule has been leavened by greater multiethnic representation in the government.[60] But the exclusive focus of political scientists on party politics in determining state strategies overlooks other forms of power that go beyond the electoral and legal systems.

The Asian state role in regulating both the economy and society according to liberal market principles is clearly recognized and encouraged by the international business community. In a recent *Business Week* article, Malaysia, Singapore, and Hong Kong were urged first and foremost to develop productive, cohesive, and stable societies and second, to discipline workers so that both the economy and society would be highly attractive and competitive in the world economy. By weighing their "strengths and weaknesses" in attracting foreign investments, the article assessed Hong Kong and Singapore as important economic centers that nevertheless possess problematic social conditions that might affect further growth. It expressed fear that the handover of Hong Kong to China "could weaken [its] legal system and dull [its] edge as [a] media center" and that Singapore's "rigid social controls, rote education, and limits on media [might] hamper [the] drive to nurture [the] entertainment and design industries."[61] However, when *Business Week* urged these reforms, it was not for improving human rights; rather, the reforms were recommended so that the most competitive countries would become "flexible, lean models for future growth."[62] These lessons—whereby the state does not so much control the technical aspects of development as secure the sociopolitical conditions conducive to global trade—are not lost on the states concerned. They indicate that there is a shift to a postdevelopmental strategy as Asian governments pay more attention to negotiating relations with their burgeoning middle classes instead of relying on the heavy use of repressive measures.

Elsewhere, the term *postdevelopment* has been taken to mean something quite different. Arturo Escobar uses it to describe "the unmaking of the Third World," that is, the failure of development "to complete the Enlightenment in Asia, Africa and Latin America."[63] For him, postdevelopment means resistance to modernization, and he points as evidence to the proliferation of hybrid cultures and social movements with alternative visions not dominated by the logics of capital and instrumental reason.[64] For Escobar, the post–World War II discursive formation of development arises out of Western agency, whereas the current postdevelopment indexes a noble third-world insurrectionary agency, a kind of "the Rest saying no to the West." But by this theoretical stroke, Escobar seems to erase the historically sedimented effects of colonial political economies and governmentality in shaping social movements in the non-West. I used the term *postdevelopmental* differently, recognizing the ongoing effects of developmental economics in formerly colonized societies but also identifying a new stage of state *engagement* (rather than disengagement) with global agencies and capital. *Postdevelopmental* should properly indicate the state strategy that comes after the developmentalist state; it can most aptly be used to describe the former Soviet Union and Maoist China, where the explicit state project was to promote developmental economics.[65] Of course, the developmentalist state was a label used to refer not only to socialist regimes implementing development economics after the revolution but also, as the above discussion of "repressive-developmentalist regimes" shows, to emerging postcolonial capitalist formations that were advised and prodded by the World Bank to intervene massively in the development of their economies.

With the increasing influx of global capital since the mid-1980s, the regimes in Malaysia, Singapore, and Hong Kong have adopted a postdevelopmental strategy that represents a shift in relations between the state, the market, and society. The old alliance between the state and local Chinese capital in Thailand, the Philippines, Indonesia, and Malaysia began to loosen as Chinese enterprises formed more ventures with foreign capital and expanded their global networks.[66] Thus, Ruth McVey notes that "to the extent that foreign capital frees domestic business from dependence on the state and helps to generate the articulation of demands by local capital, it reduces the state's autonomy from society."[67] Peter Evans identifies a similar shift in South Korea, where the "new alliance of local entrepreneurs and transnational corporations make[s] it harder to sustain the old alliance between local capital and the state."[68] This change in the partnership between the state and local capital signals a postdevelopmental state strategy that seeks a multiplicity of links with global capital and multilateral agencies: "What determines Southeast Asian policy-makers' strategic decisions will be the interplay of complex interests—bureaucratic, political, and business, national and regional—which will be expressed more and more through agencies, associations, and lobbies."[69] In other words, the postdevelopmental strategy relinquishes direct technical control over development and comes to rely on a plethora of transnational linkages to capital and multilateral agencies.

Governmentality: "The Caring Society"

Postdevelopmental strategies increasingly adopt nonrepressive cultural measures to produce a society, especially the middle classes, that is attractive to global capital. When scholars analyze politics in the Asian tiger economies, they often confine themselves to the juridico-legal mechanisms that subjugate labor to capital or to the repressive rules that suppress dissent, but they ignore the disciplining and pastoral regimes that increasingly shape the modern Asian subject. Foucault's notion of disciplinary power refers to the rules and regulations aimed at instilling self-discipline and productivity, while the pastoral modality of power concerns itself with the biological and the social existence of human beings.[70] Postdevelopmental strategies emphasize the caring aspects of state power; these aspects are directed toward the middle class because it is the middle-class citizenry whose credentials, skills, and overall well-being have been so critical to attracting foreign capital. But whereas in the West, pastoral power is dispersed through a series of nongovernmental programs that emphasize self-care,[71] in Southeast Asian liberalism, what has been called "the caring society" is integrated into the government itself and culturally constructs relations between the ruler and the ruled.

The caring society is not the same as the welfare liberalism one associates with Western societies. Whereas the latter institutionalized claims on the national product by those who could not "fairly compete"—women, the urban poor, the unemployed, the sick, and so on—the caring society institutes stability through bureaucratic benevolence and thus welcomes global capital in.[72] In other words, while the welfare state developed as a way to deal with class conflict, the postdevelopmental strategy of pastoral care seeks to produce citizens attractive to capital. A precedent for the Asian model of pastoral care may be found in Bismarkian Germany, probably the most important example of a state producing a society through caring. The German state managed not only to usher in industrial development but also to address the "social question" of class relations through a social policy that produced caring. Canada too has used the state to produce a social policy on citizenship.[73] There is therefore nothing intrinsically unique or unprecedented about the Asian model of pastoral care, which seeks to be the guarantor of social and legal conditions—stability, legitimacy, accountability—through producing citizens that have the human, social, and cultural capitals that allow them to flourish in a global economy.

Thus, the cultural idiom of Asian values is invoked for its familiar "traditional" appeal to articulate discourses and categories that regulate society while culturally authenticating policies that produce the social conditions desired by global business. In their conceptualization of English state formation as a cultural revolution, Philip Corrigan and Derek Sayer note that political states "define, in great detail, acceptable forms and images of social activity and individual and collective identity; they regulate, in empirically specifiable ways, much—very much, by the twentieth century—of social life."[74] Corrigan's and Sayer's attempt to "grasp state forms culturally and cultural forms as state-regulated" is particularly apt here, for increasingly, the "routines and rituals of rule" in ASEAN countries are mechanisms whereby regimes of cultural truth and cultural normativity increasingly regulate the life of middle-class subjects.[75] That accounts for the Western view of Southeast Asian nations as being "illiberal" and the persistence of "Asian values."[76] I will now discuss two models of these regimes of sociality that seem to dominate Southeast Asian liberalism: (1) one that produces a calculative subject who is also dependent on state benevolence; and (2) one in which society demands state accountability in terms of its overall "caring" and protection of middle-class interests.

Calculative but Dependent Subjects

Although Southeast Asian states such as Singapore and Malaysia have been labeled authoritarian or repressive, they fall far short of the police state.[77] In contrast to the fully authoritarian state, the ruling regimes in these countries tie expert knowledge in the social and human sciences to government, thereby translating the practical rationalities of liberalism into strategies and programs that shape the mentalities of their subjects, who are increasingly middle class. More than in the West, the liberal Asian state plays a pedagogical role in educating the public as to the ethico-political meaning of citizenship. Expertise in the social and human sciences is deployed to provide "a certain style of reasoning," according to Nicholas Rose. One must consider the ways in which expert language operates as "a set of 'intellectual techniques' [that] is used for rendering reality thinkable and practicable, and constituting domains that are amenable—or not amenable—to reformatory intervention."[78] In Asian democracies, narratives of cultural authenticity not only make certain regulations reasonable and familiar (and appeal to pride), they also regulate the ways responsible/good subjects accept such authoritative norms of governmentality.

The rise of the "new rich" in Asia requires new forms of civilizing and caring from the regimes that have played a major role in their formation. In ASEAN countries, the expansion of the middle classes requires governments that can produce not only the professional skills and expertise desired by multinational corporations but also the kind of cultural sensibility that is loyal to the state. For instance, Malaysia, following the example of Japan Inc., employs the concept of "communitarian capitalism," in which the state sees itself as a coordinator of both the public and the private sectors for strengthening the country.[79] Besides fostering an economic partnership between the government and capital, the caring society is geared toward the formation of middle-class subjects whose "technological proficiency" and "exemplary work ethic" will ensure "a high and escalating productivity," so that Malaysia can attain its goal of becoming a fully industrialized country by 2020.[80]

Relying on cultural forms and norms rather than on laws, this communitarian capitalism justifies social regulation in terms of religion because "you cannot legislate the empathy and affection that bind family and close friends. In the years ahead the Asian tradition of stressing these bonds will provide us with guidelines for increasingly complex information societies. The fundamentals of Eastern thought—avoiding unnecessary conflict, eschewing coercive tactics, living within one's means—will sustain us."[81] Islam is invoked to legitimize the call to establish "a fully moral and ethical society whose citizens are strong in religious and spiritual values and imbued with the highest of ethical standards."[82] Through the concept of the caring society, the government casts itself as a custodian not only of the population's welfare but also of its cultural traditions, thus wedding its goal of attaining economic competitiveness to the political disciplining of its population.

The pastoral power represented by communitarian capitalism has succeeded in reforming the subjectivity of the Malay ethnic majority, who are known as *bumiputra* and whose rise as a favored middle class was engineered by affirmative action–style state policies.[83] The new Malay (*Melayu baru*) is a middle-class subject who is self-disciplined, able, and wealth accumulating, but in a way that is cast as within the precepts of Islam rather than of capitalism. Authoritative leaders from the prime minister downward proclaim not the contradiction but rather the spiritual fit between a Malaysian can-doism (*Malaysia boleh*) and Islamic modernity. In opposing the new Malay subjectivity to its colonial representations—hardworking rather than easygoing, profit seeking rather than interest avoiding, knowledgeable rather than ignorant, cosmopolitan rather than narrow-minded[84]—government policies seek to bring Islam in line with capitalism. The array of programs designed to inculcate capitalist practices in the Malay population include preparing Malay students for college education in Western centers of science and capitalism; encouraging Muslims to save in special Islamic banks; and training them to work with ethnic Chinese and foreign businesses. The new Malay subject—the receiver of government scholarships, credit, business licenses, civil service jobs, and innumerable other perks associated with being bumiputra—has been trained to obtain credentials, to be effective on the job, and also to view these activities as within the dictates of an official Islam.

Even in religious practice, seeking wealth and prestige is presented as being in line with Islamic precepts. On television, the call to Islamic prayers, which follows the proclamation "Allah is Great," is itself followed by the invocation "Let us perform the *sorah* [Islamic prayer]! Let us follow the path of prosperity!" This is accompanied by images of Muslims at prayer in mosques, followed by pictures of Muslims receiving certificates at university convocations. While this standard call to prayer is not new, the commercially infused vocabulary of classical Islam has been used to good effect to promote the newly credentialed elite. The state investment in and nurturing of the new Malays reinforces their lack of autonomy from official definitions of what is culturally appropriate behavior for Muslims and for Malaysian citizens. The new Islamic identity has not gone unchallenged, of course. A dissident group of Muslims, called Darul Arqam, criticized state developmental projects for being based on un-Islamic capitalist principles and set up a network of villages where they implemented a communally based economy. But in an unprecedented move against a nonpolitical Muslim group, the government arrested the Darul Arqam leaders and dispersed their followers. For many upwardly mobile new Malays, the rituals and words of an official Islamic culture fused with capitalism represent a meaningful way of being modern citizens. In the government rhetoric, then, there are various levels of cultural difference. Whereas certain activities—"unnecessary conflict, coercive tactics"—are marked as foreign (Western), modern entrepreneurship is not so marked but is instead recast as an essential ingredient of the new Islam.[85]

In neighboring Singapore, experts also invoke Asian ethics to both authenticate and naturalize the authority of the state over individually directed knowledge, values, and behavior. For instance, in a debate with Huntington, political scientist Chan Heng Chee argues that a key feature of Asian political systems is the de-emphasis of individual rights but stress on respect for authority, so that opposition to those in power is "not a normal reflex."[86] Frequently, academic experts are employed to cast such a state calculation in terms of culturally distinctive reasoning. Tu Wei-ming is a Harvard professor who is often invited to Singapore to make universalizing pronouncements about Chinese culture. In a recent visit, he defined Confucianism as a sinicized Asian humanism that is "anthropocosmic," balancing self-transformation with consciousness of duty within a series of concentric circles consisting of "self, family, community, society, nation, world, and cosmos."[87] By presenting philosophical questions as pedagogical lessons on what being a Chinese subject is all about, this expert knowledge authenticates governing strategies that normalize submission to state authority as the work of heavenly principles rather than the product of technologies of calculation reflecting the logic of liberal economics. These officially sanctioned views of Chinese culture do produce meaningful effects on subjects who are proud of the achievements of their country and its focus on families, productivity, and security.

Such a liberalism imbued with quasi-religious pastoral power appears to be a strategy borrowed by the new merchant-politicians in Hong Kong. Under China's "one country, two systems" formula, the economic liberalism of Hong Kong is now guaranteed by a group of ruling tycoons who are mostly nominated by Beijing, not elected. They have suspended labor laws that give workers the right to bargain collectively and have curbed the right to public rallies. It appears that under Chinese self-rule, Hong Kong liberalism is based on a revival and an elaboration of British colonial labor regulation, which is now justified in terms of Chinese culture. When the international media points to actions against trade unions and public assemblies, and to the expulsion of illegal immigrant children from the mainland, as antiliberal,[88] they fail to note that these actions are taken in the interests of economic liberalism—to make Hong Kong more competitive and politically stable for business interests (and in the process, to differentiate Hong Kong's administrative system from that of the mainland). Tung Chee Hwa, Beijing's appointed top administrator in Hong Kong, has linked future economic growth to an unquestioning attitude toward authority. Pro-consul Tung defines "Chineseness" as respect for power holders in the family and in the government, "a belief in order and stability," and "an emphasis on obligations to the community rather than the rights of the individual."[89]

The program of collective security appears directed primarily at the middle classes, who are dependent on state employment. Tung has made home ownership the top priority of his administration. His housing program— whereby the government hopes to attain 70 percent home ownership in ten years[90]—deals with problems of both economic and social regulation. The high cost of real estate threatens Hong Kong's future growth as an Asian regional hub for multinational corporations, and economic competitiveness requires the cooling down of the housing market. At the same time, Tung's housing program is a strategy of social regulation because grown children are urged to live with and care for aged parents, a mode of governmentality that borrows from Singapore. Casting these modes of regulation as a way of being Chinese is a view that is reinforced by the Western interpretation of them as "a quasi-Confucian paternalism."[91] These programs, which regulate family support systems and control the influx of mainland Chinese, are intended to ensure that Hong Kong remains socially stabilized and economically viable in the aftermath of the transition to mainland rule.

These culturally variant constructions of pastoral power in the Asian tiger economies display different degrees of the state's capacity to shape the middle-class subject and to tie his or her achievements and aspirations closely to the government. Whereas in Malaysia and Singapore, the state has produced society and established institutions of cultural caring, the middle classes in Hong Kong, having risen primarily out of their own entrepreneurial activities, are now being subjected to a broader pastoral care that has come with the reversion to Chinese sovereignty and the hegemonic ideal of playing by Chinese cultural rules. This modality of a calculative subject who is building economic and cultural capital and who is also dependent on the government's definition of cultural normativity is a distinctive feature of these middle-range economies that are seeking a cheaper way to build economically competitive societies.

State Accountability: Trust and Security

But how do these states deal with the discontents that are inspired by liberal economies? Nicholas Rose observes: "Liberalism inaugurates a continual dissatisfaction with government, a perpetual questioning of whether the desired effects are being produced, of the mistakes of thought or policy that hamper the efficacy of government, a recurrent diagnosis of failure coupled with a recurrent demand to govern better."[92] One may well ask how subjects in Asian liberalism can engage in a continual questioning of the rule of authority when in most cases, they are dominated by one-party rule (Singapore, Malaysia, South Korea, Japan) and there are various curbs on the freedom of speech. In recent years, Taiwan has been singled out as a robust East Asian democracy where street demonstrations and fistfights in the legislature have become rather common, everyday affairs. The middle classes in the Philippines and Thailand, too, have overthrown dictatorships—but without bringing more democratic regimes to power. Nevertheless, I argue that in the so-called authoritarian states of Malaysia and Singapore, subjects do engage in a continual assessment of their rulers, but their demands for better government are expressed not so much in terms of the degree of democratic representation as in terms of the state's efficiency in ensuring overall social security and prosperity.[93]

If, as Rose maintains, in advanced democracies, individuals are regulated to "enterprise themselves,"[94] in Asian tiger economies, the state is required more and more to enterprise itself as accountable to the expectations and interests it has built up among the middle classes, who are accustomed to ever growing levels of social security and wealth accumulation. As Chan Heng Chee has argued, the legitimacy of an ASEAN state derives from "the ability of the government to deliver the goods."[95] Chan's home country of Singapore is a unique city-state of 3 million people, where Asian economic liberalism has been honed to a science. It is a telling case of Asian liberalism taken to the extreme—a model that is admired, though it is hardly reproducible, in larger countries such as Vietnam and China. Because of its infamous global image as having an authoritarian regime, and because of the periodic repressive moves of its government, analysts have tended to view Singapore as a negative model of power. But most of the quotidian aspects of life in Singapore are governed not by repression but by the unity of the application of knowledge and the positive exercise of power. A multiplicity of programs—housing, health, savings, education—produces not merely social consensus but actual arrangements and practices that reflect the liberal ethos of national efficiency and competitiveness. State-directed social regulation involves the co-optation of selected elements of the corporate and professional elites, who are nominated to run for Parliament, to serve on state committees, and to work at think tanks. Their technical expertise is used to assist in refining government policy, while their partial integration into the state provides feedback that enables the government to monitor dissension and manage society.[96] But beyond regulating society through a range of welfare and social mechanisms, the government must also be accountable to its citizens for maintaining very high standards of living and continual economic growth.

The structure of accountability in Singapore is predicated on the population's trusting in the expertise and cultural authority of the political leadership and the state's ability to deliver in terms of social stability and economic performance. Rather than focusing on individual liberties, the rational Singaporean subject holds the government accountable for universal home ownership, high-quality education, and unending economic expansion. The country prides itself on being a "home-owning democracy."[97] It has the highest rate of provision of public housing anywhere in the world. About 70 percent of the dwellers in government-built apartments are owner-occupiers.[98] Citizen grievances against the government vis-à-vis the provision of "collective welfare" have proliferated as the lower classes have demanded better-quality subsidized housing and the aspiring middle classes have demanded the ability to buy affordable housing. The government now provides subsidies for both sets of demands as a way to maintain the boast of a Confucianist state ethos. The ferocious demands of parents for quality education have made Singapore's primary-school students among the world's most competitive in science and math. Every year, Singaporeans anxiously await measures of their nation's global competitiveness. In recent years, Singapore has been ranked by a U.S.-based company as the second most profitable country in the world (after Switzerland) to do business in. This ranking is based on operations risk (general economic environment), political risk, and the remittance and repatriation of profits.[99] Singapore is an excellent example of the fact that a disciplined labor force is no longer the only essential feature for attracting foreign capital; just as important is the provision of efficient state services and resources to well-trained middle- and working-class citizens.

The technologies of security, which are interwoven through an array of programs into the very fabric of everyday life—subsidized housing, education, compulsory retirement and saving schemes, incentives for childbearing[100]—are so entrenched that perhaps the worst punishment that the government can mete out to an errant subject is not a prison whipping but a bout of bankruptcy. A new strategy of the political authorities is to file defamation suits against opposition leaders and government critics.[101] When judged guilty, defendants are punished with multimillion-dollar damages, which have effectively bankrupted individuals or forced them into exile. Through this strategy, the state exposes intransigent Singaporeans to the unaccustomed privatized management of risks, a condition more commonly found in advanced liberal societies. These defamation suits operate as public lessons that reinforce the authority of the state and the technologies of security to which Singaporean subjects have become habituated. By exposing dissident subjects to the individualized risks of advanced liberalism, the liberal Asian state makes yet another case for "Asian communitarianism."

Similarly, in Malaysia, the individual's right to dissent is balanced against the imperatives of the state to deliver on economic and social promises. The prime minister provides a defense of state-engineered liberalism when he says that in Asia, "we believe that strong, stable governments [that are] prepared to make decisions, which, though often unpopular, are nevertheless in the best interests of the nation, are a prerequisite for economic development. . . . When citizens understand that their right to choose also involves limits and responsibilities, democracy doesn't deteriorate into an excess of freedom."[102]

Although the Malaysian regime comes nowhere near providing the kind of collectivized support for the majority of its population that Singapore provides, the government nevertheless is held accountable for continuing to deliver prosperity to the bumiputra. Following racial riots in 1969, a set of affirmative-action measures directly favored the Malay majority in owning corporate stocks, being offered government jobs, and finding employment in the private sector. The extraordinary success of this policy gave rise to Malay urban workers, middle-class professionals, and a powerful corporate elite. Although some aspects of affirmative action are now being phased out, the Malay community continues to receive an array of special favors through state patronage.[103] The legitimacy of communitarian capitalism depends on the ability of the government to continue to deliver goods, services, wealth, and privileges to the Malay middle and upper classes, who are being groomed to participate in global capitalism.

Their responsiveness and accountability, rather than their expressions of cultural authenticity, are what make these governments appealing to their subjects. In short, while the Asian tigers used to govern too much through repressive measures, the shift to postdevelopmental strategies reveals that more and more, the solution to the liberal paradox of maximizing gain and minimizing government is to exercise disciplinary and pastoral powers that are cast in the principles of Islam or Confucianism. To compete in the global economy, the postdevelopmental state must produce sociopolitical order and modern technical efficiency. Given the current financial crises in South Korea and in Southeast Asia, whether the exercise of a pastoral power that is cast in the cultural logic of Confucianism or Islam is an enduring solution remains to be seen.

Variations in Western Neoliberalism

The common features and varieties of Asian liberalism not only undermine the cultural essentialism of Huntington's clash-of-civilizations model, they also challenge the rather broad cultural brush strokes with which he paints

Western civilization. Indeed, the heritage of the Enlightenment—for example, democracy and neoliberalism—are also variously experienced and structured by different Western governments. Scholars have noted that globalization has increased liberal policies to such an extent that they work against democracy in the West as well. Led by the United States, neoliberal economism has come to restrict democratic ideals in the West, and programs to increase competitiveness in the global economy are exacting high social costs. As Ralf Dahrendorf has noted, "Economic globalization . . . appears to be associated with new kinds of social exclusion. . . . The new inequality . . . would be better described as inequalization, the opposite of leveling, building paths to the top for some and digging holes for others, creating cleavages, splitting. . . . The systematic divergences of the life chances of larger social groups [are] incompatible with a civil society."[104]

At a recent meeting of the Group of Seven industrialized nations, the economic preeminence of the United States was explained in terms of cultural differences between the Americans and the Europeans and the Japanese. According to an article in the *Wall Street Journal*, "To match America's dynamism," the Europeans and the Japanese "must overcome significant differences in culture, history, and geography. While Americans tend to embrace change for its own sake, Europeans and Japanese tend to mistrust it." But the article is not just talking about the behavior of private entrepreneurs, it is describing a difference in economic neoliberalism whereby the American government is willing to tolerate economic change and "creative destruction," which it euphemizes as "flexibility in labor markets, capital markets, corporate culture." Furthermore, the article points out that the American government invests in the infrastructural conditions—transportation projects, universities, scientific research—that serve as foundations for growth in the private sector.[105] The *Wall Street Journal* celebrates the willingness of American neoliberalism to accept downsizing, privatization, and the loosening up of the labor laws, which creates tensions with the European powers, who are less willing to write off welfare policies. It appears that ideologically speaking, spreading markets and spreading democracy has come to mean practically the same thing for the United States.[106]

American neoliberalism is an extreme realization of the priority of market principles, which are now invading all areas of social life and exposing citizens to levels of risk from which they have heretofore been partially protected. Its logic entails a sustained assault on democratic institutions, such as the welfare state and labor unions, that traditionally serve as countervailing powers vis-à-vis market forces; this produces, in effect, a "politics of indifference."[107] This neoliberalism follows recent waves of corporate downsizing and restructuring that have thrown large numbers of working Americans into unemployment and poverty.[108] Middle-class people who are not dependent on state employment free their government to pursue what Japanese officials have referred to as a "slash-and-burn" system and French economist Jacques Attali calls "market dictatorship." Attali contrasts American neoliberalism with the French liberal tradition, which is also being undermined by globalization, noting that "the frantic search for money to fund elections and the scale of the criminal economy are signs of the ascendancy of the market economy over democratic ethics."[109]

With the world's economies under assault from speculation by Wall Street banks, we are witnessing a kind of hegemonic neoliberalism in which Western powers such as Germany are forced to give up their "social market economy" by pruning the welfare state while the French, under a new, socialist prime minister, try to maintain a brake on the unraveling of the social benefits that are deemed essential for preserving the "civilized [French] way of life."[110] The struggle between more or less drastic liberal measures (a struggle that, as in Asia, is also framed in terms of deep cultural differences) will determine the degree of readiness of the European Union to adopt a common currency across the continent.[111]

To put the differences in East-West neoliberalism in a nutshell, then, American neoliberalism, by excessively privileging individual rights, undermines democratic principles of social equality, whereas the dominant Asian liberal strategy, by excessively privileging collectivist security, undermines democracy by limiting individual political expression. While the European model of pastoral care and the welfare state evolved in the context of intense class conflict, the Asian model of pastoral care aims not so much at defusing class conflict as at producing citizens with the human, social, and cultural capital that will allow them to thrive in a global economy. These are some of the many traditions of liberalism—different rationalities tied to economic growth that stress different "vital" issues of culture and community—that reflect the respective histories, trajectories, and strategies of nation-states in the global economy. These varied liberal traditions dictate the formation of economic blocs—the United States, the European Union, NAFTA, ASEAN, Greater China—that are in fierce competition over trade issues; political-economic battles are increasingly cast in the civilizational discourses of Western superiority and Asian conservatism.

Conclusion

Huntington's clash-of-civilizations model is a throwback to feverish nineteenth-century imaginings about the Orient as the symbolic obverse of the West. The cultural essentialism and binarism of his theory, which opposes East and West, overlooks the logic of the political-economic imperatives that underwrite their differences and predicaments. Huntington has a nineteenth-century evolutionary view, when what is needed is original historical and cultural inquiry. Differences in economic and political rationalities are perhaps more important than civilizational differences in defining the kinds of societies in our globalized world.

Ironically, even when they reject his message that China represents a profound military threat to the West, Asian leaders like his resurrection of civilizational discourse. Saying no to the West—in wars over capitalist strategies—is only the beginning of a virtual explosion of civilizational discourses in Asia. As we shall see in the next chapter, the leaders of the Asian tiger economies are happy to talk about civilizational differences because they can feel superior to the West—if not (yet) in the realm of economics, then definitely in the language of ancient civilizations. They are busy constructing the idea of civilized empires in an affluent Asia and are embarked on a game of moral-political one-upmanship with the West. But Asian economies and societies today are more like those in the West than at any previous point in world history; thanks to Huntington, the notion of civilization, redolent of nineteenth-century themes of Orientalism and global binary oppositions, has returned as the red flag to incite global conflict.

8   Zones of New Sovereignty

Rezoning Sovereignty

I have used the concept of flexible citizenship to describe the practices of refugees and business migrants who work in one location while their families are lodged in "safe havens" elsewhere. The art of flexibility, which is constrained by political and cultural boundaries, includes sending families and businesses abroad, as well as acquiring multiple passports, second homes, overseas bank accounts, and new habits. Here, I turn the question around and look at how the art of government, which is strained by the condition of transnationality, has to further stretch the bounds of political economy and sovereignty. I will argue that the industrializing states in Southeast Asia have responded to the challenges of globalization by also becoming more flexible in their management of sovereignty.

There is a growing literature on the effects of globalization, much of it framed in terms of a state retreat in the face of inroads by global capital that has resulted in the expansion of transnational social orders. Manuel Castells, for instance, proposes that there is "a new spatial form characteristic of social practices that shape network society: the space of flows."[1] By "flows," he refers to the sequences of interaction enabled by electronic circuits, communication networks, and the social organization of globe-trotting managerial elites. Akhil Gupta and James Ferguson point to the structures of "reterritorialization" brought about by global capital and transstatal agencies that create "grids" of spatial power that discriminate by class, gender, race, and sexuality.[2] Neither model pays much attention to the role of the nation-state, since both are concerned largely with emerging forms of spatial power that do not depend on governments. In contrast, I maintain that the nation-state—with its supposed monopoly over sovereignty[3]—remains a key institution in structuring spatial order.

Despite frequent assertions about the demise of the state, the issue of state action remains central when it comes to the rearrangements of global spaces and the restructuring of social and political relations. But Saskia Sassen, for instance, maintains that global markets and supranational entities such as GATT (the General Agreement on Tariffs and Trade) and NAFTA have made serious inroads into state sovereignty. She argues that a form of "economic citizenship" has emerged that demands accountability not from governments but from global firms and markets or planetary organizations such as the United Nations.[4] Yet if we consider state power as a positive agency, the issue is no longer one of the state "losing control" but rather one of the state taking an active role in refashioning sovereignty to meet the challenges of global markets and supranational organizations.

I argue that in an era of globalization, sovereignty—"the existence of a final, highest, or supreme power over a set of people, things, or places"[5]—remains key to our understanding the shifting relations between state, market, and society. Rather than accepting claims about the end of sovereignty, we need to explore mutations in the ways in which localized political and social organizations set the terms and are constitutive of a domain of social existence. I maintain that in Southeast Asia, governments seeking to accommodate corporate strategies of location have become flexible in their management of sovereignty, so that different production sites often become institutional domains that vary in their mix of legal protections, controls, and disciplinary regimes. Anthony Giddens has usefully described civil, political, and economic rights as "arenas of *contestations* or *conflicts,* each linked to a distinctive type of surveillance, where that surveillance is both necessary to the power of superordinate groups and an axis for the operation of the dialectic of control."[6] But while European states have confronted these contestations sequentially over decades, postcolonial Asian states have had to deal with them simultaneously, mostly in an era of globalization. Newly industrializing regimes, eager to meet capitalist requirements, have evolved what I call a system of graduated sovereignty, whereby citizens in zones that are differently articulated to global production and financial circuits are subjected to different kinds of surveillance and in practice enjoy different sets of civil, political, and economic rights. By thus calibrating its control over sovereignty to the challenges of global capital, the so-called tiger state develops a system of graduated zones that also protects against pockets of political unrest.

In this chapter, I will discuss the model of graduated sovereignty and the ideological constructions of an Islamic normativity that have emerged in Southeast Asia. In the postcolonial era, the term "strong states" has been applied to the Southeast Asian regimes to describe their dominant role in directing the capitalist development of their economies, mainly through a powerful bureaucracy, public enterprises, and state monopolies.[7] While such state-centered institutions continue to exist in all Southeast Asian countries, new strategies focus more and more on forming links with global capital and producing the middle classes. Since the end of the cold war the ASEAN countries have evolved a state strategy that I refer to as "postdevelopmental." While the typical ASEAN state continues to control a (diminishing) nationalized sector of its economy, an expanding multinational sector is dominated by global capital. The postdevelopmental strategy relies on two mechanisms for attracting foreign investments and technology transfers. These are (1) the proliferation of strategic alliances with corporate actors;[8] and (2) the provision of sites that are linked to global "commodity chains" for the production of a variety of low- and high-tech goods.[9] In Malaysia, this mixed strategy requires the state to focus more and more on developing so-called smart partnerships with the private sector and foreign corporate interests. The state seeks diverse links with global capital to "maximize and balance benefits for both and for all, even if the contribution towards the partnerships may not be equal."[10] This strategy makes more flexible the relationship between state and capital, so that enterprises enjoy greater leverage in regulating labor and trade relations within the state's territory, and legal and social forms of control can be negotiable on a case-by-case basis. Malaysia is promoting this smart-partnership scheme with countries in Africa, Latin America, and Oceania. For instance, South African leaders now consider smart partnerships with foreign capital to be a strategy that will produce an "African renaissance."[11]

Under the postdevelopmental strategy, new state-capital alliances also signal a shift in relations between state and society, as the state focuses more on producing and managing populations that are attractive to global capital. Before discussing this, we need to widen our notion of sovereignty to include other forms of power that are not strictly juridical. While others view the relationship between the state and its citizens strictly in terms of political power over legal subjects, I wish to consider sovereignty as "an effect of practices" associated with law and other forms of regulation that construct relations between the state, its population, and the market.[12] Increasingly, as Asian tiger states seek to maintain their economic competitiveness and political stability, they are no longer interested in securing uniform regulatory authority over all their citizens. One can distinguish zones of graduated sovereignty in which legal controls predominate in some places and some state functions are outsourced to private enterprises in others. Through the differential deployment of state power, populations in different zones are variously subjected to political control and to social regulation by state and nonstate agencies.

The concept of governmentality is useful in describing regimes for constituting and maintaining social relations and practices within these domains. For instance, just as biotechnology has led to new ways of governing and valuing human life, globalization has induced governments to think up new ways of governing and valuing different categories of its subject population.[13] Michel Foucault uses the term *biopower* to refer to a central concern of the modern state in fostering of life, growth, and care of the population.[14] I argue that to remain globally competitive, the typical ASEAN state makes different kinds of biopolitical investments in different subject populations, privileging one gender over the other, and in certain kinds of human skills, talents, and ethnicities; it thus subjects different sectors of the population to different regimes of valuation and control. This unequal biopolitical investment in different categories of the population results in the uneven distribution of services, care, and protection; while some subjects are invested with rights and resources, others are neglected outright. Thus, globalization has induced a situation of graduated sovereignty, whereby even as the state maintains control over its territory, it is also willing in some cases to let corporate entities set the terms for constituting and regulating some domains. Sometimes, weaker and less-desirable groups are given over to the regulation of supranational entities. What results is a system of variegated citizenship in which populations subjected to different regimes of value enjoy different kinds of rights, discipline, caring, and security.

There are good reasons for using Malaysia as an illustrative example of a state that is developing a system of graduated sovereignty. Since its political independence from Great Britain in 1957, Malaysia has favored the political rights of Malays on the grounds of their status as an "indigenous" majority population and their general economic backwardness when compared with the ethnic Chinese and Indians who are descended from immigrant populations. But one can argue that from the early 1970s onward, an extensive system of graduated sovereignty has come into effect as the government has put more investment into the biopolitical improvement of the Malays, awarding them rights and benefits that are largely denied to the Chinese and Indian minorities. Special programs have awarded shares in state-held trusts, government contracts, business credit, scholarships, business licenses, university admissions, civil employment, and jobs in large firms to Malay subjects. This, in effect, has created the world's first affirmative-action system that is tied exclusively to ethnicity. The pastoral power that has been employed on behalf of the Malays has unevenly favored the middle and upper classes, and Malays as a community enjoy more rights, benefits, and claims than non-Malays. Ethnic Chinese are disciplined especially in the realms of cultural expression and economic activities,[15] while most ethnic Indians have remained plantation proletarians.

But this system of ethnic-based governmentality has been further elaborated into at least six zones of graduated sovereignty for the entire population: the low-wage manufacturing sector, the illegal labor market, the aboriginal periphery, the refugee camp, the cyber corridor, and the growth triangle. The multinational sector, which is based on semiskilled industrial labor, produces most of the manufactured goods for export. Its workforce is governed by a mix of disciplinary and repressive measures that ensure the social stability desired by foreign companies. Disciplinary mechanisms permit but limit the activities of trade unions, and policemen are quickly mobilized whenever workers engage in strikes. At the same time, state social policy ensures that the firms employ a majority of Malays in their workforce and pay minimum wages and cost-of-living allowances to avoid charges of exploitation.[16] The workers' freedom to pray during work hours also contributes to the general norms that promote self-discipline and low levels of dissent.

An immigrant labor market that draws workers from Indonesia, Bangladesh, the Philippines, and Burma has grown in response to labor shortages in the plantation and construction industries. Almost one-third of the country's eight million workers are immigrant workers.[17] They are subjected to stringent laws of employment, residence, and termination. Legal immigrants are employed in domestic service, construction, and on plantations. They enjoy limited rights of employment, but they cannot apply for citizenship. There are no labor rights for illegals who slip into the country. While Muslim illegals may be more tolerated or better treated and can often blend into the larger population by passing as Malays, non-Muslim workers, when exposed, are deported, with no rights of appeal. In the recent economic crisis, anti-immigrant sentiment has mounted, and ridding the country of illegal aliens is now considered a patriotic duty. In a cost-saving measure, the government has selected female domestics from the Philippines as the first foreign workers to be expelled. But as the currency crisis worsens in Indonesia and millions of refugees are poised to enter Malaysia, tens of thousands of Indonesian workers are being sent home. Thailand is also set to expel about one million workers from Burma and south Asia.

In contrast to the limited or nonexistent social rights afforded most locals and foreigners, a zone of superior privileges is planned for a largely Malay entrepreneurial elite. The grandly named Multimedia Super Corridor (msc) is projected to become a "springboard to serve the regional and world markets for multimedia products and services."[18] The corridor, which will link Kuala Lumpur to a new technological research center and a new international airport, is designed to facilitate the creation of another Silicon Valley in Malaysia. Besides favoring the Malay elite, the msc appears to be a project of Islamic governmentality that is intended to offset ethnic-Chinese economic power, which is linked to the transnational firms that are concentrated in Penang. Special laws, policies, and practices are being drafted to encourage investment in a new kind of Malay subject who will be fully at home in a multimedia world. Affirmative-action employment policies will be suspended to free up the capital, talent, and information that will ultimately favor the Malay corporate elite. Bill Gates, of Microsoft, and other high-technology-industry executives from the United States and Japan have been persuaded to commit themselves to building enterprises in the zone. Visas will be readily issued to foreigners known as "knowledge workers," who represent the "best minds." Students will be trained in "smart" (high-tech) schools and a new university. For these privileged few, there will be no censorship of the Internet. New practices include residents having access to distance-learning technology, to telemedical services, and to an electronic government. The msc is thus a project that involves an enormous state investment and is intended to breed and nurture a new kind of computer-literate Malay culture. Names such as Leonardo Da Vinci, Ernest Hemingway, and Stephen Spielberg are invoked as models of creativity.[19] By focusing on high-technology knowledge production and technological innovation, the project provides an alternative to the national dependence on low-wage subcontracting industries and offers an opportunity for Malaysia to link up with the transnational research and development community. Although the official explanation for the MSC is that it is a "test bed" to safely experiment with "modernization without undermining . . . traditional values,"[20] in reality it will be a superprivileged zone where the Malay elite plugs into the world of high-technology industry.

For Southeast Asian states then, ethnicity often becomes a sorting mechanism for defining the meaning of and the claims on sovereignty. For instance, the flood of boat people in the aftermath of the Indochina war brought Vietnamese (in 1975) and Cambodian (in 1979) refugees to camps throughout Southeast Asia. Vietnamese boat people, most of whom were ethnic Chinese, were kept in isolated camps in Malaysia, Indonesia, and the Philippines under the jurisdiction of the United Nations High Commission for Refugees (UNHCR). Along the Thai border, Cambodians in refugee camps had no political claims on the Thai government, and only the humanitarian norm of *nonrefoulement*—the right not to be returned to a country in which they will suffer persecution—allowed them to remain in "temporary" camps while awaiting resettlement, mainly in the United States and France.[21] In Southeast Asia, as in most Western countries receiving refugees, the prevailing practice was not to offer asylum but to emphasize state policies of control and deterrence, so that "refugee law has become immigration law, emphasizing the protection of borders rather than the protection of persons."[22] By and large, the receiving countries refused to extend asylum to the refugees (ethnic Chinese, Vietnamese, Cambodians, and Laotians) in ways that would have made them citizens. The only exception was the Chams, from Cambodia, whom the Malaysian state considers part of the Malay-Muslim diaspora and thus acceptable as citizens. This selective reception of refugees was an expression of how sovereignty is shaped by a dominant ethnicity and by the nation-state's definition of its desired ethnic composition. Refugees and citizens of undesirable ethnicity are frequently given over to the regulatory power of supranational agencies.

Also in the margins of mainstream sovereignty are the aboriginal areas, where a mix of disciplining and civilizing powers seeks to lure the aborigines away from their nomadic life in the jungle and persuade them to become settlers like the Malay peasants. Although aboriginal groups are also considered bumiputra and, like the Malays, enjoy special affirmative-action rights, in practice they have access to these rights only if they abandon the aboriginal way of life and become absorbed into the larger Malay population. Jungle dwellers who resist the civilizing mission of schools, sedentary agriculture, markets, and Islam are left to their own devices in the midst of the destruction caused by the encroaching logging companies. Generally, scattered and neglected nomads are made to adapt to development by becoming agricultural producers. Aboriginal groups in practice enjoy very limited rights vis-à-vis their territory, their livelihood, or their cultural identity. The Penan foragers of Sarawak have developed two different responses to territorial encroachment, each of which is shaped by a different sense of the Malaysian government's sovereignty. The eastern Penan have actively blockaded logging activities, and this has won them international attention; the western Penan have acquiesced to logging as part of their acceptance of Malaysian rule.[23]

Even as differentiated zones of sovereignty proliferate within national borders, there are also moves toward forming multinational zones of sovereignty. One modality is the development of growth triangles (GTs), which straddle the borders between neighboring states so as to maximize the locational advantage and attract global capital. GTs are determined by "economic geometry," in which location, the accessibility of cheap labor, the possibility of exploitation of complementary resources, and the proximity of a regional hub, such as Singapore, enhance the competitive advantage of the region in the global economy.[24] So far, three GTs have been formed by linking contiguous parts of neighboring countries. The country configurations are Indonesia-Malaysia-Singapore (Sijori), Indonesia-Malaysia-Thailand, and Brunei-Indonesia-Malaysia-Philippines. Sijori is a massive industrial park that sits astride the Riau archipelago and draws on the complementary labor and technical resources of three countries to enhance investment opportunities. From the Singaporean perspective, this growth triangle allows Singapore to retain command/control functions at home while moving "low-end" jobs offshore. It takes advantage of cheap Indonesian labor, and it also ameliorates tensions over the presence of too many guest workers within the city state. Sijori thus represents a zone of low-cost production in which Singapore capital and expertise can be used for training and managing regional workers. It represents the low end of a system of zones in which the city-state is the site of continuously upgrading human capital.[25]

Thus, growth triangles are zones of special sovereignty that are arranged through a multinational network of smart partnerships and that exploit the cheap labor that exists within the orbit of a global hub such as Singapore. It appears that GT workers are subject less to the rules of their home country and more to the rules of companies and to the competitive conditions set by other growth triangles in the region. More research needs to be done to discover the kinds of "conducive regulatory environment" and labor discipline that prevail under foreign management.[26] It is this foreign management that defines the "business environment," that is, the rules of inclusion and exclusion and the rights and privileges of workers from different countries. To help foreign enterprises exploit the advantages of its location and its setup vis-à-vis the other growth triangles, the Sijori triangle established a graded system of labor and material conditions in each of the triangle's nodes: In Singapore, one finds skilled labor and sophisticated business and control services; in Johore, skilled and semiskilled labor, recreation, and land; and in Batam and Riau, "low-cost, controlled" labor and some natural amenities (beaches).[27] By incorporating different mixes of manpower, natural resources, and regulatory conditions in graded zones, the growth-triangle model transforms previously rural or "unproductive" hinterlands into what have been called "extended metropolitan regions" (EMRs). As dense production and distribution nodes, where the cross-border flows of capital, people, and information are intensified, EMRs further refine the time-space coordinates of "flexible production" through the regional reorganization of economic activities and social sovereignty.

Indonesia represents an interesting case of a so-called emerging tiger nation, where there is a less-coherent postdevelopmental strategy and much of the manufacturing is dominated by cheap, low-skilled labor working in export-oriented industries, and where citizens enjoy different degrees of state investment and legal and social protection. Like Malaysia, Indonesia over the past two decades has transformed itself into an industrializing power. It now has an industrial labor force of seven million workers.[28] Large export-oriented industrial zones are located in Sumatra and Java; they depend on cheap labor to manufacture furniture, watches, clothing, shoes, toys, and plastic goods. Millions of young women have left their rice fields to work for less than a living wage in factories operated by Koreans that subcontract for brand-name companies such as Nike, Reebok, and The Gap. But besides making Indonesia part of the global production system, these industrial estates are institutional contexts of limited citizenship: workers are rarely protected by the state, are in fact frequently harassed by the military, and are left to adjust as well as they can to the exigencies of the market.

Indonesian workers are among the lowest paid in Asia, and the majority are young women who seem to lack the most basic human rights. In 1994, women working twelve-hour days sewing Gap outfits made less than $2.00 a day, including overtime. In the Tangerang zone, outside Jakarta, thousands of young women employed by Adidas and Nike took home much less. That year, the Indonesian Prosperity Trade Union (sbsi), calculating that the average worker needed to earn at least $2.50 a day, broke "the taboo on labor strikes" and called a national strike to protest low wages.[29] After a long struggle, the government agreed to a minimum wage of $2.00 a day, but this was unevenly enforced, coming into effect only in some urban factories. When I visited the area in mid-1996, workers claimed they needed at least $5.00 a day to survive.

The feminization of "low-end" manufacturing work depends on gendered forms of labor control and harassment. The widespread surveillance and much of the daily control of female workers center on their bodies, for instance, in the provision of food, in the granting or withholding of permission for menstrual leave, in the pressure for family planning, and in the physical confinement imposed during work hours. Examples of sexual harassment include timing visits to the toilet and using the excuse of having to verify requests for menstrual leave to conduct body searches. Workers are crammed into dormitories above or next to warehouses, thus creating firetraps. Managers punish the tardy by making them stand under the sun for hours and are quick to fire those who demand basic survival wages.[30] Whenever there is a strike, the army is deployed against the workers, no matter how peaceful they are.[31] In my visit to the Tangerang zone, I noticed that military barracks are often adjacent to factory sites, and army personnel mingle freely with security guards outside the factory gates.[32] I was told that the army could reach any factory within twenty minutes of an outbreak of worker insurrection. Indonesians think it is normal for the army to keep industrial cities secure for factories, and factory bosses routinely make "donations" to local commanders to help meet their costs.[33] In practice, these free-trade zones often operate as sovereignty-free zones, where workers are denied the most basic social protections and are generally unshielded from the onslaught of capital while remaining vulnerable to the state's repressive apparatus.

Aboriginal peoples in jungle communities also experience limited civil rights and frequent neglect by the state. Indigenous groups are labeled *orang terasing* (isolated peoples) on account of their isolation from mainstream society, their nomadic culture, and their imputed primitivity.[34] In West Kalimantan, Borneo, the indigenous Dayaks, who are not represented in the local government, are denied legal protection against crimes committed by Muslim migrants from Madura. The Dayaks are also fighting a larger battle against timber companies that are grabbing their land. Security forces are routinely used to destroy Dayak crops and jungle resources, to enforce land theft, and to torture people into accepting "compensation" for land taken to develop plantations. The Dayaks are practicing self-defense in accordance with their customary law (*adat*), which permits them to attack Madurese migrants and timber-estate developers. These clashes have produced killing fields in the jungles.[35] As in the industrial zones, the aboriginal enclaves are subject to two regulatory authorities, namely, private enterprise and the army. Citizens are exploited and controlled in such a way that capital appears to hold local sovereignty, and this sovereignty is enforced by state troops. In the market domains where capital reigns supreme, the state's function seems reduced to that of night watchman.

I have thus identified what might be called a system of graduated sovereignty that is superimposed on the conventional arrangement of nation-states in Southeast Asia. In varying degrees, Southeast Asian states have responded to globalization by assigning "different social destinies" to their populations according to the roles those populations play in making their countries competitive and profitable.[36] The MSC, in which Malaysia's elite has invested heavily, is shielded by the government, while the inhabitants of the free trade zones that are the links in global commodity chains are often stripped of their right to state protection and subjected instead to severe corporate discipline, backed by the army. Aboriginal enclaves are usually places to dump unprofitable commodities or zones to be cleared for new investment ventures. But this fragmentation of sovereignty across a range of locations has required the state to assert its ideological power to build up national legitimacy and thereby sustain economic growth, social stability, and regional interdependency. How do these new styles of governmentality, in which different categories of citizens are treated according to their ability to serve market competitiveness, take normative expression at the national and transnational levels?[37]

The New Islam as Corporate Normativity

Kuala Lumpur (or K.L.), its old Moorish buildings now overshadowed by twin towers that pierce the tropical sky (and that are currently enjoying fame as the world's tallest buildings), is a global city and a showcase for Islamic corporate power. On a palm-fringed hillock stands the Kuala Lumpur Hilton, where attendants in white suits and batik sarongs rush forward to greet well-groomed Malay executives wielding cellular phones as they step out of limousines. Women in silk *baju kurong* (the loose Malay tunic and sarong), dripping jewelry from their ears and necks, saunter in on their way to fancy receptions. These members of the corporate elite are the "preferred Malays" (as they are called by the Malaysian public)—the lucky but not always talented few who have been favored by the New Economic Policy and by the patronage of powerful politicians.[38] But with regional economic integration, the horizons of new professionals have stretched beyond Malaysia. These new professionals are joining a segregated stratosphere—one created by corporate networks, political parties, professional groupings, clubs and golf courses, think tanks, and universities—that has increased cultural commonality among elite citizens of ASEAN countries while the gulf between them and ordinary citizens in the region has widened. What we see is a revamped Islam that has come to infuse Malaysian culture, as well as influence ASEAN corporate culture.

The outward symbols and forms of Malaysian corporate and professional culture are shaped more by Madison Avenue and Hollywood than by local culture. For instance, Kuala Lumpur has caught up with Singapore as a city of shopping malls; it now boasts the world's largest swimming pool with man-made waves, which is located in a mall decorated like Las Vegas. American pop music blasts forth from shopping malls filled with boutiques such as Calvin Klein, DKNY, and Ralph Lauren. Young people are increasingly educated in Western universities through an economical "twinning" arrangement in which the first two years of a foreign curriculum are completed in Malaysia before students attend an American, Australian, or British university. A new class of superficially Westernized Malay professionals now runs the country according to American management principles, although there is still substantial room for increased efficiency and imagination. As in the United States, public universities are being downsized and corporatized, while the social sciences—for example, anthropology—are being replaced by "social administration" studies. The American corporate presence in K.L. is so pervasive that the city seems like an economic and cultural extension of California.

Perhaps not surprisingly, the headlong rush toward globalized culture has stimulated a desire for rediscovering local roots and reasserting a distinctive regional identity. New narratives about a wider religious commonality that is linked to powerful states have emerged to counter the worst excesses of flexible citizenship and consumerism. The revival of the term "civilization" by Samuel Huntington has encouraged Asian leaders to articulate a cultural logic that can guide and justify their burgeoning sense of economic power and cosmopolitanism.[39] While local scholars question Huntington's knowledge of Asian civilizations and his hawkish stance toward the East, they appreciate his validation of "enduring" Asian civilizations.

Alongside other "Asian-values" discourses circulating in insular Southeast Asia, an Islam-infused nationalism has emerged in Malaysia. This new Islamic ethos weds a religious reflowering to an unswerving allegiance to the state; it uses religion to promote a cultural kinship that can help integrate the national project into the region.[40] In recent years, the Mahathir regime has taken steps to modernize Islam through a range of strategies. First, the state has taken away some of the more abusive personal powers of the sultans and reduced their overall role as the key symbol of (an older social order of) Islam. Second, the government is trying to regulate another bastion of traditional Islamic power—the network of Islamic courts that shape the local understanding of Islamic laws. Ulamas associated with these courts often issue arbitrary *fatwas* and other Islamic injunctions, especially against certain changes in social behavior that come with secularization. The official explanation for curbing the Islamic courts is that the national standardization of Islamic law will ensure that women are not disproportionately prosecuted for violating codes governing dress and sexual behavior.[41] The larger goal appears to be state control over Islamic law as an instrument of and a rationale for national growth and security. Third, the government is claiming Islam as a force in the broader front of nationalism and state power. Political leaders argue that "an Islamic country must first ensure security and economic prosperity before getting into the details of implementing Islamic principles on the people."[42] Islam should be used to turn Malaysia into a "model state," but what the politicians have in mind is not another Iran but rather a state in which a moderate and reasonable Islam helps to strengthen the state by working and meshing smoothly with global capitalism.

The fourth strategy is a transformation of the cultural sensibility of Malaysian Islam, by emphasizing the conjunction of Islam and capitalist modernity. The prime minister Mahathir has declared that "Islam wants its followers to be self-sufficient, independent, and progressive."[43] During the decades when the government wanted to create a large Malay middle class and a corporate elite, Mahathir had sought to demonstrate that "there is no reason why the Islamic faith, properly interpreted, cannot achieve spiritual well-being as well as material success for the Malays."[44] A Malaysian scholar notes: "The values listed in the *Mid-Term Review of the Fourth Malaysia Plan* were exactly the kinds of values to raise productivity at home, increase competitiveness abroad, and ensure political stability always. Among them were 'better discipline, more self-reliance and striving for excellence' which together with 'thriftiness' and 'a more rational and scientific approach in overcoming problems' were 'values which are progressive and consistent with the needs of a modernizing and industrializing plural society.' "[45]

In insular Southeast Asia, this new role for Islam as a productive force for tolerance, inclusiveness, and economic development has culminated in claims about an "Asian renaissance." For Anwar Ibrahim, the deputy prime minister of Malaysia, a new era of Asian cultural vitality and autonomy has dawned: "The Renaissance of Asia entails the growth, development, and flowering of Asian societies based on a certain vision of perfection; societies imbued with truth and the love of learning, justice and compassion, mutual respect and forbearance, and freedom and responsibility. It is the transformation of its cultures and societies from its capitulation to Atlantic powers to the position of self-confidence and its reflowering at the dawn of a new millennium."[46]

These strong claims suggest a pan-Islamic nationalism that is built on the common Islamic links between Malaysia, Indonesia, and other Southeast Asian countries; they also recall the precolonial era (from the fourteenth to the eighteenth centuries) when Islam was the force that brought commerce and splendor to Southeast Asian trading empires.[47] Anwar Ibrahim notes that the grounds for identifying an Asian renaissance are religious revivalism, the end of socialism, and the vibrant economic transformation of the region. He claims that "centuries ago Muslim thinkers conceived and expounded the concept of *ahadiyyat a-kathra,* which presupposes the essential oneness and transcendent connectedness or the apparent diversity on the surface. Asians firmly rooted in their cultural and spiritual traditions do possess the intellectual capacity to perceive the cultural unity of Asia, its meta-culture."[48] But this notion of an Asian renaissance is mainly an Islamic one; Anwar cites "attempts by Muslim thinkers such as Al-Afghani, Syed Ahmad Khan and Iqbal, among others, to re-discover and re-articulate their Islamic heritage as an Islamic renaissance." He goes on to say that the values to be cherished and disseminated "include spirituality, family cohesion, and a sense of community which are still real in many Asian societies but less meaningful in the West."[49] Anwar's views have been disseminated in scholarly forums and through publication; they provide a framework for shaping elite thinking about Malaysian modernity. The only public dissenting voice is that of local anthropologist Shamsul A. Baharuddin, who argues that the Asian-renaissance discourse is a "kind of ideology" that is linked to the interests of the ruling class. It seeks social order and should not be confused with the Western notion of renaissance, which implies revolt against institutionalized religion, according to Shamsul.[50]

But the Asian renaissance is precisely about deinstitutionalizing an older form of religious order by imposing from above a reformed Islam that positions the ruling elite and develops their moral power in a renewed nationalism. In sharp contrast, then, to the images of Islamic radicalism in the Middle East and in the recent past in Southeast Asia,[51] the new Islam promotes new normativities in cultural behavior, technical expertise, and regional cooperation. Political leaders claim the new Islam not only flourishes in the multiethnic milieus of Southeast Asia but also fosters "economic progress in partnership with others."[52] Under the new Islam, society is exposed to the flexible operations of market principles, which includes the mass employment of young Muslim women who are frequently transported to distant workplaces where their bosses are non-Muslim South Korean or ethnic-Chinese managers. This new Islamic governmentality thus deploys gender in a way that subjects working-class Malay women to disciplinary power from another ethnic group, while "civilizing" Malay male professionals are considered to be equals of the economically successful diasporan Chinese.

Muslims are encouraged to work with fewer constraints in Chinese-dominated and westernized cities such as Singapore, Hong Kong, and Taipei. Muslim school children and businessmen are learning Mandarin to work more effectively with the Chinese communities that control commerce throughout the region. Corporate networking *has* tempered the more austere Islamic practices, and Southeast Asian Muslim yuppies are eager to be the new model of how a moderate and reasonable Islam can work successfully with global capital. For instance, in world-class hotels that cater to the every whim of patrons, rooms come equipped with both minibars and a Qur'an. An arrow on the ceiling points toward Mecca to guide Muslims in prayer. Muslim movers and shakers are at home in settings where Muslim women wearing veils rub shoulders with Westerners in swimsuits and Muslims dine alongside non-Muslims eating pork and drinking brandy. The new ease that the religiously correct, self-made new Malay expresses in mingling with international players and an international clientele has been endorsed by the new Islam, which encourages both wealth accumulation and a cosmopolitan worldliness that recalls an earlier era of Islamic trading empires and the cultural syncretism of peoples across the Malay archipelago. The new Islam also defines acceptable and unacceptable forms of "liberalism" that underlie the concept of "ASEAN solidarity"; it encourages economic liberalism and allows for the presence of the legal liberalism that is associated with "Western decadence and excessive freedom"—as long as Muslims are not participants. Thus, by promoting Muslim professional and investor classes who can participate confidently in the globalized contexts of capitalism, the rise of Islamic governmentality operates as a foil to "Chinese" economic power in the region.

"Civilizational Dialogue" and Internal Colonies

Under state sponsorship, a Center for Civilizational Dialogue has been set up at the University of Malaya to produce a new moral vision of Southeast Asian regionalism. In an obvious response to Huntington's "clash of civilizations," "civilizational dialogue" focuses on civilizational differences as well as "the affinities that exist between civilizations," according to a brochure published by the center. Disavowing Huntington's paradigm, which assumes an inevitable competition between global powers, the brochure maintains that only when one "celebrates both the similarities and the differences between civilizations" can one "evolve a truly just, humane and compassionate world civilization where there is neither the dominant nor the dominated." Nevertheless, the brochure identifies a conflict—one generated by "the globalization process, propelled as it is by powerful economic and technological forces, [which] threatens to create a hegemonic, homogeneous, materialistic civilization that is antagonistic to spiritually and ethically based civilizations."[53] This suggests an alternative hierarchy of civilizations that turns Huntington's model of a supremacist Western civilization on its head. From the (official) Malaysian perspective, Asian civilizations are ethically based and therefore superior to, but threatened by, the soulless and overweening power of Western civilization. As the center of and host to such civilizational exchanges, Malaysia prides itself on being, in the words of the center's brochure, "a nation where civilizations converge." In rather immoderate language, the brochure claims that "there is perhaps no other nation on earth where substantial numbers of Muslims, Buddhists, Confucianists, Taoists, Hindus, Christians, and Sikhs live together in relative peace and harmony. What is equally remarkable is that [in Malaysia] civilizational communities have for decades been exposed to, and interacted with, Western civilization."[54] The center will be the promoter and disseminator of civilizational discourse; it has held international conferences titled "Islam and Confucianism," "Islam, Japan, and the West," and "Civilizational Dialogue: Present Realities; Future Possibilities." The official, ideological nature of civilizational language is spelled out clearly when it is linked directly to regional and national interests: "Shared values, derived through inter-civilizational dialogue, it is hoped, will help to mold the ASEAN identity of tomorrow."[55]

Civilizational discourse that directly engages globalization processes also aids in the articulation of an enlightened set of Asian values that is friendly to economic liberalism, a concept that is redefined as "democracy with Asian flavor and characteristics." Invoking Adam Smith, Malaysian prime minister Mahathir talks about the "reasonable enlightened self-interest coming from a rationality" based on multilateral cooperation, so that ASEAN countries are helping all boats to rise "with the rising East Asian economic tide."[56] This Asian liberalism resonates with a loose sense of cultural kinship that stems from Islam and the historical legacy of trading empires. Perhaps nowhere else in the world has the sense of cultural kinship, combined with shared authoritarian values of state power, been deployed more effectively to generate an elite sense of collective dignity, one that is based on geopolitical location and common regional trade interests. As Anthony D. Smith has pointed out, the interstate groupings such as ASEAN "only help to perpetuate, if they do not inflame, the hold of national identities and nationalist aspirations, as do the new classes of international capitalism."[57]

The use of "civilization" as an overarching set of core values that are common to the "diverse cultures and communities" in Southeast Asia allows politicians to frame national and regional problems in stark East-West terms. Such talk about regional civilizational commonalities is also convenient for suppressing discussions about the class, cultural, regional, and political differences that are endemic throughout the region. Civilizational discourse maintains that ASEAN is the most "multi-religious and multi-cultural" regional grouping in the world.[58] As the Asian tigers' growth rates have risen dramatically over the past decade, the rhetoric of "ASEAN solidarity" has served to present a relatively unified position within the Asia Pacific Economic Conference (APEC), as well as a counterweight to the challenge represented by China's giant economy.

But the discourse defining an ASEAN civilizational world also lends spiritual authority to the practices of individual regimes in managing and suppressing profane others, who are excluded by such discourses. Seeking to expand its economic muscle, ASEAN recently admitted Vietnam and Burma, making ASEAN an interstatal system that tolerates or is silent about human-rights violations in a network of "internal colonies."[59] Each Southeast Asian state has its own irredentist groups: the East Timorese and Acehnese in Indonesia, the Shans and Karens in Burma, the Patani Malays in Thailand, the Dayaks in Malaysia and Indonesia, and the Moros in the Philippines. In a policy of scratching each other's backs, governments silence debates about and criticisms of human-rights violations in their ASEAN neighbors. For instance, prodemocracy activists in Malaysia who demonstrate against Indonesia's occupation of East Timor have been suppressed by the Malaysian government, which uses the excuse that such activities damage state-level relations within the region. Protests in Malaysia, Thailand, and the Philippines against the admission of the Burmese regime into ASEAN are barely reported in the local media.[60] George J. Aditjondro notes that because "all ASEAN governments have their own 'East Timors' in their backyard" ASEAN has become "a conspiracy of repressive regimes, busy protecting each other's behinds."[61] These internal colonies, then, are places where sovereign power is imposed with overwhelming coercion (as in East Timor) or is simply absent, so that a kind of low-grade struggle continues to fester (as in Patani in Thailand). Thus, processes of regional cooperation and modern state-endorsed subjectivity proceed alongside processes of fragmentation that seek to elude centralized power.

The galaxy of differentiated zones is thus unevenly integrated into the structures of state power and global capital. Technology zones and growth triangles are plugged tightly into globalization processes, while aboriginal and ethnic-minority reserves are often disarticulated from national and regional centers of power. In short, the structural logic of globalization has not resulted in the solidification of differences between civilizations but rather in the proliferation of differentiated sovereignty within and across borders. The moral regulation of the state both homogenizes and individualizes its subjects, so that while unifying images and forms associated with Islam emphasize uniformity, the cultural definition of jungle dwellers, illegals, and ethnic minorities makes them less legitimate in the social order. These zones of graduated sovereignty thus call into question the uniformity of citizenship and the kinds of political or moral claims that subjects can make on state power. More and more, the state's authority as legitimized power depends on modes of regulation that are morally justified in terms of a hegemonic cultural model that defines normal and deviant subjects even as it conceals relations of inequality between the ruler and the ruled.

For the middle classes, who are vested in the structure of the state, moralizing discourses about national unity and ASEAN solidarity continue to sustain their claims on state protection. For instance, whereas the international press attributes the recent wave of currency devaluation to reckless borrowing and lending, the building of megaprojects, and the lack of market controls in the tiger economies,[62] local politicians blame outsiders, who are viewed as having the antithesis of Asian civilizational values. Urging "ASEAN unity," Mahathir blamed international financier George Soros, whom he demonized as anti-Asia, and "anti–poor countries": "We are told that we must open up, that trade and commerce must be totally free. Free for whom? For rogue speculators. For anarchists wishing to destroy weak countries in their crusade for open societies, to force us to submit to the dictatorship of international manipulators. We want to embrace borderlessness but we still need to protect ourselves from self-serving rogues and international brigandage."[63] As the crisis spreads across the region and local currencies continue to slide, other Asians see a larger conspiracy that is motivated by Western jealousy. Expressed first through attacks on local currencies and then through regulations imposed by the International Monetary Fund (IMF), this larger conspiracy seeks to intimidate relatively healthy economies. Culture and economics become entangled as ordinary people try to understand the fiscal crisis in terms of a profound crisis in East-West civilizational values. Such a cultural understanding helps to sustain the social contract even under circumstances in which the state is increasingly unable to deliver the goods in their accustomed quantities, nor to plan its economy in a world of unruly financial markets. Will the postdevelopmental strategy protecting the interests of the middle classes become undermined, and must the tiger states once again resort to repressive measures to control social unrest?

Seedbeds of Counterpublics?

A major goal of the postdevelopmental state has been the production of a middle-class society that consists of competitive workers and consumers who are attractive to global capital. Yet the growth of the middle classes in Southeast Asia has also brought about movements that challenge the state's monopoly over the meaning of citizenship. Members of the middle classes who are frustrated with conventional party politics and the corrupted electoral systems have turned to nongovernmental organizations (NGOs) as a way of participating in public life without undue intervention by the state. Besides those NGOs associated with the United Nations, there are thousands of local NGOs working in the region that are engaged in a variety of activities; their activities range from providing social services to promoting the causes of special groups to broadly educating people about human rights. At least at the microlevel, NGOs have been able to promote the process of securing social, economic, and cultural rights for particular "target" groups, such as the poor, refugees, workers, women and children, political prisoners, and minority and aboriginal populations. These NGOs have become seedbeds for progressive

forces that are struggling against state repression and seeking a broader definition of Asian democracy. While in Indonesia, Singapore, and Malaysia, the
state seeks to control individual NGOs through periodic repression, it cannot
prevent the formation of transnational NGO networks, which act as a bulwark
against state power and focus international attention on state actions that
violate human rights.

The international discourse of human rights has been variously deployed to
shape new terms of social existence in different parts of the region. In war-
torn Cambodia, the presence of the United Nations Transitional Authority
has been a major factor in the flourishing of local NGOs, most of which are
dedicated to performing welfare-type services for the poor, the war-injured,
and the orphaned. NGOs set up by returning Cambodian expatriates also seek
to educate local people about civil liberties and political rights, such as the
right to vote and women's and children's rights, and about an American-style
multiculturalism that would transcend ethnic-based notions of citizenship.[64]
However, the recent coup in Phnom Penh and the killings of opposition
supporters that followed powerfully demonstrate the limits, in an admittedly
anarchic regime, of international condemnation, UN-type sanctions, and demands for human rights. Who is accountable for the citizens of those countries that have come under UN authority, when that authority can easily be
revoked by the state?

Elsewhere in the region, the majority of NGOs have been formed by what
Fred Chiu calls "a-systemic" public activists, that is, activists who are embroiled in local politics but who also maintain links with similar organizations
in other countries.[65] From the late 1970s onward, Hong Kong has been a site of
dynamic experimentation with alternative politics. Civic groups formed by
public-sector unionists, teachers, and social workers have successfully agitated
against massive government projects, such as nuclear plants, and become the
vehicle for a genuine democratic movement from below.[66] Many such groups
are dedicated to helping people who have been displaced and exploited by the
industrial revolution in China. Increasingly, NGOs that are organized around
religion, feminism, human rights, or environmental problems are based on
grassroots building coalitions that bypass state, corporate, and UN structures
to effect social change. For instance, the Hong Kong–based Asian Human
Rights Commission "seeks to promote greater awareness and realization of
human rights in the Asian region, and to mobilize Asian and international

public opinion to obtain relief and redress for the victims of human rights violations."[67] It sends fact-finding missions to trouble spots in, for instance, Indonesia, Cambodia, Burma, and Nepal and publishes a newsletter to disseminate information and foster solidarity among the multiplicity of NGOs that are fighting for civil, political, economic, and social rights in the region. This organization is a major regional voice in articulating human rights and condemning the violence initiated and/or supported by state authorities throughout the region.

In the setting of Malaysian communal party politics, the few NGOs that cater mainly to non-Malay interests are vital centers and are organized around consumer and environmental issues. Consumer, environmental, women's, and religious movements often seem to be the only alternative voices in a public sphere that is dominated by discourses about the nation, religion, and civilization that are carefully in line with official language. Through their activities and publications, they play an invaluable role in providing different news and perspectives than can be found in the government-controlled media, in nurturing independent thinking, and in generally educating people about their rights and obligations as citizens. In Thailand and the Philippines, NGOs have been very active in forming grassroots coalitions to fight for women's rights, for workers' rights, and for democracy as well.

Indonesia too has become a hotbed of NGOs that have been founded by lawyers, journalists, writers, feminists, environmentalists, trade unionists, and members of the new middle classes who are seeking agrarian reform, democratic freedoms, and state accountability. This politically significant development has inspired government officials to remind citizens that Indonesians are bound by duty to the nation and that Indonesia is "not a rights-based society."[68] Indeed, the Soeharto government considered NGOs such a threat that the July 1996 crackdown on the political opposition was extended into a broad attack on leaders of NGOs from labor, legal, feminist, and student organizations.[69] These groups have been active in educating a widen spectrum of Indonesians on human rights. The government went so far as to compare sixty-five NGOs to the discredited Community Party of Indonesia (PKI), accusing the group of seeking, with the help of the World Bank, to replace the existing Agrarian Law. In many cases, such intimidation included raids and the arrests of NGO leaders. The state, however, has to watch out for international reactions to its crackdown on local NGOs. The arrest of Muchtar Pakpahan, the leader of the SBSI (Indonesia's first independent mass labor movement), generated a raft of letters and faxes calling for his unconditional release from labor groups throughout the world. Groups such as the Legal Aid Society (Yayasan Lembaga Bantuan Hukum) are usually the only recourse for citizens seeking to combat state brutality, and these civil-rights fighters often find themselves in jail with their clients. But by mobilizing international support against state repression and hosting visits by foreign-based NGOs, such struggles are kept alive in the international media.[70] For instance, as a result of such contacts, articles on Indonesia's human-rights activists have been published in American press such as the *Nation*.

Asian NGOs have come to rely more and more on transnational networks with access to the same devices of power—communications technology, travel, South-South linkages—that are controlled by the ASEAN ruling elites.[71] But in a triangular relationship with their home governments, their Southern counterparts, and their Northern counterparts, Asian NGOs often have to mediate between rival conceptions of rights and sovereignty. On the one hand, they are struggling against state repression, and they would like to bring international pressure to bear on problematic policies at home. On the other hand, Asian NGOs often find themselves siding with the positions taken by their own governments and by other Southern NGOs against the human-rights stances of northern states and groups. Asian NGOs tend to stress the priority of social, economic, and cultural rights in the South against the north's exclusive focus on civil and political rights. Asian NGOs also favor forming South-South coalitions to bypass the economic and political domination of the north. For instance, at the UN World Conference on Human Rights in Vienna in 1993, Asian NGOs linked human rights to a demand for the restructuring of a north-dominated global order.[72]

Yet at the same time, Asian NGOs fighting local battles often find that North-South coalitions are much more effective at bringing international pressure to bear on government repression. One example has already been mentioned, namely, the international protest against SBSI leader Pakpahan's arrest in Indonesia. At the height of the Indonesian government's attacks on the political opposition, the cancellation of a sale of jet fighters by the United States was widely viewed as American support for human-rights activists and a great morale booster for democracy fighters. Women's groups have also found that North-South coalitions are more effective for putting pressure on their governments than South-South coalitions. At the fourth World Conference on Women in Beijing in August 1995, Asian feminists, despite their resistance to hegemonic notions of gender and family by human-rights activists, called for a "strategic sisterhood" with Western feminists.[73]

In Southeast Asia, then, NGOs have become vehicles for the middle classes to struggle for greater democracy and to define a substantive citizenship that is based on socioeconomic and cultural rights and is midway between formal citizenship and universalist human-rights prescriptions.[74] As such, they have the potential for forming counterpublics that could make up for the weak power of opposition political parties. NGOs are the late-twentieth-century equivalents of the coffee shops, universities, and salons where new discourses and practices of secularism and democracy emerged to mediate between the postabsolutist modern states of Western Europe and the private spheres of economy and family.[75] The activism of Asian NGOs shows that in Asia, the fight for democracy is being led by the middle classes (which, other than in Japan, have largely emerged only within the last twenty years).[76] They are fighting not only arbitrary state power but also the state's flexible approach to sovereignty, which sometimes denies the human rights of subjects. But unlike the public sphere in early modern Europe, the public sphere in Asia has the ability to form transnational coalitions outside state and market systems. This ability increases the power of interlinked NGOs to form potential global counterpublics and to articulate alternative visions that go beyond the Western bourgeois focus on individual rights.

Conclusion

As the economic crisis continues to gather momentum throughout Southeast Asia, political leaders are poised to react against expected social unrest. Already, in Indonesia, an emerging economic tiger has suddenly been leashed by IMF policies; millions of workers have been laid off. Labor strikes and food rioting have erupted in small and large cities across the archipelago. Many indigenous Indonesians consider ethnic Chinese, who control much of the economy, to be the cause of economic hardship. While a few tycoons, such as Liem Sioe Liong, Bob Hasan, and Mocthar Riady, have become exceedingly rich working closely with the Soeharto government, the majority of ethnic Chinese are small shopkeepers, traders, and professionals. But as the economic crisis intensifies, attacks on merchants have become indistinguishable from anti-Chinese riots; ethnic hostilities are being whipped up by army and Muslim leaders who accuse ethnic Chinese of hoarding, of raising food prices, and of sending millions of dollars overseas. The 1998 Chinese New Year celebrations were canceled (once again) for fear that a display of Chinese wealth would incite jealousy and violence. Hundreds of Chinese-owned shops, nightclubs, churches, and even homes have been looted and destroyed.[77] The country is in danger of losing its relatively small class of well-trained professionals and entrepreneurs, who have been crucial for running most of its modern industries. It appears that the export enclaves and zones of differentiated sovereignty, which have been the economic and political centerpieces of the tiger economies, have not been sufficient innovations to protect them from the anarchy of global financial markets.

Even in the more stable Malaysian and Singaporean economies, there is a growing sense that the state is less able to protect its citizens or to deliver the goods. Although not expecting rioting in the streets, political leaders there have consulted each other on how to deal with the political fallout. Can the postdevelopmental strategy, which is based on an implicit social contract between the state and the middle classes, be sustained, or will repressive measures be wielded more readily again? As before, globally induced economic circumstances will require the Asian tiger states to adjust their relations to the market and to society. This strategic flexibility, which is honed by the social turbulence engendered by capitalism, is echoed in the practices of the rich and poor. An Indonesian Chinese stockbroker, reacting to the news that the Chinese New Year celebrations in Jakarta had been cancelled, remarked, "I don't think too many of us were going to venture out over the period anyway. Some of us are looking at getting to Singapore for that time. By the sounds of it, that would be best for everyone."[78] Middle-class ethnic Chinese have joined the affluent in pulling up stakes and fleeing to safe havens in Singapore and Australia. At the same time, tens of thousands of Indonesian refugees are poised to enter Malaysia and Singapore. Threatened with deportation, a few illegals have managed to escape and have crashed the compound of the UNHCR office in K.L.; they protested that the Malaysian and Indonesian dictators "do not observe human rights. They treat humans like animals."[79] Thus, the migrations spawned by the Asian economic crisis dramatically highlight how business networks and labor markets have become the transnational domains for coding, eluding, and contesting the terms of citizenship; they also highlight the role of global capital and transstatal agencies in adjudicating questions of sovereignty.

The question remains: does the spread of social sovereignty—in the sense of codes, rules, and practices—mean that the state is undermined as a locus of sovereignty? The answer is no; the political space within which the nominal citizens dwell, work, and are subjectivized remains significant. The state has to will a piece of territory to be put outside the normal juridical order (as in setting aside of free-trade zones), and to agree to outsource state functions (as in the control of particular populations) to other regulatory agencies. The social terms, codes, and norms that constitute zones of new sovereignty are the interface between the techniques of biopower and juridical rules. As Giorgio Agamben has argued, "states of exception" such as refugee camps are enabled by the modern state; more and more they are part of its normalized system of political-juridical arrangements.[80] In an era of transnationality, the state deployment of disciplinary and pastoral forms of biopower has enlarged the space of the political. This politicization of life, whereby subject populations are included or excluded under different forms of sovereignty, is an aspect of the contradictory nature of the relation between politics and capital.

Indeed, as this book goes to press, the economic typhoon unleashed by unruly capital markets has toppled the Soeharto regime and shattered Indonesia's economy. In contrast, Asian tiger countries have responded by strengthening the hand of the state against capital flows. The Hong Kong government, in an unprecedented move, has intervened to protect the property sector from foreign speculators. In Malaysia, Mahathir has imposed even more rigid controls on capital flows; he has also moved decisively against his political rivals. Such revolts of the Asian states (and Russia) to protect society against what has been called "Anglo-Saxon capitalism" refute Western axioms about globalization, and its inevitable weakening of sovereignty.

An Anthropology of Transnationality

[handwritten annotation: Use this carefully to explore how to distinguish transnationalism & transculturalism]

This book has considered the varied practices and policies—reworked, of course, in terms of local cultural meanings—that transform the meanings of citizenship in an era of globalization. My focus on transnationality highlights the processes whereby flexibility, whether in strategies of citizenship or in regimes of sovereignty, is a product and a condition of late capitalism. This work also represents an anthropological intervention into the study of changing relations between subjects, state, and capital, and it demonstrates why a keen grasp of cultural dynamics is essential to such an analysis. By tying ethnography to the structural analysis of global change, we are able to disclose the ways in which culture gives meaning to action and how culture itself becomes transformed by capitalism and by the modern nation-state. An approach rooted in the ethnographic knowledge of a region also demonstrates that capitalism, which has been differently assimilated by different Asian countries, has become reconfigured and has taken on new cultural meanings and practices—whether at the level of the individual or the community—that valorize flexibility, difference, and transnationality.

Anthropologists can grasp the history of the present in a way that universalizing armchair theorists, who persist in their view of the world as being divided into traditional and modern halves, cannot. Indeed, the modernity-tradition model assumes an intellectual division of labor between sociology and anthropology, and anthropologists are chastised for dealing with "traditional," "disappearing" cultures, when in fact, "non-Western" cultures are not disappearing but are adjusting in very complex ways to global processes and remaking their own modernities.[1] A further mistake in the rationalist and reductionist models of the world is the tendency to view non-Western cultures and human agency as passive or, at best, ineffectual. Let us briefly consider, for example, a dominant sociological framework for grasping the dynamism of global relations and human interaction.

As formulated by Immanuel Wallerstein, the world-system theory views the world according to a tripartite scheme of core, periphery, and semiperiphery.[2] Wallerstein has been criticized for reducing capitalism to exchange relations (at the expense of production) and for his functionalist emphasis on the "needs" of core countries in shaping the global division of labor. At the same time, he downgrades the importance of political and military factors in processes of social change. Onto this system of (narrowly defined) transnational economic interdependencies Anthony Giddens has grafted a system of nation-states, seeking to emphasize the latter as a separate system of political power that counterbalances the economic power of global capital.[3] This separation of capitalism and state administrative power into disconnected entities reduces the usefulness of Giddens's approach for an understanding of globalization. Like Huntington's taxonomy of civilizations, such universalizing models based on systemic relations—economic, political, religious—all paper over the actual uneven spread of capitalism, the intertwining of capitalism and state power, the cultural forms of ruling, and the dynamism of cultural struggles in different parts of the world that do not fit their logical schemes.

More recently, totalizing discourses of globalization, which are drawn from business and management literature, represent the latest example to date of a unidirectional model that sees global forces transforming economies and societies into a single global order, which Castells calls "the network society."[4] Politics, culture, and human agency are viewed only as the effects of globalizing processes, such as trade, production, and communications, rather than as vital logics that play a role in shaping the distribution, directionality, and effects of global phenomena. In contrast, an approach that embeds global processes in a regional formation will yield a finer, more complex understanding of the reciprocal shaping of cultural logics and social and state relations in the course of uneven capitalist development.[5]

Anthropology is a field known for its distinctive methodology (regardless of the populations studied) in exploring the links between cultural and material processes in historically specific contexts and in using ethnographic understanding to explain the cultural logics that shape the relations between society, state, and capital. American anthropology has a long history of attending to local-global articulations and melding fine-grained ethnographic perspectives with an appreciation for the historical dynamics of capitalism and social change. Although earlier anthropologists were also influenced by the binarisms of modernity-tradition, core-periphery, and Europe-"people without history," their careful ethnographic study of the historical dynamics through which the multiple meanings and material practices of colonialism and capitalism are reworked point to the culturally specific ways societies have participated in global history.[6] A newer generation of anthropologists who are freeing themselves from the binarism of older models and deploying post-structuralist theories has refined the anthropological analysis of the complex interplay between capitalism, the nation-state, and power dynamics in particular times and places.[7]

But, in turning away from the overarching theories of social change, we may have rushed too quickly into the arms of cultural studies and postcolonial studies. In our post–cold war flirtations with the humanities, anthropologists have too often ceded ground to an anemic approach that takes as its object culture-as-text or that reduces cultural analysis to a North American angst-driven self-reflexivity or to an equally self-conscious, postcolonial, elite-driven discourse that ignores the structures of power in identity making and social change. A hermeneutic trend in anthropology involves witty texts that pose as a form of self-indulgent identity politics, literary works that build a stage for moral grandstanding, and studies of abstracted cultural globalization that are coupled with insubstantial claims. I am all for flirtations and skirmishes on the boundaries of knowledge and for serious interdisciplinary work, but what we want is not a resulting "lite" anthropology but rather an enlarged space for telling the stories of modernity in ways that capture the interplay between culture and the material forms of social life.[8]

The field must recapture its unique role in addressing the big questions of politics, culture, and society in ways that transcend the mechanical modernity-tradition, first world–third world, core-periphery models and the universalizing assumptions that underlie metropolitan theories of postcoloniality, modernity, and globalization. To the grounding of anthropology in political economy, cultural politics, and ethnographic knowledge, I have added a Foucauldian sensibility about power, thus offering a more complex view of the fluid relations between culture, politics, and capitalism. The different paths to modernity have depended upon political strategies that target, organize, and give meaning to bodies, populations, and the social forms of contemporary life. These biopolitical concerns have given a distinctiveness to particular cultural systems, and the kinds of capitalism they enable and produce.

Throughout, I treat culture as a contingent scheme of meanings tied to power dynamics, and I rigorously problematize even "natives' " claims about their "own" culture, since apprehension, ownership, and representation are practices embedded in strategies of positioning, control, and maneuver. I go beyond simple claims about the nonessentialized nature of culture, to show that culture-making involves not only processes of othering by dominant players but also processes of cultural self-theorizing and re-envisioning in relation to fluid power dynamics, whether at the level of interpersonal relations or at the level of national politics and geopolitical posturing. Second, this book shows that the cultural logics of family, religion, and nation are reworked in relation to capitalism, and that new practices of travel, subject making, and citizenship are interlinked with the reconfigured capitalisms we find in different parts of the world. Third, going beyond class or subaltern analysis, this book demonstrates that the varied regimes of regulation, and the strategies of multiple positioning that engage and evade these regimes, produce a more complex view of subject making. While global processes valorize mobility, flexibility, and accumulation, there are structural limits set by cultural norms, modes of ruling, and nationalist ideologies. Fourth, emerging transnational publics constitute fields of cultural normativity in intermingled spaces of Asian and Western capitalisms, thus setting the stage for the dynamic construction of new kinds of transnational ethnicized subjectivity. Fifth, in a critique of American orientalism that views Asian societies as inalienably different, I argue that Asian tigers in fact share "Western" liberal rationalities, but their liberalism uses culture as a legitimizing force—to regulate society, to attract global capital, and to engage in trade wars. Sixth, in contrast to arguments about the retreat of the state, I argue that postdevelopmental Asian states respond positively to global capital, either by engaging in transnational linkages to capital and multilateral agencies or by experimenting with graduated sovereignty as a way to make their societies more attractive to global capital. Finally, by identifying the cultural forms that are shaped by globalization at the personal, state, and regional levels in the Asia Pacific region, this book seeks to document the existence of a vibrant center of globalization, which is now quite interpenetrated by the spaces and practices we used to associate exclusively with the West. This intermingling of spaces and practices of travel, production, discipline, consumption, and accumulation is a product of globalization, but its effects are apprehended, organized, and experienced in culturally distinctive ways. I hope the arguments presented above persuade anthropologists that they have something to say about the role of culture in constituting state and society under varying conditions of globalization, and thus a vital role in provincializing metropolitan theories of universal change. Surely, in an age when the state and capital are directly engaged in the production and the destruction of cultural values, we should cultivate a kind of nomadic thinking that allows us to stand outside a given modernity, and to retain a radical skepticism toward the cultural logics involved in making and remaking our worlds.

Notes

Introduction Flexible Citizenship: The Cultural Logics of Globalization

1 I thank Fred Chiu Yen Liang of the Hong Kong Baptist University for relating this story to me.

2 Edward A. Gargan, "A Year from Chinese Rule, Dread Grows in Hong Kong," *New York Times,* 1 July 1996, A1, 6.

3 Paul Theroux, "Memories That Drive Hong Kong," *New York Times,* 11 June 1997, A21.

4 Dieter Hoffmann-Axthelm, "Identity and Reality: The End of the Philosophical Immigration Officer," in *Modernity and Identity,* ed. Scott Lash and Jonathan Friedman (Oxford: Basil Blackwell, 1992), 199.

5 Benedict Anderson, "Exodus," *Cultural Inquiry* 20 (winter 1994): 323.

6 Alternatively, Bryan S. Turner argues that uncertainties associated with globalization may "produce strong political reactions asserting the normative authority of the local and the national over the global and international." See Turner, "Outline of a Theory of Citizenship," *Sociology* 24 (May 1990): 2, 212.

7 See David Harvey, *The Condition of Postmodernity* (Oxford: Basil Blackwell, 1989), chaps. 10, 11.

8 See, for example, Martin Carnoy et al., *The New Global Economy in the Information Age* (University Park: Pennsylvania State University Press, 1993); and Manuel Castells, *The Information Age,* vol. 1., *The Rise of the Network Society* (Oxford: Basil Blackwell, 1996).

9 See Claus Offe, *Disorganized Capitalism* (Cambridge, Mass.: MIT Press, 1985); and Harvey, *Condition of Postmodernity.*

10 Arif Dirlik, *After the Revolution: Waking to Global Capitalism* (Hanover, N.H.: Wesleyan University Press, 1994), 62.

11 Alan Pred and Michael Watts, *Reworking Modernity: Capitalisms and Symbolic Discontent* (New Brunswick, N.J.: Rutgers University Press, 1992).

12 Arjun Appadurai, *Modernity at Large: Cultural Dimensions of Globalization* (Minneapolis: University of Minnesota Press, 1996), 178–99.

13 This point was also raised in Doreen Massey, "Power Geometry and a Progressive Sense of Place," in *Mapping the Futures: Local Cultures, Global Change,* ed. J. Bird et al. (London: Routledge, 1993).

14 The Asia Pacific region has been defined by Euroamerican imperialism and capitalisms and by the political struggles of peoples within the region over the past centuries. See Arif Dirlik, "Introducing the Pacific," in *What Is in a Rim? Critical Perspectives on the Pacific Region Idea,* ed. Arif Dirlik (Boulder, Colo.: Westview, 1992), 3–11.

15 See Sherry Ortner, "Theory in Anthropology since the Sixties," in *Culture/Power/ History,* ed. Nicholas B. Dirks, Geoff Eley, and Sherry Ortner (Princeton, N.J.: Princeton University Press, 1994), 388–401. For a criticism of Ortner see Talal Asad, "Introduction," in *Genealogies of Religion* (Baltimore, Md.: Johns Hopkins University Press, 1993), 5–6.

16 See Michel Foucault, *Ethics: Subjectivity and Truth,* ed. Paul Rabinow, trans. Robert Hurley et al. (New York: New Press, 1997), 1:81.

17 See Michel Foucault, "Governmentality," in *The Foucault Effect: Studies in Governmentality,* ed. Graham Burchell, Colin Gordon, and Peter Miller (Chicago: University of Chicago Press, 1991).

18 See Aihwa Ong and Don Nonini, eds., *Ungrounded Empires: The Cultural Politics of Modern Chinese Transnationalism* (New York: Routledge, 1997). The term "Asian tiger economies" refers to the rapidly developing countries of South Korea, Taiwan, Hong Kong, Singapore, Malaysia, Thailand, and the "emerging tiger" economies of Indonesia and the Philippines. Business enterprises and networks dominated by ethnic Chinese are prominent everywhere except in South Korea.

19 This concept was first articulated in Aihwa Ong, "On the Edge of Empires: Flexible Citizenship among Chinese in Diaspora," *positions* 1, no. 3 (winter 1993): 745–78.

20 An example of the former is Lucie Cheng and Edna Bonacich, eds., *Labor Immigration under Capitalism: Asian Workers in the United States before World War II* (Berkeley and Los Angeles: University of California Press, 1984). An example of the latter is Alejandro Portes and Ruben G. Rumbaut, *Immigrant America: A Portrait* (Berkeley and Los Angeles: University of California Press, 1990). European studies of immigration from the South often focus on state resistance to the integration of immigrants. See, for example, Robin Cohen, "Policing the Frontiers: The State and the Migrant in the International Division of Labor," in *Global Restructuring and Territorial Development,* ed. J. Henderson and M. Castells (London: Sage, 1987), 88–111.

21 Linda Basch, Nina Glick-Schiller, and Cristina B. Szanton, *Nations Unbound: Transnational Projects, Postcolonial Predicaments, and Deterritorialized Nation-States* (Langhorne, Pa.: Gordon and Breach, 1994).

22 Michael Kearney, "Borders and Boundaries of State and Self at the End of the Empire," *Journal of Historical Sociology* 4, no. 1 (March 1991): 52–74; Roger Rouse,

"Mexican Migration and the Social Space of Postmodernity," *Diaspora* 2, no. 2 (spring 1991): 8–23.

23 See Aihwa Ong, "Citizenship as Subject Making: New Immigrants Negotiate Racial and Ethnic Boundaries," *Current Anthropology* 37, no. 5 (December 1996): 737–62. See also Lisa Lowe, *Immigrant Acts* (Durham, N.C.: Duke University Press, 1997), for a different approach to the ways Asian Americans may interrogate the universalist claims of American citizenship.

24 See Robert Gooding-Williams, ed., "Introduction: On Being Stuck," in *Reading Rodney King, Reading Urban Uprising* (New York: Routledge, 1993), 1–12.

25 See, for instance, Steve Gregory and Roger Sanjek, eds., *Race* (New Brunswick, N.J.: Rutgers University Press, 1992). I thank Don Nonini for discussing this point with me.

26 See, for example, Mike Featherstone, "Global Culture: An Introduction," in *Global Culture: Nationalism, Globalization, and Modernity,* ed. M. Featherstone (Newbury Park, Calif.: Sage, 1990).

27 See Ulf Hannerz, "Notes on the Global Ecumene," *Public Culture* 1, no. 2 (1989): 66–75; Ang Ien, *Living Room Wars: Rethinking Media Audiences for a Postmodern World* (London: Routledge, 1996); and Stuart Hall "Cultural Identity and Diaspora," in *Identity: Community, Culture, Difference,* ed. J. Rutherford (London: Lawrence and Wishart, 1990), 222–37.

28 Appadurai, *Modernity at Large,* 3; italics in the original.

29 Benedict Anderson, *Imagined Communities: Reflections on the Origins and Spread of Nationalism,* 2d ed. (London: Verso, 1991).

30 Appadurai, *Modernity at Large,* 178–99.

31 Ibid., 48–65.

32 In her critique of David Harvey's notion of "time-space compression" (see Harvey, *Condition of Postmodernity,* chaps. 16, 17), Doreen Massey argues that the benefits of globalization are unequally distributed so that a few are able to benefit from, and "be in charge of," the mobility and intensified communication associated with late capitalism, while a large majority are too imprisoned by limited resources to take advantage of these innovations. See Massey, "Power Geometry," 61–63.

33 Barbara Crosette, "U.N. Survey Finds World Rich-Poor Gap Widening," *New York Times,* 12 July 1996, A3.

34 See, for example, Patricia Fernandez-Kelly, *For We Are Sold, I and My People* (Albany, N.Y.: SUNY Press, 1985); Aihwa Ong, *Spirits of Resistance and Capitalist Discipline: Factory Women in Malaysia* (Albany, N.Y.: SUNY Press, 1987); Diane L. Wolf, *Factory Daughters: Gender, Household Dynamics, and Rural Industrialization in Java* (Berkeley and Los Angeles: University of California Press, 1992); and Ping-chun Hsiung, *Living Rooms as Factories: Class, Gender, and the Satellite Factory System in Taiwan* (Philadelphia: Temple University Press, 1995). For a review of the field see Aihwa Ong, "The Gender and Labor Politics of Postmodernity," *Annual Review of Anthropology* 20 (1991): 279–309.

35 Harvey, *Condition of Postmodernity,* 152–53.

36 This approach has been inspired by the work of Mary L. Pratt, which links imperial topography to the ways Europeans viewed "natives" in the colonies. See Pratt, *Imperial Eyes: Travel Writing and Transculturation* (London: Routledge, 1992).

37 Inderpal Grewal, *Home and Harem* (Durham, N.C.: Duke University Press, 1996).

38 Cynthia Enloe, *Bananas, Beaches, and Bases: Making Feminist Sense of International Politics* (Berkeley and Los Angeles: University of California Press, 1990); Caren Kaplan, *Questions of Travel: Postmodern Discourses of Displacement* (Durham, N.C.: Duke University Press, 1996).

39 See Paul Gilroy, "*There Ain't No Black in the Union Jack*" (Chicago: University of Chicago Press, 1989); Gilroy, *The Black Atlantic: Modernity and Double Consciousness* (Cambridge, Mass.: Harvard University Press, 1992); and Gilroy, *Small Acts: Thoughts on the Politics of Black Cultures* (London: Serpent's Tail, 1993).

40 Stuart Hall, "What Is This Black in Black Popular Culture?" in *Stuart Hall,* ed. David Morley and Kuan-Hsing Chen (New York: Routledge, 1996), 474. See also Hall, "Cultural Identity and Diaspora"; and Gilroy, *Small Acts.*

41 Ong and Nonini, *Ungrounded Empires.*

42 See, for example, Jane Margold, "Narratives of Masculinity and Transnational Migration: Filipino Workers in the Middle East," in *Bewitching Women, Pious Men: Gender and Body Politics in Southeast Asia,* ed. Aihwa Ong and Michael G. Peletz (Berkeley and Los Angeles: University of California Press, 1995), 274–98; and Vince Rafael, "'Your Grief Is Our Gossip': Overseas Filipinos and Other Spectral Presences," *Public Culture* 9, no. 2 (December 1997): 269–91.

43 See, for example, Gloria Anzaldúa, *Borderlands/La Frontera* (San Francisco: Spinsters/Aunt Lute, 1987); Smadar Lavie and Ted Swedenburg, eds., *Displacement, Diaspora, and Geographies of Identity* (Durham, N.C.: Duke University Press, 1996); and Donald M. Carter, *States of Grace: Senegalese in Italy and the New European Immigration* (Minneapolis: University of Minnesota Press, 1997).

44 An earlier treatment of the subject can be found in Ulf Hannerz, "Cosmopolitans and Locals in World Culture," in Featherstone, *Global Culture,* 237–521.

45 James Clifford, "Traveling Cultures," in *Cultural Studies,* ed. L. Grossberg, C. Nelson, and P. A. Treichler (New York: Routledge, 1992): 104–8. See also Clifford, *Routes: Travel and Translation in the Late Twentieth Century* (Cambridge, Mass.: Harvard University Press, 1997).

46 Bruce Robbins, "Comparative Cosmopolitanisms," *Social Text* 31/32 (1992): 169–86.

47 Ibid., 179, 183. Ulf Hannerz seems to propose a hegemonic model of the cosmopolitan as a global symbol maker vis-à-vis all the locals. For him, the cosmopolitan orientation is "generally expansionist in its management of meaning," which by "simulating" local knowledge and forming "alliances" across frontiers, brings a kind of coherence to "one world culture." See Hannerz, "Cosmopolitans and Locals," 246–47, 249.

48 Pheng Cheah and Bruce Robbins, eds., *Cosmopolitics: Thinking and Feeling beyond the Nation* (Minneapolis: University of Minnesota Press, 1998).

49 Paul Rabinow, *The Anthropology of Reason* (Princeton, N.J.: Princeton University Press, 1996), 56. For an analysis of European bourgeois cosmopolitanism in relation to imperial rule and modes of racial and sexual control in the colonies see Ann L. Stoler, "Carnal Knowledge and Imperial Power: Gender, Morality, and Race in Colonial Asia," in *Gender at the Crossroads of Knowledge: Feminist Anthropology in the Postmodern Era,* ed. Michaela di Leonardo (Berkeley and Los Angeles: University of California Press, 1991): 55–101.

50 Rabinow, *Anthropology of Reason,* 56.

51 This point was also made in Akhil Gupta and James Ferguson, "Beyond 'Culture': Space, Identity, and the Politics of Difference," *Cultural Anthropology* 7, no. 1 (1992): 6–23.

52 Homi Bhabha, "Introduction," in *Nation and Narration,* ed. H. Bhabha (New York: Routledge, 1990); James Clifford, "Diasporas," *Cultural Anthropology* (summer 1994): 1–50; and Gilroy, *"There Ain't No Black."*

53 Masao Miyoshi, "A Borderless World? From Colonialism to Transnationalism and the Decline of the Nation-State," *Critical Inquiry* 19, no. 4 (summer 1993): 726–51.

54 Appadurai, *Modernity at Large,* 166–68.

55 Arturo Escobar, *Encountering Development: The Making and Unmaking of the Third World* (Princeton, N.J.: Princeton University Press, 1995), 61.

56 This call for throwing out political economy because of different hegemonies and negotiations over the meanings of capitalism is expressed in J. K. Gibson-Graham, *The End of Capitalism (As We Knew It): A Feminist Critique of Political Economy* (Cambridge, Mass.: Blackwell, 1996).

57 Katharyne Mitchell argues that while it is imperative to "examine the different forms capitalism takes in different contexts," we need to maintain "a knowledge of the structural principles undergirding a system that infects us and is infected by every other system in an *unequal exchange*" (Mitchell, "Transnational Discourse: Bringing Geography Back In," *Antipode* 29, no. 2 [1997]: 109; italics in the original).

58 For a discussion of the crisis in English national identity under Margaret Thatcher see Stuart Hall, "The Toad in the Garden: Thatcherism among the Theorists," in *Marxism and the Interpretation of Culture,* ed. Cary Nelson and Lawrence Grossberg (Urbana: University of Illinois Press, 1988), 35–73.

59 For an analysis of Chinese diasporic practices that both transgressed and participated in the structures of colonial markets and protection see Donald M. Nonini and Aihwa Ong, "Introduction: Chinese Transnationalism as an Alternative Modernity," in Ong and Nonini, *Ungrounded Empires,* 3–33; and Carl Trocki, "Boundaries and Transgressions: Chinese Enterprise in Eighteenth- and Nineteenth-Century Southeast Asia," in ibid., 61–85.

60 Nonini and Ong, "Introduction," 11.

61 In this book, I use the term "the West" as shorthand for the cluster of European and American countries—led by the United States—that have played such a major role in shaping our anglophone understanding of the world. Of course, in anthropology, French and German perspectives are also present, but they do not enjoy the hegemonic role in determining our major interests and obsessions unless and until they are translated—in both linguistic and intellectual senses—by British and American academics.

62 ASEAN is the Association of Southeast Asian Nations, a security zone formed during the Vietnam War that has now become a trading bloc seeking greater regional integration to offset China's rising economic power. ASEAN has nine members: the original member states of Malaysia, Singapore, Indonesia, Brunei, Thailand, and the Philippines, and the new member states of Vietnam, Laos, and Burma.

63 Fredric Jameson, *Postmodernism, or, The Cultural Logic of Late Capitalism* (Durham, N.C.: Duke University Press, 1991).

64 See Emily Martin, *Flexible Bodies: Tracking Immunity in American Culture from the Days of Polio to the Age of AIDS* (Boston: Beacon Press, 1994). A related approach is found in Donna Haraway's brilliant work on modern scientific knowledge as postmodern systems that promiscuously interweave nature and culture, bodies and machines, the organic and the technological. See Haraway, *Simians, Cyborgs, and Women: The Reinvention of Nature* (New York: Routledge, 1991).

65 Judith Stacey, *Brave New Families: Stories of Domestic Upheaval in Late-Twentieth-Century America* (New York: Basic Books, 1990).

66 See Donald M. Nonini, "Shifting Identities, Positioned Imaginaries: Transnational Traversals and Reversals by Malaysian Chinese," in Ong and Nonini, *Ungrounded Empires*, 203–27.

67 Sylvia Yanagisako has also noted the importance of transnational Asian families for an understanding of Asian American citizenship. See Yanagisako, "Transforming Orientalism: Gender, Nationality, and Class in Asian American Studies," in *Naturalizing Power: Essays in Feminist Cultural Analysis*, ed. S. Yanagisako and C. Delaney (New York: Routledge, 1995), 275–98.

68 A naive binarism that views the world and "Western capitalism" as abstractions that do not really enter into people's everyday lives and believes that "cultural autonomy" at the ground level should be the only contribution of anthropology is proposed in Ortner, "Theory in Anthropology." See also Clifford Geertz, *Local Knowledge* (Princeton, N.J.: Princeton University Press, 1983).

69 Our tendency to self-critique derives from our fear that anthropology as a field is more "colonizing" than other Western disciplines, which are even less mediated by non-Western forms of cultural knowledge and are more in denial about their role in the semiotics of domination and production of self-interested truth claims.

70 For a criticism of the study of "overseas Chinese" see Nonini and Ong, "Introduction," in *Ungrounded Empires*, 5–9.

71 Ien Ang, "To Be or Not to Be Chinese: Diaspora, Culture, and Postmodern Ethnicity," *Southeast Asia Journal of Social Science* 21, no. 1 (1993): 1–19.

72 See Tani Barlow, "*Zhishifenzi* (Chinese Intellectuals) and Power," *Dialectical Anthropology* 16 (1991): 209–32; Ann Anagnost, *National Past-Times: Narrative, Representation, and Power in Modern China* (Durham, N.C.: Duke University Press, 1997); Arif Dirlik and Xudong Zhang, eds., *Chinese Postmodernism* (Durham, N.C.: Duke University Press, 1997); and Lisa Rofel, *Modern Imaginaries and "Other" Modernities* (Berkeley and Los Angeles: University of California Press, forthcoming).

1   The Geopolitics of Cultural Knowledge

1 In *New World Disorder* (Berkeley and Los Angeles: University of California Press, 1992), political scientist Ken Jowitt argues that the "Leninist extinction" has had dramatic consequences in the world, but he has overlooked the overwhelming impact of globalization on the Asia Pacific region.

2 Edward Said, *Culture and Imperialism* (New York: Alfred A. Knopf, 1993).

3 See, for example, these distinguished ethnographies on poverty, suffering, and vanishing cultures in South America: Claude Levi-Strauss, *Triste Tropics* (New York: Washington Square, 1973); Sydney Mintz, *Worker in the Cane* (Baltimore, Md.: Johns Hopkins University Press, 1960); and Nancy Scheper-Hughes, *Death without Weeping* (Berkeley and Los Angeles: University of California Press, 1992).

4 See, for example, Eric Wolf, *Europe and the People without History* (Berkeley and Los Angeles: University of California Press, 1982).

5 But see Sydney Mintz, *Sweetness and Power* (New York: Penguin, 1985).

6 An example of a study that examines the powers of the weak is James Scott, *Weapons of the Weak* (New Haven, Conn.: Yale University Press, 1989).

7 George Marcus and Michael Fischer, eds., *Anthropology as Cultural Critique* (Chicago: University of Chicago Press, 1989), 158–62.

8 See, for example, W. W. Rostow, *Stages of Economic Growth: A Non-Communist Manifesto* (Cambridge, Mass.: MIT Press, 1960).

9 Modernity as the pervasive rationalization of social life is most extensively formulated by Max Weber. For the development of administrative power in the modern nation-state see Anthony Giddens, *The Nation-State and Violence*, vol. 2 of *A Contemporary Critique of Historical Materialism* (Berkeley and Los Angeles: University of California Press, 1987). Frequently, the term *modernity* is used without the need to specify global location, since it is understood that it implies the Western or a universal standard. See, for instance, Anthony Giddens, *Modernity and Self-Identity* (Stanford, Calif.: Stanford University Press, 1991); and Scott Lash and Jonathan Friedman, "Introduction," in *Modernity and Identity*, ed. S. Lash and J. Friedman (Oxford: Blackwell, 1992).

10 Rostow, *Stages of Economic Growth;* Immanuel Wallerstein, *The Modern World System* (New York: Academic Press, 1972). For a critique of the development para-

digm as a strategy of ongoing metropolitan domination see Escobar, *Encountering Development*.

11 Christopher Layne, "Pox Americana, Not Pax Americana," *New York Times*, 13 March 1993.

12 Homi Bhabha, *The Location of Culture* (London: Routledge, 1994), 252; Gilroy, "*There Ain't No Black*"; and Gilroy, *Black Atlantic*.

13 For an overview of Stuart Hall's contributions, see Morley and Chen, *Stuart Hall*.

14 Bill Ashcroft, Gareth Griffiths, and Helen Tiffins, eds., *The Empire Writes Back: Theory and Practice in Post-colonial Literature* (New York: Routledge, 1989).

15 Gayatri Chakravorty Spivak, "Can the Subaltern Speak?" in *Marxism and the Interpretation of Cultures*, ed. Cary Nelson and Lawrence Grossberg (Urbana: University of Illinois Press, 1988); and Spivak, "Diasporas Old and New: Women in the Transnational World," *Textual Practice* 10, no. 2 (1996): 262.

16 See, for example, Bill Ashcroft, Gareth Griffiths, and Helen Tiffins, eds., *The Postcolonial Reader* (New York: Routledge, 1995); Spivak, "Diasporas Old and New"; and Ruth Frankenberg and Lata Mani, "Crosscurrents: Race, 'Postcoloniality,' and the Politics of Location," *Cultural Studies* 7 (May 1993): 292–310.

17 See Morley and Chen, *Stuart Hall*, 397. Such analyses will reveal that many situations in the global periphery are still not "post" colonial.

18 Partha Chatterjee, *The Nation and Its Fragments: Colonial and Postcolonial Histories* (Princeton, N.J.: Princeton University Press, 1993), 156. See also Chatterjee, *Nationalist Thought and the Colonial World: A Derivative Discourse?* (London: Zed Books, 1986).

19 Chatterjee, *Nation and Its Fragments*, 217–18.

20 Arif Dirlik, "The Postcolonial Aura: Third World Criticism in the Age of Global Capitalism," *Critical Inquiry* 20, no. 2 (1994): 328–56.

21 See Brackette F. Williams, *Stains on My Name, Blood in My Veins* (Durham, N.C.: Duke University Press, 1992); and Akhil Gupta, *Postcolonial Developments* (Durham, N.C.: Duke University Press, 1998).

22 Postcolonial scholars always assume this is the case when we deal with non-Western populations and nation-states. See Gilroy, *Black Atlantic*; and Chatterjee, *Nation and Its Fragments*.

23 See other criticisms of unitary theories of the postcolonial in Ella Shohat, "Notes on the 'Post-Colonial,'" *Social Text* 31–32 (1992): 99–113; Dirlik, "Postcolonial Aura"; Masao, "Borderless World?"; and Aijaz Ahmad, "The Politics of Literary Postcoloniality," *Race and Class* 36, no. 3 (1995): 1–20.

24 Barlow, "*Zhishifenzi*," 211.

25 Ibid., 212. Marilyn Ivy notes that the national cultural imaginary of Japan is "a representation coeval, if not identical, with the sensibility of the modern in the putative West." See Ivy, *Discourses of the Vanishing: Modernity, Phantasm, Japan* (Chicago: University of Chicago Press, 1995), 8.

26 The treatment of "multiple modernities" as merely reactive formations to Western capitalism is a position taken by Pred and Watts, *Reworking Modernity*.

27 For a perspective on Eastern Europe see Katherine Verdery, "Theorizing Socialism: A Prologue to the 'Transnation,'" *American Ethnologist* 18, no. 3 (August 1991): 419–39.

28 Barlow, "*Zhishifenzi,*" 211; see also Perry Link, R. Madsen, and P. G. Pikowics, "Introduction," in *Unofficial China*, ed. P. Link, R. Madsen, and P. G. Pikowics (Boulder, Colo.: Westview, 1990).

29 Barlow, "*Zhishifenzi,*" 212–13. Post-Maoist strategies include seeking to represent truth in realist literary texts.

30 For a useful and concise discussion of Marxist theories of global capitalism in relation to liberation politics see Dirlik, *After the Revolution*.

31 Many of the recent struggles against the Chinese state date back to the Democracy Wall campaigns mounted by students and workers in the 1970s to add democracy to the modernization list. The struggle for democracy in China's official concept of modernity continues.

32 See Mayfair Yang, *Gifts, Favors, and Banquets* (Ithaca, N.Y.: Cornell University Press, 1989), 39.

33 See *New York Times*, 13 March 1992, 6.

34 *New York Times*, 19 April 1992, 1.

35 See Hong Kong Trade Development Council, *Recent Investment Environments of Guangdong, Fujian, and Hainan*, 2d ed. (Hong Kong: Hong Kong Trade Development Council, 1991).

36 Herbert Feith, "Repressive-Developmentalist Regimes in Asia," *Alternatives* 7 (1982): 493.

37 Such state strategies are by no means limited to Asia; the developmentalist-militarist state in South America is another variant of third-world nationalist projects of modernity, although one cannot say that South American nations see themselves in competition with North America.

38 This use of the word *Asian* is ironic because these biopolitical mechanisms— whereby subjects are regulated both as members of a population and as individuals—are not unique to Asia but are, according to Michel Foucault, distinctively modern modes of power that initially emerged in Europe. See Foucault, *Discipline and Punish: The Birth of the Prison*, trans. A. Sheridan (New York: Random House, 1977); Foucault, *History of Sexuality*, vol. 1, trans. M. Hurley (New York: Pantheon, 1978); and Foucault, "Governmentality."

39 *Wall Street Journal*, 2 March 1992.

40 *San Francisco Chronicle*, 30 December 1993, A20.

41 China has an internal migrant labor market of one hundred million people, many of whom are outside state regulation.

42 See Ann Anagnost, "Prosperity and Counter-Prosperity: The Moral Discourse on

Wealth in Post-Mao China," in *Marxism and the Chinese Experience,* ed. Arif Dirlik and Maurice Meisner (Armonk, N.Y.: M. E. Sharpe, 1989), 210–34.

43 For a lively account of the effects on village households of children working in factories see Anita Chan, Richard Madsen, and Jonathan Unger, *Chen Village: Under Mao and Deng,* rev. and enl. ed. (Berkeley and Los Angeles: University of California Press, 1992), chap. 11.

44 This account, culled from a Chinese newspaper, appears in Emily Honig and Gail Hershatter, *Personal Voices: Chinese Women in the 1980s* (Stanford, Calif.: Stanford University Press, 1988), 39.

45 *Wall Street Journal,* 3 April 1992, B1.

46 Barlow, "*Zhishifenzi,*" 219.

47 *Renmin ribao,* 19 September 1994, national ed.

48 Barlow, "*Zhishifenzi,*" 213.

49 Stephen Feld, "*He Shang* and the Plateau of Ultrastability," *Bulletin of Concerned Asian Scholars* 23, no. 3 (1991): 6.

50 This reading is given in James L. Watson, *The Renegotiation of Chinese Cultural Identity in the Post-Mao Era,* Social Science Research Center Occasional Paper 4 (Hong Kong: University of Hong Kong, 1991). But the impression that all intellectuals represent an emergent civil-society category ignores the expansion of the role of the intelligentsia within the state structure.

51 Barlow, "*Zhishifenzi,*" 222.

52 Gregory E. Guildin, ed., *Urbanizing China* (New York: Greenwood Press, 1992), 179.

53 For a recent reminder of this dichotomy within the Chinese nation see Edward Friedman, "Reconstructing China's National Identity: A Southern Alternative to Mao-Era Anti-imperialist Nationalism," *Journal of Asian Studies* 53, no. 1 (1994): 67–91.

54 Relations between the Chinese state and emigrant Chinese have passed through many cycles of rejection and embrace over the centuries. For instance, the Manchu invasion of northern China brought about the gradual collapse of the Ming dynasty in the seventeenth century, which spawned an outflow of loyalist subjects (such as Koxinga, who fought off the invaders in Taiwan) who are still celebrated as true patriots. During the Qing dynasty, Chinese who ventured abroad were considered traitors who would be beheaded upon returning to China. Following the overthrow of the dynasty in 1912, overseas Chinese played a major role, patriotically supporting Sun Yat Sen's republican efforts and providing the needed funds to resist the Japanese invasion of China in 1937. When the communists took power in 1949, overseas Chinese were once again considered traitors, and thousands of overseas Chinese were forced either to return to China or to give up claims to citizenship. Although overseas Chinese (*huaqiao*) continued to send remittances home to relatives in the People's Republic of China, it was not until the late 1970s that the Chinese state once again considered overseas Chinese to be an important

social and economic force in the transformation of the country. For a discussion of the shifting Beijing policy toward overseas Chinese in Southeast Asia throughout much of this century see Ta Chen, *Emigrant Communities in South China* (Shanghai: Kelly and Walsh, 1939); and Stephen Fitzgerald, *China and the Overseas Chinese: A Study of Peking's Changing Policy, 1949–70* (Cambridge: Cambridge University Press, 1972).

55 "Straits Chinese" refers to the creolized community descended from premodern Chinese diasporas that first settled along the Straits of Malacca and intermarried with local populations. In the nineteenth and early twentieth centuries, the Straits Chinese flourished under the British colonial administration of the Malay Peninsula and Singapore. They were later augmented by new immigrants from republican China and by the 1960s, had become culturally less distinct from later arrivals. For one account of the Straits Chinese see Victor Purcell, *The Chinese in Malaya* (Oxford: Oxford University Press, 1967).

56 I borrow the idea of a "contrast category" from Lewis C. Copeland, "The Negro as a Contrast Conception," in *Race Relations and the Race Problem*, ed. Edgar Tristram Thompson (Durham, N.C.: Duke University Press, 1939), 152–79.

57 It is as if these diasporan subjects can have no other primary cultural reference.

58 "Yi qiao da qiao, yi qiao sheng chai!" *Renmin ribao,* 7 January 1993, international edition.

59 "Qiaoxian Quanzhou, qiao pai yue ta, yue huo," *Renmin ribao,* 15 October 1991, international edition.

60 *Renmin ribao,* 2 October 1991; *Renmin ribao,* 21 November 1991, international edition.

61 *Renmin ribao,* 7 January 1993, international edition.

62 "Shui ye bu lao you zi xin, / guan shan nan duan gu xiang qing." These lines are probably by the poet Li Po. See *Renmin ribao,* 22 October 1991, international edition.

63 *Renmin ribao,* 22 October 1991, international edition.

64 *Renmin ribao,* 11 January 1992, international edition.

65 *Renmin ribao,* 11 November 1991, international edition.

66 Sheryl Wu Dunn, "Chinese Isle Bewitched (and Bothered) by Taiwan," *New York Times,* 3 February 1992, A9.

67 *South China Morning Post,* 29 November 1992.

68 Strictly speaking, Taiwanese are not considered huaqiao by the mainlanders since Taiwan is viewed as a part of China, but it seems appropriate from the analytical perspective to think of them since the Second World War as part of the offshore network of overseas Chinese communities that have developed within capitalist systems in the Asia Pacific region.

69 Orville Schell seems to suggest this view in his assessment of discos in China. See Schell, *Discos and Democracy: China in the Throes of Reform* (New York: Anchor Books, 1988), 355–56.

70 For another discussion of the role of karaoke in cementing business deals see You-tien Hsing, "Building *Guanxi* across the Straits: Taiwanese Capital and Local Chinese Bureaucrats," in Ong and Nonini, *Ungrounded Empires,* 143–66.

71 *Wall Street Journal,* 10 October 1993, 1.

72 Yang, *Gifts, Favors, and Banquets,* 71–72.

73 See especially Takeshi Hamashita, "The Tribute Trade System and Modern Asia," in *Memoirs of the Research Department of the Toyo Bunko, No. 46* (Tokyo: Tokyo University, 1988).

74 *International Herald Tribune,* 23 November 1993, 4.

75 Chatterjee, *Nationalist Thought,* 168. This statement was made primarily in reference to India.

76 Tani Barlow, "Colonial Modernity and Gendered Agency" (paper presented at the East Asian Institute, University of California, Berkeley, 3 May 1993).

77 See Rob Wilson and Arif Dirlik, eds., *Asia/Pacific As Space of Cultural Production* (Durham, N.C.: Duke University Press, 1995); and Ong and Nonini, *Ungrounded Empires.*

78 Obviously, India, Indonesia, and other major Asian countries also produce their own competing versions of modernity.

79 See Barlow, "*Zhishifenzi,*" 224.

80 "Mobile subjectivity" is proposed by Kathy Ferguson in Ferguson, *The Man Question: Visions of Subjectivity in Feminist Theory* (Berkeley and Los Angeles: University of California Press, 1993). "Nomadic" thinking is proposed by philosophers such as Gianni Vattimo. See Vattimo, *The Transparent Society,* trans. David Webb (Baltimore, Md.: Johns Hopkins University Press, 1992).

81 Minimal human rights include basic rights such as freedom from hunger and torture and the right to survive as individuals, and as a people, anywhere in the world.

2   *A "Momentary Glow of Fraternity"*

1 Arjun Appadurai, "Disjuncture and Difference in the Global Cultural Economy," in *Modernity at Large* (Minneapolis: University of Minnesota Press, 1996), 27–47.

2 A helpful distinction between nation and state is provided by T. K. Oommen, who notes that while nation and state are territorial entities, the first is a moral formation (i.e., one that invests meaning in a homeland), whereas the second is "a legally constituted system which provides its residents protection from internal insecurity and external aggression." See Oommen, "Introduction: Conceptualizing the Linkage between Citizenship and National Identity," in *Citizenship and National Identity: From Colonialism to Globalism,* ed. T. K. Oommen (Thousand Oaks, Calif.: Sage, 1997), 33.

3 See Anderson, *Imagined Communities;* and Anderson, "Exodus."

4 Anderson, *Imagined Communities,* 149–50.

5 See Frank Dikötter, *The Discourse of Race in Modern China* (Stanford, Calif.: Stanford University Press, 1992).

6 Brackette F. Williams, "Classification Systems Revisited: Kinship, Caste, Race, and Nationality as the Flow of Blood and the Spread of Rights," in *Naturalizing Powers: Essays in Feminist Cultural Analysis,* ed. Sylvia Yanagisako and Carol Delaney (New York: Routledge, 1995), 232.

7 Anthony Reid has made a careful distinction between civic and ethnic nationalisms and has examined their overlaps in Southeast Asia. See Reid, "Religion, Ethnicity, and Modernity in Southeast Asia" (paper presented at the conference "Religion, Ethnicity, and Modernity in Southeast Asia," Center for Area Studies, Seoul National University, 29–30 November 1996).

8 See Anderson, *Imagined Communities,* 149–50.

9 Louisa Schein, *Making Difference Matter: The Miao in China's Cultural Politics* (Durham, N.C.: Duke University Press, forthcoming).

10 Fitzgerald, *China and the Overseas Chinese.*

11 Vivienne Shue, *The Reach of the State: Sketches of the Chinese Body Politic* (Stanford, Calif.: Stanford University Press, 1988); and Helen F. Siu, *Furrows: Peasants, Intellectuals, and the State* (Stanford, Calif.: Stanford University Press, 1990).

12 Peter van Ness, "China As a Third World State: Foreign Policy and Official National Identity," in *China's Quest for National Identity,* ed. L. Dittmer and S. S. Kim (Ithaca, N.Y.: Cornell University Press, 1993), 194–214.

13 Dikötter, *Discourse of Race,* 162–63.

14 See Ssu-Yu Teng and John K. Fairbank, *China's Response to the West: A Documentary Survey, 1923–39* (New York: Atheneum, 1965), 164–66.

15 Barlow, "*Zhishifenzi,*" 211.

16 Stuart Hall, "The Local and the Global: Globalization and Ethnicity," in *Culture, Globalization, and the World System,* ed. Anthony King (London: Macmillan, 1991), 25–26.

17 Joel Kotkin, *Tribes: How Race, Religion, and Identity Determine Success in the New Global Economy* (New York: Random House, 1992), 197.

18 Chen Xiyu, "Research Note on the 'Chinese Economic Zone,'" *issco Bulletin* 2, no. 2 (1994): 3–4.

19 Huang Kunzhang, speech (from field notes).

20 Interview, November 1993 (from field notes).

21 Such cautions about overseas Chinese are also reported in You-tien Hsing, "Building *Guanxi* across the Straits: Taiwanese Capital and Local Chinese Bureaucrats," in Ong and Nonini, *Ungrounded Empires,* 142–66.

22 Chen, "Research Note."

23 Michael Richardson, "China's Growth: A Double Edged Sword," *International Herald Tribune,* 23 November 1993, 8.

24 Charles P. Wallace, "Asia Gets Tough, Adopts Its Own Way," *San Francisco Chronicle,* 29 May 1994, A8.

25 Lee Kuan Yew, "The Loyalty of Overseas Chinese Belongs Overseas," *International Herald Tribune,* 23 November 1993, 4.

26 Barry Wain, "Myths of the Overseas Chinese," *Asian Wall Street Journal*, 10–11 December 1993, 8.

27 Doubt about the loyalty of ethnic Chinese in Southeast Asia has a long tradition that stems from the colonial era. See, for instance, Maurice Freedman, "The Chinese in Southeast Asia: A Longer View," in *Man, State, and Society in Contemporary Southeast Asia*, ed. R. O. Tilman (New York: Praeger, 1969), 431–99.

28 "Bad" class subjects were those whose class background fell under the "five black categories" of landlord, rich peasant, bad element, counterrevolutionary, and rightist. See Yang, *Gifts, Favors, and Banquets*, 186–87; and Chan, Madsen, and Unger, *Chen Village*. Sexually deviant subjects included those who celebrated romantic love, the sexually permissive, prostitutes, and homosexuals. See Honig and Hershatter, *Personal Voices*.

29 *Chinese News Digest*, 20 September 1994, 40.

30 Anderson, *Imagined Communities*, stresses the power of print capitalism in building the imagined state but overlooks the power of television and other electronic media in undermining the sense of cultural unity and national loyalty that the Chinese officials so rightly fear.

31 "China Cracks Down on the Arts," *San Francisco Chronicle*, 4 February 1997, 10.

32 Cited in do Rosario, "Network Capitalism: Personal Connections Help Overseas Chinese Investors," *Far Eastern Economic Review*, 2 December 1993, 17.

33 Field notes, November 1993, Shantou, China.

34 Lynn White and Li Cheng, "China's Coast Identities: Regional, National, and Global," in *China's Quest for National Identity*, ed. Lowell Dittmer and Samuel S. Kim (Ithaca, N.Y.: Cornell University Press, 1993), 164.

35 Lee, "The Loyalty."

36 See Bruce Cumings, "Rimspeak," in *What Is in a Rim? Critical Perspectives on the Pacific Region Idea*, ed. Arif Dirlik (Boulder, Colo.: Westview, 1993), 29–47.

37 Lee, "The Loyalty."

38 Joel Kotkin, "Family Ties in the New Global Economy," *Los Angeles Times Magazine*, 17 January 1993, 21–22.

39 John Kao, "The Worldwide Web of Chinese Business," *Harvard Business Review* (March–April 1993): 24–37.

40 Ray Heath, "Perhaps It Is Time to Mingle," *South China Morning Post*, 23 November 1993, B1.

41 Kao, "Worldwide Web," 13.

42 *South China Morning Post*, 25 November 1993.

43 Lee, "The Loyalty."

44 Sylvia Yanagisako and Carol Delaney, eds., *Naturalizing Powers: Essays in Feminist Cultural Analysis* (New York: Routledge, 1995), 1.

45 Syed Hussein Alatas, *The Myth of the Lazy Native* (London: Frank Cass, 1977), 73–76. For another example of how these colonialist discourses were reworked in postcolonial business contexts see Ong, *Spirits of Resistance*.

46 This is Donald M. Nonini's phrase for the point I am making here.

47 See Geraldine Heng and Janadas Devan, "State Fatherhood: The Politics of Nationalism, Sexuality, and Race in Singapore," in *Bewitching Women, Pious Men: Gender and Body Politics in Southeast Asia,* ed. Aihwa Ong and Michael G. Peletz (Berkeley and Los Angeles: University of California Press, 1995), 195–215.

48 David Harvey, following A. Lipietz, calls such state-sponsored mass-production industrialization and its modes of labor regulation "peripheral Fordism." He says that regimes that practice peripheral Fordism are conducive to strong patriarchal control in shaping gender relations. See Harvey, *Condition of Postmodernity,* 155, 165. For ethnographic examples see Ong, *Spirits of Resistance.*

49 Heng and Devan, "State Fatherhood."

50 James C. Scott, *The Moral Economy of the Peasant* (New Haven, Conn.: Yale University Press, 1976). Scott was inspired by the "moral economy" concept first introduced by British historian Edward P. Thompson, who analyzed eighteenth-century food riots by English artisans and others displaced by new industries as protests against the loss of premodern social controls over market forces. See E. P. Thompson, "The Moral Economy of the English Crowd in the Eighteenth Century," *Past and Present,* no. 50 (1971).

51 Scott assumes that moral-economy concepts emerge from the precarious circumstances of peasant livelihood that foster social values of reciprocity and exchanges that can help avert disaster for individual households and the community as a whole. While I do not contest this view of peasant society, in my formulation of the moral economy of the modern Southeast Asian state, I argue that the ideology of morally justified exchanges must be continually produced and organized by the state, regardless of whether there is a preexisting set of moral values that will support such unequal collaborations between citizens and the state.

52 *Far Eastern Economic Review,* 10 December 1992.

53 George Yeo, "In Asia and Elsewhere, Small Will Be the Better Way to Govern," *International Herald Tribune,* 22 June 1994, 4. Although Yeo claims that what he calls "smaller democracy" has evolved out of the Asian experience, his views echo those of American conservatives who have for decades called for smaller government.

54 Lee Kwan Yew, interview by Barry Wain, "What Makes an Economic Miracle?" *Asian Wall Street Journal,* 3–4 December 1993, 8; emphasis added.

55 See Hall, "Toad in the Garden," 53–54.

56 See Heng and Devan, "State Fatherhood."

57 See Francis T. Seow, *To Catch a Tartar: A Dissident in Lee Kuan Yew's Prison,* Yale Southeast Asian Studies Monograph 42 (New Haven, Conn.: Yale Center for International and Area Studies, 1994).

58 The term "patri-order" was used by Brackette Williams to describe social orders regulated by racial and sexual systems that required deviant others—females, homosexuals, subordinated races—to redeem themselves, but only partially. In na-

tionalist ideologies based on ideal racial masculinity, women, if properly behaved, may become containers for, but never producers of, culture as a civilizing process. See Williams, "Introduction: Mannish Women and Gender after the Act," in *Women Out of Place: The Gender of Agency and the Race of Nationality,* ed. Brackette Williams (New York: Routledge, 1996), 10.

59 *Wall Street Journal,* 13 April 1994, A1.

60 Chatterjee, *Nation and Its Fragments.*

61 Ong, *Spirits of Resistance,* 149–50.

62 See Rob Steven, *Japan's New Imperialism* (Armonk, N.Y.: M. E. Sharpe, 1990).

63 Shintaro Ishihara, *The Japan That Can Say No* (New York: Simon and Schuster, 1990).

64 *Economist,* 28 May 1994, 13. Ironically, while the Taiwan regime is trying to maintain its political independence from mainland China, it participates in the Confucian discourse by claiming possession of a more "authentic" Confucian cultural heritage (see Allen Chun, "From Nationalism to Nationalizing: Cultural Imagination and State Formation in Postwar Taiwan," *Australian Journal of Chinese Affairs* 31 [1994]: 49–72). Taiwan emphasizes its "progressive cultural alienation from a country that is increasingly seen as brutal, lawless, corrupt, and irrelevant to Taiwan's future" (see *New York Times,* 26 June 1994, A6). Indeed, one may add that many in Southeast Asia also view China in this light, but hegemonic discourses about Greater China or "the Asian way" gloss over this fact to enforce a sense of regional cultural solidarity.

65 See Harvey, *Condition of Postcoloniality,* 168.

66 *Economist,* 5 November 1994, 18.

67 *San Francisco Examiner,* 29 May 1994, A8.

68 *Renmin ribao,* 4 April 1994, 1; my translation.

69 Kishore Mahbubani, "Live and Let Live: Allow Asians to Choose Their Own Course," *Far Eastern Economic Review,* 17 June 1993, 26.

70 Don Nonini reminded me of this point.

71 Fan Guoxiang, "A Reasonable and Practical Choice," *Beijing Review,* 14–20 March 1994.

72 *Wall Street Journal,* 13 April 1994, A6.

73 Dong Yunhu, "Fine Traditions of Human Rights in Asia," *Beijing Review,* 28 June–4 July 1993, 11–12; emphasis added.

74 Kishore Mahbubani, "*The Dangers of Decadence: What the Rest Can Teach the West,*" *Foreign Affairs* 73, no. 4 (1993): 10–15; and Mahbubani, "The United States: 'Go East, Young Man,'" *Washington Quarterly* 17, no. 2 (1994): 5–23.

75 Mahbubani, "United States," 10, 12.

76 See Hall, "Toad in the Garden," 53.

77 See Heng and Devan, "State Fatherhood"; and Chun, "From Nationalism to Nationalizing."

78 See Allen Chun, "Pariah Capitalism and the Overseas Chinese of Southeast Asia:

Problems in the Definition of the Problem," *Ethnic and Racial Studies* 12, no. 2 (1989): 233–56.

79 Ong, *Spirits of Resistance;* Ong, "Gender and Labor Politics"; Wolf, *Factory Daughters;* Hsiung, *Living Rooms as Factories;* and Ching Kwan Lee, *Women Workers and the Manufacturing Miracle: Gender, Labor Markets, and Production in South China* (Berkeley and Los Angeles: University of California Press, forthcoming).

80 In other words, relations of domination are euphemized so that the forms of violence entailed in debt, personal loyalty, submission, and so on are unrecognized as such and coded instead in the language of honor. See Pierre Bourdieu, *Outline of a Theory of Practice* (Cambridge: Cambridge University Press, 1977), 191–92.

81 *China News Digest,* 16 October 1994.

82 *Straits Times,* 23 August 1994, 19.

83 *Straits Times,* 29 May 1994, 6.

84 *Straits Times,* 29 April 1994, 17.

85 *Straits Times,* 1994.

86 *Asiaweek,* 1 December 1993, 20–25.

87 I thank Prasenjit Duara for helping me to clarify this point. See Duara, *Rescuing History from the Nation: Questioning Narratives of Modern China* (Chicago: University of Chicago Press, 1995), for an approach to the question of modernity constructed independently of the nation in China.

88 This point is made in Arif Dirlik, "The Asia-Pacific in Asian-American Perspective," in *What Is in a Rim? Critical Perspectives on the Pacific Region Idea,* ed. Arif Dirlik (Boulder, Colo.: Westview, 1993), 305–29.

89 This point is made in Yang, *Gifts, Favors and Banquets,* 38.

90 White and Li, "China's Coast Identities," 191. This claim is significant in that recent Japanese revisionist history considers the Chinese tributary system, rather than the coming of the Europeans, to be the source of Japanese and Chinese modernity. See Hamashita, "Tribute Trade System."

91 See Jameson, *Postmodernism.*

92 See Hall, "Toad in the Garden," 80.

93 do Rosario, "Network Capitalism"; emphasis added.

3 Fengshui *and the Limits to Cultural Accumulation*

1 Peninsula Peak is a pseudonym.

2 The mainland peninsula across from Hong Kong Island is called Kowloon, or Nine Dragons; according to local belief, this propitious placement has blessed Hong Kong with the capacity to generate great wealth.

3 *San Francisco Chronicle,* 27 February 1991, B1.

4 See Maurice Freedman, "The Handling of Money: A Note on the Background to the Economic Sophistication of the Overseas Chinese," *Man,* o.s., 19 (1959): 64–65. See also James L. Watson, *Emigration and the Chinese Lineage: The Mans in Hong Kong and London* (Berkeley and Los Angeles: University of California Press, 1975).

5 James A. Mackie, "Overseas Chinese Entrepreneurship," *Asia Pacific Economic Literature* 6, no. 1 (1992): 54.

6 Pierre Bourdieu, *Distinctions: The Social Judgment of Taste* (Cambridge, Mass.: Harvard University Press, 1984).

7 Bourdieu, *Outline*, 177.

8 Ibid., 171–83.

9 See Appadurai, *Modernity at Large*, 27–47.

10 See Pierre Bourdieu, "The Forms of Capital," in *Handbook of Theory and Research for the Sociology of Education*, ed. J. G. Richardson (New York: Greenwood, 1986), 241–58; and Moshe Postone, Edward LiPuma, and Craig Calhoun, "Introduction: Bourdieu and Social Theory," in *Bourdieu: Critical Perspectives*, ed. C. Calhoun, E. LiPuma, and M. Postone (Chicago: University of Chicago Press, 1993), 4–5.

11 See Ong and Nonini, *Ungrounded Empires*.

12 Bourdieu, *Distinctions*, 244–45.

13 Bourdieu, *Outline*, 172–73.

14 Bourdieu, *Distinctions*, 245.

15 See Ang, "To Be or Not to Be Chinese."

16 Bourdieu, *Distinctions*.

17 In recent years, because of the economic takeoff of most Southeast Asian economies, many have returned to settle down and are helping to run the family business or are working in private or government enterprises or in transnational enterprises that may relocate them all over Asia.

18 Theroux, "Memories."

19 See Nonini and Ong, "Introduction," in Ong and Nonini, *Ungrounded Empires*, 1–33.

20 Since the eighteenth century, and especially since the mid–nineteenth century (when Britain attacked China and gained control of Hong Kong), Chinese merchant families from the coastal cities have engaged in far-flung trade ventures in Southeast Asia and all over the Pacific. For centuries, out-migration by peasants has been a continual process. Peasants from Guangdong and Fujian Provinces migrated in large numbers to frontiers opened up by Euroamerican colonial capitalism in Southeast Asia and throughout the Asia Pacific region. See, for instance, Victor Purcell, *The Chinese in Southeast Asia*, 2d ed. (Kuala Lumpur: Oxford University Press, 1965); and Sucheng Chan, *This Bittersweet Soil: The Chinese in California Agriculture, 1860–1910* (Berkeley and Los Angeles: University of California Press, 1986). Throughout Southeast Asia, Chinese merchant families operated major businesses such as rice milling, import-export businesses, and rubber production. See T'ien Ju-kang, *The Chinese of Sarawak*, Monographs on Social Anthropology, no. 12 (London: Department of Anthropology, London School of Economics and Social Sciences, 1953); William G. Skinner, *Chinese Society in Thailand* (Ithaca, N.Y.: Cornell University Press, 1957); W. F. Wertheim, "The Trading Minorities of Southeast Asia," in *East-West Parallels* (The Hague: W. Van Hoeve, 1964), 39–82; and John T.

Omohundro, *Chinese Merchant Families in Iloilo* (Athens: Ohio University Press, 1981). Especially since the Second World War, ethnic Chinese have become a dominant presence in light manufacturing, lumbering, the urban trades, the hotel industry, and finance. See Linda Y. L. Lim and Peter Gosling, eds., *The Chinese in Southeast Asia*, 2 vols. (Singapore: Maruzen Press, 1983). By the 1970s, these entrepreneurs had begun to move out of Southeast Asia to invest abroad. See Watson, *Emigration;* and Peter Kwong, *The New Chinatown* (New York: Noonday Press, 1987).

21 Harvey, *Condition of Postmodernity*, 159.

22 For a fascinating account of the different itineraries of lower-middle-class Chinese Malaysian families see Nonini, "Shifting Identities."

23 The total number of Asian immigrants in the United States is estimated at under 10 million. Asia has become the principal source of legal immigrants to America (about 40 percent of the total).

24 See Paul Ong, Edna Bonacich, and Lucie Cheng, *The New Asian Immigration in Los Angeles and Global Restructuring* (Philadelphia: Temple University Press, 1994).

25 K. Connie Kang, "Chinese in the Southlands: A Changing Picture," *Los Angeles Times*, 29 June 1997.

26 *New York Times*, 17 October 1994, A8. See also Timothy P. Fong, *The First Suburban Chinatown: The Remaking of Monterey Park, California* (Philadelphia: Temple University Press, 1994).

27 Mike Davis, *City of Quartz: Excavating the Future in Los Angeles* (New York: Vintage, 1992), 129–30.

28 David Rieff, "The Real L.A. Story," *San Francisco Examiner Image Magazine*, 27 October 1991, 20.

29 Herb Caen, "Hong Kong's Quiet Bay Area Presence," *San Francisco Examiner*, 7 June 1987, D5.

30 Ibid.

31 *San Francisco Examiner*, August 1995, B2.

32 See Davis, *City of Quartz*, 206–9; and Fong, *First Suburban Chinatown*.

33 New Asian immigrants contributed a quarter of a million dollars to the San Francisco mayoral campaign of Democrat Art Agnos and a few years later, over a million dollars to Republican Pete Wilson in his successful 1991 campaign for governor of California.

34 Interview with a Chinatown activist, March 1994.

35 Interview by author with a prominent Hong Kong entrepreneur based in San Francisco, June 1994.

36 Fong, *First Suburban Chinatown*, 171. For a similar argument about the collusions between Vancouver officials and Pacific Rim capital using "multiculturalism" as an argument see Katharyne Mitchell, "Multiculturalism or the United Colors of Capitalism?" *Antipode* 25, no. 4 (1993): 263–94.

37 For a discussion of the naturalization of concepts such as ethnic succession in the American public consciousness see Brackette F. Williams, "Identity Politics: Suffer-

ing, Succession, and Redemption in the American Moral Order" (paper presented at the Department of Anthropology, University of California, Berkeley, 10 October 1997).

38 See David Rieff, *Los Angeles: The Capital of the Third World* (New York: Simon and Schuster, 1991).

39 In 1991, more than 60 percent of the 1.6 million Chinese Americans were born overseas (see *New York Times*, 12 June 1991, A1). For a perspective that calls for a strict separation between American-born and overseas-born Asians in order to put aside the racial issue and highlight instead the question of citizenship and democracy see Wang Ling-chi, *Asian Americans for Campaign Finance Reform in the U.S.: A Statement of Purpose* (San Francisco: ISSCO Internet Community, 1996).

40 Asians have always had a tenuous position in California. They were excluded as a racial group by the Chinese Exclusion Act of 1882. In 1924, an immigration law extended the restrictive quota on other groups from Asia. Only the end of racial exclusion in 1943 allowed for the formation of stable Chinese communities, which were under the leadership of merchants who founded home-district associations. In San Francisco, the merchant Six Companies confined itself to business affairs within Chinatown, trying to be a good citizen by keeping out of trouble with the authorities. In the 1960s, two major events changed the character of Chinese communities throughout the United States: One was the rise of Asian American awareness among college-educated children inspired by the Civil Rights Movement. The other was the Family Reunification Act, which rapidly increased the influx of Chinese immigrants, including students from Taiwan, Hong Kong, China, and Southeast Asia. These immigrants have produced an Asian American middle class whose interests are not necessarily or adequately represented by the old Chinatown leadership. See Victor Nee and Brett de Bary Nee, *Longtime Californ'* (Stanford: Stanford University Press, 1972).

41 For an account of similar conflicts in Vancouver see Katharyne Mitchell, "Transnational Subjects: Constituting the Cultural Citizen in an Era of Pacific Rim Capital," in Ong and Nonini, *Ungrounded Empires*, 228–58.

42 *Asiaweek* (San Francisco), 6 May 1995, 5.

43 Ibid.

44 Ibid.

45 *San Francisco Examiner*, 7 June 1987, D5.

46 "Asian Influence Comes of Age," *San Francisco Chronicle*, 21 August 1989, A6.

47 Ian Mak [pseud.], interview by author, San Francisco.

48 *San Francisco Focus Magazine*, August 1991, 25.

49 Kenny Pao [pseud.], interview by author, San Francisco.

50 A Hong Kong–born architect whom I interviewed who has made a fortune in California real estate maintains that he is an exception to such attempts to buy white approval. Rather than giving money to mainstream arts groups, he is a strong supporter of the Asian American film and theater movement in the city.

51 Malaysian Chinese philanthropist Tan Kah Kee is famous for building Xiamen University and many other public works in Fujian, his native province. Today, his American-educated children are organizing the campaign to contribute to the aforementioned chemistry building on the University of California, Berkeley, campus.

52 Of course, in making donations for public buildings, Asian American nouveaux riches are merely replicating a long immigrant tradition, most famously cultivated in the Bay Area by Irish, Italian, and Jewish immigrants who made good. The Chinese newcomers are following in the footsteps of the Hearsts, the Aliotos, and the Haases. For an anthropological study of a major American family dynasty and the symbolic boundaries of wealth see George Marcus with Peter Hall, *Lives in Trust: The Fortunes of Dynastic Families in Late-Twentieth-Century America* (Boulder, Colo.: Westview, 1992). However, what we are seeing today for the first time is the nonwhite arrivals scaling the social heights with wealth made in the international economy and causing reluctant, minimal adjustments in the domestic racial hierarchy. For an interesting comparison with another highly successful non-European immigrant community, the Cubans in Florida, see Alejandro Portes and Alex Stepick, *City on the Edge: The Transformation of Miami* (Berkeley and Los Angeles: University of California Press, 1993).

53 I am paraphrasing the title of Wilson and Dirlik, *Asia/Pacific As Space of Cultural Production.*

4 The Pacific Shuttle: Family, Capital, and Citizenship Circuits

1 Francis X. Clines, "In Burst of Fiendish Delight, Ukraine Topples a Monolith," *New York Times,* 31 August 1991, A1.

2 "The Silicon Valley Way of Divorce" (in Chinese), *Overseas Scholars' Monthly* (Taipei), January 1991.

3 See the two special issues of the journal *Daedalus* titled *The Living Tree: The Changing Meaning of Being Chinese Today* (120, no. 2 [spring 1991]) and *China in Transformation* (122, no. 2 [spring 1993]).

4 Edward Said, *Orientalism* (New York: Pantheon, 1978).

5 Harvey, *Condition of Postmodernity,* identifies our era as one of "flexible accumulation," but he underestimates the ways culture shapes material forces and the effects of political economy on culture.

6 This has been suggested by many scholars. See Masao, "Borderless World?"; and Anderson, "Exodus."

7 By "governmentality," Michel Foucault means the deployment of modern forms of (nonrepressive) disciplining power by the state—especially in the bureaucratic realm—and other kinds of institutions that produce rules based on knowledge/ power about populations. See Foucault, "Governmentality."

8 See Foucault, *Discipline and Punish;* and Foucault, *History of Sexuality.*

9 Nonini, "Shifting Identities," 203–7.

10 See Mayfair Mei-hui Yang, "The Modernity of Power in the Chinese Socialist Order," *Cultural Anthropologist* 3, no. 4 (1988): 416; and Tani Barlow, "Theorizing Woman: *Funu, Guojia, Jiating*," *Genders* 10 (spring 1991): 132–60.

11 Barlow, "*Zhishifenzi*," 214–15.

12 See Paul Rabinow, *French Modern: Norms and Forms of the Social Environment* (Cambridge, Mass.: MIT Press, 1989), 9–10.

13 For studies on Chinese merchant families in early modern China, when European powers dominated the coastal cities, see Mark Elvin and G. William Skinner, eds., *The Chinese City between Two Worlds* (Stanford, Calif.: Stanford University Press, 1972).

14 Fei Hsiao-tung, "Peasant and Gentry: An Interpretation of Chinese Social Structure and Its Changes," in *Class, Status, and Power*, ed. E. Bendix and S. M. Lipset (New York: Free Press, 1953), 646–47. While Fei attacks the merchant class for its lack of responsibility toward society, other scholars maintain that the "hybrid" and "modernized" offspring of the compradors were people who might have brought about a capitalist revolution in China. See Rhoades Murphey, "The Treaty Ports and China's Modernization," in Elvin and Skinner, *Chinese City*.

15 See Purcell, *Chinese in Southeast Asia;* and Carl Trocki, *Opium and Empires: Chinese Society in Colonial Singapore, 1800–1910* (Ithaca, N.Y.: Cornell University Press, 1990).

16 See Nonini and Ong, "Introduction."

17 In Southeast Asia, *huaqiao* became a generic term to refer in a diffused way to diasporan Chinese in general, regardless of their nationality. In this chapter, I use the terms *huaqiao, overseas Chinese,* and *diasporan Chinese* interchangeably.

18 Anderson, *Imagined Communities,* underplays the centrality of race in colonially inspired notions of nationalism in Southeast Asia and seeks instead to focus on the "good" kind of anti-imperialist, civic nationalism.

19 See Bourdieu, *Outline,* 90–95.

20 See Chun, "Pariah Capitalism."

21 Bourdieu, *Outline,* 190–97.

22 See, for example, Peter Berger and Hsin-huang Michael Hsiao, eds., *In Search of an East Asian Development Model* (New Brunswick, N.J.: Transaction Books, 1988); and Hung-chao Tai, ed., *Confucianism and Economic Development: An Oriental Alternative?* (Washington, D.C.: Washington Institute Press, 1989).

23 American writers who contribute to this discourse include Kotkin, *Tribes;* and James Fallows, *Looking at the Sun: The Rise of the New East Asian Economic and Political System* (New York: Pantheon, 1994).

24 Hsiung, *Living Rooms as Factories.*

25 Edward A. Gargan, "A Giant Spreads Its Roots," *New York Times,* 14 November 1995, C3.

26 Michel Foucault, *The History of Sexuality;* and Foucault, "Governmentality."

27 See Frederic C. Deyo, ed., *The Political Economy of New Asian Industrialism* (Ithaca, N.Y.: Cornell University Press, 1987).

28 Emily Siu-kai Lau, *Society and Politics in Hong Kong* (New York: St. Martin's Press, 1983).

29 Janet W. Salaff, *Working Daughters of Hong Kong: Filial Piety or Power in the Family?* (Cambridge: Cambridge University Press, 1981).

30 See Ho Ping-ti, *The Ladder of Success in Imperial China* (New York: Columbia University Press, 1962).

31 See Lau, *Society and Politics*, 95–96.

32 Edward K. Y. Chen, "The Economic Setting," in *The Business Environment in Hong Kong*, 2d ed., ed. D. G. Lethbridge (Hong Kong: Oxford University Press, 1984), 3–4.

33 Brian Wong [pseud.], interview by author, San Francisco, June 1992.

34 See Colin Gordon, "Governmental Rationality: An Introduction," in *The Foucault Effect*, ed. Graham Burchell, Colin Gordon, and P. Miller (Chicago: University of Chicago Press, 1991): 1–15.

35 Robert Miles, *Race* (London: Routledge, 1989), 84–85.

36 Ibid., 85–86.

37 Watson, *Emigration*, 50–78.

38 Chan Chi-Keung, "Exodus Threat to H.K. Credibility," *South China Morning Post*, 28 January 1988. The most the official could hope for was that the Chinese emigrants would return to Hong Kong with their shiny new Canadian and Australian passports.

39 Homi K. Bhabha, "DissemiNation: Time, Narrative, and the Margins of the Modern Nation," in *Nation and Narration*, ed. Homi K. Bhabha (New York: Routledge, 1990), 327.

40 TK.

41 "Time Running Out to Stop the Brain Drain," *South China Morning Post*, 29 December 1987.

42 Ibid.

43 Sam Seibert et al., "Hong Kong Blues," *Newsweek*, 16 April 1990, 45.

44 For more details on finance-based immigration programs see *South China Morning Post*, 20 November 1988.

45 See Siu-lun Wong, *Emigrant Entrepreneurs: Shanghai Industrialists in Hong Kong* (Hong Kong: Oxford University Press, 1988).

46 Alex Leong [pseud.], interview by author, San Francisco, March 1997.

47 Ibid.

48 For comparable practices in Chinese business families based in Singapore see Chan Kwok Bun and Claire Chiang, *Stepping Out* (Singapore: Simon and Schuster, 1994).

49 Leong, interview.

50 See, for example, Sung Lung-sheng, "Property and Family Division," in *The An-*

thropology of Taiwanese Society, ed. Emily Martin and Hill Gates (Stanford, Calif.: Stanford University Press, 1981).

51 *Towkay* is a transliteration of the Hokkien word for the head of a family business; it is commonly used in Southeast Asia to refer to Chinese entrepreneurs or any successful self-employed Chinese man. In Mandarin, the word is *toujia.*

52 See *New York Times,* 14 January 1996.

53 For a discussion of Chinese cosmopolitans in Vancouver see Mitchell, "Transnational Subjects."

54 Leong, interview, June 1994.

55 The name Ten Brothers is borrowed from the band of Robin Hood–type robbers in the Chinese classic *The Water Margin.* See *South China Morning Post,* 5 February 1994.

56 For an example of such claims see Tai, *Confucianism and Economic Development,* 18–19.

57 See Ong, "Citizenship as Subject Making."

58 See Roger Daniels. *Asian American: Chinese and Japanese in the United States since 1850* (Seattle: University of Washington Press, 1988), 129–54, 301.

59 Gunnar Myrdal, *The American Dilemma: The Negro Problem and Modern Democracy* (New York: Vintage, 1968), 184–85.

60 Scholars often miss the ways neoliberal ideas about human worth have affected processes of racial formation in the United States. See, for example, Michael Omi and Howard Winant, *Racial Formation in the United States* (New York: Routledge and Kegan Paul, 1986).

61 Actually, the ideological divide was not so clearly cut, for Chinatown movements also came to be shaped by the Great Society programs, and many Chinese American students were radicalized by the African American struggle for civil rights in the 1960s. This new ethnic consciousness, which arose out of struggle, found expression in storefront programs to provide for the health care, housing, and other needs of new immigrants. Many of its advocates saw Chinese immigrants, most of whom were poor, as victims of racist capitalism, a view that was shaped by the Marxist framework of ethnic-studies programs that were being introduced on campuses.

62 The influx of poor immigrants also continued, helped by a 1962 law that allowed for the reunification of families; it provided a new infusion of people that revitalized many Chinatowns. See Nee and Nee, *Longtime Californ'.*

63 Letter to the Editor, *San Francisco Chronicle,* 16 June 1989.

64 Asian American writers such as Frank Chin and Maxine Hong Kingston have challenged the model-minority image by exploring Chinese American identity as formed from the tension between politics and aesthetics. See Jeffery Paul Chan, Frank Chin, Lawson Fusao Inada, and Shawn Wong, eds., *The Big AIIEEEEE! An Anthology of Chinese American and Japanese American Literature* (New York: Meridian, 1991). However, such literary works, together with more recent Asian Amer-

ican performative arts, have had less impact on the national consciousness than the media-borne and corporate renditions of Asians at home and abroad.

65 Through this opening, the U.S. government hoped to attract $4 billion a year and to create as many as forty thousand jobs annually (see "Green-Card Law Means Business to Immigrants," *Wall Street Journal*, 21 February 1992, B1). The actual gains so far have fallen short of both goals. The Hong Kong investors I spoke to said that the investment figure is too steep, given that they can obtain a Canadian passport for Can$300,000. Furthermore, since the law was passed, great investment opportunities in China have sucked most of the overseas Chinese capital back to Asia. See chapter 2.

66 Hall, "Cultural Identity and Diaspora," 225–26.

67 The Japanese, of course, were the first economically significant Asians in the world economy, but other than by being featured in a few business tracts about superior Asian quality control, they have not participated as vigorously in Western discourses about Orientals as one might have expected. But some have recently become more vocal, following the example of the newly assertive Southeast Asian leaders. See Mahathir Mohamad and Shintaro Ishihara, *The Voice of Asia: Two Asian Leaders Discuss the Coming Century* (Tokyo: Kodansha International, 1995).

68 See Wang Gungwu, "Among Non-Chinese," *Daedalus* 120, no. 2 (1991): 148–52. It is interesting that the term "non-Chinese" has emerged as a category in such self-orientalizing discourses as displayed in this special issue of *Daedalus,* which is titled *The Living Tree.* The term seems to herald the elevation of Chineseness to the global status enjoyed by Westerners vis-à-vis less-developed parts of the world, which are commonly referred to as the conceptual and geographic South. By taking the East out of the underdeveloped category, this discursive move reinforces the model of global binarism.

69 See Tai, *Confucianism and Economic Development;* Tu Wei-ming, "The Rise of Industrial East Asia: The Role of Confucian Values," *Copenhagen Papers in East and Southeast Asian Studies* (April 1988): 81–97; and Tu, "Cultural China: The Periphery as the Center," *Daedalus* 120, no. 2 (1991): 1–32.

70 See Salaff, *Working Daughters;* Susan Greenhalgh, "De-orientalizing the Chinese Family Firm," *American Ethnologist* 21, no. 4 (1994): 746–76; Lee Ching Kwan, "Factory Regimes of Chinese Capitalism: Different Cultural Logics in Labor Control," in Ong and Nonini, *Ungrounded Empires,* 115–42; and Hsiung, *Living Rooms as Factories.*

71 Lau, *Society and Politics,* 118.

72 Ibid., 119.

73 Lynn Pan, *Sons of the Yellow Emperor: A History of the Chinese Diaspora* (Boston: Little, Brown, 1990), 366–67.

74 This view is promoted in the bestseller *Rising Sun,* by Michael Crichton (New York: Ballantine, 1992), and is suggested by James Fallows in Fallows, *Looking at the Sun.*

75 David Murdock, keynote speech delivered at the Asia Society conference "The Asian American Experience: Looking Ahead," Los Angeles, October 1991.

76 Michael Woo, keynote speech delivered at the Asia Society conference "The Asian American Experience: Looking Ahead," Los Angeles, October 1991.

77 Ibid.

78 See Edna Bonacich, "A Theory of Middleman Minorities," *American Sociological Review* 38 (1973): 583–94.

79 Fred Y. L. Chiu, "Non-mediating Forces versus Mediating Forces—New 'Subjecthood' in Local/Regional Resistances against Nation/Global Systemic Drives" (paper presented at the workshop "Nation-States, Transnational Publics, and Civil Society in the Asia-Pacific," University of California, Berkeley, 28–30 June 1996).

80 Woo, keynote speech.

81 As a politician with a tiny Asian support base, Woo depended primarily on votes from multiethnic constituencies, especially Anglos and African Americans. There was something about his bridge-building metaphor that was reminiscent of the Confucian norm of relations between older and younger brothers, which he seemed to suggest as a model for city politics. This representation apparently found some acceptance among Los Angeles citizens because despite the failure of interethnic coalitions during the 1992 class and racial rioting, Michael Woo remained for a time the most popular candidate in the mayoral race.

82 See Stuart Hall and David Held, "Citizens and Citizenship," in *New Times: The Changing Face of Politics in the 1990s,* ed. Stuart Hall and M. Jacques (New York: Verso, 1989), 173–88.

83 Citizenship rights are public entitlements, but does a citizen have the material and cultural resources to choose between different courses of action in public life? For Woo, Asian American citizenship seems irrevocably tied to Pacific Rim capital.

84 The academic terms were coined in Freedman, "Handling of Money"; and Wertheim, "Trading Minorities."

85 Nonini, "Shifting Identities."

86 Clifford, "Traveling Cultures," 108.

87 Roger Rouse ("Thinking Through Transnationalism: Notes on the Cultural Politics of Class Relations in the Contemporary United States," *Public Culture* 7, no. 2 [1996]: 353–402) maintains that American class formation and cultural politics must be analyzed in relation to global capitalism, and yet he neglects to consider the role of foreign capitalists in reworking American race and class relations. Also, while he claims flexible subjectivities are fostered among the working classes by "the bourgeoisie" (391), he does not discuss the flexible strategies of the latter in dealing with both global capitalism and the regulatory power of the nation-state.

88 Ong and Nonini, *Ungrounded Empires.*

89 See, for example, Michael Lind, "To Have and Have Not: Notes on the Progress of American Class War," *Harpers',* June 1995, 35–47.

5   *The Family Romance of Mandarin Capital*

1 Joan Vincent, *Anthropology and Politics* (Tucson: University of Arizona Press, 1990), 329–99. Vincent traces this theoretical destination back to the 1950s, when Eric Wolf and Sydney Mintz, under the supervision of Julian Steward (*The People of Puerto Rico* [Urbana: University of Illinois Press, 1956]), reworked the community-study approach within hierarchical systems of political economies. In the 1970s, Immanuel Wallerstein (*The Modern World-System*) explained the world system in rather taxonomic terms. In the following decade, Wolf (*Europe*) and Mintz (*Sweetness and Power*) in different ways plotted the cultural histories of conquest, colonialism, the division of labor, trade, and consumption in making diverse political economies that were also contexts of cultural making. By then, many anthropologists of different persuasions, including Marxists and symbolic analysts, had come to assume a global-local axis (which Vincent called "Europe and the Third World in a single paradigm") as background and frame for their ethnographies.

2 Vincent, *Anthropology and Politics*, 409.

3 In her first book, *African Elite: The Big Men of a Small Town* (Chicago: University of Chicago Press, 1971), Vincent drew critical attention to the strategic importance of "men in motion" circulating through small towns in East Africa as agents in the expansion of British capital; the movements of these indigenous men became inseparable from the "moving frontier" of imperial capitalism. See Vincent, *Teso in Transformation: The Political Economy of Peasant and Class in Eastern Africa* (Berkeley and Los Angeles: University of California Press, 1982), 9–11.

4 Vincent, *Teso in Transformation*, 259–62.

5 Karl Marx, *The Eighteenth Brumaire of Louis Bonaparte* (1869; reprint, New York: International Publishers, 1963), 124. Marx described the nineteenth-century French peasantry as atomized household units that did not enter into social relations with each other. Unaware of the wider relations that exploited them as a collectivity, they were incapable of enforcing class interests in their own name.

6 This insight was later echoed in Massey, "Power Geometry."

7 There is a huge literature on this topic, but among the more innovative are Wolf, *Peasants* (Englewood Cliffs, N.J.: Prentice Hall, 1996); Scott, *Weapons of the Weak*; and Ranajit Guha and Gayatri Chakravorty Spivak, eds., *Selected Subaltern Studies* (New York: Oxford University Press, 1988).

8 To Marx, the "stupefied seclusion" of the French peasantry under the Bonaparte dynasty was compounded by the priest—"the anointed bloodhound of the earthly police"—as the ideological instrument of the government (Marx, *Eighteenth Brumaire*, 125, 129–30). Marxist approaches to the problems of cultural consciousness among third-world peasants are dominated by notions of ideological mystification, as, for example, in Eric Wolf, *Peasants*, and a variant of ideological mystification that incorporates the concept of a resistant peasant subculture, as, for example, in Scott, *Moral Economy*.

9 For cultural approaches to relations of production and consumption in our highly technologized, late-capitalist world see Harvey, *Condition of Postmodernity;* Jameson, *Postmodernism;* and Donald M. Lowe, *The Body in Late-Capitalist USA* (Durham, N.C.: Duke University Press, 1995).

10 Lowe, *Body in Late-Capitalist USA,* 15. See also Jameson, *Postmodernism.*

11 See Ong, "Gender and Labor Politics."

12 As Gayatri C. Spivak has claimed in 1988 (Spivak, "Can the Subaltern Speak?"). She maintains that subalterns can neither be depicted by nor spoken for by elites whose relations of domination prevent them from portraying the "real" interests of subalterns.

13 Lowe, *Body in Late-Capitalist USA,* 8. Like Donald Lowe, I do not see a problem in combining both Marxist and Foucauldian approaches as a way to better grasp the constitution of contemporary social consciousness. See, for example, Ong, *Spirits of Resistance.*

14 See Fredric Jameson, *The Political Unconscious: Narrative as a Socially Symbolic Act* (Ithaca, N.Y.: Cornell University Press, 1981).

15 Cristina S. Blanc, "The Thoroughly Modern 'Asian': Capital, Culture, and Nation in Thailand and the Philippines," in Ong and Nonini, *Ungrounded Empires,* 261–86.

16 See Ariel Dorfman and Armand Mattelart, *How to Read Donald Duck: Imperialist Ideology in the Disney Comic,* trans. David Kunzie (New York: I. G. Editions, 1975).

17 Of course, American popular culture continues to be widespread throughout the region, and Japanese mass culture is growing in appeal among young Taiwan and Hong Kong Chinese. Nevertheless, I maintain that whatever cultural forms are used and borrowed from the United States or Japan, they are often deployed and woven within cultural scripts about Chinese ethnicity or national identity, depending on the particular programs.

18 Gordon, "Governmental Rationality," 14.

19 Ibid., 16.

20 See Mahathir Mohamad and Shintaro Ishihara, "Will East Beat West?" *World Press Review,* December 1995, 6–11. For a fuller discussion of this idea see Aihwa Ong, "Strategic Sisterhood or Sisters in Solidarity? Questions of Communitarianism and Citizenship in Asia," *Indiana Journal of Global Legal Studies* 4, no. 1 (1997): 1–29.

21 Lynn Hunt, *The Family Romance of the French Revolution* (Berkeley and Los Angeles: University of California Press, 1992), 4.

22 Ibid., viii.

23 Hall, "Toad in the Garden."

24 Hunt, *Family Romance,* 1.

25 James Mackie, "Changing Patterns of Chinese Big Business in Southeast Asia," in *Southeast Asian Capitalists,* ed. Ruth McVey (Ithaca, N.Y.: South East Asia Program, Cornell University, 1992), 161. Most of the international financing for this elite Chinese minority came from the wider network of overseas Chinese investments,

and the increased mobility of capital has served to decrease Chinese leeway vis-à-vis local governments.

26 Ibid.; see other chapters in McVey, *Southeast Asian Capitalists.*

27 Interview by author, Singapore, August 1994.

28 *Business Week,* 29 November 1993.

29 Interview by author, Singapore, August 1994.

30 Joel Kotkin, "Family Ties in the New Global Economy," *Los Angeles Times Magazine,* 17 January 1993, 21–22.

31 Sigmund Freud, *Totem and Taboo: Some Points of Agreement between the Mental Lives of Savages and Neurotics,* in *The Standard Edition of the Complete Psychological Works,* vol. 13, trans. James Strachey (London: Hogarth Press, 1958). See Hunt, *Family Romance,* 1–16, for a fascinating analysis of Freud's "primal scene" and its subthemes.

32 "Confucian capitalist" has also been used to describe the South Korean founder of Hyundai, one of Asia's wealthiest industrialists, but it has been used more to refer to his "stern domination" and even "autocratic predilections" than to the positive fraternal values that have been attributed to Chinese capitalists (*Far Eastern Economic Review,* 22 June 1995, 60).

33 Jonathan Friedland, "Kuok the Kingpin," *Far Eastern Economic Review,* 7 February 1991, 46.

34 In Southeast Asia, whereas contemporary scholarly and media discussions about the rise of entrepreneurs are becoming ever more common, there is a deafening silence on the history of anti-imperialist struggles and the patriots who fought and died for national independence.

35 Jonathan Friedland, "Friends of the Family," *Far Eastern Economic Review,* 7 February 1991, 48–49.

36 *Forbes,* 18 July 1994, 12.

37 George L. Mosse, *Nationalism and Sexuality: Middle-Class Morality and Sexual Norms in Modern Europe* (Madison: University of Wisconsin Press, 1985), 10–13.

38 I borrow the term "middling" from Paul Rabinow. Rabinow (*French Modern*) talks about the "middling modernity" of middlebrow expertise in shaping social knowledges, norms, and sensibilities in modern society.

39 William Barnes, "Chinese Out of Thais' Closet," *South China Morning Post,* 26 February 1994, 4.

40 See Ong and Nonini, *Ungrounded Empires,* chaps. 5, 9.

41 "Anwar: Be Committed to Ethical Values," *New Straits Times,* 7 August 1994, A1.

42 See "Singapore Charges Scholar, Herald Tribune," *San Francisco Chronicle,* 19 November 1994, 8.

43 Mark Clifford, "Profile K. S. Lo: Milk for the Millions," *Far Eastern Economic Review,* 9 June 1994, 78.

44 Mark Clifford, "Heir Force," *Far Eastern Economic Review,* 17 November 1994, 78.

45 See Richard Robison, *Indonesia: The Rise of Capital* (Sydney: Allen and Unwin, 1986), for a discussion of the state-private capital alliances in Indonesia.

46 See Adam Schwarz, *A Nation in Waiting: Indonesia in the 1990s* (Sydney: Allen and Unwin, 1994), 109–14, for an account of Liem's vast family business and long-term links with Soeharto.

47 Ibid., 108.

48 Ali is a common Malay name and Baba refers to the Straits Chinese men who under colonialism often played the role of comprador to British concerns.

49 S. Jayasankaran, "Taking Stock: Malaysia's Rashid Hussain: At the Crossroads," *Far Eastern Economic Review*, 20 April 1995, 76–77.

50 Edward A. Gargan, "The Master Builder."

51 *Far Eastern Economic Review*, 8 February 1991, 47.

52 Chan and Chiang, *Stepping Out*, 15, 98, 354.

53 Claire Chang, interview by *Asian Wall Street Journal*, 25 November 1993, 5.

54 Joh Keng Swee, foreword to Chan and Chiang, *Stepping Out*, viii–ix.

55 Jim Scott maintains that in Southeast Asian peasant societies, the unequal exchanges between peasants and their clients are morally justified in terms of the patrons' guarantees of their social and economic security (see Scott, *Moral Economy*).

56 *International Herald Tribune*, 22 June 1994, 4.

57 See Chua Beng Huat, *Communitarian Ideology and Democracy in Singapore* (London: Routledge, 1995).

58 See Heng and Devan, "State Fatherhood."

59 Nonini, "Shifting Identities."

60 Lee, "Factory Regimes."

61 Interview by author, Shenzhen, P.R.C., November 1993.

62 See Nora Lee, "Duplicitous Liaisons," *Far Eastern Economic Review*, 20 April 1995, 64–65.

63 See Lisa Rofel, " 'Yearnings': Televisual Love and Melodramatic Politics in Contemporary China," *American Ethnologist* 21, no. 4 (1994): 700–722.

64 See Lee, "Factory Regimes."

65 This term was first used in Mayfair Yang, "The Gift Economy and State Power in China," *Comparative Studies in Society and History* 31 (1989): 25–54, where the author comments on the practice of accumulating network capital in contemporary China as a way to bypass and subvert state regulations. See also Yang, *Gifts, Favors, and Banquets*.

66 See Bourdieu, *Outline*, 171–83.

67 See Siu-lun Wong and Janet W. Salaff, "Network Capital: Emigration from Hong Kong" (paper presented at the conference "The Transnationalization of Chinese Capitalism," National University of Singapore, 8 August 1994).

68 I am grateful to Connie Clark, a graduate student in anthropology at the University of California, Berkeley, for keeping me abreast of developments in these women's lives. Clark, who was conducting dissertation research in Shenzhen, introduced me

to these women and, together with Ching Kwan Lee, showed me various aspects of working women's lives during my field trip.

6 "A Better Tomorrow"? The Struggle for Global Visibility

1 Arjun Appadurai, "Disjuncture and Difference," in *Modernity at Large*, 27–47. For a useful summary of these approaches, see Smadar Lavie and Ted Swedenburg, "Introduction: Displacement, Diaspora, and Geographies of Identity," in Lavie and Swedenburg, *Displacement, Diaspora*, 1–25.

2 Castells, *Rise of the Network Society*, 336–37.

3 See Paul Rabinow, "Representations Are Social Facts: Modernity and Postmodernity in Anthropology," in Rabinow, *Anthropology of Reason*, 28–58.

4 Roland Robertson, "Mapping the Global Condition: Globalization as the Central Concept," in *Global Culture: Nationalism, Globalization, and Modernity*, ed. Mike Featherstone (Newbury Park, Calif.: Sage, 1990), 22. For an economistic notion of the world system see Wallerstein, *Modern World-System*. For the political view that focuses on the modern nation-state and its ordering by global norms concerning its sovereignty see Giddens, *Nation-State and Violence*.

5 See Craig Calhoun, "Introduction: Habermas and the Public Sphere," in *Habermas and the Public Sphere*, ed. Craig Calhoun (Cambridge, Mass.: MIT Press, 1992). Philip Huang criticizes the "value-laden" teleology of Habermas's concept of the public sphere as being nowhere justified. He suggests instead a value-neutral term, "public realm." See Huang, "Public Sphere/'Civil Society' in China? The Third Realm between State and Society," *Modern China* 19, no. 2 (1993): 224.

6 See Calhoun, *Habermas*, for discussions of the exclusions of other publics implied in Habermas's ideal-type model.

7 For examples of how cultural politics engage the state see Ong and Nonini, *Ungrounded Empires*.

8 Castells, *Rise of the Network Society*, 416.

9 Calhoun, "Introduction." Calhoun continues: "Within this network there might be a more or less even flow of communication. In nearly any imaginable case there will be clusters of relatively greater density of communication within the looser overall field . . ." (37–38).

10 John B. Thompson, *The Media and Modernity: A Social Theory of the Media* (Stanford, Calif.: Stanford University Press, 1995), 245.

11 Castells, *Rise of the Network Society*, 330.

12 Massey, "Power Geometry," 59.

13 Thompson, *Media and Modernity*, 247.

14 Habermas sees modern society as split between two distinct institutionalized orders: the system-integrated world that engages in material reproduction (the market and the state) and the lifeworld that specializes in symbolic reproduction (the family and the public sphere). See Jürgen Habermas, *The Theory of Communicative Action*, vol. 1, *Reason and the Rationalization of Society*, trans. Thomas McCarthy

(Boston: Beacon, 1984). For a feminist critique of this formulation see Nancy Fraser, "What's Critical about Critical Theory? The Case of Habermas and Gender," in *Unruly Practices* (Minneapolis: University of Minnesota Press, 1989), 113–43.

15 Postmodernism is characterized by cultural differentiation, heterogeneity, and styles that privilege irony and parody.

16 I use the term *social consciousness* in the Marxist sense of a social consciousness that is determined by social beings and not vice versa.

17 Craig Calhoun, "Tiananmen, Television, and Public Sphere: Internationalization of Culture and the Beijing Spring of 1989," *Public Culture* 2, no. 1 (winter 1989): 54–72.

18 Mayfair Yang has written about mainland Chinese audiences who consume films about expatriate Chinese in the United States. See Yang, "Mass Media and Transnational Subjectivity in Shanghai: Notes on (Re)Cosmopolitanism in a Chinese Metropolis," in Ong and Nonini, *Ungrounded Empires,* 287–323.

19 See Barbara Ryan, "Blood Brothers and Hong Kong Gangster Movies: Popular Culture and Commentary on 'One China,'" in *Asian Popular Culture,* ed. John Lent (Boulder, Colo.: Westview, 1995), 61–76.

20 Ibid., 64–65.

21 In the Jackie Chan police stories, however, Chan plays a Hong Kong policeman working for the colonial state. I thank Shu-mei Shi for pointing this out to me.

22 Ryan, "Blood Brothers," 73–74.

23 Of course, this movie can be viewed as a political allegory of the eventual "fall" of Hong Kong to communist rule, but its theme of political events disrupting family relations remains prominent.

24 Louis Cha writes under the pen name Jin Yong. See *Far Eastern Economic Review,* 5 September 1996, 39.

25 The last name echoes the title of the movie *Tequila Sunrise,* which is also about brotherhood and sacrifice.

26 I am grateful to Brackette Williams for pointing out these intertextual echoes of Western movies.

27 In 1997, revenues to the company were running 300 percent ahead of 1996. See "The Global Mall," *Wall Street Journal,* 26 June 1997, A10. American mass culture, as depicted on TV and in films, popular songs, and magazines, has been influential among young people in the region since the 1960s. See Leo Ching, "Imaginings in the Empires of the Sun: Japanese Mass Culture in Asia," in *Asia/Pacific as Space of Cultural Production,* ed. Rob Wilson and Arif Dirlik (Durham, N.C.: Duke University Press, 1995), 262–83.

28 Castells, *Rise of the Network Society,* 341.

29 See Ang, *Living Room Wars,* for a discussion of the inherently contradictory nature of the media's role in shaping our identities and fantasies.

30 Castells, *Rise of the Network Society,* 339. For a discussion of TV programs in Shanghai see Yang, "Mass Media," 299.

31 *Hemisphere,* July 1993, 21–24. For an interesting discussion of the new popular

music in Singapore that selectively appropriates and questions cultural authenticity in self-parodies of orientalism, see C. J. W. L. Wee, "Staging the New Asia: Singapore's Dick Lee, Pop Music, and a Counter-modernity," *Public Culture* 8, no. 3 (spring 1994): 492.

32 Ien Ang notes that to foster national unity, the government of multiracial Malaysia requires advertising agencies to feature "pan-Asian" models in their television commercials. See Ang, *Living Room Wars*, 145. Here, the state and business are allied in the cultural coding of "ethnic" identity for a specific national audience.

33 Murdoch is the world's biggest media magnate. Besides Star TV, his News Corporation owns larger corporations such as 20th Century–Fox, Fox subsidiaries, and a part of British Sky Broadcasting.

34 Mike Levin, "Star TV Takes Over after MTV Asia Goes off the Air," *Billboard*, 14 May 1994, 8–9.

35 Ibid.

36 For decades, Eurasian models have been highly successful in Japan for the same reason. Currently, in Hong Kong, recruiters are looking for tall, northern Chinese beauties, who are considered more "feminine" than Hong Kong women and whose build is more in keeping with Western ideals (Arif Dirlik, personal communication, 29 June 1996).

37 *Hemisphere*, July 1993, 24.

38 Chinese-dominated mass media, especially film, TV, radio, and magazines, is much more widespread and popular in China, Southeast Asia, and west Asia than is Japanese media, despite the latter's earlier development and technological sophistication. Japanese mass culture has had very limited transnational crossover compared to overseas-Chinese mass media. Japanese media has difficulty representing non-Japanese cultural forms either in transcultural terms or in English, which is still the lingua franca throughout much of Asia. In any case, Japanese media industries are almost exclusively focused on the domestic market.

39 See, for instance, essays by R. Srivatsen and by Pradip Krishen in *Public Culture* 4, no. 1 (fall 1991).

40 For images of modern Muslim subjects, see Aihwa Ong, "State versus Islam: Malay Families, Women's Bodies, and the Body Politic in Malaysia," in Ong and Peletz, *Bewitching Women, Pious Men*, 159–94.

41 Wee, "Staging the New Asia," 492.

42 Bernard Wysocki Jr., "Global Mall," A1.

43 In this sense, normativity is the effect of technologies of governmentality. See Nikolas Rose, "Governing 'Advanced' Liberal Democracies," in *Foucault and Political Reason*, ed. Andrew Barry, Thomas Osborne, and Nicholas Rose (Chicago: University of Chicago Press, 1996), 41.

44 *Wall Street Journal*, 19 April 1995, A1.

45 For a discussion of flexibility as the modus operandi of contemporary corporate and knowledge industries see Martin, *Flexible Bodies*.

46 G. Pascal Zachary, "Malaysia Bosses: High Tech Firms Shift Some Skilled Work to Asian Countries," *Wall Street Journal*, 30 September 1994, A1.

47 *Wall Street Journal*, 5 December 1994, A10.

48 Ibid.

49 Zachary, "Malaysian Bosses."

50 There are twenty-eight Levi Strauss outlets in Malaysia alone. The company advertises premovie commercials for a hit movie starring teenage heartthrob Brad Pitt. See Wysocki, Jr., "Global Mall."

51 G. Pascal Zachary, "Exporting Rights," *Wall Street Journal*, 28 July 1994, A1, A5.

52 For an account of the *salaryman* culture's distinctive practices see Anne Allison, *Nightwork: Sexuality, Pleasure, and Corporate Masculinity in a Tokyo Hostess Club* (Chicago: University of Chicago Press, 1994).

53 *Forbes*, 1996 list of the world's top ten billionaires.

54 *New York Times*, 14 November 1995, C1.

55 *Wall Street Journal*, 13 April 1994, A1, A6.

56 Edward A. Gargan, "The Master Builder of Malaysia," *New York Times*, 27 March 1996, C1, C6.

57 *Wall Street Journal*, 13 April 1994, A1, A6.

58 This process of cultural accumulation on the world stage is replicated at the national level as well. Recently, through a huge investment of funds in museums, galleries, and exhibitions, Singapore has declared itself the "new art capital of Asia" (overtaking Tokyo and Shanghai).

59 Stuart Hall, "Old and New Identities: Old and New Ethnicities," in *Culture, Globalization, and the World-System: Contemporary Conditions for the Representation of Identity*, ed. Anthony D. King (Binghamton: Department of Art and Art History, State University of New York at Binghamton, 1991), 53.

60 *New York Times*, 3 March 1994, A9.

61 Davis, *City of Quartz*, 137–38.

62 *New York Times*, 3 March 1994, A9.

63 See, for instance, David Palumbo-Liu, "Los Angeles, Asians, and Perverse Ventriloquisms: On the Functions of Asian America in Recent American Imaginary," *Public Culture* 3 (1994): 365–84.

64 Interview by author, June 1991.

65 Ibid.

66 Ibid.

67 Ibid.

68 Ibid.

69 See Karen B. Sacks, "How Did Jews Become White Folks?" in *Race*, ed. Steven Gregory and Roger Sanjek (New Brunswick, N.J.: Rutgers University Press, 1994), 78–102.

70 "Whiteness" represents mainstream normalized "American" character. It is the historically produced symbol of "original" producer classes who possessed "Ameri-

can" culture in opposition to colored interlopers. Successive immigrant groups, depending on their class background, are variously incorporated within what is manifested as a racially stratified society. See Brackette F. Williams, "The Symbolics of Ethnic Historical Traditions and 'Suffering': Some Implications for the Doctrine of Equal Citizenship in the United States" (manuscript).

71 Williams, "The Symbolics."

72 Ibid.

73 William Safire, *New York Times,* 21 October 1996.

74 *New York Times,* 30 March 1997, A1.

75 Robin Madrid, personal communication, 20 March 1997. Madrid, a student at American University, is completing her dissertation on Muslim groups and civil society in Indonesia. The Indonesian students also wondered why Riady could not channel some of this "soft money" to nongovernment organizations back home.

76 Between 1965 and 1966, an estimated half-million Indonesians were killed in a bloodbath instigated by the military against communists, peasants, members of mass organizations, and their sympathizers. The CIA was alleged to have provided a list of top communists to be killed. Tens of thousands of communist suspects were sent to the Indonesian gulag. See Audrey R. Kahin and George McT. Kahin, *Subversion as Foreign Policy: The Secret Eisenhower and Dulles Debacle in Indonesia* (New York: New Press, 1995), 217, 227–30. For a further discussion of American influence in these events see Frederick Bunnell, "American 'Low Posture' Policy toward Indonesia in the Months Leading to the 1965 'Coup,' " *Indonesia* 50 (October 1990).

77 See Aihwa Ong, "The Invisible Costs of Soeharto's Empire," *AnthroWatch* 4, no. 2 (November 1996): 7–8.

78 *New York Times,* 27 January 1997, A1.

79 I owe this phrasing to Don Nonini.

80 In a discussion of tourism, Edward M. Bruner notes that many Western people make a desperate effort not to see third-world people in their midst, preferring to spend large sums on travel to view them in their proper "space/place" on the other side of the world. Bruner goes on to note that "for a large segment of the Western elite, . . . the essential paradox remains—in First World cities the Other is a social problem; in Third World places the Other is an object of desire." See Bruner, "Tourism in the Balinese Borderzone," in Lavie and Swedenburg, *Displacements, Diasporas,* 160. In his travels, the tourist seeks a disembodied, decontextualized, sanitized, hypothetical other while overlooking the poverty and suffering of third-world subjects who dwell downtown.

81 David Palumbo-Liu makes a similar argument in *Asia/America: Body, Psyche, Space* (Stanford, Calif.: Stanford University Press, forthcoming), chap. 8.

82 Wang Ling-chi, professor of ethnic studies at University of California, Berkeley, and a leading spokesperson for Asian Americans on the West coast.

83 Henry Der, *San Francisco Examiner,* 22 December 1996, C6. Der is an Asian American civil-rights activist.

84 I owe this insight to Brackette Williams.

85 About 60 percent of Asian Americans are foreign born.

7   Saying No to the West: Liberal Reasoning in Asia

1 English translation by the Decca Record Company, London, 1960. Puccini, *Turandot*, Rome Opera House orchestra and chorus, Erich Leinsdorf, sound recording, AG13-3970.

2 Whereas Persia was the Orient to the French, one imagines that to the Italians, ever since the travels of Marco Polo, China has always been the true seat of oriental despotism.

3 The latter is Puccini's well-known opera about Butterfly/Ciociosan, a young geisha who is married and then abandoned by Pinkerton, an American naval officer. Pinkerton returns with his American wife to claim Butterfly's son. Ciociosan gives up her son to be raised as an American and then kills herself.

4 But see Joseph Kerman, *Opera as Drama*, new and rev. ed. (Berkeley: University of California Press, 1988).

5 A *Turandot* character more similar to Ciociosan is Liu, the "slave girl" who, despite unrequited love, sacrifices herself for Calaf and thus foreshadows the moral transformation that is to come for Turandot.

6 These operas have, of course, been joined by the Andrew Lloyd Webber musical *Ms. Saigon*, an updated version of *Madam Butterfly* for less highbrow, younger audiences. The play *M. Butterfly*, by Asian American David Huang, is a rebuke and a reversal of such orientalist fantasies, but it has made not a dent in the popularity of the two Puccini operas. See Dorinne Kondo, "*M. Butterfly:* Orientalism, Gender, and a Critique of Essentialist Identity," *Cultural Critique* 18 (1990): 5–29.

7 Samuel P. Huntington, "The Clash of Civilizations?" *Foreign Affairs* 72, no. 3 (summer 1993): 22–49. Huntington's thesis is now a book titled *The Clash of Civilizations and the Remaking of the World Order* (New York: Simon and Schuster, 1996).

8 See Richard Bernstein and Ross H. Munro, "The Coming Conflict with China," *Foreign Affairs* 76, no. 2 (March/April 1997). Bernstein and Munro maintain that China will be the chief American rival of the indefinite future, but they deny that China has plans to dominate the world. However, the Washington elite tends to take their argument as a prediction of an inevitable military clash with China. *Foreign Affairs* has since published an issue titled "The China Threat."

9 See "America's Dose of Sinophobia," *Economist*, 29 March 1997, 35.

10 "For the relevant future, there will be no universal civilization, but instead a world of different civilizations, each of which will have to learn to co-exist with the others" (Huntington, "Clash?" 49).

11 Others who have indirectly contributed to different parts of the debate include Chalmers Johnson and James Fallows. See Johnson, *MITI and the Japanese Miracle* (Stanford, Calif.: Stanford University Press, 1982); and Fallows, *Looking at the Sun.*

12 Rostow, *Stages of Economic Growth.*

13 "With the end of the Cold War, international politics moves out of its Western phrase, and its centerpiece becomes the interaction between the West and non-Western civilizations, and among non-Western civilizations" (Huntington, "Clash?" 23). Huntington also argues that to modernize is not the same thing as to westernize when there is no adoption of Western democratic values and institutions concerning democracy and human rights (41).

14 Ibid., 49.

15 Bryan S. Turner, *Orientalism, Postmodernism and Globalism* (London: Routledge, 1994), 46, 96.

16 Huntington, "Clash?" 24.

17 Ibid., 29–30.

18 The orientalist themes of the Orient as stagnant, backward, irrational, and despotic go back to Aristotle, but social-science views have been mainly shaped by nineteenth-century theorists, most prominent of whom are Karl Marx, with his theory of "the Asiatic mode of production" (see *Karl Marx: Pre-capitalist Economic Formations,* trans. J. Cohen, ed. and intro. E. J. Hobsbawm [New York: International Publishers, 1964]), and Max Weber (see Weber, *The Sociology of Religion* [Boston: Beacon Press, 1966]).

19 Huntington, "Clash?" 27; Samuel P. Huntington, "The West: Unique, Not Universal," *Foreign Affairs* 75, no. 6 (November/December 1996): 38–39.

20 Weber, *Sociology of Religion,* 268–69. For a critique of Weber's evaluation of Oriental deficiencies see Turner, *Orientalism,* pt. 1.

21 Huntington, "Clash?" 49.

22 Asad, "Introduction," 18.

23 Talal Asad, "Are There Histories of Peoples without Europe? A Review Article," *Comparative Studies in Society and History* 29, no. 3 (1987): 594–607.

24 Ibid., 604. The original quote, phrased somewhat differently, is in Marx, *The Eighteenth Brumaire,* 15.

25 Ronald Takaki, *Iron Cages: Race and Culture in Nineteenth-Century America* (New York: Oxford University Press, 1981), 253–79.

26 James C. Thomson, Peter W. Stanley, and John Curtis Perry, *Sentimental Imperialists: The American Experience in East Asia* (New York: Harper, 1981).

27 See Lisa Lowe, *Critical Terrains: French and British Orientalisms* (Ithaca, N.Y.: Cornell University Press, 1991).

28 *Straits Times Weekly,* 13 March 1993, overseas ed., 14.

29 Huntington, "Clash?" 45.

30 Huntington, "The West," 41.

31 See Ulrich Beck, *Risk Society* (London: Sage, 1992).

32 Huntington, "The West."

33 Huntington, "Clash?" 49.

34 Ibid., 37.

35 Huntington, "The West," 37–41.

36 Barry Hindess, "Liberalism, Socialism, and Democracy—Variations on a Governmental Theme," in *Foucault and Political Reason*, ed. Andrew Barry, Thomas Osborne, and Nicholas Rose (Chicago: University of Chicago Press, 1996), 66.

37 *Straits Times Weekly*, 13 March 1993, overseas ed., 14.

38 See John Rawls, *Theory of Justice* (Cambridge, Mass.: Harvard University Press, 1971).

39 Chantal Mouffe, "Democratic Citizenship and the Political Community," in *Dimensions of Radical Democracy: Pluralism, Citizenship, Community*, ed. Chantal Mouffe (London: Verso, 1992), 266. For more on the individualism versus communitarian debates see Will Kymlicka, "Liberalism and Communitarianism," *Canadian Journal of Philosophy* 18, no. 2 (June 1988), and Daniel Bell, *Communitarianism and Its Critics* (Oxford: Clarendon Press, 1993).

40 Hindess, "Liberalism, Socialism, and Democracy," 71–72.

41 Huntington thus conveniently ignores the civic-republican philosophy in the West that puts a strong emphasis on the common good.

42 See Karl Marx, *Capital*, vol. 1 (1867; reprint, New York: International Publishers, 1972).

43 Foucault, "Governmentality," 89.

44 Graham Burchell, "Liberal Government and Techniques of the Self," in *Foucault and Political Reason*, ed. Andrew Barry, Thomas Osborne, and Nicholas Rose (Chicago: University of Chicago Press, 1996), 26; italics in the original.

45 For a Foucauldian analysis of advanced liberalism see Rose, "Governing 'Advanced' Liberal Democracies."

46 Ibid., 39.

47 Ibid., 46–47.

48 Ibid.

49 Song Qiang et al., *Zhongguo keyi shuo bu* (Beijing: Zhonghua Gongshang Lianhe Chubanshe, 1996).

50 Quotes are from Peter Gries, review of *Zhongguo keyi shuo bu*, by Song Qiang et al., *China Journal* 37 (January 1997): 181. MFN is the "most favored nation" clause that gives a preference in the American market to the trading country in question.

51 Mahathir and Ishihara, *Voice of Asia*.

52 Ishihara, *Japan That Can Say No*.

53 Song Qiang et al., *Zhongguo hai shi neng shuo bu* (Beijing: Xinhua Shudian, 1996).

54 Andrew Barry, Thomas Osborne, and Nicholas Rose, "Introduction," in *Foucault and Political Reason*, ed. Andrew Barry, Thomas Osborne, and Nicholas Rose (Chicago: University of Chicago Press, 1996), 13.

55 Richard Robison and David S. G. Goodman, "The New Rich in Asia: Economic Development, Social Status, and Political Consciousness," in *The New Rich in Asia* (London: Routledge, 1996), 5.

56 Barrington Moore Jr., *The Social Origins of Dictatorship and Democracy* (New York: Beacon Press, 1966), 433–52.

57 Edward G. Verlander, "The Seeds of Empire," letter to the editor, *New York Times*, 30 June 1997, A14.

58 See Feith, "Repressive-Developmentalist Regimes."

59 For an overview of industrial strategies and state accommodations in Asia see Deyo, *Political Economy*; Gordon White, ed., *Developmental States in East Asia* (New York: St. Martin's Press, 1988); and Richard Appelbaum and Jeffrey Henderson, eds., *States and Development in the Pacific Rim* (Newbury Park, Calif.: Sage, 1992).

60 Harold Crouch, *Government and Society in Malaysia* (Ithaca, N.Y.: Cornell University Press, 1996), 236–47. For a discussion of a more complex Southeast Asian regime see Schwartz, *Nation In Waiting*.

61 "Time for a Reality Check in Asia," *Business Week*, 2 December 1996, 58, 62.

62 Ibid., 67.

63 Escobar, *Encountering Development*.

64 Ibid., 212–26.

65 Stephen Collier's insights and clarifications have been helpful in my formulation of the concept of postdevelopmental state strategy. A graduate student in anthropology at the University of California, Berkeley, he is conducting research on the transition from socialism in Russia.

66 See Richard Robison, "Authoritarian States, Capital-Owning Classes, and the Politics of NICs: The Case of Indonesia," *World Politics* 41 (1988): 52–74; and *Southeast Asian Capitalists*, ed. Ruth McVey (Ithaca, N.Y.: South East Asia Program, Cornell University, 1992).

67 Ruth McVey, "The Materialization of the Southeast Asian Entrepreneur," in *Southeast Asian Capitalists*, ed. Ruth McVey (Ithaca, N.Y.: South East Asia Program, Cornell University, 1992), 30.

68 Peter Evans, *Embedded Autonomy: States and Industrial Transformation* (Princeton, N.J.: Princeton University Press, 1995), 16.

69 McVey, "Materialization," 32. Peter Evans calls this new state alliance with foreign capital "embedded autonomy" (Evans, *Embedded Autonomy*).

70 For Michel Foucault's discussion of pastoral power see Foucault, "Omnes et Singulatim," in *The Tanner Lectures on Human Values*, vol. 2, ed. Sterling M. McMurrin (Salt Lake City: University of Utah Press, 1981), 225–54. For his concept of disciplining power, see Foucault, *Discipline and Punish*.

71 See Barbara Cruikshank, "Revolutions Within: Self-Government and Self-Esteem," in *Foucault and Political Reason*, 19–36. See also Michel Foucault, "The Subject and Power," in *Michel Foucault: Beyond Structuralism and Hermeneutics*, ed. Hubert L. Dreyfus and Paul Rabinow (Chicago: University of Chicago Press, 1983), 208–28.

72 Don Nonini urged me to make this clarification.

73 See G. Steinmetz, *Regulating the Social: The Welfare State and Local Politics in Imperial Germany* (Princeton, N.J.: Princeton University Press, 1993); and K. G. Banting, *The Welfare State and Canadian Federalism* (Kingston, Ont.: McGill-

Queen's University Press, 1987). I thank Ashraf Ghani for suggesting these comparative references.

74 Philip Corrigan and Derek Sayer, *The Great Arch: English State Formation as Cultural Revolution* (Oxford: Basil Blackwell, 1985), 3.

75 Ibid.

76 Of course, the pastoral modality of state power has not totally normalized society. One should not underestimate the importance of recent middle-class uprisings that fought for political and economic rights in South Korea, that overthrew the Marcos regime in the Philippines, that protested military coups in Thailand, and that struggled and died for democracy in Tiananmen Square. In all Asian countries, the new middle classes have also founded a multiplicity of local nongovernmental organizations dedicated to protecting fundamental human rights and to resisting state power. See chapter 8.

77 See Chua, *Communitarian Ideology;* and Crouch, *Government and Society.* The charge of authoritarian rule is more accurate for Indonesia, where there is the form of democracy but little substantive content, and political repression is much more frequent and extensive. See Schwarz, *Nation in Waiting.*

78 Rose, "Governing 'Advanced' Liberal Democracies," 42.

79 Mahathir and Ishihara, "Will East Beat West?", 11.

80 Khoo Boo Teik, *Paradoxes of Mahathirism* (Kuala Lumpur: Oxford University Press, 1995), 328.

81 Mahathir and Ishihara, "Will East Beat West?" 10.

82 Khoo, *Paradoxes,* 328.

83 *Bumiputra,* or "princes of the soil," refers to the Malays' claim to be the original inhabitants of Malaysia, which has a multiethnic population of about twenty million. All Malays are Muslims.

84 See Khoo, *Paradoxes,* 24–41, where the author enumerates the moral problems of Malay culture as viewed by Mahathir Mohamad.

85 Unlike the Malay middle classes, the ethnic Chinese, who are economically and culturally more independent of the state structure, are politically too weak to pose a significant challenge to state power. Much of their energy is invested in economic interests and structures that can free them from the disciplining of the state and in eluding political-cultural control through plotting emigration strategies or participating in transnational business.

86 *Straits Times Weekly,* 13 March 1993, overseas ed., 14. Chan is currently the Singapore ambassador to the United States and is thus a major translator of Singaporean political rationalities.

87 Tu Wei-ming, *A Confucian Perspective on Human Rights,* The Inaugural Wu The Yao Memorial Lectures, 1995 (Singapore: UNI Press, 1995), 20–22, 24.

88 See, for instance, Wang Hui Ling, "Sowing Seeds of Potential Discord," *New Straits Times,* 25 July 1997, 50.

89 Bruce Gilley, "Hong Kong Handover: Is Hong Kong Having an Identity Crisis?" *Asian Wall Street Journal*, 17 June 1997.

90 Edward A. Gargan, "A New Leader Outlines His Vision for Hong Kong," *New York Times*, 2 July 1997, A1.

91 Ibid.

92 Rose, "Governing 'Advanced' Liberal Democracies," 47.

93 Although obviously, criticism of the government in terms of the degree of democratic representation also is expressed among the few but lively opposition members of Parliament and activist groups in both countries.

94 Rose, "Governing 'Advanced' Liberal Democracies," 57.

95 *Straits Times Weekly*, 13 March 1993, overseas ed., 14.

96 See Garry Rodan, "Expect Asia's Values to Turn Out Much Like Everyone Else's," *International Herald Tribune*, 4 August 1997, 8.

97 Chua, *Communitarian Ideology*, ix–x.

98 Ibid., 129.

99 "Singapore Ranked Second Again for Profitability," *Straits Times*, 8 August 1997, 40.

100 Chua, *Communitarian Ideology*, 116.

101 For a recent case see "Singapore Leader Is Accused of Lying," *New York Times*, 20 August 1997, A5.

102 Mahathir and Ishihara, "Will East Beat West?" 8.

103 See Crouch, *Government and Society*.

104 Ralf Dahrendorf, "Economic Opportunity, Civil Society, and Political Liberty," *Development and Change* 27 (1996): 229–49.

105 "Dynamic Model: U.S. Economy Shows Foreign Nations Ways to Grow Much Faster," *Wall Street Journal*, 19 June 1997, A1, A12.

106 As Stephen Collier pointed out to me.

107 Stephen Gill, "Globalization, Democratization, and the Politics of Indifference," in *Globalization and Critical Reflections*, ed. James H. Mittelman (Boulder, Colo.: Lynne Reinner Publishers, 1996), 205–28.

108 See Katherine S. Newman, *Falling from Grace: The Experience of Downward Mobility in the American Middle Class* (New York: Free Press, 1988).

109 Jacques Attali, "The Crash of Western Civilization: The Limits of the Market and Democracy," *Foreign Policy* 107 (summer 1997): 70.

110 *Wall Street Journal*, "Dynamic Model."

111 See, for example, John Vinocur and John Schmid, "The German Crisis: The Shadows Darken," *International Herald Tribune*, 4 August 1997, 1.

8 Zones of New Sovereignty

1 Castells, *Rise of the Network Society*, 412–18.

2 Gupta and Ferguson, "Beyond 'Culture,' " 23. See also Akhil Gupta, " 'The Song of

the Non-aligned World: Transnational Identities and the Reinscription of Space in Late Capitalism," *Cultural Anthropology* 7, no. 1 (1992): 63–79; and Lisa Malkki, "Citizens of Humanity: Internationalism and the Imagined Community of Nations," *Diaspora* 3, no. 1 (1994): 41–68.

3 Robert Latham ("States, Global Markets, and Social Sovereignty" [paper presented at the Social Science Research Council conference "Sovereignty and Security," Notre Dame, Ind., 18–20 April 1998]) challenges this notion of the sovereign nation-state.

4 Saskia Sassen, *Losing Control? Sovereignty in an Age of Globalization* (New York: Columbia University Press, 1995), xiv.

5 Latham, "States, Global Markets." Latham defines sovereignty in broad terms against the agency-focus model. He maintains that sovereignty "should refer to the construction and maintenance of structures of relations that set the terms for—or are constitutive of—a domain of social existence" (2).

6 Giddens, *Nation-State and Violence*, 205; italics in the original.

7 See McVey, "Materialization," 3–34.

8 Yilmaz Akyüz and Charles Gore, "The Investment-Profits Nexus in East Asian Industrialization," *World Development* 24, no. 2 (1996): 461–70; and Peter Evans, "The Eclipse of the State? Reflections on Stateness in an Era of Globalization," *World Politics* 50 (October 1997): 66.

9 The phrase "commodity chains" refers to the global production networks through which commodities are designed, produced, and marketed in a multiplicity of national sites. See Gary Gereffi, "New Realities of Industrial Development in East Asia and Latin America: Global, Regional, and National Trends," in *States and Development in the Asian Pacific Rim*, ed. Richard P. Appelbaum and Jeffrey Henderson (Newbury Park, Calif.: Sage, 1992), 85–112.

10 "Work towards Tangible Gains, Dr. M. Tells Participants," *Straits Times*, 29 July 1997, 1.

11 "Third Langkawi International Dialogue: Now It's How to Make It Work," *Straits Times*, 27 July 1997, 8.

12 The phrase "an effect of practices" is from Bill Maurer, "Cyberspatial Sovereignties: Offshore Finance, Digital Cash, and the Limits of Liberation," *Indiana Journal of Global Legal Studies* (forthcoming). Maurer argues that the coconstruction of state, sovereignty, market, and subject "throws into relief the *moral* claims subjects make in any momentary configuration of these power effects. Such moral claims tend to hide or naturalize the very terms—sovereignty, the market, the rule of law—from which they draw their moral force" (italics in the original).

13 See Giorgio Agamben, *Homo Sacer: Sovereign Power and Bare Life*, trans. Daniel Heller-Roazen (Stanford, Calif.: Stanford University Press, 1998). I thank Paul Rabinow for alerting me to this reference.

14 See Foucault, *History of Sexuality*. According to Foucault, biopower "brought life and its mechanisms into the realm of explicit calculations and made knowledge/power an agent of the transformation of human life" (143).

15 Nonini, "Shifting Identities," 207–8.

16 Ong, *Spirits of Resistance.*

17 "Malaysia Arms Its Borders against Flood of Refugees," *San Francisco Chronicle,* 31 March 1998, B2.

18 MIMOS, "Malaysia's Multimedia Super Corridor." http://www.jaring.my.

19 "Conduit to Fully Tap Creativity," *New Straits Times,* 30 July 1997, 6.

20 Bernard Wysocki Jr., "Malaysia Is Gambling on a Costly Plunge into a Cyber Future," *Wall Street Journal,* 10 June 1997, A10.

21 For perspectives on refugee camps in Southeast Asia see Barry S. Levy and Daniel C. Sussott, *Years of Horror, Days of Hope: Responding to the Cambodian Refugee Crisis* (Millwood, N.Y.: Associated Faculty Press, 1992); and J. W. Tollefson, *Alien Winds: The Reeducation of America's Indochinese Refugees* (New York: Praeger, 1989).

22 T. Alexander Aleinikoff, "State-Centered Refugee Law: From Resettlement to Containment," in *Mistrusting Refugees,* ed. E. Valentine Daniel and John C. Knudsen (Berkeley and Los Angeles: University of California Press, 1995), 263.

23 See Peter Brosius, "Prior Transcripts, Divergent Paths: Resistance and Acquiescence to Logging in Sarawak, East Malaysia," *Comparative Studies in Society and History* (forthcoming).

24 Tradenet Malaysia, "News and Reports: Growth Triangles," http://tradenetmala. com.

25 Scott Macleod and T. G. McGee, "The Singapore-Johore-Riau Growth Triangle: An Emerging Extended Metropolitan Region," in *Emerging World Cities in the Asia Pacific,* ed. Fu-chen Lo and Yue-man Yeung (Tokyo: United Nations University Press, 1996), 440, 442, 449.

26 "Project ASEAN as Closely-Linked: Don" *New Straits Times,* 25 February 1997, 19.

27 Macleod and McGee, "Singapore-Johore-Riau," 443.

28 Merril Goozner and Uli Schmetzer, "Asian Workers Fighting Back Low Wages: Terrible Working Conditions Foster Strikes," *Chicago Tribune,* 7 November 1994.

29 Merril Goozner, "Western Firms Exploit Working Conditions," *Buffalo News,* 20 November 1994.

30 Ibid.

31 Charles Wallace, "Relief Elusive for Asia's Labor Pains," *Los Angeles Times,* 13 December 1994.

32 In 1993, a young worker at a watch factory in Surabaya was abducted, gang-raped, and murdered after leading a strike to demand that a U.S.$.25 meal allowance be added to the U.S.$.84 daily wage. The murder provoked a national outcry, which led to the arrests of some people. There was widespread belief that the military was implicated.

33 Richard Borsuk, "Fear of Unrest Grows in Indonesian City," *Wall Street Journal,* 20 February 1998, A12.

34 See Tania Li, "Constituting Tribal Space: Indigenous Identity and Resource Politics

in Indonesia" (paper presented at the University of California, Berkeley, 17 October 1997). See also Nancy Peluso, *Rich Land, Poor People: Resource Control and Resistance in Java* (Berkeley and Los Angeles: University of California Press, 1995).

35 Sinapan Samydorai, "The Killing Fields of West Kalimantan," *Human Rights Solidarity* (Hong Kong) 7, no. 2 (April–July 1997): 5–7, 29. *Human Rights Solidarity* is the newsletter of the Asian Human Rights Commission.

36 Robert Castel observes the emergence, in neoliberal states, of "differential modes of treatment of populations, which aim to maximize the returns on doing what is profitable and to marginalize the unprofitable" (Castel, "From Dangerousness to Risk," in *The Foucault Effect*, ed. Graham Burchell, Colin Gordon, and Peter Miller [Chicago: University of Chicago Press, 1992], 294). While Indonesia and the tiger countries are not neoliberal economies, the strategy of differentiation among populations in relation to market forces has produced the system of graduated sovereignty.

37 It might be added that the European states played this role of favoring corporate elites even more blatantly during their period of consolidation.

38 There is growing resentment among Malay professionals against these "preferred Malays" for gaining power not entirely on their own merits but through even more exclusive political favors than the Malay professionals themselves have enjoyed.

39 Huntington, *Clash of Civilizations.* The book is widely displayed in Southeast Asian bookstores.

40 Tu Wei-ming has been the proponent of a Confucian version of universalism that is also closely linked to corporate capitalism. He recently lectured Singaporeans that Confucianism is not the possession of any single nation but is rather a "transvaluated" values system. With globalization, Confucianism has not rejected Enlightenment values but rather has absorbed "instrumental rationality, material progress, social engineering, empiricism, pragmatism, scientism, and competitiveness. . . ." Tu notes that the "Confucian personality" can be realized more fully in a liberal-democratic society than in an authoritarian one. By redefining Confucianism as an ethos that has absorbed the Western rationalities of competition, technical efficiency, and economic progress, he frames the moral choices and self-actualization encouraged by Confucianism within an instrumentalist, market-oriented framework, not the framework of human rights. See Tu, "Confucian Perspective," 27, 29.

41 See Aihwa Ong, "Muslim Feminists in the Shelter of Corporate Islam," *Citizenship Studies* (forthcoming).

42 "Anwar: Carry Out Islamic Laws Wisely, Objectively," *New Straits Times,* 27 July 1997.

43 Cited in Khoo, *Paradoxes,* 165.

44 Ibid., 179.

45 Ibid., 181.

46 Anwar Ibrahim, *The Asian Renaissance* (Kuala Lumpur: Times Publications, 1997), back cover.

47 See Anthony Reid, *The Land below the Wind,* vol. 1 of *Southeast Asia in an Age of Commerce, 1450–1680* (New Haven, Conn.: Yale University Press, 1985).

48 *Far Eastern Economic Review,* 50th Anniversary Issue (Hong Kong, 1996), 187.

49 "When Asia Awakes," *New Straits Times,* 29 July 1997, 10.

50 Ibid., 11.

51 For Islamic radicalism in Malaysia see Clive Kessler, *Politics and Islam in a Malay State* (Ithaca, N.Y.: Cornell University Press, 1976).

52 "The New Face of Islam," *Time,* 23 September 1996, international ed., 18.

53 Center for Civilizational Dialogue, *The Center for Civilizational Dialogue* (Kuala Lumpur: University of Malaya, n.d.).

54 Ibid.

55 Ibid.

56 "Future Belongs to All of Mankind," *New Straits Times,* 4 December 1996, 12, 15.

57 Anthony D. Smith, *National Identity* (Reno: University of Nevada Press, 1993), 169.

58 Center, *Center for Civilizational Dialogue.*

59 George J. Aditjondro, "All in the Name of 'ASEAN Solidarity,'" *Sydney Morning Herald,* 14 November 1996. Only a globally condemned military coup in Phnom Penh made the ASEAN leadership hesitate about including Cambodia in the new lineup.

60 For an exception see *Aliran Monthly* 17, no. 2 (1997): 29–40.

61 Aditjondro, "All in the Name."

62 *Wall Street Journal,* 5 August 1997, 1. This article blamed "a grave lack of economic discipline" for the financial storm sweeping through the region and predicted a decline in growth rates from 9 percent to 4 percent.

63 "Currency Speculators Out to Undermine 'Asian Economies,'" *New Straits Times,* 25 July 1997, 29; and "Dr. M: It's Soros," *New Straits Times,* 27 July 1997, 1.

64 See Kathryn A. Poethig, "Ambivalent Moralities: Cambodian Americans and Dual Citizenship in Phnom Penh" (Ph.D. diss., Graduate Theological Union, Berkeley, Calif., 1997).

65 Fred Y. L. Chiu, "From the Politics of Identity to an Alternative Cultural Politics: On Taiwan's Primordial Inhabitants' A-systemic Movement," in *Asia/Pacific as Space of Cultural Production,* ed. Rob Wilson and Arif Dirlik (Durham, N.C.: Duke University Press, 1995), 112–46.

66 Fred Y. L. Chiu, "Rearing Tigers: Politics and the Body Social in Colonial Hong Kong" (paper presented at the conference "Cultural Politics of Cosmopolitanism: Critiques of Modernity in the Non-West Context," Chinese University of Hong Kong, 1996.

67 Editorial, *Human Rights Solidarity.*

68 T. Mulya Lubis, "The Future of Human Rights in Indonesia," in *Indonesia Assessment 1992: Political Perspectives on the 1990s,* ed. Harold Crouch and Hal Hill (Canberra: Research School of Pacific Studies, Australian National University, 1992), 116.

69 See Aihwa Ong, "The Invisible Costs of Soeharto's Empire," *AnthroWatch* 4, no. 2 (November 1996): 7–8.

70 During the 1996 crackdown, I participated in a visit to Indonesia organized by Global Exchange, a San Francisco–based NGO, which drew human-rights activists from Holland and the Philippines.

71 Francis Loh, "ASEAN NGOs in the Post–Cold War World," in *Asia—Who Pays for Growth?* ed. Jayant Lele and Wisdom Tettey (Aldershot, England: Dartmouth, 1996), 52.

72 Ibid., 49–50.

73 But for a criticism of the implicit Western moral bias in this concept see Ong, "Strategic Sisterhood?"

74 James Holston and Arjun Appadurai note that the substantive rights struggled for by immigrants and the disenfranchised can be independent of formal citizenship. See Holston and Appadurai, "Cities and Citizenship," *Public Culture* 8, no. 2 (winter 1996): 187–204.

75 See Calhoun, "Introduction."

76 By comparison, the growth of the bourgeoisie in Europe took place over several generations.

77 For a fairly comprehensive list of all anti-Chinese incidents in Indonesia in the first month and a half of 1998 see "Recent Anti-Chinese Violence," *Indonesian Archives Digest,* 19 February 1998. This article makes the point that the attacks began for economic, not political, reasons, but the violence has become increasingly tinged with ethnic and religious overtones as leaders linked to the government have sought to channel public discontent away from the government.

78 "Lunar New Year Celebrations Banned As They Could Spark Jealousy," *South China Morning Post,* 21 January 1998, Internet ed.

79 "Immigrants Remain under U.N. Care in Malaysia," *New York Times,* 1 April 1998, A4.

80 Agamben, *Homo Sacer,* 169–70.

Afterword   An Anthropology of Transnationality

1 This modern-traditional division of the world's societies is very evident in Anthony Giddens, *In Defense of Sociology* (London: Polity, 1996). Giddens maintains that because anthropology deals with "nonmodern" cultures, it is dealing with an "evaporating" subject (122).

2 Wallerstein, *Modern World System.*

3 Giddens, *Nation-State and Violence.*

4 Castells, *Rise of the Network Society.*

5 See Ashraf Ghani, "Space as an Arena of Represented Practices," in *Mapping the Futures: Local Cultures, Global Change,* ed. J. Bird et al. (London: Routledge, 1993).

6 See chapter 5. This tradition is associated with anthropological training at Columbia University, the University of Chicago, and Johns Hopkins University. For a

summary see Vincent, *Anthropology and Politics.* A short list of leading works might suffice here: Steward, *People of Puerto Rico;* Eric Wolf, *Peasant Wars of the Twentieth Century* (New York: Harper and Row, 1969); Wolf, *Europe;* Marshall Sahlins, *Stone Age Economics* (Chicago: Aldine-Atherton, 1972); Sahlins, *Culture and Practical Reason* (Chicago: University of Chicago Press, 1976); Sydney Mintz, *Caribbean Transformations* (Chicago: Aldine, 1974); Mintz, *Sweetness and Power;* Scott, *Moral Economy;* Scott, *Weapons;* June Nash, *We Eat the Mines and the Mines Eat Us* (New York: Columbia University Press, 1979); and Vincent, *Teso in Transformation.* This important tradition is inexplicably ignored in Sherry Ortner's representation of political economy in Ortner, "Theory in Anthropology."

7 See Michael Taussig, *The Devil and Commodity Fetishism in South America* (Chapel Hill: University of North Carolina Press, 1980); Ann Stoler, *Capitalism and Confrontation in Sumatra's Plantation Belt, 1870–1979* (New Haven, Conn.: Yale University Press, 1985); Jean Comaroff, *Body of Power, Spirit of Resistance* (Chicago: University of Chicago Press, 1985); Scott, *Weapons;* Ong, *Spirits of Resistance;* Michael G. Peletz, *A Share of the Harvest* (Berkeley: University of California Press, 1988); William Roseberry, *Anthropologies and Histories* (New Brunswick: Rutgers University Press, 1989); James Ferguson, *The Anti-politics Machine: 'Development,' Depoliticization, and Bureaucratic State Power in Lesotho* (Cambridge: Cambridge University Press, 1990); Williams, *Stains on My Name;* John Comaroff and Jean Comaroff, *Ethnography and the Historical Imagination* (Boulder, Colo.: Westview, 1992); Katherine Verdery, *What Was Socialism? What Comes After?* (Princeton, N.J.: Princeton University Press, 1995); and Gupta, *Postcolonial Developments.*

8 This is a point that Don Nonini and I raised in Nonini and Ong, "Introduction."

Bibliography

Agamben, Giorgio. *Homo Sacer: Sovereign Power and Bare Life.* Trans. Daniel Heller-Roazen. Stanford, Calif.: Stanford University Press, 1998.

Ahmad, Aijaz. "The Politics of Literary Postcoloniality." *Race and Class* 36, no. 3 (1995): 1–20.

Alatas, Syed Hussein. *The Myth of the Lazy Native.* London: Frank Cass, 1977.

Aleinikoff, T. Alexander. "State-Centered Refugee Law: From Resettlement to Containment." In *Mistrusting Refugees,* ed. E. Valentine Daniel and John C. Knudsen. Berkeley and Los Angeles: University of California Press, 1995.

Allison, Anne. *Nightwork: Sexuality, Pleasure, and Corporate Masculinity in a Tokyo Hostess Club.* Chicago: University of Chicago Press, 1994.

Anagnost, Ann. "Prosperity and Counter-prosperity: The Moral Discourse on Wealth in Post-Mao China." In *Marxism and the Chinese Experience,* ed. Arif Dirlik and Maurice Meisner, 210–34. Armonk, N.Y.: M. E. Sharpe, 1989.

——. *National Past-Times: Narrative, Representation, and Power in Modern China.* Durham, N.C.: Duke University Press, 1997.

Anderson, Benedict. *Imagined Communities: Reflections on the Origins and Spread of Nationalism.* 2d ed. London: Verso, 1991.

——. "Exodus." *Cultural Inquiry* 20 (winter 1994): 324–25.

Andrew, Barry, Thomas Osborne, and Nicholas Rose. "Introduction." In *Foucault and Political Reason,* ed. Andrew Barry, Thomas Osborne, and Nicholas Rose, 1–18. Chicago: University of Chicago Press, 1996.

Ang, Ien. "To Be or Not to Be Chinese: Diaspora, Culture, and Postmodern Ethnicity." *Southeast Asia Journal of Social Science* 21, no. 1 (1993): 1–19.

——. *Living Room Wars: Rethinking Media Audiences for a Postmodern World.* London: Routledge, 1996.

Anwar Ibrahim. *The Asian Renaissance.* Kuala Lumpur: Times Publications, 1997.

Anzaldúa, Gloria. *Borderlands/La Frontera.* San Francisco: Spinsters/Aunt Lute, 1987.

Appadurai, Arjun. "Disjuncture and Difference in the Global Cultural Economy." In *Modernity at Large,* 27–47. Minneapolis: University of Minnesota Press, 1996.

———. *Modernity at Large: Cultural Dimensions of Globalization.* Minneapolis: University of Minnesota Press, 1996.

Appelbaum, Richard, and Jeffrey Henderson, eds. *States and Development in the Pacific Rim.* Newbury Park, Calif.: Sage, 1992.

Asad, Talal. "Are There Histories of Peoples without Europe? A Review Article." *Comparative Studies in Society and History* (1987): 594–607.

———. "Introduction." In *Genealogies of Religion: Discipline and Reasons of Power in Christianity and Islam.* Baltimore, Md.: Johns Hopkins University Press, 1993.

Ashcroft, Bill, Gareth Griffiths, and Helen Tiffins, eds. *The Postcolonial Reader.* New York: Routledge, 1995.

———. *The Empire Writes Back: Theory and Practice in Post-Colonial Literature.* New York: Routledge, 1989.

Attali, Jacques. "The Crash of Western Civilization: The Limits of the Market and Democracy." *Foreign Policy* 107 (summer 1997): 54–64.

Bah Kah Choon. "Narrating Imagination." In *Imagining Singapore,* ed. Ban Kah Choon, Ann Pakir, and Tong Chee Kiong, 23–24. Singapore: Times Academic Press, 1992.

Banting, K. G. *The Welfare State and Canadian Federalism.* Kingston, Ont.: McGill-Queen's University Press, 1987.

Barlow, Tani. "*Zhishifenzi* [Chinese Intellectuals] and Power." *Dialectical Anthropology* 16 (1991): 209–32.

———. "Theorizing Woman: *Funu, Guojia, Jiating.*" *Genders* 10 (spring 1991): 132–60.

———. "Colonial Modernity and Gendered Agency." Paper presented at the East Asian Institute, University of California, Berkeley, 3 May 1993.

Basch, Linda, Nina Glick-Schiller, and Cristina B. Szanton. *Nations Unbound: Transnational Projects, Postcolonial Predicaments, and Deterritorialized Nation-States.* Langhorne, Pa.: Gordon and Breach, 1994.

Beck, Ulrich. *Risk Society.* London: Sage, 1992.

Bell, Daniel. *Communitarianism and Its Critics.* Oxford: Clarendon Press, 1994.

Berger, Peter, and Hsin-huang Michael Hsiao, eds. *In Search of an East Asian Development Model.* New Brunswick, N.J.: Transaction Books, 1988.

Bernstein, Richard, and Ross H. Munro. "The Coming Conflict with China." *Foreign Affairs* 76, no. 2 (March/April 1997).

Bhabha, Homi K. "Introduction." In *Nation and Narration,* ed. Homi K. Bhabha. New York: Routledge, 1990.

———. "DissemiNation: Time, Narrative, and the Margins of the Modern Nation." In *Nation and Narration,* ed. Homi K. Bhabha, 291–322. New York: Routledge, 1990.

———. *The Location of Culture.* London: Routledge, 1994.

Blanc, Cristina S. "The Thoroughly Modern 'Asian': Capital, Culture, and Nation in

Thailand and the Philippines." In *Ungrounded Empires,* ed. Aihwa Ong and Donald Nonini, 261–86. New York: Routledge, 1997.

Bonacich, Edna. "A Theory of Middleman Minorities." *American Sociological Review* 38 (1973): 583–94.

Bourdieu, Pierre. *Outline of a Theory of Practice.* Cambridge: Cambridge University Press, 1977.

——. *Distinctions: The Social Judgment of Taste.* Cambridge, Mass.: Harvard University Press, 1984.

——. "The Forms of Capital." In *Handbook of Theory and Research for the Sociology of Education,* ed. J. G. Richardson, 241–58. New York: Greenwood, 1986.

Brosius, Peter. "Prior Transcripts, Divergent Paths: Resistance and Acquiescence to Logging in Sarawak, East Malaysia." *Comparative Studies in Society and History* (forthcoming).

Bruner, Edward M. "Tourism in the Balinese Borderzone." In *Displacements, Diasporas, and the Geographies of Identity,* ed. Smadar Lavie and Ted Swedenburg, 157–79. Durham, N.C.: Duke University Press, 1996.

Bunnell, Frederick. "American 'Low Posture' Policy toward Indonesia in the Months Leading to the 1965 'Coup.'" *Indonesia* 50 (October 1990).

Burchell, Graham. "Liberal Government and Techniques of the Self." In *Foucault and Political Reason: Liberalism, Neo-liberalism, and Rationalities of Government,* ed. Andrew Barry, Thomas Osborne, and Nicholas Rose. Chicago: University of Chicago Press, 1996.

Calhoun, Craig. "Introduction: Habermas and the Public Sphere." In *Habermas and the Public Sphere,* ed. Craig Calhoun, 1–50. Cambridge, Mass.: MIT Press, 1992.

——. "Tiananmen, Television, and Public Sphere: Internationalization of Culture and the Beijing Spring of 1989." *Public Culture* 2, no. 1 (winter 1989): 54–72.

Carnoy, Martin, et al. *The New Global Economy in the Information Age.* University Park: Pennsylvania State University Press, 1993.

Carter, Donald M. *States of Grace: Senegalese in Italy and the New European Immigration.* Minneapolis: University of Minnesota Press, 1997.

Castel, Robert. "From Dangerousness to Risk." In *The Foucault Effect,* ed. Graham Burchell, Colin Gordon, and Peter Miller, 281–98. Chicago: University of Chicago Press, 1992.

Castells, Manuel. *The Rise of the Network Society.* Vol. 1 of *The Information Age.* Oxford: Basil Blackwell, 1996.

Center for Civilizational Dialogue. *The Center for Civilizational Dialogue.* Kuala Lumpur: University of Malaya, n.d.

Chan, Anita, Richard Madsen, and Jonathan Unger. *Chen Village: Under Mao and Deng.* Rev. and enl. ed. Berkeley and Los Angeles: University of California Press, 1992.

Chan, Jeffery Paul, Frank Chin, Lawson Fusao Inada, and Shawn Wong, eds. *The Big*

AIIEEEEE! An Anthology of Chinese American and Japanese American Literature. New York: Meridian, 1991.

Chan, Sucheng. *This Bittersweet Soil: The Chinese in California Agriculture, 1860–1910.* Berkeley and Los Angeles: University of California Press, 1986.

Chan Kowk Bun and Claire Chiang. *Stepping Out: The Making of Chinese Entrepreneurs.* Singapore: Simon and Schuster, 1994.

Chatterjee, Partha. *Nationalist Thought and the Colonial World: A Derivative Discourse?* London: Zed Books, 1986.

——. *The Nation and Its Fragments: Colonial and Postcolonial Histories.* Princeton, N.J.: Princeton University Press, 1993.

Cheah, Pheng, and Bruce Robbins, eds. *Cosmopolitics: Thinking and Feeling beyond the Nation.* Minneapolis: University of Minnesota Press, 1998.

Chen, Edward K. Y. "The Economic Setting." In *The Business Environment in Hong Kong.* 2d ed., ed. D. G. Lethbridge, 1–51. Hong Kong: Oxford University Press, 1984.

Chen, Ta. *Emigrant Communities in South China.* Shanghai: Kelly and Walsh, 1939.

Chen Xiyu. "Research Note on the 'Chinese Economic Zone.'" *ISSCO Bulletin* 2, no. 2 (1994): 3–4.

Cheng, Lucie, and Edna Bonacich, eds. *Labor Immigration under Capitalism: Asian Workers in the United States before World War II.* Berkeley and Los Angeles: University of California Press, 1984.

Ching, Leo. "Imaginings in the Empires of the Sun: Japanese Mass Culture in Asia." In *Asia/Pacific as Space of Cultural Production,* ed. Rob Wilson and Arif Dirlik, 262–83. Durham, N.C.: Duke University Press, 1995.

Chiu, Fred Y. L. "Rearing Tigers: Politics and the Body Social in Colonial Hong Kong." Paper presented at the conference "Cultural Politics of Cosmopolitanism: Critiques of Modernity in the Non-West Context." Chinese University of Hong Kong, 1996.

——. "From the Politics of Identity to an Alternative Cultural Politics: On Taiwan's Primordial Inhabitants' A-systemic Movement." In *Asia/Pacific as Space of Cultural Production,* ed. Rob Wilson and Arif Dirlik, 112–16. Durham, N.C.: Duke University Press, 1995.

——. "Non-mediating Forces versus Mediating Forces—New 'Subjecthood' in Local/Regional Resistances against Nation/Global Systemic Drives." Paper presented at the workshop "Nation-States, Transnational Publics, and Civil Society in the Asia-Pacific." University of California, Berkeley, 28–30 June 1996.

Chua Beng-huat, *Communitarian Ideology and Democracy in Singapore.* London: Routledge, 1995.

Chun, Allen. "Pariah Capitalism and the Overseas Chinese of Southeast Asia: Problems in the Definition of the Problem." *Ethnic and Racial Studies* 12, no. 2 (1989): 233–56.

——. "From Nationalism to Nationalizing: Cultural Imagination and State Formation in Postwar Taiwan." *Australian Journal of Chinese Affairs* 31 (1994): 49–72.

Clifford, James. "Traveling Cultures." In *Cultural Studies*, ed. Lawrence Grossberg, Cary Nelson, and Paula A. Treichler, 96–116. New York: Routledge, 1992.

——. "Diasporas." *Cultural Anthropology* (summer 1994): 1–50.

——. *Routes: Travel and Translation in the Late Twentieth Century.* Cambridge, Mass.: Harvard University Press, 1997.

Cohen, Robin. "Policing the Frontiers: The State and the Migrant in the International Division of Labor." In *Global Restructuring and Territorial Development,* ed. J. Henderson and Manuel Castells, 88–111. London: Sage, 1987.

Comaroff, Jean. *Body of Power, Spirit of Resistance: The Culture and History of a South African People.* Chicago: University of Chicago Press, 1985.

Comaroff, John, and Jean Comaroff. *Ethnography and the Historical Imagination.* Boulder, Colo.: Westview, 1992.

Copeland, Lewis C. "The Negro as a Contrast Conception." In *Race Relations and the Race Problem: A Definition and an Analysis,* ed. Edgar T. Thompson, 152–79. Durham, N.C.: Duke University Press, 1939.

Corrigan, Phillip, and Derek Sayer. *The Great Arch: English State Formation as Cultural Revolution.* Oxford: Basil Blackwell, 1985.

Crichton, Michael. *Rising Sun.* New York: Ballantine, 1992.

Crouch, Harold. *Government and Society in Malaysia.* Ithaca, N.Y.: Cornell University Press, 1996.

Cruikshank, Barbara. "Revolutions Within: Self-Government and Self-Esteem." In *Foucault and Political Reason,* 19–36.

Cumings, Bruce. "Rimspeak." In *What Is in a Rim? Critical Perspectives on the Pacific Region Idea,* ed. Arif Dirlik, 29–47. Boulder, Colo.: Westview, 1993.

Dahrendorf, Ralf. "Economic Opportunity, Civil Society, and Political Liberty." *Development and Change* 27 (1996): 229–49.

Daniels, Roger. *Asian American: Chinese and Japanese in the United States since 1850.* Seattle: University of Washington Press, 1988.

Davis, Mike. *City of Quartz: Excavating the Future in Los Angeles.* New York: Vintage, 1992.

Deyo, Frederic C., ed. *The Political Economy of New Asian Industrialism.* Ithaca, N.Y.: Cornell University Press, 1987.

Dikötter, Frank. *The Discourse of Race in Modern China.* Stanford, Calif.: Stanford University Press, 1992.

Dirlik, Arif. "Introducing the Pacific." In *What Is in a Rim? Critical Perspectives on the Pacific Region Idea,* ed. Arif Dirlik, 3–11. Boulder, Colo.: Westview, 1992.

——. "The Asia-Pacific in Asian-American Perspective." In *What Is in a Rim? Critical Perspectives on the Pacific Region Idea,* ed. Arif Dirlik, 305–29. Boulder, Colo.: Westview, 1992.

——. "The Postcolonial Aura: Third World Criticism in the Age of Global Capitalism." *Critical Inquiry* 20, no. 2 (1994): 328–56.

——. *After the Revolution: Waking to Global Capitalism.* Hanover, N.H.: Wesleyan University Press, 1994.

Dirlik, Arif, and Xudong Zhang, eds. *Chinese Postmodernism.* Durham, N.C.: Duke University Press, 1997.

Dong Yunhu. "Fine Traditions of Human Rights in Asia." *Beijing Review,* 28 June–4 July 1993, 11.

Dorfman, Ariel, and Armand Mattelart. *How to Read Donald Duck: Imperialist Ideology in the Disney Comic.* Trans. David Kunzie. New York: I. G. Editions, 1975.

Duara, Prasenjit. *Rescuing History from the Nation: Questioning Narratives of Modern China.* Chicago: University of Chicago Press, 1995.

Elvin, Mark, and G. William Skinner, eds. *The Chinese City between Two Worlds.* Stanford, Calif.: Stanford University Press, 1972.

Enloe, Cynthia. *Bananas, Beaches, and Bases: Making Feminist Sense of International Politics.* Berkeley and Los Angeles: University of California Press, 1990.

Escobar, Arturo. *Encountering Development: The Making and Unmaking of the Third World.* Princeton, N.J.: Princeton University Press, 1995.

Evans, Peter. *Embedded Autonomy: States and Industrial Transformation.* Princeton, N.J.: Princeton University Press, 1995.

——. "The Eclipse of the State? Reflections on Stateness in an Era of Globalization." *World Politics* 50 (October 1997): 67–87.

Fallows, James. *Looking at the Sun: The Rise of the New East Asian Economic and Political System.* New York: Pantheon, 1994.

Fan Guoxiang. "A Reasonable and Practical Choice." *Beijing Review,* 14–20 March 1994.

Featherstone, Mike. "Global Culture: An Introduction." In *Global Culture: Nationalism, Globalization, and Modernity,* ed. Mike Featherstone, 1–14. Newbury Park, Calif.: Sage, 1990.

Fei Hsiao-tung. "Peasant and Gentry: An Interpretation of Chinese Social Structure and Its Changes." In *Class, Status, and Power,* ed. Reinhard Bendix and Seymour M. Lipset, 646–47. New York: Free Press, 1953.

Feith, Herbert. "Repressive-Developmentalist Regimes in Asia." *Alternatives* 7 (1982): 491–506.

Feld, Stephen. "He Shang and the Plateau of Ultrastability." *Bulletin of Concerned Asian Scholars* 23, no. 3 (1991): 6.

Ferguson, James. *The Anti-politics Machine: "Development," Depoliticization, and Bureaucratic State Power in Lesotho.* Cambridge: Cambridge University Press, 1990.

Ferguson, Kathy. *The Man Question: Visions of Subjectivity in Feminist Theory.* Berkeley and Los Angeles: University of California Press, 1993.

Fernandez-Kelly, Patricia. *For We Are Sold, I and My People.* Albany, N.Y.: SUNY Press, 1985.

Fitzgerald, Stephen. *China and the Overseas Chinese: A Study of Peking's Changing Policy, 1949–70.* Cambridge: Cambridge University Press, 1972.

Fong, Timothy P. *The First Suburban Chinatown: The Remaking of Monterey Park, California.* Philadelphia: Temple University Press, 1994.

Foucault, Michel. *Discipline and Punish: The Birth of the Prison.* Trans. A. Sheridan. New York: Vintage, 1979.

——. *History of Sexuality.* Vol. 1. Trans. M. Hurley. New York: Pantheon, 1978.

——. "On Governmentality." *Ideology and Consciousness* 6 (autumn 1979): 18.

——. "The Subject and Power." In *Michel Foucault: Beyond Structuralism and Hermeneutics,* ed. Hubert L. Dreyfus and Paul Rabinow, 208–28. Chicago: University of Chicago Press, 1983.

——. "Governmentality." In *The Foucault Effect: Studies in Governmentality,* ed. Graham Burchell, Colin Gordon, and Peter Miller, 87–104. Chicago: University of Chicago Press, 1991.

——. *Ethnics: Subjectivity and Truth.* Vol. 1. Ed. Paul Rabinow. Trans. Robert Hurley et al. New York: New Press, 1997.

——. "Omnes et Singulatim." In *The Tanner Lectures on Human Values.* Vol. 2, ed. Sterling M. McMurrin, 225–54. Salt Lake City: University of Utah Press, 1981.

Frankenberg, Ruth, and Lata Mani. "Crosscurrents: Race, 'Postcoloniality,' and the Politics of Location." *Cultural Studies* 7 (May 1993): 292–310.

Fraser, Nancy. "What's Critical about Critical Theory? The Case of Habermas and Gender." In *Unruly Practices,* 113–43. Minneapolis: University of Minnesota Press, 1989.

Freedman, Maurice. "The Handling of Money: A Note on the Background to the Economic Sophistication of the Overseas Chinese." *Man,* o.s., 19 (1959): 64–65.

——. "The Chinese in Southeast Asia: A Longer View." In *Man, State, and Society in Contemporary Southeast Asia,* ed. R. O. Tilman, 431–99. New York: Praeger, 1969.

Freud, Sigmund. *Totem and Taboo: Some Points of Agreement between the Mental Lives of Savages and Neurotics.* In *The Standard Edition of the Complete Psychological Works.* Vol. 13. Trans. James Strachey. London: Hogarth Press, 1958.

Friedman, Edward. "Reconstructing China's National Identity: A Southern Alternative to Mao-Era Anti-imperialist Nationalism." *Journal of Asian Studies* 53, no. 1 (1994): 67–91.

Gayatri C. Spivak. "Can the Subaltern Speak?" In *Marxism and the Interpretation of Cultures,* ed. Cary Nelson and Lawrence Grossberg, 271–313. Urbana: University of Illinois Press, 1988.

Geertz, Clifford. *The Religion of Java.* Chicago: University of Chicago Press, 1960.

——. *Local Knowledge.* Princeton, N.J.: Princeton University Press, 1983.

Gereffi, Gary. "New Realities of Industrial Development in East Asia and Latin America: Global, Regional, and National Trends." In *States and Development in the Asian Pacific Rim,* ed. Richard P. Appelbaum and Jeffrey Henderson, 85–112. Newbury Park, Calif.: Sage, 1992.

Ghani, Ashraf. "Space as an Arena of Represented Practices." In *Mapping the Futures: Local Cultures, Global Change,* ed. Jon Bird et al., 49–59. London: Routledge, 1993.

Gibson-Graham, J. K. *The End of Capitalism (As We Knew It): A Feminist Critique of Political Economy.* Cambridge, Mass.: Blackwell, 1996.

Giddens, Anthony. *The Nation-State and Violence.* Vol. 2 of *A Contemporary Critique of Historical Materialism.* Berkeley and Los Angeles: University of California Press, 1987.

——. *Modernity and Self-Identity.* Stanford, Calif.: Stanford University Press, 1991.

——. *In Defense of Sociology.* London: Polity, 1996.

Gill, Stephen. "Globalization, Democratization, and the Politics of Indifference." In *Globalization: Critical Reflections,* ed. James H. Mittelman, 205–28. Boulder, Colo.: Lynne Reinner Publishers, 1996.

Gilroy, Paul. *"There Ain't No Black in the Union Jack."* Chicago: University of Chicago Press, 1989.

——. *The Black Atlantic: Modernity and Double Consciousness.* Cambridge, Mass.: Harvard University Press, 1992.

——. *Small Acts: Thoughts on the Politics of Black Cultures.* London: Serpent's Tail, 1993.

Goh Keng Swee, foreword to *Stepping Out: The Making of Chinese Entrepreneurs,* by Chan Kwok Bun and Claire Chiang. Singapore: Simon and Schuster Asia, 1994.

Gooding-Williams, Robert, ed. "Introduction: On Being Stuck," *Reading Rodney King, Reading Urban Uprising,* 1–12. New York: Routledge, 1993.

Gordon, Colin. "Governmental Rationality: An Introduction." In *The Foucault Effect: Studies in Governmentality,* ed. Graham Burchell, Colin Gordon, and Peter Miller, 1–15. Chicago: University of Chicago Press, 1992.

Greenhalgh, Susan. "De-orientalizing the Chinese Family Firm." *American Ethnologist* 21, no. 4 (1994): 746–76.

Gregory, Steve, and Roger Sanjek, eds. *Race.* New Brunswick, N.J.: Rutgers University Press, 1992.

Grewal, Inderpal. *Home and Harem.* Durham, N.C.: Duke University Press, 1996.

Gries, Peter. Review of *Zhongguo keyi shuo bu,* by Song Qiang et al. *China Journal* 37 (January 1997): 181–83.

Guha, Ranajit, and Gayatri Chakravorty Spivak, eds. *Selected Subaltern Studies.* New York: Oxford University Press, 1988.

Guildin, Gregory E., ed. *Urbanizing China.* New York: Greenwood Press, 1992.

Gupta, Akhil. "The Song of the Non-aligned World: Transnational Identities and the Reinscription of Space in Late Capitalism." *Cultural Anthropology* 7, no. 1 (1992): 63–79.

——. *Postcolonial Developments: Agriculture in the Making of Modern India.* Durham, N.C.: Duke University Press, 1998.

Gupta, Akhil, and James Ferguson. "Beyond 'Culture': Space, Identity, and the Politics of Difference." *Cultural Anthropology* 7, no. 1 (1992): 6–23.

Habermas, Jürgen. *The Theory of Communicative Action.* Vol. 1. *Reason and Rationalization of Society.* Trans. Thomas McCarthy. Boston, 1984.

Hall, Stuart. "The Toad in the Garden: Thatcherism among the Theorists." In *Marxism and the Interpretation of Cultures,* ed. Cary Nelson and Lawrence Grossberg, 35–57, 58–73. Urbana: University of Illinois Press, 1988.

———. "Cultural Identity and Diaspora." In *Identity: Community, Culture, Difference,* ed. J. Rutherford, 222–37. London: Lawrence and Wishart, 1990.

———. "The Local and the Global: Globalization and Ethnicity." In *Culture, Globalization, and the World System,* ed. Anthony King, 19–39. London: Macmillan, 1991.

———. "Old and New Identities, Old and New Ethnicities." In *Culture, Globalization, and the World System: Contemporary Conditions for the Representation of Identity,* ed. Anthony D. King, 41–68. Binghamton: Department of Art and Art History, State University of New York at Binghamton, 1991.

———. "What Is This Black in Black Popular Culture?" In *Stuart Hall,* ed. David Morley and Kuan-Hsing Chen, 465–75. New York: Routledge, 1996.

Hall, Stuart, and David Held. "Citizens and Citizenship." In *New Times: The Changing Face of Politics in the 1990s,* ed. Start Hall and M. Jacques, 173–88. New York: Verso, 1989.

Hamashita, Takeshi. "The Tribute Trade System and Modern Asia." In *Memoirs of the Research Department of the Toyo Bunko, No. 46.* Tokyo: Tokyo University, 1988.

Hannerz, Ulf. "Notes on the Global Ecumene." *Public Culture* 1, no. 2 (1989): 66–75.

———. "Cosmopolitans and Locals in World Culture." In *Global Culture,* ed. Mike Featherstone, 237–521. Newbury Park, Calif.: Sage, 1990.

Haraway, Donna. *Simians, Cyborgs, and Women: The Reinvention of Nature.* New York: Routledge, 1991.

Harvey, David. *The Condition of Postmodernity.* Oxford: Basil Blackwell, 1989.

Heng, Geraldine, and Janadas Devan. "State Fatherhood: The Politics of Nationalism, Sexuality, and Race in Singapore." In *Bewitching Women, Pious Men: Gender and Body Politics in Southeast Asia,* ed. Aihwa Ong and Michael G. Peletz, 195–215. Berkeley and Los Angeles: University of California Press, 1995.

Hindess, Barry. "Liberalism, Socialism, and Democracy—Variations on a Governmental Theme." In *Foucault and Political Reason,* ed. Andrew Barry, Thomas Osborne, and Nicholas Rose, 65–80. Chicago: University of Chicago Press, 1996.

Ho Ping-ti. *The Ladder of Success in Imperial China.* New York: Columbia University Press, 1962.

Hoffmann-Axthelm, Dieter. "Identity and Reality: The End of the Philosophical Immigration Officer." In *Modernity and Identity,* ed. Scott Lash and Jonathan Friedman, 196–217. Oxford: Basil Blackwell, 1992.

Holston, James, and Arjun Appadurai. "Cities and Citizenship." *Public Culture* 8, no 2 (winter 1996): 187–204.

Hong Kong Trade Development Council. *Recent Investment Environments of Guang-*

dong, Fujian, and Hainan. 2d ed. Hong Kong: Hong Kong Trade Development Council, 1991.

Honig, Emily, and Gail Hershatter. *Personal Voices: Chinese Women in the 1980s.* Stanford, Calif.: Stanford University Press, 1988.

Hsing, You-tien. "Building *Guanxi* across the Straits: Taiwanese Capital and Local Chinese Bureaucrats." In *Ungrounded Empires,* ed. Aihwa Ong and Donald M. Nonini, 143–66. New York: Routledge, 1997.

Hsiung, Ping-chun. *Living Rooms as Factories: Class, Gender, and the Satellite Factory System in Taiwan.* Philadelphia: Temple University Press, 1995.

Huang, Philip. "Public Sphere/'Civil Society' in China? The Third Realm between State and Society." *Modern China* 19, no. 2 (1993): 216–40.

Hunt, Lynn. *The Family Romance of the French Revolution.* Berkeley and Los Angeles: University of California Press, 1992.

Huntington, Samuel P. "The Clash of Civilizations?" *Foreign Affairs* 72, no. 3 (summer 1993): 22–49.

——. "The West: Unique, Not Universal." *Foreign Affairs* 75, no. 6 (November/December 1996): 28–46.

——. *The Clash of Civilizations and the Remaking of World Order.* New York: Simon and Schuster, 1996.

Ishihara, Shintaro. *The Japan That Can Say No,* trans. Frank Baldwin. New York: Simon and Schuster, 1990.

Ivy, Marilyn. *Discourses of the Vanishing: Modernity, Phantasm, Japan.* Chicago: University of Chicago Press, 1995.

Jameson, Fredric. *The Political Unconscious: Narrative as a Socially Symbolic Act.* Ithaca, N.Y.: Cornell University Press, 1981.

——. *Postmodernism, or The Cultural Logic of Late Capitalism.* Durham, N.C.: Duke University Press, 1991.

Johnson, Chalmers. *MITI and the Japanese Miracle.* Stanford, Calif.: Stanford University Press, 1982.

Jowitt, Ken. *New World Disorder: The Leninist Extinction.* Berkeley and Los Angeles: University of California Press, 1992.

Kahin, Audrey R., and George McT. Kahin. *Subversion as Foreign Policy: The Secret Eisenhower and Dulles Debacle in Indonesia.* New York: New Press, 1995.

Kao, John. "The Worldwide Web of Chinese Business." *Harvard Business Review* (March–April 1993): 24–37.

Kaplan, Caren. *Questions of Travel: Postmodern Discourses of Displacement.* Durham, N.C.: Duke University Press, 1996.

Kearney, Michael. "Borders and Boundaries of State and Self at the End of the Empire." *Journal of Historical Sociology* 4, no. 1 (March 1991): 52–74.

Kerman, Joseph. *Opera as Drama.* New and rev. ed. Berkeley: University of California Press, 1988.

Kessler, Clive. *Politics and Islam in a Malay State.* Ithaca, N.Y.: Cornell University Press 1976.

Khoo Boo Teik, *Paradoxes of Mahathirism.* Kuala Lumpur: Oxford University Press 1995.

Kondo, Dorinne. "*M. Butterfly:* Orientalism, Gender, and a Critique of Essentialist Identity." *Cultural Critique* 18 (1990): 5–29.

Kotkin, Joel. *Tribes: How Race, Religion, and Identity Determine Success in the New Global Economy.* New York: Random House, 1992.

——. "Family Ties in the New Global Economy." *Los Angeles Times Magazine,* 17 January 1993, 21–22.

Kwong, Peter. *The New Chinatown.* New York: Noonday Press, 1987.

Kymlicka, Will. "Liberalism and Communitarianism." *Canadian Journal of Philosophy* 18, no. 2 (June 1988).

Lash, Scott, and Jonathan Friedman. "Introduction: Subjectivity and Modernity's Other." In *Modernity and Identity,* ed. Scott Lash and Jonathan Friedman, 1–30. Oxford: Blackwell, 1992.

Latham, Robert. "States, Global Markets, and Social Sovereignty." Paper presented at the Social Science Research Council conference, "Sovereignty and Security," Notre Dame, 18–20 April 1998.

Lau, Emily Siu-kai. *Society and Politics in Hong Kong.* New York: St. Martin's Press, 1983.

Lavie, Smadar, and Ted Swedenburg, eds. *Displacement, Diaspora, and Geographies of Identity.* Durham, N.C.: Duke University Press, 1996.

——. "Introduction: Displacement, Diaspora, and Geographies of Identity." In *Displacement, Diaspora, and Geographies of Identity,* ed. Smadar Lavie and Ted Swedenburg, 1–25. Durham: Duke University Press, 1996.

Lee, Ching Kwan. *Women Workers and the Manufacturing Miracle: Gender, Labor Markets, and Production in South China.* Berkeley and Los Angeles: University of California Press, forthcoming.

——. "Factory Regimes of Chinese Capitalism: Different Cultural Logics in Labor Control." In *Ungrounded Empires,* ed. Aihwa Ong and Donald M. Nonini, 115–42. New York: Routledge, 1997.

Levi-Strauss, Claude. *Tristes Tropiques.* New York: Washington Square, [1955] 1973.

Levin, Mike. "Star TV Takes Over after MTV Asia Goes off the Air." *Billboard,* 14 May 1994, 8–9.

Levy, Barry S., and Daniel C. Sussott. *Years of Horror, Days of Hope: Responding to the Cambodian Refugee Crisis.* Millwood, N.Y.: Associated Faculty Press, 1992.

Li, Tania. "Constituting Tribal Space: Indigenous Identity and Resource Politics in Indonesia." Paper presented at the University of California, Berkeley, 17 October 1997.

Lim, Linda Y. L., and Peter Gosling, eds. *The Chinese in Southeast Asia.* Vols. 1 and 2. Singapore: Maruzen Press, 1983.

Lind, Michael. "To Have and Have Not: Notes on the Progress of American Class War." *Harpers*, June 1995, 35–47.

Link, Perry, Richard Madsen, and Paul G. Pikowics. "Introduction." In *Unofficial China*, ed. Perry Link, Richard Madsen, and Paul Pikowics. Boulder, Colo.: Westview, 1990.

Loh, Francis. "ASEAN NGOs in the Post–Cold War World." In *Asia—Who Pays for Growth?* ed. Jayant Lele and Wisdom Tettey. Aldershot, U.K.: Dartmouth, 1996.

Lowe, Donald. *The Body in Late-Capitalist USA*. Durham, N.C.: Duke University Press, 1995.

Lowe, Lisa. *Critical Terrains: French and British Orientalisms*. Ithaca, N.Y.: Cornell University Press, 1991.

——. *Immigrant Acts: On Asian American Cultural Politics*. Durham, N.C.: Duke University Press, 1996.

Lubis, T. Mulya. "The Future of Human Rights in Indonesia." In *Indonesia Assessment 1992: Political Perspectives on the 1990s*, ed. Harold Crouch and Hal Hill. Canberra: Research School of Pacific Studies, Australian National University, 1992.

Mackie, James A. "Overseas Chinese Entrepreneur." *Asia Pacific Economic Literature* 6, no. 1 (1992): 41–64.

——. "Changing Patterns of Chinese Big Business in Southeast Asia." In *Southeast Asian Capitalists*, ed. Ruth McVey, 161–90. Ithaca, N.Y.: South East Asia Program, Cornell University, 1992.

Macleod, Scott, and Terry G. McGee. "The Singapore-Johore-Riau Growth Triangle: An Emerging Extended Metropolitan Region." In *Emerging World Cities in the Asia Pacific*, ed. Fu-chen Lo and Yue-man Yeung, 417–64. Tokyo: United Nations University Press, 1996.

Mahathir, Mohamad, and Shintaro Ishihara. *The Voice of Asia: Two Asian Leaders Discuss the Coming Century*, trans. Frank Baldwin. Tokyo: Kodansha International, 1995.

——. "Will East Beat West?" *World Press Review*, December 1995, 6–11.

Mahbubani, Kishore. "The Dangers of Decadence: What the Rest Can Teach the West." *Foreign Affairs* 73, no. 4 (1993): 10–15.

——. "The United States: 'Go East, Young Man.'" *Washington Quarterly* 17, no. 2 (1994): 5–23.

Malkki, Lisa. "Citizens of Humanity: Internationalism and the Imagined Community of Nations." *Diaspora* 3, no. 1 (1994): 41–68.

Marcus, George, with Peter Hall. *Lives in Trust: The Fortunes of Dynastic Families in Late-Twentieth-Century America*. Boulder, Colo.: Westview, 1992.

Marcus, George, and Michael Fischer, eds. *Anthropology as Cultural Critique*. Chicago: University of Chicago Press, 1989.

Margold, Jane. "Narratives of Masculinity and Transnational Migration: Filipino Workers in the Middle East." In *Bewitching Women, Pious Men: Gender and Body*

Politics in Southeast Asia, ed. Aihwa Ong and Michael G. Peletz, 274–98. Berkeley and Los Angeles: University of California Press, 1995.

Martin, Emily. *Flexible Bodies: Tracking Immunity in American Culture from the Days of Polio to the Age of AIDS.* Boston: Beacon Press, 1994.

Marx, Karl. *Capital.* Vol. 1. 1867. Reprint, New York: International Publishers, 1967.

———. *The Eighteenth Brumaire of Louis Bonaparte.* 1869. Reprint, New York: International Publishers, 1963.

———. *Karl Marx: Pre-capitalist Economic Formations.* Trans. J. Cohen. Ed. and intro. E. J. Hobsbawm. New York: International Publishers, 1964.

Masao Miyoshi. "A Borderless World? From Colonialism to Transnationalism and the Decline of the Nation-State." *Critical Inquiry* 19, no. 4 (summer 1993): 726–51.

Massey, Doreen. "Power Geometry and a Progressive Sense of Place." In *Mapping the Futures: Local Cultures, Global Change,* ed. Jon Bird et al. London: Routledge, 1993.

Maurer, Bill. "Cyberspacial Sovereignties: Offshore Finance, Digital Cash, and the Limits of Liberation." *Indiana Journal of Global Legal Studies* (forthcoming).

McVey, Ruth. "The Materialization of the Southeast Asian Entrepreneur." In *Southeast Asian Capitalists,* ed. Ruth McVey, 7–33. Ithaca, N.Y.: South East Asia Program, Cornell University, 1992.

Miles, Robert. *Race.* London: Routledge, 1989.

Mintz, Sydney. *Worker in the Cane.* Baltimore, Md.: Johns Hopkins University Press, 1960.

———. *Caribbean Transformations.* Chicago: Aldine, 1974.

———. *Sweetness and Power.* New York: Penguin, 1985.

Mitchell, Katharyne. "Multiculturalism or the United Colors of Capitalism?" *Antipode* 25, no. 4 (1993): 263–94.

———. "Transnational Subjects: Constituting the Cultural Citizen in an Era of Pacific Rim Capital." In *Ungrounded Empires,* ed. Aihwa Ong and Donald M. Nonini, 228–58. New York: Routledge, 1997.

———. "Transnational Discourse: Bringing Geography Back In." *Antipode* 29, no. 2 (1997).

Moore, Barrington, Jr. *The Social Origins of Dictatorship and Democracy.* New York: Beacon Press, 1966.

Morley, David, and Kuan-Hsing Chen, eds. *Stuart Hall,* New York: Routledge, 1996.

Moose, George L. *Nationalism and Sexuality: Middle-Class Morality and Sexual Norms in Modern Europe.* Madison: University of Wisconsin Press, 1985.

Mouffe, Chantal. "Democratic Citizenship and the Political Community." In *Dimensions of Radical Democracy: Pluralism, Citizenship, Community,* ed. Chantal Mouffe, 225–39. London: Verso, 1992.

Mulya, Lubis T. "The Future of Human Rights in Indonesia." In *Indonesia Assessment 1992: Political Perspectives on the 1990s,* ed. Harold Crouch and Hal Hill. Canberra: Research School of Pacific Studies, Australian National University, 1992.

Murphey, Rhoades. "The Treaty Ports and China's Modernization." In *The Chinese City between Two Worlds,* ed. Mark Elvin and G. William Skinner, 17–72. Stanford, Calif.: Stanford University Press, 1974.

Myrdal, Gunnar. *The American Dilemma: The Negro Problem and Modern Democracy.* New York: Vintage, 1968.

Nash, June. *We Eat the Mines and the Mines Eat Us.* New York: Columbia University Press, 1979.

Nee, Victor G., and Brett de Bary Nee. *Longtime Californ': A Documentary Study of an American Chinatown.* Stanford, Calif.: Stanford University Press, 1972.

Newman, Katherine S. *Falling from Grace: The Experience of Downward Mobility in the American Middle Class.* New York: Free Press, 1988.

Nonini, Donald M. "Situated Identities, Positioned Imaginaries: Transnational Traversals and Reversals by Malaysian Chinese." In *Ungrounded Empires,* ed. Aihwa Ong and Donald M. Nonini, 203–27. New York: Routledge, 1997.

Nonini, Donald M., and Aihwa Ong. "Introduction: Chinese Transnationalism as an Alternative Modernity." In *Ungrounded Empires,* ed. Aihwa Ong and Donald M. Nonini, 1–33. New York: Routledge, 1997.

Offe, Claus. *Disorganized Capitalism.* Cambridge, Mass.: MIT Press, 1985.

Omi, Michael, and Howard Winant. *Racial Formation in the United States.* New York: Routledge and Kegan Paul, 1986.

Omohundro, John T. *Chinese Merchant Families in Iloilo.* Athens: Ohio University Press, 1981.

Ong, Aihwa. *Spirits of Resistance and Capitalist Discipline: Factory Women in Malaysia.* Albany: State University of New York Press, 1987.

——. "The Gender and Labour Politics of Postmodernity." *Annual Review of Anthropology* 20 (1991): 279–309.

——. "On the Edge of Empires: Flexible Citizenship among Chinese in Diaspora." *positions* 1, no. 3 (winter 1993): 745–78.

——. "State versus Islam: Malay Families, Women's Bodies, and the Body Politic in Malaysia." In *Bewitching Women, Pious Men,* ed. Aihwa Ong and Michael G. Peletz, 159–94. Berkeley and Los Angeles: University of California Press, 1995.

——. "The Invisible Costs of Soeharto's Empire." *AnthroWatch* 4, no. 2 (November 1996): 7–8.

——. "Citizenship as Subject Making: New Immigrants Negotiate Racial and Ethnic Boundaries." *Current Anthropology* 37, no. 5 (December 1996): 737–62.

——. "Strategic Sisterhood or Sisterly Solidarity? Questions of Communitarianism and Citizenship in Asia." *Indiana Journal of Global Legal Studies* 4, no. 1 (1997): 1–29.

——. "Muslim Feminists in the Shelter of Corporate Islam." *Citizenship Studies* (forthcoming).

Ong, Aihwa, and Donald M. Nonini, eds. *Ungrounded Empires: The Cultural Politics of Modern Chinese Transnationalism.* New York: Routledge, 1997.

——. *Bewitching Women, Pious Men: Gender and Body Politics in Southeast Asia.* Berkeley and Los Angeles: University of California Press, 1995.

Ong, Paul, E. Bonacich, and Lucie Cheng. *The New Asian Immigration to Los Angeles and Global Restructuring.* Philadelphia: Temple University Press, 1994.

Oommen, T. K. "Introduction: Conceptualizing the Linkage between Citizenship and National Identity." In *Citizenship and National Identity: From Colonialism to Globalism,* ed. T. K. Oommen, 13–51. Thousand Oaks, Calif.: Sage, 1997.

Ortner, Sherry. "Theory in Anthropology since the Sixties." In *Culture/Power/History,* ed. Nicholas B. Dirks, Geoff Eley, and Sherry Ortner, 372–411. Princeton, N.J.: Princeton University Press, 1994.

Palumbo-Liu, David. "Los Angeles, Asians, and Perverse Ventriloquisms: On the Functions of Asian America in Recent American Imaginary." *Public Culture* 3 (1994): 365–84.

——. *Asia/America: Body, Psyche, Space.* Stanford, Calif.: Stanford University Press (forthcoming).

Pan, Lynn. *Sons of the Yellow Emperor: A History of the Chinese Diaspora.* Boston: Little, Brown, 1990.

Peletz, Michael G. *A Share of the Harvest: Kinship, Property, and Social History among the Malays of Rembau.* Berkeley and Los Angeles: University of California Press, 1988.

Peluso, Nancy. *Rich Land, Poor People: Resource Control and Resistance in Java.* Berkeley and Los Angeles: University of California Press, 1992.

Poethig, Kathryn A. "Ambivalent Moralities: Cambodian Americans and Dual Citizenship in Phnom Penh." Ph.D. diss., Graduate Theological Union, Berkeley, 1997.

Portes, Alejandro, and Ruben G. Rumbaut. *Immigrant America: A Portrait.* Berkeley and Los Angeles: University of California Press, 1990.

Portes, Alejandro, and Alex Stepick. *City on the Edge: The Transformation of Miami.* Berkeley and Los Angeles: University of California Press, 1993.

Postone, Moshe, Edward LiPuma, and Craig Calhoun. "Introduction: Bourdieu and Social Theory." In *Bourdieu: Critical Perspectives,* ed. Craig Calhoun, Edward LiPuma, and Moshe Postone, 1–12. Chicago: University of Chicago Press, 1993.

Pratt, Mary L. *Imperial Eyes: Travel Writing and Transculturation.* London: Routledge, 1992.

Pred, Alan, and Michael Watts. *Reworking Modernity: Capitalisms and Symbolic Discontent.* New Brunswick, N.J.: Rutgers University Press, 1992.

Purcell, Victor. *The Chinese in Malaya.* Oxford: Oxford University Press, 1967.

——. *The Chinese in Southeast Asia.* 2d ed. Kuala Lumpur: Oxford University Press, 1965.

Rabinow, Paul. *French Modern: Norms and Forms of the Social Environment.* Cambridge, Mass.: MIT Press, 1989.

——. *The Anthropology of Reason.* Princeton, N.J.: Princeton University Press, 1996.

Rafael, Vince. "'Your Grief Is Our Gossip': Overseas Filipinos and Other Spectral Presences." *Public Culture* 9, no. 2 (December 1997): 269–91.

Rawls, John. *Theory of Justice.* Cambridge, Mass.: Harvard University Press, 1971.

Reid, Anthony. *The Land below the Winds.* Vol. 1 of *Southeast Asia in an Age of Commerce, 1450–1680.* New Haven, Conn.: Yale University Press, 1988.

——. "Religion, Ethnicity, and Modernity in Southeast Asia." Paper presented at the conference "Religion, Ethnicity, and Modernity in Southeast Asia," Center for Area Studies, Seoul National University, 29–30 November 1996.

Rieff, David. "The Real L.A. Story." *San Francisco Examiner Image Magazine,* 27 October 1991.

——. *Los Angeles: The Capital of the Third World.* New York: Simon and Schuster, 1991.

Robbins, Bruce. "Comparative Cosmopolitanisms." *Social Text* 31/32 (1992): 169–86.

Robertson, Roland. "Mapping the Global Condition: Globalization as the Central Concept." In *Global Culture: Nationalism, Globalization, and Modernity,* ed. Mike Featherstone, 15–30. Newbury Park, Calif.: Sage, 1990.

Robison, Richard. *Indonesia: The Rise of Capital.* Sydney: Allen and Unwin, 1986.

——. "Authoritarian States, Capital-Owning Classes, and the Politics of NICs: The Case of Indonesia." *World Politics* 41 (1988): 52–74.

Robison, Richard, and David S. G. Goodman. "The New Rich in Asia: Economic Development, Social Status, and Political Consciousness." In *The New Rich in Asia,* 1–16. London: Routledge, 1996.

Rofel, Lisa. " 'Yearnings': Televisual Love and Melodramatic Politics in Contemporary China." *American Ethnologist* 21, no. 4 (1994): 700–722.

——. *Modern Imaginaries and "Other" Modernities.* Berkeley and Los Angeles: University of California Press (forthcoming).

Rose, Nicholas. "Governing 'Advanced' Liberal Democracies." In *Foucault and Political Reason,* ed. Andrew Barry, Thomas Osborne, and Nicholas Rose, 37–64. Chicago: University of Chicago Press, 1996.

Roseberry, William. *Anthropologies and Histories: Essays in Culture, History, and Political Economy.* New Brunswick, N.J.: Rutgers University Press, 1989.

Rostow, W. W. *Stages of Economic Growth: A Non-Communist Manifesto.* Cambridge, Mass.: MIT Press, 1960.

Rouse, Roger. "Mexican Migration and the Social Space of Postmodernity." *Diaspora* 2, no. 2 (spring 1991): 8–23.

——. "Thinking through Transnationalism: Notes on the Cultural Politics of Class Relations in the Contemporary United States." *Public Culture* 7, no. 2 (1996): 353–402.

Ryan, Barbara. "Blood Brothers and Hong Kong Gangster Movies: Popular Culture and Commentary on 'One China.' " In *Asian Popular Culture,* ed. John Lent, 61–67. Boulder, Colo.: Westview, 1995.

Sacks, Karen B. "How Did Jews Become White Folks?" In *Race,* ed. Steven Gregory and Roger Sanjek, 78–102. New Brunswick, N.J.: Rutgers University Press, 1994.

Sahlins, Marshall. *Stone Age Economics.* Chicago: Aldine-Atherton, 1972.

——. *Culture and Practical Reason.* Chicago: University of Chicago Press, 1976.

Said, Edward. *Orientalism.* New York: Pantheon, 1978.

——. *Culture and Imperialism.* New York: Alfred A. Knopf, 1993.

Salaff, Janet W. *Working Daughters of Hong Kong: Filial Piety or Power in the Family?* Cambridge: Cambridge University Press, 1981.

Samydorai, Sinapan. "The Killing Fields of West Kalimantan." *Human Rights Solidarity* (Hong Kong) 7, no. 2 (April–July 1997): 5–7, 29.

Sassen, Saskia. *Losing Control? Sovereignty in an Age of Globalization.* New York: Columbia University Press, 1995.

Schein, Louisa. *Minzu Modern: The Miao and the Feminine in China's Cultural Politics.* Durham, N.C.: Duke University Press (forthcoming).

Scheper-Hughes, Nancy. *Death without Weeping: Everyday Violence in Rural Brazil.* Berkeley and Los Angeles: University of California Press, 1992.

Scott, James C. *The Moral Economy of the Peasant.* New Haven, Conn.: Yale University Press, 1976.

——. *Weapons of the Weak.* New Haven, Conn.: Yale University Press, 1989.

Seow, Francis T. *To Catch a Tartar: A Dissident in Lee Kuan Yew's Prison.* Yale Southeast Asian Studies Monograph 42. New Haven, Conn.: Yale Center for International and Area Studies, 1994.

Schell, Orville. *Discos and Democracy: China in the Throes of Reform.* New York: Anchor Books, 1988.

Schlesinger, Philip. "Europeanness: A New Cultural Battlefield?" In *Nationalism,* ed. J. Hutchinson and A. D. Smith. New York: Oxford University Press, 1994.

Schwarz, Adam. *A Nation in Waiting: Indonesia in the 1990s.* Sydney: Allen and Unwin, 1994.

Shohat, Ella. "Notes on the 'Post-Colonial.'" *Social Text* 31–32 (1992): 99–113.

Shue, Vivienne. *The Reach of the State: Sketches of the Chinese Body Politic.* Stanford, Calif.: Stanford University Press, 1988.

Siu, Helen F. *Furrows: Peasants, Intellectuals, and the State.* Stanford, Calif.: Stanford University Press, 1990.

Skinner, William S. *Chinese Society in Thailand.* Ithaca, N.Y.: Cornell University Press, 1957.

Smith, Anthony D. *National Identity.* Reno: University of Nevada Press, 1993.

Song Qiang, et al. *Zhongguo hai shi neng shou bu.* Beijing: Xinhua Shudian, 1996.

Spivak, Gayatri Chakravorty. "Can the Subaltern Speak?" In *Marxism and the Interpretation of Cultures,* ed. Cary Nelson and Lawrence Grossberg, 271–316. Urbana: University of Illinois Press, 1988.

——. "Diasporas Old and New: Women in the Transnational World." *Textual Practice* 10, no. 2 (1996): 245–69.

Stacey, Judith. *Brave New Families: Domestic Upheaval in Late-Twentieth-Century America.* New York: Basic Books, 1990.

Steinmetz, George. *Regulating the Social: The Welfare State and Local Politics in Imperial Germany.* Princeton, N.J.: Princeton University Press, 1993.

Steven, Rob. *Japan's New Imperialism.* Armonk, N.Y.: M. E. Sharpe, 1990.

Steward, Julian, ed. *The People of Puerto Rico*. Urbana: University of Illinois Press, 1956.

Stoler, Ann L. *Capitalism and Confrontation in Sumatra's Plantation Belt, 1870–1979*. New Haven, Conn.: Yale University Press, 1985.

——. "Carnal Knowledge and Imperial Power: Gender, Morality, and Race in Colonial Asia." In *Gender at the Crossroads of Knowledge: Feminist Anthropology in the Postmodern Era*, ed. Michaela di Leonardo, 55–101. Berkeley and Los Angeles: University of California Press, 1991.

Sung Lung-sheng. "Property and Family Division." In *The Anthropology of Taiwanese Society*, ed. Emily Martin and Hill Gates. Stanford, Calif.: Stanford University Press, 1981.

Tai, Hung-chao, ed. *Confucianism and Economic Development: An Oriental Alternative?* Washington, D.C.: Washington Institute Press, 1989.

Takaki, Ronald. *Iron Cages: Race and Culture in Nineteenth-Century America*. New York: Oxford University Press, 1981.

Taussig, Michael. *The Devil and Commodity Fetishism in South America*. Chapel Hill: University of North Carolina Press, 1980.

Teng, Ssu-Yu, and John K. Fairbank. *China's Response to the West: A Documentary Survey*. New York: Atheneum, 1965.

T'ien Ju-kang. *The Chinese of Sarawak*. Monographs on Social Anthropology, no. 12. London: Department of Anthropology, London School of Economics and Social Sciences, 1953.

Thompson, E. P. "The Moral Economy of the English Crowd in the Eighteenth Century." *Past and Present*, no. 50 (1971): 76–136.

Thompson, John B. *The Media and Modernity: A Social Theory of the Media*. Stanford, Calif.: Stanford University Press, 1995.

Thomson, James C., Peter W. Stanley, and John Curtis Perry. *Sentimental Imperialists: The American Experience in East Asia*. New York: Harper, 1981.

Tollefson, J. W. *Alien Winds: The Reeducation of America's Indochinese Refugees*. New York: Praeger, 1989.

Trocki, Carl. *Opium and Empires: Chinese Society in Colonial Singapore, 1800–1910*. Ithaca, N.Y.: Cornell University Press, 1990.

——. "Boundaries and Transgressions: Chinese Enterprise in Eighteenth- and Nineteenth-Century Southeast Asia." In *Ungrounded Empires*, ed. Aihwa Ong and Donald M. Nonini, 61–85. New York: Routledge, 1997.

Tu Wei-ming. "The Rise of Industrial East Asia: The Role of Confucian Values." *Copenhagen Papers in East and Southeast Asian Studies* (April 1898): 81–97.

——. "Cultural China: The Periphery as the Center." *Daedalus* 120, no. 2 (1991): 1–32.

——. *A Confucian Perspective on Human Rights*. The Inaugural Wu The Yao Memorial Lectures, 1995. Singapore: UNI Press, 1995.

Turner, Bryan S. "Outline of a Theory of Citizenship." *Sociology* 24 (May 1990): 189–217.

——. *Orientalism, Postmodernism, and Globalism*. London: Routledge, 1994.

van Ness, Peter. "China as a Third World State: Foreign Policy and Official National Identity." In *China's Quest for National Identity,* ed. Lowell Dittmer and Samuel S. Kim, 194–214. Ithaca, N.Y.: Cornell University Press, 1993.

Vattimo, Gianni. *The Transparent Society.* Trans. David Webb. Baltimore, Md.: Johns Hopkins University Press, 1992.

Verdery, Katherine. "Theorizing Socialism: A Prologue to the 'Transnation.'" *American Ethnologist* 18, no. 3 (August 1991): 419–39.

——. *What Was Socialism? What Comes After?* Princeton, N.J.: Princeton University Press, 1995.

Vincent, Joan. *African Elite: The Big Men of a Small Town.* Chicago: University of Chicago Press, 1971.

——. *Anthropology and Politics.* Tucson: University of Arizona Press, 1990.

——. *Teso in Transformation: The Political Economy of Peasant and Class in Eastern Africa.* Berkeley and Los Angeles: University of California Press, 1982.

Wallerstein, Immanuel. *The Modern World System.* New York: Academic Press, 1974.

Wang Gungwu. "Among Non-Chinese." *Daedalus* 120, no. 2 (1991): 148–52.

Wang Ling-chi. *Asian Americans for Campaign Finance Reform in the U.S.: A Statement of Purpose.* San Francisco: ISSCO Internet Community, 1996.

Watson, James L. *Emigration and the Chinese Lineage: The Mans in Hong Kong and London.* Berkeley and Los Angeles: University of California Press, 1975.

——. *The Renegotiation of Chinese Cultural Identity in the Post-Mao Era.* Social Science Research Center Occasional Paper 4. Hong Kong: University of Hong Kong, 1991.

Weber, Max. *The Sociology of Religion.* Boston: Beacon Press, 1966.

Wee, C. J. W. L. "Staging the New Asia: Singapore's Dick Lee, Pop Music, and a Counter-modernity." *Public Culture* 8, no. 3 (spring 1994): 489–510.

Wertheim, W. F. "The Trading Minorities of Southeast Asia." In *East-West Parallels,* 39–82. The Hague: W. Van Hoeve, 1964.

White, Gordon, ed. *Developmental States in East Asia.* New York: St. Martin's Press, 1988.

White, Lynn, and Li Cheng. "China's Coast Identities: Regional, National, and Global." In *China's Quest for National Identity,* ed. Lowell Dittmer and Samuel S. Kim, 154–93. Ithaca, N.Y.: Cornell University Press, 1993.

Williams, Brackette F. *Stains on My Name, Blood in My Veins: Guyana and the Politics of Cultural Struggle.* Durham, N.C.: Duke University Press, 1992.

——. "Classification Systems Revisited: Kinship, Caste, Race, and Nationality as the Flow of Blood and the Spread of Rights." In *Naturalizing Power: Essays in Feminist Cultural Analysis,* ed. Sylvia Yanagisako and Carol Delaney, 201–38. New York: Routledge, 1995.

——. "Introduction: Mannish Women and Gender after the Act." In *Women Out of Place: The Gender of Agency and the Race of Nationality,* ed. Brackette F. Williams, 1–36. New York: Routledge, 1996.

——. "The Symbolics of Ethnic Historical Traditions and 'Suffering': Some Implications for the Doctrine of Equal Citizenship in the United States." Unpublished manuscript.

———. "Identity Politics: Suffering, Succession, and Redemption in the American Moral Order." Paper presented at the Department of Anthropology, University of California, Berkeley, 10 October 1997.

Wilson, Rob, and Arif Dirlik, eds. *Asia/Pacific as Space of Cultural Production*. Durham, N.C.: Duke University Press, 1995.

Wolf, Diane L. *Factory Daughters: Gender, Household Dynamics, and Rural Industrialization in Java*. Berkeley and Los Angeles: University of California Press, 1992.

Wolf, Eric. *Peasants*. Englewood Cliffs, N.J.: Prentice Hall, 1966.

———. *Peasant Wars of the Twentieth Century*. New York: Harper and Row, 1969.

———. *Europe and the People without History*. Berkeley and Los Angeles: University of California Press, 1982.

Wong, Siu-lun. *Emigrant Entrepreneurs: Shanghai Industrialists in Hong Kong*. Hong Kong: Oxford University Press, 1988.

Wong, Siu-lun, and Janet W. Salaff. "Network Capital: Emigration from Hong Kong." Paper presented at the conference "The Transnationalization of Chinese Capitalism," National University of Singapore, 8 August 1994.

Yanagisako, Sylvia. "Transforming Orientalism: Gender, Nationality, and Class in Asian American Studies." In *Naturalizing Powers: Essays in Feminist Cultural Analysis*, ed. Sylvia Yanagisako and Carol Delaney, 275–98. New York: Routledge, 1995.

Yanagisako, Sylvia, and Carol Delaney, eds. *Naturalizing Power: Essays in Feminist Cultural Analysis*. New York: Routledge, 1995.

Yang, Mayfair Mei-hui. "The Modernity of Power in the Chinese Socialist Order." *Cultural Anthropologist* 3, no. 4 (1988): 416.

———. "The Gift Economy and State Power in China." *Comparative Studies in Society and History* 31 (1989): 25–54.

———. *Gifts, Favors, and Banquets: The Art of Social Relationships in China*. Ithaca, N.Y.: Cornell University Press, 1989.

———. "Mass Media and Transnational Subjectivity in Shanghai: Notes on (Re)Cosmopolitanism in a Chinese Metropolis." In *Ungrounded Empires*, ed. Aihwa Ong and Donald M. Nonini, 287–323. New York: Routledge, 1997.

Newspapers

Asian Wall Street Journal (Hong Kong)
International Herald Tribune (Hong Kong)
New Straits Times (Kuala Lumpur)
New York Times (New York)
Renmin ribao (Beijing)
San Francisco Chronicle (San Francisco)

San Francisco Examiner (San Francisco)
South China Morning Post (Hong Kong)
Straits Times (Singapore)
Straits Times Weekly (overseas edition)
Wall Street Journal (New York)

Index

Aditjondro, George J., 232

Anderson, Benedict, 2, 56

Ang, Ien, 24, 92, 277 n.32

Anthropology, 5–6, 22–24, 29–32, 241–42; and the comparative approach, 30–32, 240–41; and "crisis of representation," 30–31; and culture concept, 80; as nomadic thinking, 24, 54, 256 n.80; and self-critique, 22, 250 n.69

Anthropology and Politics (Vincent), 139

Anwar Ibrahim, 227–28

Appadurai, Arjun, 10–11

Art of government, 6–7, 26, 195. *See also* Liberalism

Asad, Talal, 190

ASEAN (Association of Southeast Asian Nations), 18, 62–64, 213, 232, 250 n.62; and solidarity, 229–31; and state strategy, 217

Asian Americans: as bridge builders, 132–34; as a category, 130; as foreigners, 179–80; location in the United States, 179; versus Asian immigrants, 179–80

Asian development model, 36–38, 253 n.38

Asian Human Rights Commission, 234

Asian immigrants (in the United States): and anti-immigrant sentiments, 98–103; in California, 264 n.40; and cultural competence, 101–3; as "economic animals," 101–3; and green cards, 130, 269 n.65; as *homo economicus,* 107, 130, 133–34; from Hong Kong, 87–88; as "model minorities," 33, 101, 174, 179; and money politics, 100, 108; and monster houses, 102; and philanthropy, 103–8, 265 n.52; and politicking, 175–76; and politics of location, 96–103; and strategies of positioning, 108; and symbolic capital, 102, 107–8; versus Asian Americans, 175–76, 179–80. *See also* Asian Americans; Overseas Chinese

Asian Pacific Economic Council (APEC), 197

Asian Pacific Leadership Council, 175–76

Asian tigers, 24, 35, 246 n.18; and civilizational discourse, 213; as liberal formations, 195–96; in the postcolonial era, 35; and transnational firms, 198–99

Aihwa Ong is Professor of Anthropology at the University of California, Berkeley. She is the author and editor of several books, including *Spirits of Resistance and Capitalist Discipline: Factory Women in Malaysia* (1987).

Library of Congress Cataloging-in-Publication Data

Ong, Aihwa.

Flexible citizenship : the cultural logics of transnationality / Aihwa Ong.

   p.   cm.

Includes bibliographical references and index.

ISBN 0-8223-2250-1 (alk. paper). — ISBN 0-8223-2269-2 (pbk. : alk. paper)

1. Chinese—Foreign countries—Cultural assimilation.   2. Intercultural communication—Asia.   3. Cultural relations.   I. Title.

DS732.O54   1999

303.48'2—DC 21   98-33678